Monsters of Contact

Monsters of Contact

HISTORICAL TRAUMA IN CADDOAN ORAL TRADITIONS

Mark van de Logt

University of Oklahoma Press : Norman

Also by Mark van de Logt
War Party in Blue: Pawnee Scouts in the U.S. Army (Norman, Okla., 2010)

The Caddo stories "The Young Men and the Cannibals" and "Coyote and the Six Brothers" were previously published in George A. Dorsey, *Traditions of the Caddo* (Lincoln: University of Nebraska Press, 1997). Reprinted with permission of the University of Nebraska Press.

Earlier versions of some chapters in this book were previously published as:
"'The Whirlwind Is Coming to Destroy My People!': Symbolic Representations of Epidemics in Arikara Oral Tradition," by Mark van de Logt, reprinted from *American Indian Quarterly* 39:1 (2015), 52–72.
"The Old Man with the Iron-Nosed Mask: Caddo Oral Tradition and the De Soto Expedition, 1541–42," by Mark van de Logt, reprinted from the *Journal of Western Folklore* 75:2 (2016), 123–54.
"'I Was Brought to Life to Save My People from Starvation and Their Enemies': Pahukatawa and the Pawnee Trauma of Genocide," by Mark van de Logt, reprinted from the *American Indian Culture and Research Journal* 40:3 (2016), 23–46, by permission of the American Indian Studies Center, UCLA © 2017 Regents of the University of California.

Library of Congress Cataloging-in-Publication Data

Name: Van de Logt, Mark, 1968– author.
Title: Monsters of contact : historical trauma in Caddoan oral traditions / Mark van de Logt.
Description: Norman : University of Oklahoma Press, 2018. | Includes bibliographical references and index.
Identifiers: LCCN 2017052924 | ISBN 978-0-8061-6014-6 (hardcover) | ISBN 978-0-8061-6750-3 (paper)
Subjects: LCSH: Caddoan Indians—Folklore. | Monsters—Folklore. | Oral tradition—North America
Classification: LCC E99.C13 V36 2018 | DDC 398.2089/9793—dc23
LC record available at https://lccn.loc.gov/2017052924

The paper in this book meets the guidelines for permanence and durability of the Committee on Production Guidelines for Book Longevity of the Council on Library Resources, Inc.

Copyright © 2018 by the University of Oklahoma Press, Norman, Publishing Division of the University. Paperback published 2020. Manufactured in the U.S.A.

All rights reserved. No part of this publication may be reproduced, stored in a retrieval system, or transmitted, in any form or by any means, electronic, mechanical, photocopying, recording, or otherwise—except as permitted under Section 107 or 108 of the United States Copyright Act—without the prior written permission of the University of Oklahoma Press. To request permission to reproduce selections from this book, write to Permissions, University of Oklahoma Press, 2800 Venture Drive, Norman, OK 73069, or email rights.oupress@ou.edu.

For Roger C. Echo-Hawk

"It seems strange indeed that the ancient peoples [supposedly] would spend so much time writing about the inner mysteries of life and find little time to record the events and incidents of their times."

> Vine Deloria Jr., *Spirit and Reason: The Vine Deloria Jr. Reader*

"However it was, and whatever the rhythm was, fate rewarded us, because when you want to see associations you will always find them, everywhere and in everything, the world explodes in a network, a maelstrom of connections, and everything refers to everything, everything explains everything."

> Umberto Eco, *Foucault's Pendulum*

Contents

List of Illustrations	ix
Preface	xi
Acknowledgments	xv
Introduction: Different Tribes, Different Monsters	1

Part I. Storytelling

1. Caddoan Storytellers and Storytelling Traditions	31

Part II. Oral Traditions as History

2. "The Whirlwind Is Coming to Destroy My People": Smallpox and the Arikaras	59
3. "The Spiders Who Recovered the Chief's Grandson": A Wichita Tale of Encounters with the Spanish and French in Texas	75
4. Death of the Flint Monster: A Skiri Pawnee Story of Post-Contact Warfare	103
5. The Old Man with the Iron-Nosed Mask: Caddo Oral Tradition and the De Soto Expedition, 1541–42	129

Part III. Oral Traditions and Ethnohistorical Analysis

6. From "Monster" to Savior: Scalped Men, Pahukatawa, and the Pawnee Trauma of Genocide	157
Conclusion: "We Na Netsu Ut" (Now the Gut Passes)	183
Notes	189
Bibliography	223
Index	241

Illustrations

FIGURES

Oral history and tradition diagram	12
Roaming Scout, 1907	37
James Rolfe Murie, circa 1900	48
Burgess Hunt, 1912	52
Arikara doctor treating patient, circa 1875	71
Arikara ledger drawings depicting doctors' society dance, circa 1876	73
Painting of the destruction of Mission San Sabá, circa 1765	93
Scale mailed cape and detail	108
Winter count depiction of Alights on the Cloud in iron shirt	115
Caddo mortar and pestle, circa 1900	131

MAP

The Caddoan Nations, 1650–Present	4

Preface

> A story is like a little seed. From it all sorts of other stories branch off for you. A story gives you life. Now that I am old, people invite me to come and eat good things with them and then they ask me to tell stories. So these stories keep me alive.
>
> Old-Man-That-Chief, Pawnee[1]

This book is about unmasking a number of monsters in Caddoan (Pawnee, Arikara, Wichita, and Caddo) oral traditions. These monsters include a murderous whirlwind in the Arikara creation account, a masked cannibal man in a Caddo story, an evil child-abducting witch-woman in a Wichita tale, terrifying scalped men in Pawnee and Arikara stories, and the mysterious man-slaying Flint Monster in Pawnee tradition.

Unraveling the meaning of these stories has long been the realm of folklorists, ethnologists, anthropologists, linguists, literary scholars, religious studies experts, and psychoanalysts. The contributions of these scholars have provided us with deeper insights into the mental, literary, and imaginative world of these peoples. Their work has been invaluable.

In contrast, historians have been far less active when it comes to analyzing oral traditions. Indeed, mainstream historians are generally reluctant to use supposedly "ancient" oral traditions as historical sources and too often treat them as fantasy rather than history. Yet treating them as historical accounts is exactly the methodology used in this book.

This project began a few years ago as a result of an accidental discovery. While contemplating the Arikara creation story, I realized that the monstrous whirlwind that appears in several accounts actually represents the smallpox epidemics of the 1700s, especially that of 1780–81 (see chapter 2). Intrigued by this discovery, I began analyzing monster images in the stories—often called myths—of other Caddoan peoples. In several of them, I found further evidence that these stories were in fact based on actual historical events. Suddenly a whole new area of inquiry opened up to me.

Analyzing these Caddoan texts for their historical content is not easy. Like the protagonists in the stories, I often confronted a mystery. My quest to find out what really happened or what was really described in these accounts led me on an uncertain path. This path, like the trail followed by the heroes in the Caddoan stories, is full of challenges, unexpected twists and turns, treacherous obstacles, and the occasional dead end. Fortunately, unlike the heroes in the stories, I did not have to worry that I would be swallowed up by a monster—I have only my credibility to lose.

It is difficult to understand the symbolic language of these stories. They are riddled with images and meanings that are largely unfamiliar to us today. Although the texts offer clues, the sources do not provide the historian much in the form of indisputable facts. As everyone knows, facts are indispensable for historians. They are the bricks and mortar with which historians construct their stories of the past. With these Caddoan stories, however, the facts are in dispute.

The texts themselves are of problematic provenance. There are often multiple and conflicting versions. In most cases, the stories were recorded many years later, so the contents may have changed over time. Sometimes the original owner of a story (indeed, stories were often regarded as personal property) had passed away, and the tradition survived only in imperfect form as it was retold by others. Occasionally storytellers conflated two or more stories. Outside influences, such as government officials, missionaries, and other agents of acculturation, may have prompted storytellers to alter or leave out significant portions of the text. Sometimes storytellers borrowed themes or passages from non-Native stories. Another major problem relates to the accuracy of a story's translation into English: did the recorders use accurate translations that reflect the true meaning of its passages? In quite a few cases, oral traditions contained scenes of a sexual nature, too spicy for many early twentieth-century publishers, who censored these passages by printing them in Latin. Sadly, in most cases the original Native texts were not preserved, making modern-day comparative analysis impossible.

Because of the factors outlined above, this book is largely interpretive. To some it may fall short of standard expectations of historical analysis. Readers who are satisfied with only ironclad conclusions will most likely be disappointed. Those readers willing to go on an adventurous expedition of discovery, where the outcomes are uncertain, may find in these pages things that are intriguing, engaging, and, I hope, convincing. I leave it up to the skeptics to come up with more plausible explanations. If they cannot, my hypotheses—and there are many in this book—will stand. If, however, they are able to produce better explanations, I will comfort myself with the idea that I at least challenged them to look further. That said, I would never have permitted the publication of this book if I did not stand behind my own conclusions.

It is hard to exaggerate the significance of the tribal traditions. They are not dead remnants of vanished civilizations. Nor are they "children's stories," as nineteenth-century non-Native audiences sometimes believed. The stories form the most complete record of a tribe's religious ideas, values, collective memory, and history. As long as these stories are told, many American Indians believe, the people live on. The tales that the elders passed on to subsequent generations have since become valuable objects, comparable to little sacred bundles. The men and women who shared the stories understood their significance. Telling these stories not only brought the past back to life; Roaming Scout, a Pawnee priest, said they could also lengthen the life of the storyteller: "That is what one old man—one of those who used to live here—wanted: that his stories, that these stories that I am giving you, be carried on to ensure long life."[2]

I hope that these stories continue to inspire readers, especially those belonging to the Caddoan nations. May they provide joy and pleasure. Above all, however, I hope that readers find my analysis instructive and that it encourages them to think more appreciatively about these important cultural treasures.

Acknowledgments

Like the storytellers of old, the historian constructs a story from various sources, incorporating bits and pieces of information that he or she happens to stumble upon. To be sure, I spent much time in libraries, parsing documents and texts, but just as important were the conversations I had along the way. Often these conversations took place in offices, over the phone, or by email. But sometimes, as in earlier times, they occurred around the fireplace; over a cold beer in a pub, saloon, or restaurant; or at someone's dinner table. In any case, numerous people, whether they realized it or not, helped me write this book. It is only proper to acknowledge them here.

First I wish to express my deepest debt to the various Caddoan communities in Oklahoma and North Dakota. I will forever be grateful for the friendship and support of Walter and Pauline Echo-Hawk, Marie Morning-Star Eppler, Adrian Spottedhorsechief, Eagle Thomas Knife Chief, and numerous other members of the Pawnee Nation of Oklahoma for their confidence in my scholarly work. The honor that President Marshall Gover and other members of the Pawnee community bestowed on me when I visited them in the spring of 2014 was one of the most rewarding experiences of my professional career. Gary McAdams of the Wichita Nation of Oklahoma kindly furnished me with information on Burgess Hunt and gave me valuable feedback on Wichita oral traditions. My friend Loren Yellowbird of the National Park Service at Fort Union in North Dakota has shown a keen interest in my work on the Arikaras and has cheerfully shared his ideas with me. He may not realize it, but he has influenced everything I have written about the Arikaras since we met nearly a decade ago.

I also received help and encouragement from several scholars on Caddoan history, including the late Robert S. Weddle of Dallas, Texas, who was very helpful with my discussion of the San Sabá massacre. Paul E. Hoffman at

Louisiana State University–Baton Rouge shared his thoughts on the De Soto expedition. Historian Richard Flint, a researcher at Archaeology Southwest in Tucson, Arizona, helped me identify sources on the types of weapons and armor carried into the West by the Spanish conquistadores. I owe special thanks to linguist and Caddo expert Wallace Chafe of the University of California–Santa Barbara for his encouragement and wisdom when I was completing the chapter on the Caddo tradition of the masked cannibal and for being a supporter of my speculations in general. Joel Kitchens, research librarian at Texas A&M University–College Station, kindly helped me locate sources on Spanish missions in Texas, and more importantly, he patiently listened to my ideas and showed remarkable self-control when I shared several crack-brained ones. I am also most grateful to John Romano, my friend and former colleague at Benedictine College in Atchison, Kansas, for translating Latin passages in some of the Caddoan stories.

Other people who lent me their ears while I worked on this project and who, in countless small ways, helped me improve my thinking on the subject include George Moses and Michael Smith at Oklahoma State University, Rani Andersson of the University of Helsinki, Gilles Havard of the École des hautes études en sciences sociales in Paris, Jan Ullrich and Wilhelm Meya of the Lakota Language Consortium, Anne Grob of the American Studies program at the Universität Leipzig, Rainer Hatoum of the Freie Universität Berlin, Christina Burke of the Philbrook Museum of Art in Tulsa, Oklahoma, and Candace Greene of the Smithsonian Institution in Washington, D.C. I also wish to express my gratitude to my colleagues in the Liberal Arts Department at Texas A&M University at Qatar, especially Troy Bickham for his unwavering support; Paul Lee, Jessica Herzogenrath, Mysti Rudd, Leslie Seawright, Nancy Small, Joseph Williams, Michael Telafici, Sherry Ward, Deanna Rasmussen, Jim Rogers, Philip Gray, Hassan Bashir, Trinidad Rico, Curtis Farmer, Khadija El Cadi, Amy Hodges, Bea Amaya, Elizabeth Schmidt, John Littlefield, Fatma Hassan, and Lorelei Blackburn for their comments and companionship; and Adam Cath and his amazing library staff for all their assistance. I am also grateful to Qatar Foundation for its generous financial support, which allowed me to meet fellow monster scholars at conferences and to visit archival collections and libraries around the world.

Earlier versions of several chapters in this book were published in professional journals. I would like to thank the following journal editors for granting permission to publish sections of these articles in this book: Lindsey Claire Smith of *American Indian Quarterly*, Tok Thompson of the *Journal* of *Western Folklore*, and Pamela Grieman and Judith DeTar of the *American Indian Culture and Research Journal.*

Thanks also to various anonymous readers of this manuscript, whose comments, criticisms, and suggestions improved the book, and to Alessandra Jacobi Tamulevich at University of Oklahoma Press for her patience and steadfast support of this project. I think it is safe to say that I wouldn't have finished it without Alessandra's cheerleading.

My greatest thanks, however, go out to my friend Roger C. Echo-Hawk. Throughout the process of completing this book, Roger was both my greatest supporter *and* my greatest critic. His own work on oral traditions has deeply influenced my own thinking on this subject. Roger never stopped believing in this book, and when I shared a new finding with him, his enthusiasm gave me the confidence and energy necessary to continue. Throughout, Roger also remained a critical scholar, who would not hesitate to challenge my ideas when warranted. As I bounced ideas off him, I often learned that Roger had already written about the subject, and he never failed to share his own research with me. As a fellow historian, Roger also shares my sense of awe for the amazing accomplishments of past civilizations, whether American Indian, European, or somewhere else. Whatever the flaws of this book, they would be far greater if it had not been for Roger. For these reasons, I wish to dedicate this book to him.

Monsters of Contact

Introduction

Different Tribes, Different Monsters

Monsters have captured the human imagination as far back as humanity can remember. It is hard to picture present-day pop culture without bloodthirsty vampires, moon-mad werewolves, tormented mutants who—like Frankenstein's monster—turn against their creators (one might include genetically modified apes and poorly programmed robots as well), zombies, Jurassic predators, aliens, body snatchers, alien body snatchers, mutant lizard-like Godzillas, intergalactic monsters, monstrous animal plagues, ghosts, goblins, evil spirits, cannibal psychopaths, diabolical creatures of darkness, fantastic demons, and even cuddly, child-friendly monsters like those in *Monsters, Inc.*, *Hotel Transylvania*, and the popular *Shrek* quadrilogy. But monsters are not just a Hollywood phenomenon. Monsters are universal: they can be found in the oral traditions of every culture in the world. And just as diverse as the world's monster population are the theories that explain their existence.

This book tries to explain the origins of several monsters that appear in the oral traditions of the Caddoan Indians, an American Indian language family that today consists of four nations: Caddos, Wichitas, Pawnees, and Arikaras.[1] I argue that the monsters that appear in the traditions of these nations are not merely unique but also represent a specific kind of historical trauma. In fact, the "monstrous traumas" discussed here are all related to some aspect of European contact: war, invasion, death, disease, enslavement, starvation, social upheaval, capitalism, and colonialism. The monsters discussed in this book are devastating whirlwinds, vengeful man-eating animals that punish people for their sins, cannibals who kill their victims with iron-nosed masks, an evil witch-woman who abducts little children, terrifying scalped men who have returned from the dead, and a menacing monster whose skin is made of flint.

Everyone agrees that monsters are real; we merely disagree about exactly what monsters are and where they come from. To some they are figments of the human imagination sparked by deep and dark desires, at once attractive and terrifying. For others they are simply an evolutionary response to the unknown, and it is true that anxiety and fear have kept many of us out of trouble. The fear of ghosts, for example, might be (partially) explained by the fact that human corpses, especially of those who died unexpectedly, can carry the risk of contagion or infection. There are also all-too-human monsters: evil Nazi death camp guards, sociopathic or psychopathic serial killers, predatory child molesters, deranged dictators—the list goes on and on.

This book concerns itself with a number of Caddoan Indian monsters. What attracted me to these particular monsters was my discovery that despite their strange appearance, they are almost certainly of natural (rather than supernatural) origin. Indeed, in the cases presented here, I connect these monsters to very real historical persons and events. This realization led me to the conclusion that not all American Indian oral traditions are abstract *myths* but that some are in fact *histories*. Looking back now, this finding seems obvious. I should have paid more careful attention earlier when American Indian friends told me that these stories were true accounts of things that really happened.

THE CADDOAN NATIONS

At the time of contact, the Caddoan tribes occupied a region stretching from eastern Texas to South Dakota. The southernmost branch of the Caddoan language family, the Caddo Indians, resided in what is now eastern Texas, Louisiana, Arkansas, and southeastern Oklahoma. The territory of the Wichitas and Kitsais stretched from northern Texas across Oklahoma and into Kansas. The Pawnees occupied an area comprising northern Kansas and central Nebraska. The Arikaras resided along the Missouri River in what is today South Dakota. Presently, only four of these groups continue to exist as federally recognized nations. The Kitsais were absorbed into the Wichita tribe in the late nineteenth century and no longer form a clearly distinguishable subgroup.

Apart from linguistic similarities, these groups also shared certain basic cultural traits. The most important of these is corn horticulture. Corn was their most important source of subsistence. In their gardens, Caddoan women also grew a whole range of other crops: beans, squashes, sunflowers, and pumpkins. The men engaged in hunting—bison among the Arikaras, Pawnees, Wichitas, and Kitsais; deer among the Caddos. Farming allowed the Caddoans to settle in (semi-)permanent towns, villages, or hamlets. Types of dwellings varied. The Caddos and Wichitas constructed beehive-shaped lodges from thatched grass, although certain Caddo groups also made structures with clay-plastered walls. The Pawnees and Arikaras constructed homes made of earth supported by a wooden frame. However, it appears that all the Caddoan tribes also used tepees when traveling. A distinct feature of Caddo settlements was the construction of mounds, a form of ceremonial architecture they shared with Mississippian cultures. Because the Caddoan tribes relied on corn horticulture, their ceremonial life involved the cultivation of crops, the changing of the seasons, and determining the cycle of planting and harvesting. Obviously, there were major differences between their forms of religious expression, but sacred bundles (which contained objects that referred to the creation of a tribe or ceremony) played an important role in all of them. Authority was shared between chiefs and priests, and status in society depended on one's spiritual powers. The Pawnees, Arikaras, and Wichitas were the "original" Plains Indians, whose presence on the plains far predated the arrival of the tribes of the Siouan and Algonkian linguistic stocks, with the possible exception of the Mandans and Hidatsas.[2]

A look at the map shows a clear south–north distribution of the Caddoan nations, which caused some authors to speculate that the Caddoans had southern, possibly even Mexican, origins. There are several reasons to consider this theory. The heavy reliance on corn horticulture and an elaborate ceremonial system associated with corn cultivation suggests southern origins. The Skiri (or Skidi) Pawnee and Arikaras occasionally practiced human sacrifice, which prompted anthropologists Clark Wissler and Herbert Spinden to suggest Mexican ties as well. Ethnobotanist Melvin Gilmore further strengthened the southern hypothesis when he discovered that the Arikaras cultivated a species of tobacco (*Nicotiana quadrivalvis*) that was originally found only in Mexico. Despite these theories, it is possible that these customs simply reached the Caddoans through trade and diplomatic channels.[3]

The present-day division into four nations obscures the fact that in the past there were many more Caddoan groups. For example, the four bands of the Pawnee Indians (Chawi, Pitahawirata, Kitkehahki, and Skiri) once were politically separate and autonomous tribes. Geopolitical circumstances forced these tribes to cooperate more closely for common defense against enemy tribes. The Chawi, Pitahawiratas, and Kitkehahkis first formed a "South Band" confederacy in response to pressure from the Osages and other enemy tribes. In the nineteenth century, the Skiri Pawnees joined the confederacy in response to increased pressure from the Lakota Sioux. Although band divisions remained

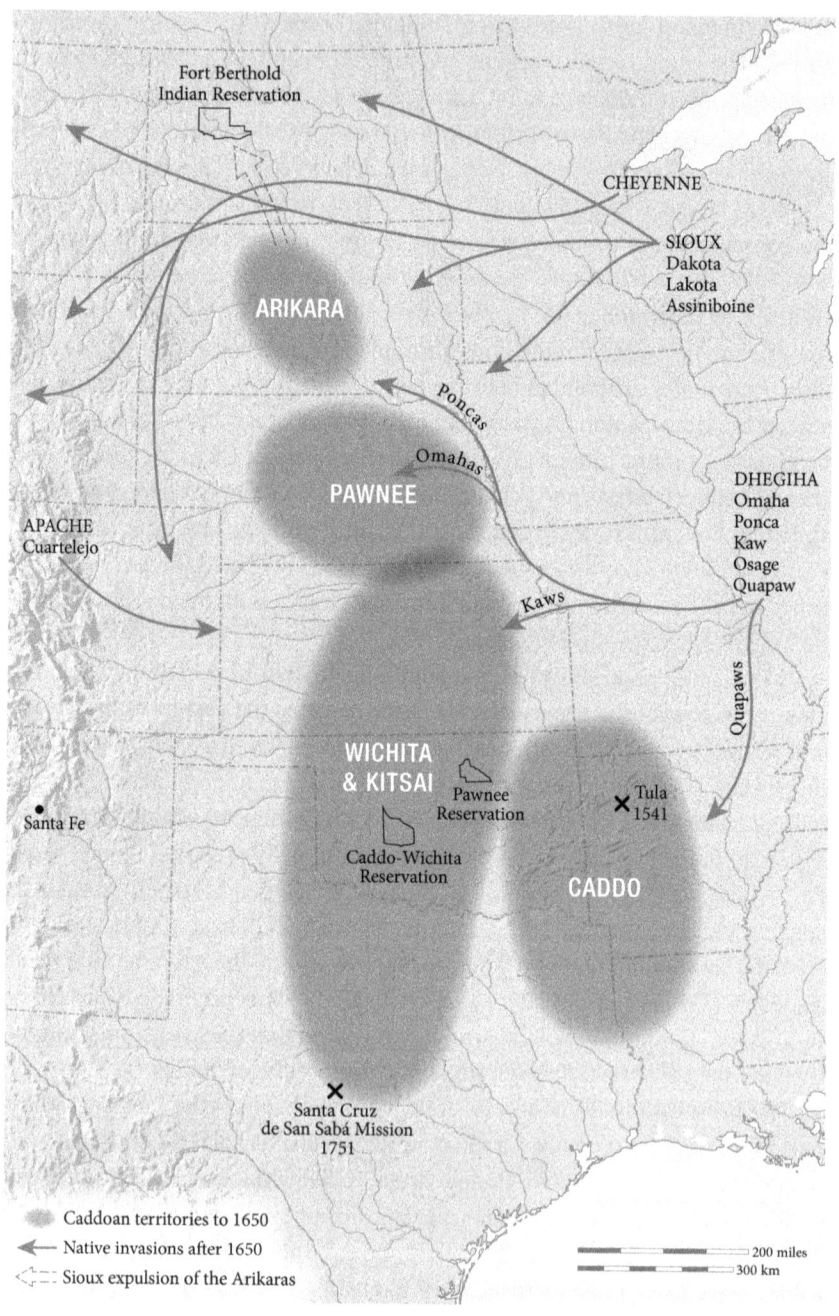

The Caddoan Nations, 1650–Present. Map by Carol Zuber Mallison. Copyright © 2018, University of Oklahoma Press.

visible to the Pawnee people, the U.S. government lumped them all together for administrative convenience.

The Arikara Indians (also known as the Sahnish or "Rees") were closely related to the Pawnees. Scholars disagree as to when the Arikaras and the Pawnees separated from each other. According to different theories, this separation occurred in phases between about 1450 and 1550.[4] At first, separate groups formed their own communities, but they were forced to unite after several devastating epidemics in the eighteenth century made them vulnerable to harassment by the Lakota Sioux. The Arikaras became the northernmost group of Caddoans. Still, the Arikaras and the Pawnees remained relatively close, and despite being separated for centuries, they shared many cultural similarities.[5] Indeed, the close linguistic and cultural ties between the Skiri Pawnees and Arikaras caused both sides to claim common ancestry. "The Skidi claim that the Arikara are Skidi," George Dorsey wrote in 1904, "while, in turn, the Arikara look upon the Skidi as part of themselves."[6]

Similarly, the Caddo Indians consisted of several independent tribes and nations. In the seventeenth and eighteenth centuries, there were eleven Hasinai tribes and four Cadohadacho tribes. The Natchitoches confederacy consisted of the Natchitoches and Doustioni tribes. Finally there were several groups dispersed among the others: the Adais, Cahinnios, Ouachitas, Yatasis, and Eyeish. All these groups shared similar cultures and ways of life, and they were forced to unite in the late eighteenth and early nineteenth century.[7] Although the Caddos are usually considered a southeastern tribe, Caddo stories often show an interesting mix of both southeastern and Plains influences.[8]

The Arikara creation story throws some light on the division of the Caddoan language family into separate groups. According to the account, the people emerged from the ground in different stages. These groups followed a northern route along the Missouri River. Once they established themselves on the river, an angry whirlwind scattered them about, creating new tribes in the process. Pawnee historian Roger Echo-Hawk takes the Arikara creation account even further back into deep time, suggesting that the obstacles the Caddoan people encountered after emerging from the earth included passages across the Bering Strait land corridor, the formidable Rocky Mountains, and possibly the Grand Canyon.[9]

The Caddoan tribes shared many of the same monsters, including witches, unnaturally fierce and powerful animals, (horned) water monsters, cannibals, and snake-tongued squirrels. However, Caddoan separations also resulted in linguistic, cultural, and geographic differences, as well as new sets of monsters unique to each tribe. These monsters include murderous whirlwinds in Arikara traditions, a cannibal man wearing an iron-nosed mask in Caddo tradition, a witch-woman and her four headless guards in Wichita tradition, the mysterious Flint Monster in Pawnee tradition, and scalped men in Pawnee and Arikara lore. Because these monsters are unique to these groups, it seems logical that they reflect different historical experiences. The theme of this book is these monsters' connections to very real historical events and processes.

ORAL TRADITIONS AS HISTORICAL SOURCES: A CRITICAL PERSPECTIVE

Although ethnohistorians such as myself have relied on oral traditions in their scholarship, the use of oral traditions as historical sources remains controversial among mainstream historians. Ethnohistorians place American Indian experiences and perspectives at the center of inquiry, and for this reason oral traditions are considered indispensable.[10] Together with winter counts, ledger drawings, petroglyphs, painted buffalo hides and other material artifacts, religious rituals and ceremonies, songs and dance, and other forms of cultural expression, oral traditions allow us to include a genuine "Indian voice" in our histories. But the use of oral traditions to reconstruct Native history is not without criticism. Indeed, quite a few conventional scholars reject oral traditions as credible sources. Skepticism about the historical value of oral traditions dates back at least to the nineteenth century. The debate hit the United States in 1915, when anthropologist Robert Lowie wrote a scathing critique of John Swanton and R. B. Dixon's 1914 article "Primitive American History," in which they used oral traditions, especially origin myths, to fill in gaps in the archaeological, linguistic, and written records.[11] Lowie protested the acceptance of oral traditions as historical records: "I cannot attach to oral traditions any historical value whatsoever under any circumstances whatsoever," he wrote. How, Lowie asked, can one reject certain parts of a tradition—such as monsters and fantastic elements—and accept others as true? Although oral traditions may "furnish a starting-point for linguistic, archaeological, or other investigations," Lowie exclaimed, only conventional scientific approaches will yield any true history.[12]

Lowie's warning shot caused Swanton and Dixon to return fire. Dixon replied that Lowie's position that there is no historical value to oral traditions was "amazingly extreme." Dixon believed that Lowie's "unqualified statements" were dangerous to the profession. "That oral tradition is, as in the instances Dr. Lowie quotes, sometimes grotesquely inaccurate is well known," Dixon retorted, "[but] that it is sometimes extraordinarily accurate and often generally correct is equally a matter of record."[13] Swanton seconded Dixon's opinion. Based on his own experiences, Swanton declared that in nine out of ten cases, "supplementary evidence" supported the oral traditions. "In cases which we cannot check up we therefore find a preponderance of probability that the tradition of origin has a historical basis."[14]

Stung by the responses in the war of words that he himself had unleashed, Lowie published a new commentary. Although more scholarly this time, it was not less belligerent: "I held then, as I do now, that those who attach an historical value to oral traditions are in the position of the circle-squarers and inventors of perpetual-motion machines, who are still found besieging the portals of learned institutions." The only value oral traditions had, according to Lowie, was as "revelations of the cultural status of the people who cherish them." In short, it was the way American Indians presented social, cultural, and psychological worldviews, not their historical content, that was significant. Lowie thought the belief that "people know best about themselves" was a fallacy, especially when the events related had taken place long before the narrators were born.[15] Anything beyond the immediate observation of the narrator was suspect and most likely false, he reasoned. Furthermore, Indians tended to remember insignificant historical facts while failing to record, or failing to record accurately, "the most momentous happenings." Indeed, Lowie thought, any kind of accuracy was most likely accidental. For example, there was a reasonable chance that a tribe guessed correctly from which of the four directions it had migrated in the distant past. Finally, Lowie again protested the idea of accepting what was not absurd as true while rejecting what was obviously "ridiculously false." Such cherry-picking techniques were subjective and could lead only to prejudiced conclusions.[16]

Lowie's basic arguments would resurface periodically, albeit in less ethnocentric terms. While not dismissing oral traditions altogether, anthropologist A. Irving Hallowell nevertheless believed that they had an expiration date. In 1937, while discussing the Saulteaux Indians, Hallowell wrote, "One hundred and fifty years is the outside limit of any genuine historic past so far as the Berens River [Saulteaux] Indians are concerned." Anything beyond that time, the Saulteaux simply referred to as "long ago." Without any clear historical markers, Hallowell wrote, "we are plunged into a bottomless mythological epoch that lacks temporal guide posts of any conventional sort." At that point, "temporal concepts actually lose most, if not all, chronological significance."[17]

Historian George E. Hyde concurred with Hallowell. In his classic history of the Oglala Lakotas, Hyde wrote about the problem of piecing together American Indian history based on oral traditions. According to Hyde, "Nothing very useful can be obtained on the history of their people back of the year 1850." Hyde blamed this not on poor memory but on "the frailty of human nature."[18] Hyde believed that the expiration date was even shorter than Hallowell's estimate. In *The Pawnee Indians*, Hyde wrote, "These Indians did not have a real memory for events farther back than about ninety years."[19] Despite these claims, Hyde nevertheless continued to include oral tradition in his books when there were no other sources available. Hyde's fellow contemporary historian Bernard DeVoto was even more blunt. "I don't trust an Indian tradition further than grandpa, if that far," DeVoto exclaimed privately in 1948.[20]

The debate on the historicity of oral traditions resumed in the mid-1950s, when folklorists debated the origins of myths. While most folklorists believed that myths had some underlying historical foundation, others, most notably Lord Raglan and Stanley Edgar Hyman, believed that myths had grown out of rituals rather than history. "Tradition never preserves historical facts," proclaimed Lord Raglan. Echoing Lowie, who claimed that American Indians did not truly understand history as a linear record of a people's past, Raglan wrote, "Since history depends upon written chronology, and the savage has no written chronology, the savage can have no history. And since interest in the past is induced solely by books, the savage can take no interest in the past; the events of the past are, in fact, completely lost." In short, because oral traditions lack periodization and chronology, events become timeless rather than fixed to a specific place in history. Apart from Raglan's use of the word "savage" (or Lowie's use of the word "primitive"), there is much that chills the present-day scholar. Obviously both men were products of their time, as much as we are of ours. Still, the ethnocentric nature of their ideas is clear: written history is supposedly more reliable than, and superior to, oral tradition; Indians supposedly do not really have a historical sense; and their ability to pass on stories accurately is, according to Lowie and Lord Raglan, extremely limited. In fact, like Hallowell, Lord Raglan rejected the idea that nonliterate peoples could retain memories for more than three fifty-year generations: "After much consideration I have fixed on the term of one hundred and fifty years as the maximum." Unless these traditions were put into writing, Raglan argued, they ceased to be historical.[21]

The debate on the historicity of oral traditions found no clear-cut winners and disappeared into the background in subsequent decades. But it resurfaced after the discovery of the Kennewick Man in July 1996. The controversy over Kennewick Man is by now well-known. A forensic examiner concluded that the remains of the unidentified man were prehistoric, but the morphology of the skeletal remains was Caucasoid in appearance. Based on this discovery, the news media erroneously reported that the first humans in the Americas were Caucasian, causing much consternation among local American Indian people, who immediately demanded repatriation of the remains under provisions of the Native American Graves Protection and Repatriation Act (NAGPRA), which had been in force since 1990. Soon archaeologists and American Indians were engaged in a legal battle over ownership of the remains of Kennewick Man. The debate revolved around two models of explanation: Western science versus Native American forms of knowledge. Many American Indians felt that their forms of knowledge, including tribal oral traditions, should be considered scientific evidence or perhaps even superseded such evidence. At the opposite end were scholars who, like Lowie and others before them, argued that oral traditions were unreliable, that they did not pass scientific scrutiny, and that therefore they were unusable.[22]

A proponent of the latter view is archaeologist Ronald J. Mason, who wrote a book on the subject. Mason laments the intrusion of "political correctness" in academia and insists that oral traditions and other Native forms of knowledge are not equal or superior to Western science and historiography. That does not preclude the possibility that oral traditions have valid information, but usually they tell us more about the narrators of the story than about what actually happened in the past. Not even American Indians can agree on the content and meaning of oral traditions. Indeed, as anthropologist Alice Beck Kehoe correctly pointed out, "There is no monolithic indigenous *history*, there are indigenous *histories*."[23] If so, which one is correct?

Mason's basic argument against the historicity of oral traditions can be summed up as follows. First, oral traditions are not as valid as scientific statements because they are "sanctioned by heritage" only and not by "critical reasoning and empiricism." Therefore "the veracity of oral traditions [is] highly dubious." Second, nonliterate people "do not 'know' their ancestors' histories, but [know] only what they have been told by their proximate progenitors." In other words, oral traditions "reflect the concerns of their contemporary reciters more than conditions and events of the past." Third, the idea that oral traditions can be understood from only a Native perspective shields them from scientific investigation and criticism. In fact, by claiming that the stories are sacred, Native peoples effectively block access to these stories for scholars and scientists. They "see the use of oral traditions by Western historians as a form of cultural appropriation." Fourth, oral traditions that discuss events in the past for which there are no other records cannot be verified. They are therefore "worthless as history." Fifth, verbal and written accounts of the past are not equally valid. And lastly, although archaeology and Western historiography grew out of the "Western cultural tradition" and are therefore "ethnocentric," the idea that "alternative histories" are more correct is false. These alternative histories are often ethnocentric as well.[24]

Mason scorns both "radical" defenders of American Indian oral traditions, such as the late Vine Deloria Jr., as well as "moderates" who call for compromise and cooperation. The latter, according to Mason, have in effect betrayed science in favor of ideology and platitudinous political correctness. He equally despises the eagerness with which postmodernists "surrender all claims to objectivity." Mason compares historians who believe in the historicity of oral traditions to unfortunate travelers who are lured to disaster by Siren calls.

Oral traditions are unreliable for many reasons, according to Mason. The most important is that oral traditions change each time they are related. They are "not fixed and immutable." They are "a living thing that changes shape, expands, shrinks, and expands again, an amoebalike creature with powers to make us laugh, and cry, and clench our fists." Indeed, oral traditions are so powerful that they can "make us believe in something that never happened."[25]

According to Mason, there is no reason to assume that preliterate peoples were not immune to the ravages of time and the sociopolitical circumstances in which the stories were passed on. Indeed, ancient Homeric poems and Norse sagas changed as their narrators performed them before audiences. Not even collective memories are particularly accurate; they too are subject to barely perceptible social and political mood swings within a culture. In fact, strict adherence to Homer and Norse sagas essentially prevented scholars from investigating other explanations that might prove to be more historically plausible. Homer might have Hellenized the story of Troy, and Norse sagas might be historical fiction, much like *Gone with the Wind* fictionalizes the American Civil War. There is also an important difference between the functions of history and myth. The first seeks to "record as accurately as possible the behavior of communities in the past," while the latter does not seek knowledge but "action [that is] essential for the very existence of the community."[26]

Because oral traditions have been exposed to human shortcomings and the eroding influences of time, the conclusions made by scholars who use them must also be fragile. Like Lowie, Mason asks how one can discern between fact and fiction in these accounts. Usually the conclusions by such scholars are supported by a great deal of enthusiasm but very little hard evidence. The presence of the fantastic in the stories serves as a good example of the ambiguous nature of such research. Quoting Lowie, Mason asks, "How can the historicists winnow out fabulous monsters and dragons and call the residue fact? . . . If part of the narrative is fiction, why not the whole?" Indeed, most of what appears to be true in the stories is usually the result of coincidence rather than historical accuracy.[27]

Still, Mason is willing to accept speculation in research on the condition that the speculative nature of the research is clarified. However, this is nothing more than "reasoned guessing." Still, even guesses "may lead serendipitously to something more tangible," Mason admits. This is to be preferred if the alternative is immobility. To decipher "hidden meanings," one can make use of "suggestion, something to stir up useful conjecture in the hope of learning something more tangible." However, scholars who employ this technique must make it absolutely clear that they are guessing so that their uncritical audiences understand that these are not facts or ironclad conclusions. "After all, even Sigmund Freud is alleged to have observed that sometimes a cigar is simply a cigar." Archaeologists may suggest only "informed conjectures." They must present as much empirical data as possible in a step-by-step argumentation that links historical and ethnographic information to prehistoric and archaeological data. Quite correctly, Mason warns against "enthusiasm for one's own conclusions," because they might lead researchers to bypass the stringency required of scholarly investigation. Still, speculation has its place, "provided it is offered for what it is and nothing more."[28]

The last warning is appropriate. As Mason points out, presenting one's speculations as fact entails certain dangers. "An accompanying handicap of this kind of symbolic speculation is that it leads too facilely to a belief that no one knows more than one does—or, perhaps more regrettably, that its consumers will think they have learned something."[29] Although Mason occasionally acknowledges that oral traditions may contain some historical facts, he concludes that the true value of oral histories is not in their accuracy but in the fact that they are "'windows' into the psyches of their tellers and the societies of which they are presumed to speak."[30]

ORAL TRADITION AS HISTORY: A DEFENSE

Despite Mason's thoughtful treatment of the problem, I disagree with him on several essential points. In particular, this book takes issue with Mason's statement that it is arbitrary to accept some parts of oral traditions as true while rejecting the most fantastic, bizarre, and inexplicable things in these accounts as false. Instead, the analysis presented in this study is aimed at explaining the fantastic.

This book also takes issue with scholars who view the fantastic elements in oral traditions as psychological reflections rather than as true depictions (albeit in abstract form) of traumatic events. According to these scholars, monsters, dragons, ghosts, cannibals, vampires, werewolves, elves, goblins, trolls, magical beings, and ogres (the variations seem endless) can be understood only in psychological or metaphysical terms: they are not history.[31]

In contrast, in the five case studies in this book, I argue that certain Caddoan Indian monsters are based on real events. These monsters are not phantasms but are depictions and descriptions of very real dangers. Just as Godzilla is a metaphor for nuclear war, so one could recognize Native monsters in tsunamis, diseases, epidemics, earthquakes, volcanoes, droughts, wars, famines, floods, fires, and so forth. Some scholars have argued, persuasively I think, that tales of vampires and werewolves were actually inspired by stories of people infected with rabies transmitted by bats and dogs. Why stop there?[32]

In short, I believe that monsters are real. They just tend to survive as metaphors in art and (oral) literature.

Perhaps I should qualify this: I believe that the monsters in the following case studies are based on historical fact. Monster metaphors in American Indian oral traditions pose a vexing problem. Proving that they are based on actual historical events is not easy. Still, this book is an attempt to make the hidden history visible.

Scholars distinguish between *oral history* and *oral tradition*. Oral history consists of descriptions of events by people who actually witnessed them. The descriptions become oral traditions after the original witnesses pass away and their stories are carried on by others. Whereas "hard" scientists such as Mason believe that most oral traditions are mythology, I argue that there are distinctions. I tried to visualize my ideas (which are hardly new or innovative) in the following diagram:

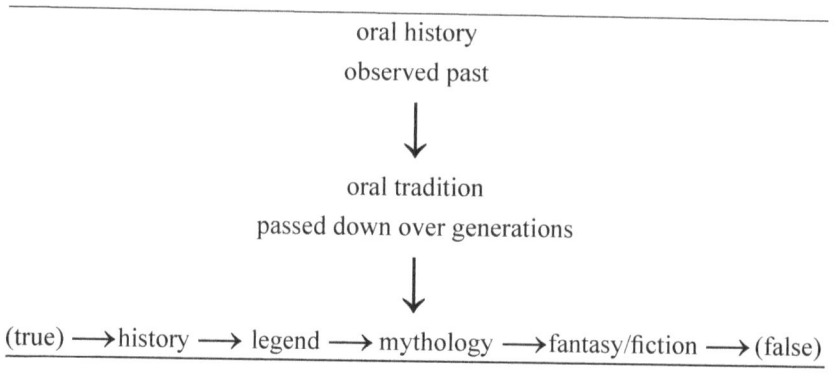

Note that sacred stories are not exempt but rather implied in this organization. American Indians might consider sacred stories to be true and therefore belonging in the category "history," while non-Natives might consider them "myths," or "fiction." Also note that it is possible for a story to change from history into legend and from legend into myth; this often happens. This book suggests that the case studies presented here started out as true history but eventually morphed into legend and myth. This book is actually an attempt to accomplish the reverse. My purpose is to save some of these stories from mythology and to restore them to their original purpose as works of history.

Of course, as with all categorizations, this one is inadequate. Some stories overlap. Some are mixtures of two or even all three categories, which raises Lowie's worst nightmare: if it is possible for a story to contain both historical, legendary, mythological, and/or fictional elements, how can one distinguish between one and the other? The short answer is that one cannot do so out of hand. One has to investigate each story individually to see which is which. I started my research on the assumption that everything was real. If it was, then the burden of proof to explain the fantastic and magical was on me.

Historicizing oral traditions is controversial not only among historians but also among American Indian people. I find myself caught between two camps: those—mostly American Indians—who take these stories as literally true, and those—mostly Western-trained non-Native scientists—who demand supporting evidence before they are willing to give oral traditions any credence. The literalist camp includes such distinguished scholars as the late Vine Deloria Jr. The "science" camp includes equally highly respected scholars such as the aforementioned Ronald J. Mason. Frequently, centrists find themselves scorned or ridiculed by both camps. Luckily, the centrist camp is not without champions. They include Native Americans as well as Western scientists.

Perhaps the most erudite defender of oral traditions as history was Belgian-born Africanist Jan Vansina. Vansina's book *Oral Tradition: A Study in Historical Methodology* was a landmark when first published in 1965. Twenty years later, he updated his theory and reissued his book under the title *Oral Tradition as History* (1985). Both books provide well-constructed arguments in support of historicizing oral traditions. Vansina's acknowledgment that some traditions are blatantly false does not mean that all are "automatically unreliable, even though all have limitations." Indeed, as sources, they are irreplaceable, because they are sources "from the inside." In fact, if not for oral traditions, "we would know very little about the past of large parts of the world, and we would not know them from the inside." In short, oral traditions are "an indispensable source for reconstruction," especially when used in conjunction with other kinds of sources. They are not less than written sources; they are just as important: "They correct other perspectives just as much as other perspectives correct them."[33]

Vansina explains that historians "should attempt to complete his oral sources by outside sources that can be checked and certified as independent." Such outside sources include documents and other written records, archaeological findings, and linguistic and ethnographic evidence. Such cross-references can confirm both the oral traditions and the written sources. "This does not mean that a written source is *a priori* better than an oral one," Vansina insists. "It means that, when a written document and a tradition converge, both are part of the proof." When the oral and written sources converge, the "evidence now is of a wholly different order of plausibility than if just one of the two were available."[34]

This book puts Vansina's advice into practice by starting out with the oral tradition, followed by a search of the written historical record for confirmation. While the results are admittedly speculative, I believe that reasonable support for my claims exists in the historical record. Of course, there is the risk of taking one's own conclusions too far. That danger lurks at both ends, however, for many mainstream historians tend to dismiss oral traditions far too easily. As Vansina observes, "Consciously or not, one wants to prove, and the temptation to argue beyond what the evidence really warrants is equally strong in either direction."[35]

Vansina's approach is distinctly ethnohistorical. Like Vansina, I support placing oral traditions at the starting point of historical inquiry. Even if they cannot be conclusively confirmed by conventional historical records, oral traditions nevertheless remain vitally important. "As long as traditions are not independently confirmed the evidence they present can best be described as 'on probation,'" Vansina writes. Indeed, such evidence has value: "It has a certain plausibility and forms a hypothesis that should be tested first, before any other hypothesis is considered." In short, "A body of tradition thus becomes an agenda for research."[36]

Certain historians contend that oral traditions are useless because they were distorted by contemporary influences. After all, the stories reflect the styles and concerns of the storyteller (who has his or her own "agenda" in seeking status, prestige, or money), the stylistic tastes of the collector-translator, and the biases of the scholar who interprets the stories. Vansina acknowledges the impact of the present: "Yes, oral traditions are documents *of the present*, because they are told in the present." However, "they also embody a message from the past, so they are expressions *of the past* at the same time." Indeed, Vansina warns scholars: "To ignore the impact of the present as some historians have done is . . . reductionistic." There is no escaping the fact that traditions "must always be understood as reflecting both past and present in a single breath."[37]

Stepping into Vansina's footsteps, anthropologist Peter Nabokov carried on the defense of American Indian oral traditions in *A Forest of Time: American Indian Ways of History* (2002). When Nabokov wrote his study, calls for integrating Indian ways of history were still "wishful thinking" because of deep-seated skepticism among many academics. "Seriously weaving Indian ways of history into America's academic and publishing systems," Nabokov wrote, "remains an uphill battle."[38]

Nabokov feels that academic skepticism is unwarranted because American Indians often took great pains to remember their history correctly. Scholar and Omaha Indian Francis LaFlesche said that among the Plains Indians, "'The burden of memorizing and transmitting with accuracy, from one generation to another' fell to specially designated individuals chosen from key social units." Meanwhile, the Pima Indians "stayed alert to youngsters who demonstrated an aptitude for recollecting traditions." They would become "recognized historians" who could "engage in the male-only 'smoke talk' of history recounting." Further back in time, French traveler Antoine Le Page du Pratz noted the existence of historians among the Natchez of seventeenth-century Louisiana: "I have been told that there were also graduates in the telling of myths. . . . These graduates, of whom there were several in each town, were evidently the repositories of learning, the keepers of the sacred myths, the historians, and the guardians of the supernatural mysteries."[39] Nabokov's findings are supported by several linguists, who point out that tribal historians were highly respected: "Good speech makers, good story tellers, good singers, and prolific song composers were admired," says linguist-ethnographer Wick R. Miller. Furthermore, Miller points out, American Indians were far more cognizant than modern-day Americans that words had power and had to be used very deliberately.[40]

Nabokov does not see a problem in the fact that there are occasionally many different—even conflicting—versions of one story. After all, conventional Western sources also often contain conflicting versions of the same thing. He believes that multiple versions of oral traditions provide "benefit and unending pleasure." Indeed, they keep the study of history interesting. For this reason also, Nabokov asserts, "Most of today's non-Indian ethnohistorians are less inclined to ask oral traditions to clinch any literalist reconstructions than to explore how this material can complement, contextualize, or provide reinterpretations for written constructions of shallower pasts." In other words, most historians mainly use oral traditions to complement or confirm other sources of information.[41] Like Vansina, however, Nabokov is inclined to put some stock into oral traditions, even if there is no other evidence that would corroborate them. Indeed, Nabokov writes that tools, tent covers, rock "art," tribal ceremonies and rituals, and other nonwritten artifacts used as mnemonic devices to record history can be of similar value as oral traditions.[42]

In a perceptive study titled *When They Severed Earth from Sky: How the Human Mind Shapes Myth* (2004), Elizabeth Wayland Barber and Paul T. Barber show the processes by which history becomes "myth." Barber and Barber reject a strictly psychological approach to the understanding of myths. Myths are not a reflection of the human psyche through natural imagery; it is the other way around: actual events were the foundation of myths, but our minds gave these events a psychological twist as they were told, remembered, and retold.[43]

In short, myths "were not intended as fiction in our sense, but as carriers of important information about real events and observations." This information "can survive intact for thousands of years."[44] The only problem is that preliterate minds had to find ways to preserve these memories so that they could be passed on to subsequent generations. To remember stories, humans resort to all kinds of tricks: they leave out unessential information or information that is already widely known; they add new images to aid in memory of an event; they compress multiple characters or events into single elements; they compress time; they add their own explanations for why an event happened; and often they erroneously conflate two or more events into a single explanation. Barber and Barber identified nearly fifty such processes—organized into four fundamental categories: "silence, analogy, compression, and restructuring"—that make stories hard to understand for distant literate generations, who, because they know how to write, have lost the ability to decode these stories. Consequently, "we often dismiss [myths] as silly or try to reinterpret them with psychobabble."[45]

Barber and Barber's theory is significant because it explains how events become mythologized. Their work contains several insightful reinterpretations of, and plausible explanations for, certain myths, such as vampires, the Promethean myth, and others. For example, intestinal gases made "vampires" look plump, as if they had been feasting recently. These gases also explained why their mouths could be bloody and why their corpses made sounds when stakes were driven through their hearts. The same postmortem gases responsible for vampires' appearances explain how dead women "gave birth" in their coffins and why corpses could suddenly sit upright. The Barbers link the dragons in the Beowulf and Siegfried legends to ancient mound graves. When treasure-seeking grave robbers dug their way into such mounds ("caves"), they sometimes released flammable methane gases coming from entombed bodies. Torches carried by the grave robbers could cause fiery explosions. Hence came the story of cave-dwelling and fire-breathing dragons guarding buried treasures of gold. Although Barber and Barber's theories have met with criticism from various corners in academia, their interpretations are not so easy to discount.

Although bolstered by Nabokov and Barber and Barber, my own position corresponds most closely with those of Pawnee historian and scholar Roger C. Echo-Hawk. Echo-Hawk was involved in formulating what would eventually become NAGPRA, which instigated the current debate on Native forms of knowledge. Therefore, his interpretation of how the law views the relationship between Native American traditions and science is important.[46]

According to Echo-Hawk, NAGPRA in essence mandates that rather than fighting each other, scientists and Native people work together. So Echo-Hawk rejects the "bibliocentric" approach of Lowie, Mason, and others and suggests treating oral traditions as "respectable siblings" of written documents. However, Echo-Hawk suggests "comparable status" between scientific facts and oral traditions rather than "equal status." Just as scientific facts must be scrutinized and evaluated, so must oral traditions. While scientists "as a rule aim for a higher degree of certainty than that called for under NAGPRA," Echo-Hawk insists that "applying a lower threshold of a preponderance of the evidence does not mean that a lower standard of scholarship should be employed." In practical terms, this means that not all oral traditions are equal. Some may be "personal visionary experiences of a religious nature [that] are subject to highly idiosyncratic interpretation and should [therefore] not be submitted or accepted as evidence on cultural affiliation under NAGPRA." According to Echo-Hawk, NAGPRA does not offer "carte blanche empowerment of the view that all oral traditions ought to be accepted as literal history."

Echo-Hawk identifies two analytical standards to test the historicity of oral traditions: compatibility and reasonability. Compatibility requires that "the historical content of the oral or written information should be compatible with the general context of human history derived from other types of evidence." In short, to determine the viability of an oral tradition, authentic information must be corroborated by archaeological, linguistic, ethnographic, or conventional forms of historical evidence.

Reasonability requires that "the oral information must present a perspective on historical events that would be accepted by a reasonable observer." The evidence, in this case an oral tradition, must "pass a level of scrutiny that might be applied by a well-informed third party with no vested interest in the outcome." In short, the oral tradition must be subjected to basic standards of criticism. Echo-Hawk admits that "[if] an oral tradition about ancient times cannot be supported by other evidence, skepticism and even rejection is warranted." However, just because part of an oral tradition cannot be proven beyond reasonable doubt, that should not automatically discredit the entire tradition. Echo-Hawk acknowledges that traditions are subject to change over time. Yet these changes usually relate to minor details that narrators use to "liven up" their stories (a process he calls "memorability"). Very often the core ideas and elements of the story remain. Therefore it may still be possible to salvage historical information from such oral traditions.[47]

Just as archaeologists and physical anthropologists allow the artifacts they uncover to inform us, so can one hear in oral traditions "echoes of the actual voices of the people who made those artifacts." Because a "bibliocentric research agenda imposes needless limits upon legitimate scholarship about the ancient past," Echo-Hawk advocates for a "peaceful coexistence and mutual interdependence" between written and spoken words, offering "more useful paradigms" to broaden our understanding.

ON SACRED TEXTS AND POSTCOLONIAL SCHOLARSHIP

If Western scientists question the *methods* that ethnohistorians use to historicize American Indian oral traditions, some American Indians question the *purpose* of this work. To some American Indians, attempting to historicize and rationalize oral traditions is to deny their sacred aspects and metaphysical meanings. By substituting American Indian understandings of these stories with secular and distinctly non-Indian models of explanation, researchers are in fact taking ownership of these stories away from Native people. They are, in effect, appropriating or colonizing American oral traditions by giving them non-Native meanings.

Although I disagree with the above position (strictly speaking, any form of analysis or interpretation is a form of colonization), I do wish to pause here to explain the significance of storytelling to many American Indian people.

After all, stories were not simply meant for entertainment. As Peter Nabokov phrased it, they "were central to tribal identity and continuity."⁴⁸ Dakota Sioux author-scholar-literary critic Elizabeth Cook-Lynn wrote that the "recording of Native views . . . has always been the purpose of storytelling, especially that storytelling that tells one generation of listeners what the previous generation has come to know through the long tenancy of the tribe in a specific geography."⁴⁹

Pawnee-Otoe author Anna Lee Walters explains why many Native people hesitate to see their stories in writing:

> First is the suspicion that they will be appropriated by the larger society like so much other cultural appropriation that has already occurred. Second, the material is often considered sacred and not for the knowledge of outsiders. Third, the "fixed" quality of written histories carries with it some very complex ideas about how this will affect the "living" state of the people and their continuity. Fourth, tribes often fear distortions of their histories. Concerns go on and on.⁵⁰

Considering past colonial academic practices, Walters's concerns are understandable. Not only do oral traditions lose their vitality by being printed (so they become frozen), but there is the very real danger that non-Indians might interpret these stories falsely or incorrectly. In this regard I wish to emphasize that the interpretations presented in this book are mine only; they do not necessarily reflect Caddoan viewpoints and interpretations.

Walters's statement begs the question how Caddoan Indians view non-Native research on their oral literature. I've encountered roughly three attitudes in Native American communities. One group simply does not care what non-Native scholars do. A second group welcomes the work of outsiders, as long as it is done respectfully. This group invites the contributions of outsiders, which might deepen the understanding and appreciation of tribal history and culture. A third group, however, rejects any meddling in tribal traditions by outsiders. It views non-Native scholars as trespassers whose real intention, whether consciously or not, is to disown American Indians of their cultural heritage and to colonize their past. Quite frequently, this group considers any interpretation or analysis of oral traditions by non-Natives as colonialist and/or sacrilegious. Which of these attitudes is supreme often varies over time, but it is not uncommon for non-Native scholar to be confronted by all three attitudes at the same time.

Which group should one listen to?

One does not have to consider members of the first group, because they do not care what academics are doing or saying. Their interest in scholarly work may be of a passing nature only. Fortunately, this group is small. In my experience, most American Indians care a great deal about how their past is remembered and represented.

Members of the second group are not just a source of encouragement; they are often also constructive critics of a work in progress. Indeed, my own work has improved significantly through the critical comments, suggestions, and recommendations of Native people. To be sure, cooperation is not always easy for historians, who are more comfortable around the ghosts of the past than among the living of the present. Still, stepping out of the isolated universe of books and archives benefits not only the scholar but Native peoples as well.

More problematic for the non-Native scholar are members of the third group. Their complaints strike at the legacy of hundreds of years of white-dominated scholarship that tended to ignore, stereotype, and stigmatize American Indian peoples. In the name of science, some scholars invaded indigenous communities in search of knowledge. According to Elizabeth Cook-Lynn, such scholars behaved "like the professional burglar, breaking into a house, rifling through certain drawers that he has good reason to think contain the jewelry and money, and triumphantly bearing his loot away." Indeed, the work of Frank Hamilton Cushing among the Zuni immediately comes to mind.[51]

To ignore this group opens one up to the charge of colonialism, a term as powerfully devastating in present-day academia as the charge of racism or sexism was a few decades earlier. However, adhering to the position of this group means that the scholar cannot do the work of trying to understand or elucidate the past. This is a difficult dilemma for any conscientious person working in the field. In truth, however, I have found that this group, though sometimes vocal, does not usually represent the majority view. Furthermore, its voices are reminders of a time when scholars did not concern themselves with the beliefs and sensitivities of the Native peoples they studied. The protests of this group serve as a reminder that one must always conduct oneself with humility and sincerity, and that one's work is serious business to American Indian people today.

Still, American Indian critics have a point. By definition, historians colonize the past. They do not let history speak for itself; they act as spokespersons for the past. Historians select the sources they want to use; they weigh the evidence and interpret its meanings; they present evidence in one way, even though it is often possible to present it in many different ways. In defense of my colleagues, however, I do not believe that they are colonizers in terms of intent. Their intentions are not to dominate or control but to further knowledge and understanding and to satisfy their own intellectual curiosity. To be sure, historians get (usually modest) material and professional gains from their work. In my case, my work counts toward tenure, job security, and promotion, which in turn allow me to live in relative comfort. The dilemma cannot be fully resolved. Still, if I have to choose between being called a "colonialist" historian by some and not being a historian at all, I will suffer the risk of getting branded occasionally.[52]

Touching upon the relationship between scholarship and tradition, Echo-Hawk defends the responsibilities of the historian-scientist. Although many Native Americans, especially religious leaders, resent the idea that their oral traditions must be subjected to critical investigation before they can serve as legitimate sources of history, Echo-Hawk believes that "scholars must stand their ground . . . when they are urged to accept origin stories as literal history." He affirms that scholars have an obligation to subject their sources "to critical examination no matter how much it may anchor any specific cultural pattern." However, one should not dismiss American Indian worldviews expressed in oral traditions because they are linked to historical patterns. Rather than dismissing one history for another, we should compare the stories we tell about ourselves, reconcile competing ideologies, and "seek creative ways to selectively structure our worldviews to accommodate conflicting interpretations of human history."[53]

Sadly, as a result of colonialism, many American Indian tribes have lost not only their language but also their understanding of tribal oral literature. "The truth is," writes Elizabeth Cook-Lynn, "our literatures have suffered the oppression of colonial intrusion, much knowledge is forgotten or ignored, and we as Native people have often been confused or disillusioned as to what it all means in terms of contemporary lives." Native understanding has been replaced by "master narratives" imposed by Western artists and scholars. Following in the footsteps of Lakota scholar-philosopher Vine Deloria Jr., intellectuals such as Cook-Lynn have changed direction: "The 'master narrative' is coming under closer scrutiny, and the return to tradition is becoming more important in the Native American story."[54]

How to deal with this problem of colonial master narratives? Anthropologist Raymond Fogelson once suggested that there are three forms of ethnohistory. The first is ethnohistory as it is done by non-Indians. In the second form, which Fogelson calls ethno-ethnohistory, non-Indian scholars present

Indian interpretations and viewpoints. Finally, Fogelson quips, there is ethno-ethno-ethnohistory, which entails the writing of Native history from a Native perspective, done by Native writers"[55] The oral traditions discussed in this book belong to the last of Fogelson's categories. For this reason, several chapters of this book begin with summaries of the original traditions as they were published by Dorsey and others. This ethno-ethno-ethnohistory is followed by ethnohistory, or my reflections on these stories.

MONSTER THEORIES

If my attempt at historicizing oral traditions sounds somewhat unconventional, interpreting monster lore is common practice. Indeed, the field of monster studies is booming currently, and there are many different theories on what monsters truly represent. The publication of *Monster Theory: Reading Culture* (1996), edited by medievalist Jeffrey Jerome Cohen, did much to popularize the field. Cohen's monsters are psychological creatures sprung out of "fear, desire, anxiety, and fantasy." They embody displacement (unease) and receive their vitality from uncertainty. Because uncertainty is always present, the monster in effect becomes immortal. Often such monsters are portrayed as sexually free and uninhibited. Even though this gives them a certain appeal, there is an associated danger: "We distrust and loathe the monster at the same time we envy its freedom, and perhaps its sublime despair." Such monsters warn us against the temptations that will unleash the monster within us.[56]

Although Cohen touches upon very important aspects of monster theory, there are several problems with his theoretical model when it is applied to the Caddoan monsters discussed in this book. Cohen's theory is Eurocentric: the monsters he analyzes—Frankenstein, Dracula, and so on—are typically the monsters of European tradition. His theory is also influenced by Freudian, Jungian, and Foucaultian views. His references to sex and sexuality, for example, are more typical of European monsters; they do not seem to apply to any of the Caddoan monsters described in this book. Unlike Cohen's occidental monsters, the monsters in this book are not timeless but *fixed* to a particular age or point in time. Furthermore, I believe they are not necessarily timeless phenomena but instead relate to specific *events*.

Likewise, in his book *Monsters: Evil Beings, Mythical Beasts, and All Manner of Imaginary Terrors* (2009), anthropologist David D. Gilmore argues that monsters are figments of our imagination rather than based on real experiences. The mind needs monsters, he writes, because without them, our societies would not function optimally. Because monsters are creations of the human mind, they share certain universal characteristics. Comparing monster lore across the world, Gilmore concludes that the catalog of monsters in human folklore, fiction, and art is rich and diverse, but the basic fear, often represented by the mouth of the monster, is the "primal fear of being eaten." Deeply influenced by Freudian theory, Gilmore's work helps us *understand* and *suppress* inappropriate behavior, such as aggression and unbridled sexual desire.

Following Rene Giraud's theory of violence and the sacred, philosopher Richard Kearney, in his book *Strangers, Gods, and Monsters: Interpreting Otherness* (2003), argues that monsters and strangers serve useful functions in divided societies. Societies blame their internal problems (sins) on strangers and begin to project monstrous qualities on outsiders. Having found a convenient scapegoat, societies often sacrifice these "monsters" in a ceremony of expiation, in which they cast away the sins and, temporarily, restore unity. Interestingly, sometimes the sacrificial victim becomes a god in the process, as was the case with Jesus Christ.[57] As this book shows later, this theory seems to apply to Pahukatawa, a scalped man who became one of the most prominent sacred powers in Pawnee tradition.

Philosopher Stephen T. Asma traces the anatomy and evolution of monster metaphors in his masterful history *On Monsters: An Unnatural History of Our Worst Fears* (2009). Unlike psychoanalysts, Asma believes that monsters are rooted in reality but that they are also shaped by our imagination: "If we find monsters in our world, it is sometimes because we have brought them with us."[58] The great appeal of Asma's theory is his analysis of how monsters changed over time. Ancient monster stories were hero stories in which the hero imposed his cultural, physical, and military superiority upon an enemy. Medieval thinkers believed that monsters were creations of an omnipotent God, who sent them to test the resolve of the faithful and to weed out sinners. The great minds of the rational era looked at monsters more scientifically and soon discovered that these monsters were not God's work but rather accidental creations. Despite efforts to debunk monsters, the scientific age gave birth to a series of new miscreants, such as Frankenstein's monster.[59] In the twentieth century, Sigmund Freud, Carl Gustav Jung, and other psychologists looked at monsters in a different way: "Having worn out their welcome in religion, natural history, and travelers' tales, the monsters settled into their new abode of human psychology."[60] Psychologists consider human emotions, psychoses (including existentialist Angst), and instincts as instrumental forces in the creation of monsters. Finally, postmodernism directed the study of monsters in yet another direction: "Instead of asking what makes a monster, it asks what makes it *seem* a monster." The answer was that certain elites use monster labels and epithets (including racial demonization) to establish power and dominance over others.

Like Asma, I believe that the monsters described in this book have their origin in reality and that they are not always fabrications of the mind. Unlike Asma, I think it is hard to discern an evolution in the nature of monsters among the Caddoans. But as the example of Pahukatawa shows, it would be reasonable to presume that Caddoan monster typology did evolve over time.

That does not mean that the psychological models have no analytical value. Although the Caddoan monsters in this book originated in real events, the Caddoan peoples did associate them with the lawlessness, barbarity, destruction, and chaos of the time before civilization. They may have viewed them as punishments by the sacred powers for their transgressions or sins. Fortunately, in the Caddoan traditions, there is very often a hero who defeats the monster and restores order. The hero's weapon is usually *tradition*, or more precisely, a return to old ways.

One should not exaggerate the role of tradition, however. In many stories, help appeared. In the Wichita tradition, Coyote received help from Spider-Man (whom I identify as a Frenchman), who represents a force not from the past but from the modern age. The hero in the Pawnee tradition defeats the Flint Monster with what I identify as a gun. Pahukatawa was based on a real figure (a scalped man) but was influenced by Morning Star and Jesus Christ. He embodies both old and new. In short, non-Indians appeared not only as monsters; in several stories they appeared as powerful and mysterious benefactors as well.

Because I believe that the Caddoan monsters in this book represent traumatic historical disasters related to European contact, it is useful to see what anthropologists have to say on the subject of disaster. Susanna M. Hoffman argues that disasters are not merely physical events but are cultural events as well: "Disaster exposes the way in which people construct or 'frame' their peril (including the denial of it), the way they perceive their environment and their subsistence, and the ways they invent explanation, constitute their morality, and project their continuity and promise into the future."[61] Disasters, in short, challenge old cultural precepts. They force people to respond to and reflect upon what has happened. People must make sense of what has happened, and their explanations reflect certain cultural ideas and values. Not only do societies have to adapt physically to perceived hazards—for example, by changing the architecture of houses in an earthquake-prone area—

but they must also adapt mentally to arm themselves against future disasters: "These cultural adaptations include innovation and persistence in memory, cultural history, worldview, symbolism, social structural flexibility, religion, and the cautionary nature of folklore and folk tales."[62]

However, as the example of the Arikara Whirlwind will show, it is also possible that people react to disasters conservatively. The Arikaras blamed a devastating whirlwind (diseases) upon religious declension. Whirlwind reminded people of their duty to worship properly. Hoffman notes that people often resort to "disaster symbolism" to explain their misfortune: "Peoples' explanations of disaster tend to rely on creative, often mythological, imagination." Quite frequently, "The disaster becomes a 'monster,' either in the guise of a formless terror or the frightful second side of an otherwise kind god."[63]

Anthony Oliver-Smith concurs that disasters are cultural constructs. He distinguishes between two forms of disasters. The first are sudden and unexpected disasters, of a hitherto unknown kind. Such disasters "are portrayed as nonroutine [unpredictable], destabilizing, causing uncertainty, disorder, and sociocultural collapse." They "endanger [old] worldviews and systems of meaning." The second type consists of cyclical or recurrent disasters. Disasters of the second type are not unfamiliar to people, and they have devised strategies to cope with them. Societies must adapt to these hazards. Consequently, "Disasters, and how well or poorly systems fare in them, are a gauge of the success or failure of the total adaptation of the community."[64]

Oliver-Smith's theory applies to the monsters in this book. Whirlwind, the masked cannibal man, the Flint Monster, and the child-snatching witch-woman are examples of the first type. They were new phenomena that took the Caddoans by surprise and forced them to reconsider their views of the universe. The scalped men are disasters of the second type, because they formed an extended threat to which the people adapted. Pahukatawa, in fact, can be viewed as a significant cultural adaptation whose development was cut short when the threat of genocidal warfare ceased to exist.

Although I am indebted to the aforementioned scholars for their insights in monster theory, this book is unique in the sense that it deals exclusively with Caddoan monsters and that it treats these not as figments of the darkest corners of human imagination but as representations of very real traumatic historical events. It attempts to explain these monsters rationally, albeit through the lens of interpretation, and treats oral traditions as historical sources comparable in status to Euro-American sources. Indeed, rather than using oral traditions to confirm details from Euro-American documents, it does the reverse by using non-Caddoan sources to support our understanding of Caddoan monster traditions. In the process, both sources—Caddoan and Euro-American—complement each other and enrich our understanding of the past.

EVALUATING THE FINDINGS

My writing this book was purely accidental. I did not look for an idea: the idea found me. While rereading the story of Mother Corn and Whirlwind in the Arikara creation account in preparation for a class, I was struck by an intriguing insight: what if the disease-causing Whirlwind was in fact a description of certain "virgin soil" epidemics that devastated Arikara society in the late 1700s? This question led me to write the first chapter of this book (which first appeared as an article in *American Indian Quarterly* and which here appears as chapter 2). It then prompted me to investigate monster stories among other Caddoan tribes. At first I was looking for similar symbols that would describe epidemics, but I soon noticed that each of these tribes had very different sets of monsters that were not associated with diseases. Could these monsters represent some other kind of disaster? As I read these stories more closely, something in the accounts occasionally captivated me and made me want to explore further. Thus the "iron nose" of the cannibal's mask in the Caddo tradition made me search for the time when the Caddo first came into contact with iron. The scaled flint skin of the monster in Pawnee tradition reminded me of European-made coats of mail introduced by the Spanish. Finally, a "pole that explodes" in a Wichita account reminded me of a cannon. With these ideas in mind, I set out to find historical events that matched the contents of the stories. After long and sometimes frustrating searches, I was fortunate on a few occasions to find the actual events in non-Indian sources.

Indeed, critics might quickly point out that I went searching the documentary record, hoping to find something that would confirm my suspicions. That attitude, they would correctly point out, may have prejudiced me in advance. I am aware of this fact, and the reader too must be made aware of it. However, while I was *hoping* to find something, I was not truly *expecting* to find anything at all. Ultimately, it is up to the reader to consider the validity of my findings. Incidentally, historians who use oral traditions to seek confirmation of their findings in written records are guilty of the same prejudice.

In essence, I reversed the order in which most ethnohistorians usually do their work. Early ethnohistorians, such as Mildred M. Wedel, looked at traditional colonial sources and tried to analyze these from an American Indian perspective, using insights from anthropology and ethnology. Often such historians scoured oral traditions later to find evidence in support of their earlier analyses of Euro-American sources. For this book, I started with the oral traditions and then went looking in Euro-American sources for evidence that would validate my findings. Although this method is exhausting and frustrating, by placing the American Indian sources at the center of inquiry, it is more ethnohistorical than the more common European bibliocentric approach. I should point out here that this method is not new. Robert S. McPherson and other ethnohistorians have used similar methodologies.[65]

In any event, after comparing the oral traditions with one another and with conventional historical records, I made several important discoveries. The first is that although these tribes were linguistically and culturally related, they had very different sets of monsters. These differences in monster iconography can be explained by the fact that each tribe had a different history. In other words, the monsters represent unique historical experiences. Usually the monsters represent a certain historical trauma. Thus Whirlwind in the Arikara creation story represented epidemic diseases of the eighteenth century that devastated the Arikara people. Similarly, the cannibal man with the iron-nosed mask was a member of the De Soto expedition, which contacted and tormented some of the Caddo Indians in 1541. The story of the witch-woman who captured the chief's son was related to events leading to the San Sabá Massacre of 1758. Several historical figures could have been the model for the Flint Monster in Pawnee tradition. Most likely he was a coat-of-mail-wearing enemy, possibly Spanish, but more likely he was an American Indian enemy. Finally, the appearance of scalped men took place at a time when the Sioux waged a devastating war of extermination against the Pawnees. Out of these unfortunate beings emerged Pahukatawa, a new culture hero who exhibited both traditional and Christian traits. Pahukatawa offered inspiration and solace to the Pawnee people at a time when they needed it most.

This leads me to suspect that, despite the fantastic content of these stories, there is a historical core to many American Indian oral traditions. To be sure, the stories are not histories in the Western, Rankean sense of the word. They are not "objective," and they are certainly not void of the magical and supernatural. Many of them probably did change over time. Some of them may be composites of multiple stories. Yet it would be too easy to dismiss them as mere phantasms or products of the imagination. I strongly believe that the stories described in the following pages were inspired by real events. As Vine Deloria wrote, "It seems strange indeed that the ancient peoples [supposedly] would spend so much time writing about the inner mysteries of life and find little time to record the events and incidents of their times."[66]

Finally, the stories analyzed in this book have a time-depth that is relatively shallow. They do not, as is often thought, refer to ancient times before the arrival of whites but rather to the time after contact. The Arikara creation account is especially noteworthy because it shows that it was an ongoing history, from its cosmic origins to the relative present.

It is true that I selected the stories for this book. I chose these stories because they promised some level of success. I believe that the evidence and the commonsense arguments I make compensate for the enthusiasm I hold for my own conclusions. In any case, for an idea to take its place in academic discourse, it must be stated first. I would rather be criticized for confusing the debate than not have my ideas discussed at all. After all, it is in the arena of debate that new understanding might be generated.

Even Mason, who criticized a too liberal use of oral traditions, admitted that perhaps speculation is to be preferred "if immobility is to be avoided." To decipher "hidden meanings," Mason suggests, one can make use of "suggestion, something to stir up useful conjecture in the hope of learning something more tangible." However, Mason also says that the scholar who employs this technique must make it absolutely clear that he is speculating so that his uncritical audience understands that these are speculations and not facts or ironclad conclusions. I am most happy to meet Mason on this point. I am not so arrogant as to claim finality. Rather I present probability. However, I am convinced that my conclusions are correct, and I will continue to believe this until proven otherwise. I leave it up to others to present more plausible explanations than the ones given in the chapters that follow.[67]

This study is divided into three parts. Part I, "Storytelling," offers an elaborate introduction to the problem of historicizing oral traditions. Part II, "Oral Traditions as History," includes four case studies that historicize a number of Caddoan myths, one from each of the Caddoan tribes. Part III, "Oral Traditions and Ethnohistorical Analysis," shows how oral traditions can be used to throw new light on well-known historical events. One of the chapters deals with Pahukatawa, a Pawnee prophet who was murdered and mutilated by the Sioux during intertribal wars of the nineteenth century. These wars were an indirect result of the chain of events caused by European invasion and colonization. This period witnessed a dramatic rise in the number of scalped men, who were a different kind of contact monster. Interestingly, in the figure of Pahukatawa we see the transformation of a "monstrous" scalped man into an important deity.

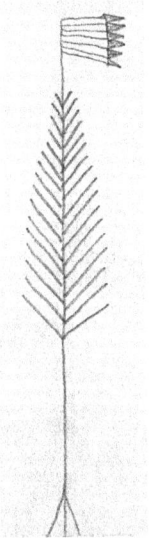

Part I
Storytelling

ONE

Caddoan Storytellers and Storytelling Traditions

One cannot overstate the significance of tribal traditions. They are not dead relics of supposedly vanished civilizations; nor are they "childish" accounts, as nineteenth-century audiences tended to believe. These stories form the most complete record of a tribe's religious ideas, values, collective memory, and history. As long as these stories are told, the people and their culture live on. The men and women who shared the stories to preserve them understood their significance. When they were published in books, the tales that the elders wished to pass on to subsequent generations became fixed on paper. This chapter details the significance of the art of storytelling for the Caddoan nations.

"PERFORMING" ORAL TRADITIONS

Folklorist John Miles Foley wrote that oral traditions "dwarf written literature in both size and diversity." Foley added that oral traditions are more accurately performances that often include dramatic narrative techniques, such as humor, intonation, irony, facial expressions, silent pauses, and gestures. Mythographer Dennis Tedlock explained that the "speaking storyteller is not a writer who fears to make use of the shift key, but an actor on a stage."[1] As these performances are committed to paper to satisfy Euro-American "print-oriented" and "text-determined" audiences, such subtleties are inevitably lost. Indeed, as texts are translated for publication, they are also edited and interpreted, with the possible result that important elements from both performance and story are lost.[2] To recapture some of the original flavors and meanings of storytelling performances, many folklorists today recommend close collaboration with Native communities. In such research, both parties should act as equal partners rather than reducing Native collaborators to "performers" and turning academics into authoritative "interpreters."[3]

Apart from mutually beneficial outcomes from collaboration, scholars should cooperate with Native communities for another reason. In many cases, non-Native scholars failed to credit the work of Native collaborators. Anthropologist Ralph Linton, for example, committed intellectual robbery when he published five scholarly articles on the Pawnees without ever mentioning James R. Murie, upon whose field notes the papers were based. Because of such abuses, many Indian tribes demand to exert some control over how their oral traditions are represented. Collaboration, therefore, is now considered an essential part of the research process.[4]

However, the pendulum swings both ways. Scholars might now run into Native prejudices suggesting that only Natives are equipped to conduct this kind of analysis. Barre Toelken, one of the leading scholars of American Indian oral traditions, rejected this notion categorically: "I do not subscribe to the notion that Indian DNA carries any built-in cultural depth or ability to articulate complex cultural meanings," he wrote. Yet Toelken believed that scholars were culturally indebted to Native people and that showing sensitivity to what they believed was appropriate: "This kind of serious attention and propriety requires respect, not adulation; it requires us to share, not intrude and plunder; it requires us to listen for Native voices, not trumpet our own assumptions."[5] Whenever possible, I tried to follow Toelken's advice and asked Native people for their input and comments. Regrettably, few were able to provide me with answers to my queries. I suppose that centuries of colonialism are largely to blame for the erosion of knowledge among the Caddoan peoples.

The stories told by George Dorsey's Native collaborators belonged to various genres, and they were important for many different reasons. Surely, many were told to provide entertainment on long fall or winter nights. But even those told for entertainment contained important cultural messages. As Toelken points out, such stories "dramatize ritual and social order; they record and maintain cultural values, providing moral examples, giving instruction, and imparting culturally important information; they express and embody artistic values; [and] they preserve historical records with an eye for culturally significant detail."[6] As mentioned earlier, this study is less interested in the artistic-ceremonial quality of these stories and more concerned with their historical content.

Although oral traditions often reach far back into time, folklorists like to point out that they are not "fossil records." In fact, they are *living* works of art. Stories are only (re)told if they continue to be "relevant" and understandable to the people. "When an orally transmitted story ceases to make sense or be interesting," Toelken writes, "people simply quit telling it, and it is no longer there."[7]

One way stories retain their relevance is that their meanings or interpretations shift to reflect present-day concerns. To the ethnohistorian who mines these oral traditions for historical information, this poses a major problem: if the meaning (and content) of stories can change, how does one determine in what ways they have changed? The answer is both simple and unsatisfying: without different recordings of the same story over time, one probably cannot. At the same time, the optimist in me believes that many of these stories were preserved fairly close to the originals over the ages. They were recorded when the tradition of storytelling was still strong, so the stories were still close to their original meanings.[8] To be sure, this is a major assumption. Ultimately, though, we have little choice in this matter: we can work only with the texts that have survived. Furthermore, while my findings may be unapologetically interpretive, the assumption that the stories have changed beyond recognition is equally unsubstantiated and presumptive.

Incidentally, the Greek word *mythos* means "word" or "story," not "error," the meaning that is often used nowadays. Indeed, many mythographers believe that "myth may constitute the highest form of truth, albeit in metaphorical guise." However, because the word "myth" is now often associated with falsehood, I try to avoid it in this book as much as possible. In any case, folklorist Alan Dundes distinguished between three types of stories or, as he called them, "prose narratives": folktales (narratives that are regarded as fiction), myths (truthful accounts of things that happened in the remote past), and legends (also considered true but set in a less remote era, "when the world was much as it is today").[9]

The study of myths has a long history, and mythographers and folklorists have suggested many theories over the centuries. In the nineteenth century, scholars suspected that myths were allegories of natural processes or spiritual qualities, or that they resulted from biographies of human beings who were deified in the process (a theory called euhemerism). Others suspected that myths were fabricated by elites to control the masses. In the twentieth century, scholars believed that myths had either historical, sociological, psychological, or structural causes. Depending on the school of thought, myths explain enigmatic phenomena, are forms of symbolic expression, are projections of the subconscious, are attempts to integrate people into social systems, are forces that steer human behavior or legitimate social institutions, or are forms of religious communication.[10] Freud argued that they reflected unconscious desires and dreams. Jung believed they were expressions of a shared human unconscious determined by archetypal patterns of thought and symbol. Anthropologist Clyde Kluckhohn reasoned that myths helped people cope with changes and anxieties. Ernst Cassirer thought they were excited responses to special aspects of the world. Alfred Radcliffe-Brown maintained that they were mechanisms of the social order. Mircea Eliade suggested that their function was to temporarily reinstate the creative past and allow people to revisit and reconnect with the world of the ancestors. Claude Lévi-Strauss revolutionized the field by suggesting that all myths reproduce a common structure of mind and society. Bronislav Malinowski proposed the theory of functionalism, which gave myths distinct functions: they expressed, enhanced, and codified beliefs; safeguarded and enforced morality; and vouched "for the efficiency of ritual and [contained] practical rules for the guidance of man."[11] Generally, in the twentieth century, myths were no longer treated as representations of the past but as keys to understanding present-day cultures. Historical and euhemeristic explanations (the theory that the gods of myths were actual historical persons who had been deified) had lost ground.[12]

I must clarify that I am not a folklorist; nor do I have a desire to trespass on the venerable field of folklore. Still, in the process of writing this book, I had to familiarize myself with folklore theories on oral traditions. I found much of value there, but also much that I found too constricting for my purposes. Therefore, in this book I do not rely on certain theories dear to folklorists, especially tale and motif type indexes that emphasize similarities between oral traditions from around the world.[13] Although I recognize that such similarities exist, I emphasize the distinctiveness of the Caddoan monsters. For example, while it may be true that the Pawnee Flint Monster story has parallels with the Old English Beowulf saga, I do not believe that they are different versions of the same story or that they describe the same archetypal processes.[14] For similar reasons, I largely ignore Claude Lévi-Strauss's structuralist approach. Although I recognize the ingenuity with which Lévi-Strauss analyzed American Indian myths, I feel that structuralism ignores the fact that real historical events are at the basis of the Caddoan monster stories.

More recently, scholars have emphasized the cultural context in which oral traditions are performed as well as the ways they have been (or should be) preserved. They quickly point out that myths have a kind of plasticity that allows them to change over time to remain relevant. By changing itself, a myth "is adapted to a new situation, armed to withstand a new challenge." As Th. P. van Baaren phrased it, "The character of myth is opposed to disappearance, but not, in view of what we said about its plasticity, to change

... as a rule it is the myth which will change.... In this situation the invention of writing has wrought havoc, because this invention has made it possible to fix the text of a myth more or less permanently."[15]

Modern scholars such as Barre Toelken, Dell Hymes, Dennis Tedlock, Brian Swann, and Arnold Krupat therefore pay close attention to the cultural context in which oral traditions are produced. They argue that oral traditions should be analyzed emically, meaning "from inside the originating culture, beginning if possible with the Native language itself, and drawing on ethnographic data."[16] Wherever possible, I used emic sources and commentaries. Unfortunately, in the case of the Caddoan stories, no original recordings exist; nor have the Native-language texts survived. Only in a few instances was I able to get emic explanations for the events described in this book. In most cases, I had only interpretation to fall back on.

Hymes and Tedlock pioneered ethnopoetics, the idea that storytelling is a performing art and that the character of the storyteller, the audience, and the occasion of the performance must be considered when analyzing the oral tradition. They criticized the way in which past storytelling performances were collected, translated, and written down. (One of the early collectors, anthropologist Franz Boas, already lamented the "loss of spirit" when an oral tradition was committed to paper.) Although their approach promises more accurate results, it is difficult to apply with oral traditions that have survived only in written form, such as the Caddoan monster traditions discussed in this book. What makes matters worse in the case of the Caddoan traditions is that we do not really know in what context and circumstances these texts were produced. For this reason, some ethnopoetic scholars dismiss older publications as useless because of their limitations. I, however, concur with William M. Clements, who warned that to use the older published traditions indiscriminately is "foolish" but that "not to use them at all seems foolish also."[17]

Although I respect the work of Toelken, Hymes, Tedlock, Swann, Krupat, and other scholars of oral traditions, I do not emphasize performance here because of the simple fact that such performance contexts were never recorded. Furthermore, I might offend these scholars by viewing symbols slightly more literally than they do. Although many of the events, characters, and phenomena in the stories under consideration here are symbolic, metaphoric, or idiomatic, I try to link the symbol to real persons or very real things. I am not content to simply assume that because a character in a story is named Coyote, he is automatically some kind of archetypal trickster figure.[18] In such cases, I searched the historical sources to see if there once lived a person by that name who matched the person in the story (see chapter 3, for example). Theorists and ethnopoeticists might find this approach strange, because they claim that their theories provide sufficient explanation for these characters. However, because I try to show that these myths are in fact histories of a different kind, I had to search other sources for corroborative evidence. Likewise, I was not content to accept blindly that the hero in one of the stories presented in this book simply transformed into a "red bird with black streaks running down its eyes" (see chapter 4). Rather than accepting that this person magically morphed into a cardinal, I looked for other explanations. While my hypotheses may require more imagination than the reader is willing to exercise, I nevertheless believe that my explanations fit the Caddoan tendency to use symbols that physically resemble the original. In short, in some cases my interpretation of symbols tends to be less abstract and more literal.

I wish to pause here to remind readers that the principal purpose of this book is to explain the presence of tribe-specific monsters in Caddoan traditions. It is, first and foremost, a book of *history*—more specifically a *history of Caddoan monsters*. Next, it is aimed at historians who, until now, have viewed American Indian oral traditions as subsidiary historical documents only, rather than as actual histories in their own right. For these reasons, anthropologists, archaeologists, and folklorists will find much to criticize in this book. Anthropologists will decry the lack of emic or tribal perspectives. Archaeologists may question my tendency for speculation. And although I often borrow from their work, folklorists will be frustrated with my lack of attention to theory. Indeed, finding theories too constricting in historical research, I am not at all interested in presenting a theory on the nature of American Indian oral traditions, even though I am aware that my conclusions may have consequences in this area.[19]

Of course, Native ways of "doing history" are different from those of non-Natives. Indeed, most non-Natives call these stories myths, not histories. Arnold Krupat observed that Western historiography "fetishizes" fact: "We neither accept Their historical criteria as consistent with truth, nor do we translatively mediate between Their language and our own."[20] Indeed, Krupat is willing to accept some oral traditions as forms of history:

> It is unlikely that anyone trained in Western modes of thought will accept accounts of "mystical happenings" as factual and accurate. But that is not necessary. What is necessary is that we stop using terms like "myth," "anecdotes," and "mystical happenings," as standing in simple and subordinate opposition to "history"—a category that We think cannot exist apart from empirical, factual accuracy.[21]

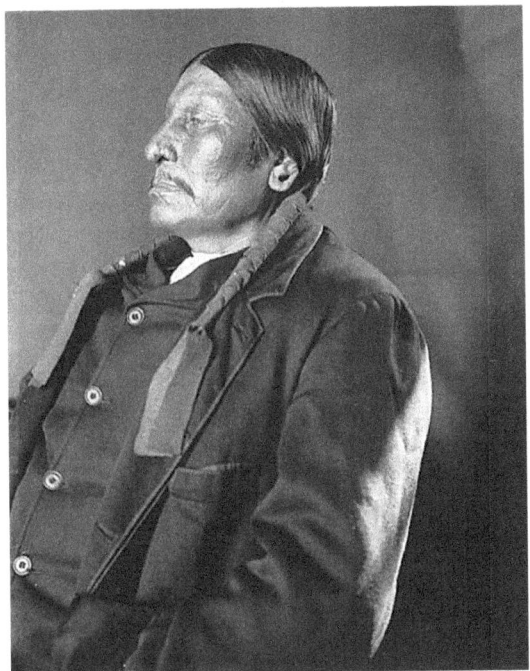

Roaming Scout (Ki-Ri-Ki-Ri-See-Ra-Ki-Wa-Ri, circa 1845–1916), June 1907. At the turn of the twentieth century, Roaming Scout was a Skiri Pawnee religious leader and one of the most knowledgeable sources on Pawnee culture and history. Courtesy Smithsonian Institution, NAA GN01218.

Thus Krupat firmly believes that Native peoples preserved history in their oral traditions. However, their understanding of historiography is different from that of non-Natives. According to Krupat, American Indians favor truth over fact. In Native historiography, "the interpretative truth of the narrative is what determines its historicity."[22] This viewpoint may be hard to accept for most mainstream historians, but it at least introduces them to the idea that some of these oral traditions are histories, albeit a different kind of history.

AMERICAN INDIAN STORYTELLING CONVENTIONS

According to Caddoan sources, telling stories not only brought the past back to life; stories could literally lengthen the life of the storyteller. At least that was the message from Roaming Scout, a Pawnee priest, when he passed on sacred stories that he had learned from elders to interpreter James Murie. "That is what one old man—one of those who used to live here—wanted," Roaming Scout told Murie, "that his stories, that these stories that I am giving you, be carried on to ensure long life."[23]

Old-Man-That-Chief, also a Pawnee, expressed a similar view. To Old-Man-That-Chief, who was known as a prolific storyteller, stories were not just a source of vitality; they literally provided him with the means of living. "A story is like a little seed," he told anthropologist Gene Weltfish in the 1930s:

> From it all sorts of other stories branch off for you. A story gives you life. Now that I am old, people invite me to come and eat good things with them and then they ask me to tell stories. So these stories keep me alive.[24]

To be sure, there were differences between American Indian and European story genres and the method of preserving them. "God gave special ways to the white man and special ways to the Indian," Caddo elders told author Cecile Elkins Carter. God's gift included the way Indians preserved history: white people wrote stories down, but Indians memorized them. "You know a white man when he gets these things [stories, he] puts it in a file and writes it down; sometimes [when] he forgets it he can find it," Cheyenne tribal historian John Stands In Timber said. "But an Indian has to keep it in his head."[25]

To be sure, memorization occasionally led to a confusion of historical events. Sometimes events were conflated or combined.[26] Often details were left out, making it difficult to identify a certain story with a specific historical event. To American Indians, that was not necessarily a problem. As John Stands In Timber explained, "The white man usually tells more details even if it isn't important; the Indians remember the main things."[27] Although Indians and whites might remember things in different ways, Lakota storyteller Luther Standing Bear charged that whites were guilty of the far more serious offense of blatantly falsifying history. Whites did so, according to Standing Bear, by ridiculing Indian memories. To Standing Bear, stories were the "libraries" of his people: "In each story there was recorded some event of interest or importance, some happening that affected the lives of the people." Among these events of interest were "calamities, discoveries, achievements, and victories to be kept." Not all of these stories were historical, but some "taught the virtues—kindness, obedience, thrift, and the rewards of right living." According to Standing Bear, there were also "stories of pure fancy in which I can see no meaning." Perhaps these were "so old that their meaning has been lost in the countless years, for our people are old." Still, Standing Bear was certain that these stories allowed people to "enrich their minds" and "keep their history on the leaves of memory." Sadly, the books written by unfriendly whites had "robbed" his people "of both history and memory."[28]

An additional issue sometimes affected the way stories were remembered. That was the taboo about speaking the names of the (recently) deceased. The dead, one of Frank B. Linderman's Crow collaborators said, "have gone to their Father, Ah-badt-dadt-deah, and like Him are sacred." Linderman observed that this "custom makes the gathering of tribal history extremely difficult."[29]

Although each tribe had its own ideas about stories, most agreed that stories should be told only at certain times in the year, usually wintertime, when the nights were long and people huddled together for conversation. Among some tribes, violating storytelling taboos could open one up to misfortune, such as snake and scorpion bites. To some, winter was the best time to tell stories "because over winter nights the creatures featured in these narratives are hibernating or sluggish and won't know that they are being talked about or, worse, made fun of."[30]

Dorsey wrote that the Skiri Pawnees avoided telling stories in the summer because the Snake Star and Coyote Star stood close together in the summer sky. If people told Coyote stories in summer, Snake might whisper to Coyote that the people were talking about him and Coyote and Snake might retaliate by sending snakes after the people.[31]

The Pawnees considered fall, right after the season's harvest was brought in, to be a good time to tell stories, because it was "not too cold not too hot. Just nice to have a fire." In her field notes, Weltfish described one storytelling gathering. A chief invited people to his home for a feast by telling them that they should bring empty plates. People who were not invited were nevertheless welcome to attend, and they received plates for dinner. Seating arrangements were prescribed: chiefs, for example, sat along the west wall of the lodge. The guests trickled in around eight o'clock in the evening. The eldest men in attendance were expected to talk about "how things used to be and came to be." But first, the women of the lodge cooked up an elaborate meal. After everyone had eaten, the women retired to their beds, from where they listened to the men telling the stories. Customarily, the leader told the first story, followed by the old men. One man brought a stick (a cane) and gave it to the man who was to speak. When the story ended, the stick passed to the next storyteller. Such gatherings usually lasted until midnight, but occasionally they continued well into the morning. Weltfish explained that a storytelling session was not a mere leisure pastime. "Through it was transmitted history, climatology, theology, the logistics of war, topography, and many other important facets of Pawnee knowledge," Weltfish wrote. "Such a session was an invaluable preamble to setting out on the winter hunt."[32]

Most tribes honored good storytellers. In fact, among the Caddoan tribes, talented speakers and storytellers were praised and admired.[33] Incidentally, the greatest Cheyenne historian, according to Stands In Timber, was an Arikara who had married into the Cheyenne Nation. His name was Stands All Night (or Standing All Night), and the Cheyennes respected him for his exceptional knowledge of Cheyenne history and tribal lore. He was reportedly born in the 1760s and was well over one hundred years old when he died in 1869.[34]

Speaking of Pawnee orators, Weltfish pointed out how much the Pawnees respected the power of language. "The reputation of being an orator was coveted, and a man, when once recognized as such, was sure to wield great influence," Weltfish wrote. "An orator when addressing a council upon a question in which he was thoroughly interested, seemed to appreciate fully the dignity of his position, and identifying himself with the cause he advocated, and addressing himself directly to the person he was attempting to answer or convince, his speech would become vividly dramatic."[35]

Weltfish also described how the Pawnees had sessions at which the most compelling storytellers displayed their storytelling skills. The "old time stories" received the most attention because they described people's "experiences as they moved from place to place abroad in the land in times past."[36] Dorsey explained that the Arikaras had regular "story-telling contests," in which storytellers challenged one another, in a friendly manner, to tell better stories.[37] The Wichitas sometimes challenged one another in telling war stories. In one Wichita tradition, Coyote defeated a powerful being in a storytelling contest by inventing war stories. In short, storytelling was powerful stuff. To illustrate the power of war stories, Kadas, a Wichita storyteller, said that when a warrior made a gift, it was customary for him "to go off, then come back, then tell a war-story and then give away whatever he had to give."[38]

Sometimes stories were introduced in a special way. Caddo storytellers often began their stories by stating, "Bah'nah 'ahyá' tiki" (It is said that long ago; the equivalent to "Once upon a time"), to indicate that the story was not something the speaker had witnessed but something he or she had heard from others. The phrase *bah'nah* (It is said) would often return in the story. Because Dorsey believed such phrases unnecessarily interrupted the "flow" of the story, he eliminated them from the final text.[39]

The Wichitas conducted little ceremonies when "life stories" were told. They offered smoke to all the sacred powers before beginning a tale, explaining that the speaker was about to relate their stories. If the narrator told the stories of their lives correctly, he or she would receive their reward, symbolized by "a light fog early on the following morning." However, if the narrator told a story incorrectly and misrepresented the sacred powers, there would be a "day of excessive cold." It was common for a narrator to break down in tears at the end of a story in which he had "followed as nearly as may be in the footsteps of the hero" whose life he had recounted, and "young listeners strike their front teeth with the nail of the thumb, thus indicating their desire that their teeth may always be sound, and that, having heard the story, they may live happily and enjoy good luck and live to old age and do wonderful deeds, such as were performed by the hero of the tale." After the story, there would be another round of smoke and food offerings by the narrator "to the heroes of the tales he had just recounted." He also offered small morsels of food to Man-never-known-on-Earth, the "chief of all the gods," to Morning Star (east), to South Star (south), to the meteors (west), to the Pole Star and the Seven Stars (north), and finally to Mother Earth.[40]

Stories often ended with a conclusive statement. The Pawnees used the phrase "We na netsu ut" (Now the gut passes) when they were done telling a Coyote story. The phrase referred to the custom of passing a piece of dried meat and fat stuffed into buffalo entrails to someone else when the people were marching on the trail.[41]

Stories were often the personal property of an individual. They often included (sacred) songs and rituals that gave the person additional power. In his *Traditions of the Skidi Pawnee*, Dorsey addressed the issue of private ownership of stories. Because the owner had paid for these stories, they "now form an intrinsic part of his life." Thus whenever he told a story, he would give up "a certain part of his life, levying a direct contribution upon its termination." Therefore a younger storyteller might say that he would not tell a story, for he was not yet ready to die. Older men who had lived long lives, by contrast, might be more willing to share. "My life is no longer of use," an old priest once said. "There is no reason why I should not tell you all that I know." Of course, the stories "did not always remain the exclusive property of the priesthood." They found their way among the ordinary people, who could recount them, albeit imperfectly. When laypeople recounted such stories, they lost much of their original meaning. "Thus," Dorsey wrote, "by a gradual process of deterioration, they come to be regarded as of no especial religious significance, and are told as tales are told."[42]

Dorsey's observation that the texts that he published (and that I treat as historical sources) have "no especial religious significance" is important, because some Caddoan people today view these texts as sacred. To them,

Dorsey's publications are little sacred bundles or sources of spiritual power that allow them to connect with the mental and spiritual world of their ancestors. For this reason some people might consider my work with these texts sacrilegious. They might insist on a literal interpretation of the texts. They might even argue that I have no right to work with them.

Even though I share a deep-seated respect for these stories, I nevertheless believe that my work with them is justified by the fact that the old storytellers wished to have them preserved and published. They are, as Dorsey's comments above imply, at most profane renditions of the sacred. That does not make them less true. Nor does it make their *content* less sacred. It merely makes them profane in *form*. Stripped of the songs and rituals, they are simply accounts. Most Caddoan people, I think, do not take the fundamentalist position and are open to the idea of interpretation because they believe that the stories use symbolism to convey a deeper meaning or reality.

CLASSIFYING CADDOAN STORIES

Scholars disagree on how to classify American Indian stories. Stories can be organized by content, by style, and in numerous other ways. As a result, there are many different classification systems.

When Dorsey began collecting Caddoan stories, he tried to present them to his audiences in an organized way. He quickly realized that this was not easy. In the introduction to *Traditions of the Skidi Pawnee* (1904), Dorsey admitted his failure in coming up with a satisfying system of classification: "An attempt has been made to classify the tales here presented, but only, it is feared, with partial success."[43] His arrangement consisted of "Cosmogonic" traditions, stories of "Boy-Heroes," stories related to sacred powers or "Medicine," "Animal Tales," "People [Who] Marry Animals or Become Animals," and "Miscellaneous" stories. Dorsey also mentioned a separate category of "Coyote Tales" but ended up including these in "Animal Tales."

For his *Traditions of the Arikara* (1904), Dorsey dropped the classification scheme in the table of contents, but in his introduction, he nevertheless provided a justification for his arrangement. The first two stories, he explained, were about the creation of the land. The next set of stories dealt with the creation of the Arikara people, followed by a set of "transformer stories" in which a culture hero rids the earth of monsters. Next are "rite myths," which explain the origin of a ceremony or a particular rite, followed by "miscellaneous" stories, animal and trickster stories, stories in "which the element of superstition or strange beliefs play a prominent part," and finally "war tales."

The Pawnee Mythology (1906) included stories from the four different Pawnee bands. Dorsey organized these stories into four categories. First there were "True Stories of the Heavenly Beings." Then there were "Tales of Ready-to-Give" (a Pawnee culture hero). Third in Dorsey's classification came stories on "The Origin of Medicine Ceremonies or Power." Finally there were "Coyote Tales." Dorsey understood that this classification was problematic, because one narrator might consider a story "true" while a narrator from a different band, who told a slightly different version, might say that it belonged in another category: "Hence it is that in one or two instances one version of a tale is found in one group, while another version is found in another group."[44]

The Pawnees divided the above categories into "true" and "false" (fictional) stories. True stories, Dorsey wrote, "relate to things or events which actually happened." False stories were "invented . . . by the old men, for the purpose of impressing some moral precept, illustrating some phase of ethical life, or of conveying a warning, etc." Stories of the heavenly beings were always true, as were those of the origins of medicine ceremonies and power. Tales of "Ready-to-Give" and other heroes might or might not be true, but Coyote tales were always fictional. That did not mean that Coyote tales were not valuable. They were, because they taught important moral lessons. But although he was always secondary to most of the heroes in Dorsey's second group, Coyote could be a powerful force of transformation who was as much a creator as he was a trickster.[45]

Writing about Arikara oral traditions, linguist Douglas Parks basically followed Dorsey's classification system of true stories and (fictional) tales. Parks further divided true stories into "sacred" and "non-sacred" stories. Tales consisted primarily of entertaining stories, such as trickster tales, animal tales, and adventure stories.

Dorsey found a similar categorization among the Wichitas. "Old" stories were those that dealt with the shaping of the world. The Wichitas considered these true stories. Stories of the present were spoken of as "new."[46]

I find many of these attempts at categorization problematic. After analyzing the stories in this book, I came to the conclusion that each story should be considered on its own merits rather than as a member of a specific category. Very often, stories relate a historical event but link it to a cosmogonic or cosmological phenomenon. For example, the Pawnee story of the Flint Monster (see chapter 5) is based on a real historical event, but Dorsey nonetheless listed it as a cosmogonic tale because it also explained the creation of birds. The story of the Flint Monster, then, cannot be easily placed into one single category.

My concern in this book is primarily with content rather than style and literary form. More precisely, I am concerned with *historical* content. I do not analyze stylistic, rhetorical, or other forms of literary expression, except that I consider certain monsters as metaphors that represent real historical events and phenomena. Beyond that, I do not really venture.

I also take issue with other conclusions drawn by Dorsey. Discussing Wichita traditions, Dorsey argued that they had a dual purpose: to teach young people to be brave and ambitious, and to show audiences that monsters no longer existed. Wonderful Man had destroyed them, "so that human beings might be human beings and animals exist as animals, to serve as food for man." It was now up to young people, to emulate Wonderful Man. The stories taught them that "bravery and greatness were something which depended upon individual effort, no matter how low or mean might have been his origin, and at the same time, that there might descend upon him the same longevity and good fortune as was possessed by the hero of the tale."[47] I take issue with Dorsey's idea that monsters no longer existed. My point is closer to that of G. K. Chesterton, whose famous dictum was that monster tales showed not merely that dragons existed but that they could be killed.[48]

Analyzing Caddo sun myths, historian Carla Gerona observed that there are often several different versions of the same story. The stories vary because they were told by different storytellers, in different time periods, and recorded by different observers. Thus each account must be read against the context it was told in. Storytellers came from different bands. Some had been influenced by Christianity or contact with other tribes. "Moreover, the people who shared and recorded the accounts had their own purpose in doing so, and each account reflected someone's truth and someone's history," Gerona writes. This of course raises the issue of which story is more authentic. Gerona's answer is that each story is authentic in its own right: "There is more than one way to understand, present, and record history."[49]

COLLECTING THE STORIES

As Lowie, Mason, folklorists, and other scholars of oral traditions have pointed out, the context in which stories were told is extremely important when analyzing them and when using them as historical accounts. Regrettably, Dorsey's papers contain no information on any of the storytellers that would allow us to the reconstruct the context or trace the genealogy of the stories. Indeed, in some cases not even the name of the storyteller was recorded. For example, the names of the storytellers are unknown in twelve of the seventy Caddo stories in Dorsey's collection.

In his introduction to the reissue of *Traditions of the Caddo*, linguist Wallace Chafe observed two more problems with Dorsey's work with Native oral traditions. First, Dorsey failed to include the songs that were part of many of the accounts. After publishing the Caddo traditions in 1905, Dorsey arranged for German ethnomusicologist Erich von Hornbostel to transcribe the songs that had been collected as part of the traditions. Unfortunately, Hornbostel never published his work, and its whereabouts are now unknown. The second major problem with Dorsey's work is that he did not record the stories in the Native language. Indeed, he edited the stories to give them "a more literary flavor than they must have had when dictated by his Oklahoma consultants." Not until much later did Dorsey come to realize "the importance of recording oral traditions in their language of origin."[50]

Although little is known about Dorsey's interpreters James Murie and Burgess Hunt, we know even less about the people who told them the stories. In some cases, only the name of a storyteller is mentioned. In quite a few cases, we do not even know that. Where information on the storyteller exists, I have included it in the chapter that treats the account.

Most of these storytellers wanted to preserve history for posterity. According to Douglas R. Parks and Raymond J. DeMallie, they left two types of texts: "those written by native people, and those dictated (and sometimes sound-recorded) by native people."[51] Unfortunately, we possess only English versions of the stories discussed in this book. The happy exception is an account of Pahukatawa by Skiri Pawnee holy man Roaming Scout.

While we don't know much about the Caddoan storytellers, we know more about the man who collected their stories. George Dorsey (1868–1931) was one of the founding fathers of American anthropology. His relative obscurity as one of anthropology's founding fathers may be attributed to the fact that he was not part of Franz Boas's intellectual circle. Nonetheless, Dorsey was the first to graduate with a PhD in anthropology from Harvard University, where he studied under Frederick Ward Putnam. In 1896 Dorsey became curator of anthropology at the Field (Columbian) Museum in Chicago. He fulfilled this position, with occasional leaves of absence to do other work, until his resignation in 1915. During these two decades, he also accepted professorships at Northwestern University and University of Chicago.[52]

As curator he undertook numerous travels around the United States, and indeed the world, to collect artifacts and information about indigenous peoples. Initially his focus was on securing Native American artifacts for the museum. His great sense of urgency to acquire objects was driven by competition from tourists, traders, art dealers, and rival collectors from institutions such as the National Museum of Natural History (Smithsonian) in Washington, D.C., and the American Museum of Natural History in New York. In a report from 1901, Dorsey complained that it was becoming more difficult to secure good ethnological material because this material became more valuable to Indians as the old cultures passed away, and because the Indians had learned that these objects were highly desirable to whites. If objects were still available, Dorsey wrote, they had to be obtained immediately: "I need not say that all material retained in the life of the Indian is to a certain extent limited in amount and so it would soon become a question of our having to take what other institutions had left behind, or in a majority of categories of objects[,] getting nothing."[53]

The urgency with which Dorsey collected artifacts has caught the attention and ire of modern-day scholars. Concerning Dorsey's expeditions into the Northwest Coast in 1897, Douglas Cole wrote that Dorsey's modus operandi had "the character of a fervid rip-and-run operation."[54] Indeed, Dorsey's methods were unethical not merely by today's standards but by those of his own era as well. On January 31, 1900, Dorsey wrote to assistant curator of ethnology Stephen Simms that there were three options available to the collector if the owner was not present: "[You can] hunt up the old man and keep hunting until you find him; give the old woman such price for it as she may ask for it running the risk that the old man will be offended; or steal it." He added, "I tried all three plans and I have no choice to recommend."[55]

It seems, however, that Dorsey changed his attitudes and developed a greater appreciation of American Indian rights after his visit to the Southwest in 1900. Dorsey's attention also shifted from collecting artifacts to collecting information. According to DeMallie and Parks, the 1900 expedition "was apparently Dorsey's introduction to ethnographic fieldwork and [it] represents a significant breakthrough in his career."[56] In fact, Dorsey became an advocate for indigenous religious rights against government agents and missionaries. For example, in 1906 he told F. W. Antelope, a Northern Arapaho collaborator, to perform ceremonies without permission from the Indian agent. "You Indians are not slaves to do the bidding of the Indian agent," he wrote. Indeed, the United States Constitution guaranteed freedom of religious expression: "The Arapaho ceremony is a kind of worship, as much so as a Methodist camp meeting, and the Indian agent has no moral or legal right to stop your sun dance." The Arapahos should never allow the agent "to bluff you into believing he can stop your dances by threatening to call out troops."[57]

While traveling in Oklahoma in 1901, Dorsey met James R. Murie (Skiri Pawnee) and Cleaver Warden (Arapaho). This encounter shifted Dorsey's focus entirely to the plains region. Between 1902 and 1907, Dorsey worked closely with Warden, Murie, and Richard Davis (Cheyenne) to record Plains Indian stories and collect ethnographic data. This half decade of work resulted in numerous publications as well as numerous unpublished works. For the Caddoan traditions that are important for this book, Dorsey relied greatly on James R. Murie. Together, Dorsey and Murie collected the great body of stories that ultimately led to the publication of Arikara, Pawnee (both Skiri and South bands), Wichita, and Caddo stories. In fact, as DeMallie and Parks point out, "The Wichita and Caddo volumes stand as the only collections of the mythology of those peoples."[58]

Apparently, Dorsey planned to write a comparative analysis of Caddoan mythology at some point. He never got around to it. For uncertain reasons, Dorsey abandoned his work on the Plains tribes to pursue other projects. Lack of funding may have been one reason, but one also suspects that the zeal with which he pursued projects also led him to lose interest when exciting new ones loomed in the distance. A consequence of this sudden course change is that much of his most important work remains unpublished.[59]

Ultimately, despite his shortcomings—especially those in his early years as a collector of artifacts—Dorsey is now recognized as one of the pioneers of American anthropology. Although much of his work has remained unpublished, it is nevertheless an invaluable source for present-day scholars. "If he had not attempted too much," biographers DeMallie and Parks wrote, "Plains scholarship today would be the poorer for it."[60]

Before heaping too much praise on Dorsey, however, it must be pointed out that he could not have done his work without help from Native collaborators. Indeed, Dorsey was lucky to find several highly capable Indians, such as James Murie of the Pawnees and Burgess Hunt of the Wichitas, who did most of the work to collect, translate, and interpret Caddoan stories. Their contributions loom as large, if not larger, than Dorsey's.

JAMES ROLFE MURIE

James Rolfe Murie was the mixed-blood son of Anna Murie, a Skiri Pawnee woman, and James Murie Sr., a Scottish immigrant who served as an officer of the famous Pawnee Scout Battalion. James Jr. was born in 1862, when the tribe still lived according to its traditional lifestyle in Nebraska. He attended an agency school at Genoa before moving to Oklahoma with the rest of the Pawnee people in 1874. At age sixteen he entered Hampton Normal and Agricultural Institute in Virginia. Like most Indian students, Murie received instruction in the English language, Christian religion, and a practical trade.

James Rolfe Murie (1862–1920), also known as Sa-Ku-Ru-Ta (the Coming Sun), circa 1900. For years, Murie worked with George A. Dorsey and other anthropologists as a collector of stories and artifacts and as interpreter and translator of Pawnee and Arikara stories. Courtesy Smithsonian Institution, NAA GN01266B.

Murie chose to become a printer. He also began publishing articles in the *Southern Workman*, the school's newspaper. While at Hampton he was confirmed in the Episcopal Church. The Christian faith had firmly established itself in him when he left the school. In 1893 he wrote that he wanted the Pawnees "to put their superstitious ideas aside, and believe in the white man's Great Spirit."[61]

After graduating from Hampton in 1883, Murie returned home and eventually became a teacher at the Pawnee Agency boarding school. In 1884 he accompanied twenty-one children to Haskell Institute in Lawrence, Kansas, where he became a "disciplinarian and Drill-Master" for the students. In short, Murie was firmly committed to "civilizing" his people. After a few years he returned to the Pawnee community. Unable to be reinstated as a teacher, he took up farming. Several years later he worked as a clerk and interpreter at the agency, and in 1896 he took a clerking position in a bank in the town of Pawnee. Although he would take occasional leave of absences to do ethnographic work, Murie worked at the bank for twenty years.[62]

Murie's work in ethnography began when he provided some stories and ethnographic information to George Bird Grinnell in the 1880s. In the mid-1890s he began working with Alice Cunningham Fletcher, who was recording information on the Pawnee calumet ceremony. This work, based on the testimony of a Pawnee *kurahus* (old man or priest), was eventually published under the title *The Hako: A Pawnee Ceremony* (1904). A few years earlier Murie had met George Dorsey, who in 1902 hired him as a full-time assistant to collect information on Pawnee culture, religion, and mythology. Murie also purchased sacred bundles on behalf of Dorsey for display at the Field Museum of Natural History in Chicago.[63]

Douglas Parks, Murie's biographer, argues that until his work with Fletcher and Dorsey, Murie was not very interested in the stories and customs of his people, preferring "to be like a white man" instead. Gradually, however, his work transformed him. Part of the reason may have been Dorsey's insatiable requests for more information. Dorsey probably encouraged Murie to obtain as many stories as possible. He may have given Murie instructions similar to those he gave to Cheyenne collaborator Richard Davis in 1902; Dorsey urged Davis to "get stories from women as well as from men," to be sure that they were as detailed and as long as possible, and, if he found a good storyteller, to "get everything he knows before you go to another man." Blind men, Dorsey believed, were especially good storytellers. "Cover the ground thoroughly and make your money go as far as possible," he concluded.[64]

In addition to collecting stories, Murie also gathered information from Pawnee elders. His most important source was Roaming Scout, a Skiri Pawnee priest, former army scout, and arguably the most knowledgeable man on Skiri religion and culture at that time. With grants secured by Dorsey, Murie also collected traditional stories from the Arikara Indians in North Dakota.

Murie's collections of Pawnee stories (two volumes) and Arikara traditions were published under Dorsey's name. Murie also wrote several other important works; only one of these, *Pawnee Indian Societies* (1914), appeared during his lifetime. Two other manuscripts were published posthumously under his own name. These were *Skidi Pawnee Society* (1940), edited by Alexander Spoehr, and *Ceremonies of the Pawnee* (1981, two volumes), edited by Douglas R. Parks. Most of Murie's work was used by other scholars, including anthropologist Ralph Linton, who published information from Murie's work without crediting Murie properly. Several of Murie's writings, mostly in collaboration with Dorsey, remain unpublished.

Apart from ethnographic work, Murie was also active in tribal government, acting as an interpreter and a delegate to Washington on several occasions. But it was his ethnographic work for which he will forever be remembered. Most scholars now agree that Murie's work is unparalleled in its significance.[65]

Despite the praise of modern-day scholars, Murie is not popular in certain quarters of the Pawnee community today. A number of Pawnees accused Murie of fraud, deception, and dishonesty. In her book *"Some Things Are Not Forgotten": A Pawnee Family Remembers*, Martha Royce Blaine recorded a conversation in which two elders accused Murie of abusing his guardianship role over young Pawnee children and so enriching himself.[66] According to the late Garland James Blaine, Murie was known among some Pawnees as "The Thief." Murie "grew to be mistrusted" by the Pawnees, possibly because he obtained information and artifacts from Pawnee elders and transmitted these to Dorsey and others.

Perhaps the charge of dishonesty stems from Murie's initial opposition to traditional Pawnee culture, which contrasts his later efforts to preserve it. Martha Royce Blaine published a letter from Murie to Indian agent D. J. M. Wood, in which he voiced his opposition to the Pawnee Ghost Dance. Rather than seeing the Ghost Dance as a revitalization movement, Murie, who had not long before returned from Hampton Institute, rejected it as superstition and a deviation from the true Christian religion. He had attended one of the dances for three days to see if was in accordance with Christian belief or if it went against it. "Major I am glad to say that I found some good true hearts who only put their trust in our God and his son, Christ," Murie reported. But there were others—Murie called them "weak minded" people—who did not. Murie argued that it was the mind leaving the body, not the soul, when people fainted from exhaustion and intensity during the dance. For this reason, Murie urged good Christians not to follow the Ghost Dance. "O what a shame it is that my poor people should be led in this way by an untutored Indian," Murie lamented. "Where is the Preacher and the Missionary? What are they here for? Ah, my heart aches to think about it. Ah, if I had only prepared to preach to my people I should today feel proud that I had a battle to fight for my Saviour."[67]

The evidence provided by Blaine seems to indicate that Murie was bidding for the approval of white authority figures and that he was seeking to benefit either financially or otherwise from his cooperation with whites. Undoubtedly, Murie benefited not merely financially from his work on Pawnee culture and ceremonial life: the knowledge he eventually acquired about Pawnee customs also elevated him to a position of authority within the Pawnee community. Perhaps this explains some of the hostility toward him within some circles of present-day Pawnee society.

There is also a different reading of Murie's attitudes. After all, Murie was one of those tragic cases of a young man who, forced by circumstances beyond his control, was sent to school to adopt the ways of a society that did not truly accept Indians. Upon his return home, Murie found himself an outsider. Eventually Murie's work became not so much an attempt to gain recognition by whites, or a means to become a man of authority among the Pawnees, but rather a genuine attempt to reconnect with the world of his mother. Roaming Scout's teachings clearly stirred a deep sense of awe for the Pawnee mental world in Murie. Rather than seeing him as a selfish and cynical egotist, I am more inclined to see him as a man who struggled to preserve what was left of Pawnee culture. Regardless of his motivations, there is no doubt that the world today owes much to Murie's work.

BURGESS HUNT

Among the Wichitas, Dorsey was fortunate to find a reliable and skilled collaborator in Burgess Hunt. Unfortunately, whereas Murie's life has been fairly well documented, much less is known about Hunt. But with the generous help of Wichita tribal member Gary McAdams, it was possible to obtain some information about his life from Marjorie Louise Brown Botone, Hunt's great-granddaughter.[68]

Hunt's date of birth is uncertain. His great-granddaughter stated that he was of Wichita, Kitsai, and Pawnee descent and that he was probably born in Pawnee country in 1873. Wichita records show that his father was Lone Chief (aka Running Chief), who was Pawnee, and his mother was Ke-ah-sun-ne-kah-daw, a Wichita. Most official records list his birth date somewhere between 1874 and 1880. Caddo County census records of the Wichita and Caddo Indians at the Kiowa Agency in the 1910s listed him as "Burgess Hunt Seger" or "Segar." Although the census records did not mention any siblings, Marjorie remembered that he had four brothers whose names all ended in "Chief." He also had one sister. The Wichita people considered Hunt a chief as well, because a flagpole base erected in 1945, one year after his death, listed him as such.[69]

Burgess Hunt (circa 1873–1944), also known as Qsa-Hi-Wa-Ski-A-Gu-Na-Ur-I-Sa (Morning Star Spirit), October 1912. Hunt recorded and translated numerous Wichita stories, which were included in *The Mythology of the Wichita* in 1904. Courtesy Smithsonian Institution, NAA GN01312A.

In his youth, Hunt attended school at Camp Creek, at the Kiowa, Comanche, and Wichita Agency. He later went to school in Carlisle, Pennsylvania, but he may have attended Indian School in Lawrence, Kansas, as well. He had a great talent with languages. According to his granddaughter, Hunt was fluent in Pawnee, Caddo, Cheyenne, Arapaho, English, and, of course Wichita. Because the Wichitas shared an agency with the Comanches, it is possible that he could speak the Comanche language as well.[70]

Hunt was an intellectual who loved to read. He taught his great-granddaughter to read long before she began first grade. Botone remembered how he encouraged her to read, saying that by reading you could learn of places and things while sitting in your chair at home. She remembered reading *National Geographic*, the *Kansas City Star*, and the *Chicago Tribune*, which may indicate that Hunt subscribed to these publications. He also encouraged her to write things down. He believed in writing things down. Consequently, Botone did a great deal of writing in her younger years, but sadly, most of these writings are now lost. She thinks that Hunt may have been a journalist with some kind of connection to the *New York Times*. After his second marriage, Hunt resided two and a quarter miles north of Binger, Oklahoma.[71]

Apart from reading, Hunt had a passion for sports, baseball especially. His great-granddaughter recalled that he was an accomplished baseball player. She said they used to have friendly arguments about baseball because she was a Yankees fan and he rooted for the Cubs. He also used to tell her about his travels to Ontario, Chicago, New York City, and Washington, D.C. She remembers him telling her about the first time he was in New York, walking downtown with a friend. The friend looked up at the tall buildings—and fell over backward.[72]

Hunt married twice. His first wife was Sit-ko-po, also known by the English name Josephine Hunt Segar. They had four children: Noble Hunt Segar, Henry Segar, Louisiana Segar (who died at the age of eighteen in 1922), and Hiram Segar (who died in infancy in 1908). Hunt's second wife was Mary Washington Wilson, who was a Caddo. She and Hunt had two children: Cecil Segar and Angie Segar.[73]

Hunt was an active member of the Native American Church. This is not surprising, as the Kiowa-Comanche Agency was a center of the peyote religion, with influential leaders such as Comanche chief Quanah Parker and Caddo religious leader John Wilson. Perhaps Hunt played an important role in acting as a missionary for the peyote religion; his great-granddaughter remembers him going to peyote meetings in both Pawnee and Comanche country.[74]

Hunt was employed at the Kiowa, Comanche, and Wichita Agency. Photographer Annette Ross Hume took his portrait when she visited the agency.[75] De Lancey W. Gill photographed him in October 1912, together with John Tatum. The picture shows him dressed in a suit and with cropped hair.[76]

In 1900 Dorsey began working with Hunt. Dorsey described him as a "well-educated Wichita of full blood." Their collaboration lasted three years. During this time, Hunt collected and translated numerous stories, which Dorsey eventually published under the title *The Mythology of the Wichita* (1904). Hunt himself contributed one story to this collection: "The Woman Who Married a Star."[77]

After working with Dorsey, Hunt continued to serve as an interpreter and source for other scholars. In 1935 he served as one of the main sources on the Wichitas for Wilbur S. Nye's classic book *Carbine and Lance: The Story of Old Fort Sill* (1937).

Did Dorsey credit Hunt enough for his role in collecting, transcribing, and translating *The Wichita Mythology?* Hunt's great-granddaughter has read Dorsey's book many times and always gets mad because her great-grandfather received so little credit for the work. Of course, he is credited for the one story, and Dorsey mentions him once in the preface. Gary McAdams, who interviewed Marjorie in May 2015, added, "Would there have been a book without Burgess? Translating Wichita to English is not an easy task. He must have had excellent command of both languages."

Hunt contracted tuberculosis and died in a sanatorium at Shawnee, Oklahoma, on August 22, 1944, at the approximate age of seventy. He was buried in a cemetery near his home in Binger, Oklahoma.

A WORD OF CAUTION

Considering these problems with Dorsey's work, as well as the criticisms voiced by Lowie, Mason, and others, readers should use these stories with caution. As stated in the previous chapter, readers must be aware that the stories discussed in this book were likely subject to change. A story may be a composite of multiple other stories. Over time, as a result of faulty memory, different narrators may have added or removed certain ideas, events, characters, or passages.

In addition, a story may indeed tell us more about the people who are telling it than about the actual historical event it is supposed to describe. Nevertheless, the stories selected for analysis here start from the assumption that some of the events described within them may be based on historical fact. Still, the context in which a story was told would affect *how* it was told. For example, a narrator might have changed a story to make it more appealing to his audience or to make a certain political or moral point. The narrator might have changed or withheld information that he found too sensitive or embarrassing to share, especially around non-Indian audiences. The interpreter, because of a lack of expertise in one of the languages, might have unintentionally changed the meaning of certain words, passages, or indeed the entire story. The interpreter, too, might have changed or withheld information that he found too sensitive or embarrassing to share with non-Indian audiences. Finally, the editor might have changed the texts for the same reasons as narrators and interpreters might have changed them: to adjust them to the tastes and sensitivities of the audience. Everyone familiar with George A. Dorsey's works knows how he censored certain sexually tainted passages by publishing them in Latin only. However, one must not exaggerate Dorsey's editorial interference either. In his *Traditions of the Skidi Pawnee*, Dorsey wrote, "The language of the tales follows the form employed by the Indian interpreters, save as respects correction of grammatical errors."[78]

Lastly, there is the very real danger to read too much into a story. Sometimes a cigar is indeed simply a cigar. Still, this book provides plausible explanations, posited as hypotheses, for the different traditions under discussion.

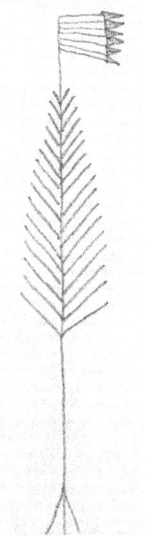

Part II
Oral Traditions as History

TWO

"The Whirlwind Is Coming to Destroy My People"

Smallpox and the Arikaras

The Whirlwind passed the people and it turned back and came to Mother-Corn. It said to her: "You slighted me in your smoke. I became angry. I have left behind me diseases, so that the people will become sick and die. You wanted your people to live forever, but I have left sickness behind, so that it will fall upon the people who are proud and dress fine."

From "The Origin of the Arikara," as told by Star (1904)[1]

In 1922 ethnobotanist Melvin Randolph Gilmore (1868–1940) arrived at the Fort Berthold Indian Reservation to document the Mother Corn ceremony of the Arikaras. This ceremony reenacted episodes from the Arikara creation story. During one of its high points, the Arikaras re-created the arrival of a devastating whirlwind that scattered and killed people in punishment for their failure to make smoke offerings to it. Fortunately, Mother Corn appeared in the form of a cedar tree to provide the people with shelter, and from the sky, Neešaanu NačitákUx (the Great Chief Above) fell to the earth in the form of a rock, upon which the people climbed for safety.

As they were conducting the ceremony, something went wrong. Despite careful preparations by Four Rings, Pat Star, and several other Arikara priests and doctors, one of the participants made a small error. That night, as if Whirlwind had been angered again, a terrible and a destructive hailstorm swept through the campsite. Tents were destroyed, and the roof of Gilmore's automobile was severely damaged. Many of the participants were certain that the powers had created the storm because of the error made during the ceremony earlier that day.[2]

The events that summer of 1922 reminded the Arikaras that the spirits of the past were still present. Although Arikara folklore was full of monsters, such as scalped men, cannibals, witches, water monsters, spirits, ghosts, and man-eating animals, none was as powerful as the Whirlwind of the creation story.

Seeking to connect events in Arikara oral traditions to actual historical events, this chapter contends that the monstrous Whirlwind (as well as a few other symbols, such as snakes and bears) in fact represented a series of epidemics that struck the Arikaras in the eighteenth century, especially the great smallpox epidemic of 1780–81. If this hypothesis is correct, this also means that the Arikara creation account does not merely tell the story of Arikara creation in the distant past (the beginning of time) but in fact covers Arikara history at least as far as 1781.

Before delving into the oral traditions about Whirlwind, snakes, and bears, however, I must point out that to many present-day Arikaras, these are sacred texts. The Arikara story of their creation, especially, is sacred history. Explaining the historical processes behind these stories, as I try to do in this chapter, may appear controversial to people who prefer the literal interpretation of these texts. It is not my intention to question the integrity of these oral traditions or the mysterious supernatural powers behind them. On the contrary: I acknowledge that these texts are of great mystical and spiritual power. My purpose is merely to suggest links between the sacred and the historical, and the mysterious and the real. Even if Whirlwind and the other monsters represented diseases, this does not at all deny the existence of the supernatural forces behind them.

"THE OLD MEN THEN TOLD US THIS STORY": A NOTE ON THE ARIKARA SOURCES

Analyzing Arikara oral traditions poses many challenges. The stories were not recorded until the late nineteenth and early twentieth century. One of the most important collections was made in the first decade of the twentieth century when George Dorsey sent James Murie to visit the Arikaras to record the stories. They were published by Dorsey in *Traditions of the Arikara* (1904).[3]

This was a time of tremendous change for the Arikaras. Their tribal lands were allotted after 1902 despite spirited resistance from Arikara elders. Worse, Arikara population numbers were dwindling rapidly, from an estimated 8,800 around 1700, to circa 2,200 in 1835, to fewer than 1,000 by 1865. In 1904, when Dorsey published his collection of Arikara stories, the Arikara population reached its nadir; only 379 names appeared on the tribal census roll. As the older generation of Arikaras passed away, their knowledge of the old traditional ways disappeared with them.

Meanwhile, missionaries and Indian agents were also undermining traditional ways. Using coercion, Indian agents discouraged Arikara elders from practicing their traditions as well as their forms of healing and worship. From his office in Chicago, George Dorsey watched with alarm as Arikara culture came under threat of extinction. In 1902, as he was preparing his ethnographic work among the Arikaras, Dorsey wrote to the commissioner of Indian affairs about the devastation wrought upon Arikara culture by agents of "civilization." "To me," Dorsey wrote, "one of the most pitiable things which I have ever seen in all my dealings with the Indians is that of a tribe like the Arikara, for instance, who have been hounded by the missionaries and by their agents for a period of thirty or forty years, and who have been made to think that they have absolutely no right on this earth to think about their own gods, who have literally been compelled to hide away all their religious paraphernalia; and whatever of their rites or ceremonies they have held they have held with fear and trembling—and yet, the Arikara are truly Indians in that feeling and belief as are any Indians of this Continent.[4]

When Dorsey wrote his letter, Arikara cultural survival indeed looked bleak. Yet Arikara elders desired to preserve the old ways. It was in this context that they sat down with Murie to share their stories. Indeed, the first three decades of the twentieth century would witness a revival of Arikara culture and history. Assisted by historians, ethnologists, and artists, Arikara people recorded and documented their stories, ceremonies, and history.

Unfortunately, because the accounts were recorded at a relatively late date, they may have been subject to change over time. New themes and elements found their way into the narratives. For example, Hand's version contains a reference to a mysterious tall man "whose hair from his mouth reached down to his waist. . . . They thought this man was from the heavens."[5] It appears that Hand was describing Jesus Christ, with whom the Arikaras had been familiar through the work of Congregational and Catholic missionaries. Thus, although the accounts appear to have changed over time, it is difficult to document those changes without earlier comparative materials. Of course, many Arikaras today will contend that the above reference to Jesus was always an integral part of the story.[6]

Another problem was the fact that most of the storytellers had only secondhand knowledge of the creation story. The Arikara creation story was sacred history and therefore had been the exclusive property of a priest. Ordinary people, such as the Arikara storytellers contacted by Murie, had only imperfect knowledge of the details of the story. This fact may explain the differences between the various accounts.

Even more problematic is the fact that neither Murie nor Dorsey provided any biographical information on the storytellers that would give the stories additional context. We know little more than their names: Hand (who contributed two versions), Star, Four Horns, and Hawk. It is impossible to determine which of these was the most authoritative. Additional versions by Two Crows, Two Hawks, Bear's Tail, and Four Rings pose similar problems. These versions were published elsewhere but fail to provide adequate biographical information as well.[7]

The provenance of the stories is obscure. They were handed down over the generations. Four Horns, one of Murie's Arikara sources, recalled how he first heard the telling of the creation story. "I sacrificed several buffalo to Mother-Corn," Four Horns said. "I used to sit and listen to the songs. Finally the old men gave me a seat with them, so I learned to sing the bundle songs. The old men then told us this story."[8]

Unfortunately, we do not have the original versions of the stories in the Arikara language. We have only the free translations in English. Consequently, it is possible that some details were lost in translation. Without the original texts in the Arikara language, the accuracy of the translations cannot be verified and a complete analysis of the exact meaning of the stories is not possible.[9]

Despite these issues, this chapter maintains that the stories are nevertheless useful ethnohistorical sources. For the creation story, Murie provided no less than five versions, which allows the researcher to confirm those points upon which the stories agree. The story of Whirlwind is basically corroborated by most storytellers. The different versions also allow the scholar to reconstruct the complete story with additional information from the other accounts. As for the accuracy of the translations, it ought to be pointed out that Murie was familiar with the Arikara language because it was closely related to Murie's own Skiri Pawnee language. Furthermore, based on the quality of his other ethnographic work, there is no reason to assume that Murie did not do his research conscientiously and reliably. In addition, young, Western-educated, and bilingual Arikara interpreters contributed to the accuracy of the translations. Finally, the Arikara storytellers themselves strongly emphasized accuracy when they told stories; remember that pre- and non-literate societies placed great emphasis on correct memorization of events and stories.[10]

ARIKARA SOCIETY AND RELIGION BEFORE THE EPIDEMICS

The Arikaras are a Plains Indian tribe closely related to the Pawnees, from whom they separated, in stages, between 1450 and 1550. It is important to note that this separation was probably a lengthy process, with different groups leaving the Pawnees at different times, resulting in the establishment of multiple more or less autonomous groups that even displayed a diversity of dialects. Following these separations, the Indian groups that would eventually become the Arikara tribe established their villages along the Missouri River in present-day South Dakota. Like their Pawnee relatives, their religious complex centered around sacred bundles that represented the various powers of the universe. For the Arikaras, the supreme powers were Neešaanu NačitákUx, Mother Corn, and the four semi-cardinal sacred directions. These were the powers responsible for creation, for keeping the universe in balance, and for dictating the seasons, which determined the cycles of corn cultivation and buffalo hunts.

The Arikara confederation (it may be too soon to talk about a tribe) grew fast.[11] Between 1675 and 1780, the Arikaras reportedly established more than sixty villages along both banks of the Missouri River in South Dakota. Although these settlements were not all occupied simultaneously, they were fairly large, with an average of forty lodges. Archaeologist Donald Lehmer estimated the peak of Arikara population at circa 8,800, but Preston Holder speculated that there may have been as many as 15,000 Arikaras in the 1700s.[12] In 1714 Étienne de Veniard, sieur de Bourgmont, reported that there were forty-two Arikara villages on the Missouri. "They are very numerous," wrote Bourgmont, who added that, considering their great numbers, they lived in one of the "most beautiful [healthful] countries to be seen."[13] In 1743 fur traders Francois and Louis-Joseph de la Vérendrye met several Arikara bands and reported that they were "the only tribe sufficiently brave not to stand in dread" of the powerful "Snake" Indians.[14] The identity of the "Snake" Indians has never been positively established, but it is quite possible that these were the Shoshone or Comanche Indians, who were regulars on the plains at this time.[15]

These sources show that the Arikaras were a relatively healthy and numerous people. They were so successful that they began to intimidate their Mandan neighbors to the north. Sadly for the Arikaras, their rise to prominence was cut short by a series of devastating epidemics between 1750 and 1781. These diseases, introduced by Europeans, ravaged the Arikara people at a pivotal moment in the development of their tribal identity.

Although European fur traders introduced many new things to the Indians of the plains, including guns, horses, and a variety of other objects, none of these items appear to have left a mark in surviving Arikara oral tradition.[16] This is not true for the appearance of crowd-type diseases and the arrival of new tribes who were displaced as a result of European immigration.[17] These new tribes entered the plains in two separate waves. The first wave occurred during the late 1600s and consisted of the Kaws, Osages, Omahas, Poncas, Iowas, Otoes, and Missourias. These tribes did not leave an imprint in Arikara oral tradition, primarily because these Indians adopted the sedentary lifestyle of the Arikaras and because their relations with the Arikara people were relatively friendly. Among the peoples of the second wave were the Plains Apaches, Kiowas, Comanches, Plains Crees, Plains Ojibwas, Blackfeet, Assiniboines, Arapahos, Gros Ventres, Cheyennes, and Sioux. Although these tribes entered the plains from different directions, at slightly different times, and for different reasons, eventually they all adopted nomadic lifestyles that challenged the horticultural lifestyle of tribes like the Arikaras. The sudden influx of these peoples upset the traditional balance of power on the plains. Intertribal warfare increased as nomadic tribes competed with each other for access to horses, guns, hunting grounds, and slaves. The Arikaras and other horticultural tribes were soon swept up into this cycle of violence.[18]

The arrival of the Sanánat (Sioux) proved especially disruptive for the Arikaras. Sioux–Arikara relations were complex. The Santees and the Yanktonais were generally friendly. But the Yanktons were not. Arikara relations with the Lakota bands were even more complex. The seven Lakota bands or subtribes (Oglalas, Brules, Minneconjous, Hunkpapas, Sans Arcs, Blackfeet, and Two Kettles) had loose social and political organizations in which chiefs had little coercive authority. Internal disagreements often resulted in bands breaking up. Families or individuals easily moved between bands. There were often divisions and disagreements on the issue of war and peace with the Arikaras. In general, the Arikaras and the various Lakota bands were at a state of enmity with each other. This state was interrupted only when a temporary truce was concluded to conduct trade. Apart from corn, horses were the objects that the Sioux desired most from the Arikaras during the first half of the eighteenth century.[19] Because of the Sioux presence, the Arikaras were forced to bolster village defenses. Still, until the epidemics of the 1750s and 1780s, the Arikaras were quite able to resist the Sioux.[20]

The arrival of the Sioux is not recorded in the Arikara creation story. The Sioux are mentioned only in conjunction with the epidemics that weakened the Arikaras militarily, thus allowing the Sioux to rise to dominance. Furthermore, whereas the epidemics were depicted as whirlwinds or ferocious man-eating animals, the Sioux simply appear in human form. The Arikara creation accounts imply that the Sioux did not become a major problem until Whirlwind scattered the people across the earth. Until the epidemics, the Arikaras viewed the Sioux as a nuisance rather than a lethal threat to tribal survival. Consequently, the Sioux do not appear in symbolic form in the Arikara creation accounts. Although Sioux arrival was disruptive, what caused the Sioux to become dangerous were the epidemics that disproportionately weakened the Arikaras.[21]

"WHEREVER THE WIND TOUCHED THE PEOPLE, DISEASE WOULD BE LEFT": THE IMPACT OF THE EPIDEMICS

Scholars identified several epidemics that affected the Arikaras in the eighteenth century: smallpox or measles (1750–52) and influenza (1761), followed again by smallpox or measles (1762–66). The most devastating epidemic, however, was the smallpox outbreak of 1780–81.[22] As a result of the epidemics, the Arikara population had declined by an estimated 80 to 90 percent by 1781.[23]

The symptoms of the diseases, especially smallpox, tell a story of tremendous suffering: fevers, vomiting, severe head and body aches, painful skin rashes, sores in the mouth, and sores on the face, soles of the feet, palms of the hands, forearms, neck, legs, and back. Patients sometimes died bleeding from the gums, eyes, nose, and other orifices. Survivors carried the disfiguring scars of the disease on their faces and bodies for the rest of their lives.[24]

In addition, the epidemics struck whole villages at once, incapacitating entire populations and preventing men from hunting and women from tending their fields. Starvation often followed, further increasing the risk of new infections. During an epidemic there were not enough healthy people to take care of the sick, cook, light fires, fetch water, or bury the dead. Secondary infections, such as colds and pneumonia, were common side effects that further reduced a victim's chances for survival. Survivors bore not only the scars of the disease on their bodies but also the sad memory of having watched loved ones suffer and die from a terrible scourge.[25]

After the epidemic of 1780–81, the surviving Arikaras gathered in a handful of villages to rebuild their lives. The process proved to be very difficult. Whereas the old village system, based on the bundle complex, had provided each group with a sense of community and identity, the new villages threw together people of diverse backgrounds and traditions. Many of the survivors spoke different dialects, causing a confusion of tongues. Worse, families from different villages competed with one another for political control.[26] When

Lewis and Clark visited the Arikaras in October 1804, they noticed bitter rivalries within the Arikara tribe. In his journal, Clark wrote, "We have every reason to believe that a jellousy [sic] exists between the Villages."[27]

In contrast, Sioux social organization was less affected by the diseases, although the Sioux too suffered greatly. Sioux social organization was more flexible, allowing groups to break up at the first signs of infection. Hence Sioux population numbers rebounded more quickly than those of the sedentary Arikaras, who lived in more compact villages, which provided fertile breeding grounds for infectious diseases.[28] As a consequence of the epidemics, Arikara power declined while that of the Sioux increased in relative terms. Indeed, the decline of Arikara power emboldened the Sioux, who began to push the Arikaras northward.[29]

Archaeologists uncovered evidence for this increasing Sioux boldness when they excavated an Arikara village site in Walworth County, South Dakota. The site had been established around 1750 but was abruptly abandoned shortly before 1785. In the village, the archaeologists found the remains of seventy-one people who had been killed in a terrible massacre. Many corpses had been mutilated. After the tragedy, the village was abandoned. The massacre reveals that the Arikaras were no longer the formidable military power they once had been. The reasons for the decline are written in the archaeological record. In the years before the massacre, the village became successively smaller as a result of depopulation caused by infectious diseases, until Larson Village, according to the archaeologists, "reached the threshold below which defense of the village was no longer possible."[30]

The epidemics thus reduced the Arikaras from a military power of the first rank to a secondary power at best. Sioux pressure forced the Arikaras to give up their villages on the Cheyenne River in present-day South Dakota in 1796 and move upriver.[31] Although they clung tenaciously to their independence, the Arikaras were now frequently at the mercy of the Sioux, who often forced them to trade at unfavorable terms.[32]

"I HAVE LEFT BEHIND ME DISEASES, SO THAT THE PEOPLE WILL BECOME SICK AND DIE": EPIDEMICS IN ARIKARA ORAL TRADITION

At first glance, no accounts of these monstrous epidemics appear to have survived in Arikara oral tradition. Could it be a case of collective amnesia caused by the sheer psychological traumatic impact of these events, similar to the one Raymond Fogelson described for the Cherokees after their removal to Indian Territory?[33] Although this is possible, Arikara traditions do offer clues. In this case, however, the epidemics appear in symbolic form.

The most powerful of these symbols is Whirlwind. Hand, one of Dorsey's sources, said that "the Whirlwind was a disease and wherever the wind touched the people, diseases would be left."[34] Four Horns emphasized the destructive nature of the storm. "We must hurry," Four Horns narrated, "for the big Black-Wind is coming, taking everything it meets."[35] In Star's account, Whirlwind addressed Mother Corn directly. "You wanted your people to live forever," Whirlwind said, "but I have left sickness behind, so that it will fall upon the people who are proud and dress fine; but always remember when you offer smoke to the gods to give me smoke towards the last, so that I shall not visit the people very often.[36]

Only in Bear's Tail's account does Whirlwind have a slightly less negative role. Bear's Tail's account is somewhat anomalous but ought to be mentioned nonetheless. According to Bear's Tail, as they traveled west following their emergence from the ground, the Arikara people came upon a thick timber that blocked their way. "A Whirlwind came and made a pathway through the timber," said Bear's Tail. "The Whirlwind did not hurt the people, although it was mad, for the powers had not called on it for help." Clearly, Bear's Tail conflated two parts of the story: one that involved the people's crossing through a dense forest, and the other of an angry Whirlwind.[37]

In most accounts, when Whirlwind struck the people, it scattered them and changed their language, thus forming new tribes.[38] Among these were the Cheyennes, the "Pichia" (an unidentified tribe), the "Wooden Faces" (Iroquois), and the enigmatic "Witchcraft-People," who lived in the south. Interestingly, Star does not mention the Sioux, unless these are the aforementioned Pichia.[39]

Although Whirlwind characters appear in the traditions of other Caddoan tribes, they do not have the same devastating qualities. In Skiri Pawnee tradition, Whirlwind was actually the sack in which Lightning carried the people to earth. In this case, Whirlwind symbolizes the uterus from which humanity springs and thus represents a creative rather than destructive force.[40] White Horse, a Pitahawirata Pawnee, told the story of a ghost woman who had returned from the dead to live with her husband. When her husband treated her badly, she turned into a whirlwind and disappeared: "As the man lifted his hand to strike her again she disappeared and where she was sitting a whirlwind formed, and the whirlwind arose and went straight up in the lodge and whirled around and went out of the opening at the top of the lodge." She returned, in her whirlwind shape once more, to tell her mourning husband that he had wronged her and that she would never come back.[41] Big Crow, a Kitkehahki Pawnee, told the story of a "Ghost-Man" who lived in graveyards and who was surrounded by whirlwinds. In fact, he cured people by enveloping them in the vortex. One time, however, he fell down, leaving only his bones on the ground. "This," Big Crow said, "is why we call whirlwinds 'ghosts' or 'spirits.'"[42] Whirlwinds seemed to represent ghosts or the spirits of the deceased in Caddo tradition as well.[43] Although Wichita traditions do not specifically mention whirlwinds, one account refers to cannibals calling upon wind to prevent a hero from traveling onward; another Wichita story mentions a magic bowstring that caused destructive winds. But winds do not have an exclusively negative connotation in Wichita accounts. Indeed, in a few Wichita stories, Wind fathers children or places children upon the earth.[44] In none of these Caddoan traditions did whirlwinds represent or cause murderous infectious diseases.

Although Whirlwind was the great disease-causing power in the Arikara creation account, animals personified the diseases in other Arikara stories.[45] Two Hawks tells of an attack by snakes upon an Arikara village after two foolish boys killed a mysterious snake. While hunting, the Arikaras passed a pretty little snake. The elders told the people to make sacrifices of deer meat and moccasins to the snake. The two foolish boys, watching jealously as the snake lay coiled up on the pile of presents, complained bitterly that they were poor and needed help while this snake received presents from the people. In anger they killed the animal. Soon all kinds of snakes came down both sides of the Missouri River. Armed with clubs, the people fought them off. One of the foolish boys was killed, while the other was bitten all over. The snakes eventually went away, but not until they had killed many people.[46]

It is possible that the snakes in this story refer to an enemy tribe. Perhaps these were the Snake People mentioned by the Vérendrye brothers in 1743. If so, they could possibly be the Shoshones or Comanches, who also entered the plains around this time. However, the story describes bite marks left by the snakes, which may represent the wounds and punctured skin caused by smallpox lesions. It is tempting to associate the scar-covered body of the surviving foolish boy—who had been bitten by the snakes "all over"—with the pitted scars left by smallpox pustules.[47]

In another story, also told by Two Hawks, the attackers were bears. According to this story, the bears attacked the village after a jealous man shot a bear who had seduced his wife. The bears tore many people to pieces. Only those people who hid in their cellars were saved.[48]

Unlike the wounds in the snake story, the wounds inflicted by the bears cannot be so readily associated with a particular disease. Perhaps the story of the bears refers more accurately to an unidentified enemy tribe. The only disease that could provide a possible explanation for the violence of the attack is rabies. However, scholars are entirely unfamiliar with a rabies epidemic at any time in history, and this disease seems an unlikely candidate.[49]

What makes the attack by "bears" such an appropriate symbol for a contagious disease is the sheer violence with which the people were attacked. Furthermore, the "bear" not only attacked the man who had killed the bear but attacked the people indiscriminately. In short, the random nature of the bear attack seems to reflect the indiscriminating attack by a contagious disease. If this is indeed the case, perhaps the people who "hid in their cellars" may be those who quarantined themselves from infected fellow Arikaras.[50]

The use of these metaphors implies that the magnitude of the suffering caused by the epidemics was so dramatic that they could be described only in symbolic or cosmological terms. Undoubtedly, many Arikaras (such as the storytellers whose accounts were published in Dorsey's *Traditions of the Arikaras*) believed that the disasters were punishments for a variety of offenses against the supernatural: taboo violation, witchcraft, religious declension, or failure to treat sacred things in the proper manner.[51]

In other accounts, disease and death appear in the form of dogs. In what may be the most authoritative theological Arikara text, Arikara priest Four Rings described this event:

> It is said that when the smoke offerings first were made to all the powers and elements of the world there were two dogs sleeping at the time which were forgotten, and so no smoke offering was made to them. They awoke and found that they had been forgotten and they were aggrieved and angry because of it. Therefore they said to the people: "You neglected to make smoke offerings to us when all other beings were remembered. In punishment for your neglect of us we shall bite you. And we shall never leave you, we will always abide with you, and we shall follow you forever." The names of the two dogs were Sickness and Death. Wheretofore it was said: "Sickness and Death shall be among the people always."[52]

Interestingly, sometimes the dogs appear in conjunction *with* Whirlwind. In one story, a dog came to warn the people that Whirlwind was coming to destroy them and offered to sacrifice himself so that the people would live. After that, whenever diseases came, the Arikaras would sacrifice a dog and offer its meat to the different powers in the heavens so that these "would send a storm that would drive away the disease from the villages."[53]

"I SHALL ALSO FIX IT SO THAT ALL ANIMALS SHALL MAKE GREAT MEDICINE-MEN OF YOU": THE EFFECTS OF THE EPIDEMICS ON ARIKARA RELIGION

Rather than causing the Arikaras to lose confidence in their religion, the epidemics may actually have *reinforced* Arikara faith. Many of the stories show that it was faith and religion that eventually helped them weather the storms of disease. In Star's account, Mother Corn appealed to Neešaanu directly: "Nesaru and the gods," she cried out, "I want help, for the Whirlwind is coming to destroy my people!"[54] In the story "How the People Escaped the Buffalo," Hawk explained that when Whirlwind came, the people "prayed to Mother [Corn] to help them, and she turned around and told them to give presents and smoke to the Whirlwind." Although the Whirlwind "scattered some of the people over the country," most people simply "went on again."[55]

In most stories, the people were saved by Mother Corn, and indeed by Neešaanu himself. Mother Corn turned herself into a cedar tree, and Neešaanu fell from the sky in the shape of a rock. The people found shelter in the tree and on top of the rock and so escaped the wrath of Whirlwind. The message was clear: if failure to properly observe religious customs caused disease and death, then faith was the way to redeem and save oneself.[56]

The bear and snake stories also served as powerful warnings to the people not to neglect their duties toward the mysterious powers. In the bear story told by Two Hawks, peace and tranquility returned only after the man who had wounded the bear had been killed. In this story, the man represented someone whose pride had endangered the entire community.

The 1780–81 epidemic may have increased the role of doctors in Arikara society and religion. Although the sacred bundle ceremonies conducted by the priests to ensure bountiful harvests, successful hunts, and growth and stability among the people remained supreme, the emergence of medicine societies may indicate that doctoring became more important as a result of the epidemics. After Whirlwind left behind diseases, the work of medical specialists became increasingly important.

According to Hand's version of the Arikara oral tradition, Neešaanu gave three things to the people: Mother Corn (who taught the people how to live)

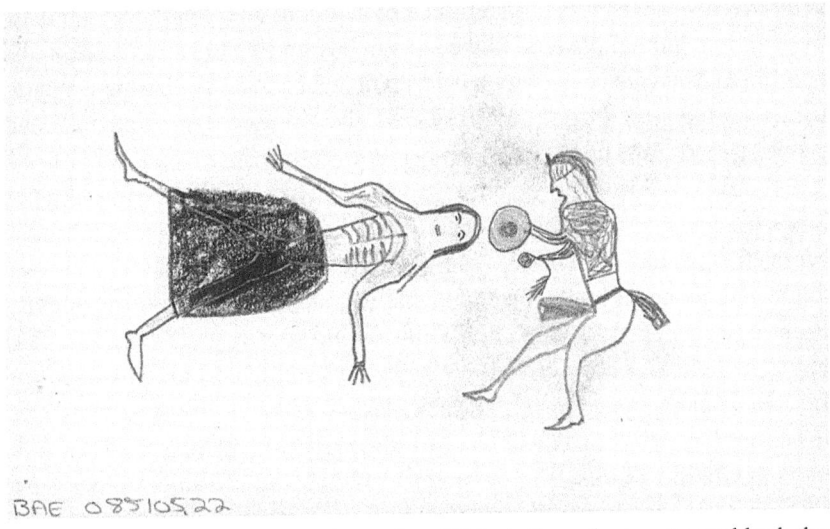

An Arikara doctor treating a patient, circa 1875. Arikara doctors treated both the physical symptoms and the spiritual causes of diseases and injuries. Courtesy Smithsonian Institution, NAA MS 154,064A (INV 08510522).

and the office of the chief; and after Whirlwind introduced sickness and death, Neešaanu created the "medicine-men." Of these three gifts, the doctors played an important role in the day-to-day lives of ordinary Arikaras. Although the story suggests that the doctors came *after* Whirlwind, Hand refers to "medicine men" before the coming of Whirlwind. Still, this leaves the possibility that doctors became more significant after the introduction of new infectious diseases.[57]

Four Horns's account also suggested the growing importance of doctors after the epidemics of the 1700s. In Four Horns's version, Whirlwind appears in the shape of an angry big Black-Wind. After this wind passed, a dog appeared. It promised to help the people in the future. "I shall be the one that you shall kill, and my meat shall be offered to the gods," the dog said. But the dog also called on other animals to make medicine men of some people. "My father is the Sun," he said: "He has given me all this power. I will give my power to all animals, then I will stay with the people, so they will not forget my promise to them."[58] In short, according to Four Horns the animals received their curative powers from the dog after Whirlwind had introduced diseases and death among the people.

Other Arikara traditions suggest that the doctors may have eventually harnessed the destructive powers of Whirlwind. In a story told by Many Fox,

Whirlwind's power was counteracted by a young man who received help from certain animal powers. In the story, a boy and a girl were accidentally left behind when the people crossed a river on their annual buffalo hunt. Whirlwind took the girl and gave her its power. The girl used it to kill and devour people. Because she had to look after her little brother, Whirlwind-girl planned to kill him too. Fortunately, some owls took pity on the little boy and gave him sacred power. When his sister came to kill him, the boy promised to give her the first woman he married. Whirlwind-girl agreed. When the boy returned to the people, he had owl power and distinguished himself in battle against enemies. A grateful Arikara chief allowed him to marry his daughter. The boy then gave his new wife to his Whirlwind sister, but Many Fox does not explain what happened to her. The next day, Whirlwind-girl gave her power to her brother. This power, she said, would enable him to kill the enemy and remain unharmed himself. "My brother," Whirlwind-girl said, "When I am coming do not let my people be afraid of me, for I shall always hear their prayers and shall always heed them. I shall not destroy them, but will always comfort them."[59]

This story suggests that diseases lost some of their terror. The Arikaras believed that they now had doctors who could control the worst effects of the diseases. For example, Hawk told Murie that Owl had the power to cure. In fact, "Owl and the Whirlwind are enemies," Hawk said. "The Whirlwind left sickness, while the Owl gave roots and herbs to cure diseases."[60] Scholars have observed similar adaptations among other tribes. Most recently, Paul Kelton argued that the Cherokees "incorporated smallpox into their cosmology" and "constructed rituals to deal with threatened or actual epidemics of the disease, and gave constructive advice to their followers about avoiding exposure."[61] The Arikaras also made smallpox and other new infectious diseases part of their sacred history through the metaphors of Whirlwind and ravenous beasts, and they too devised new ways to fight these dangers through doctors' societies.

Not surprisingly, the different doctors' societies became prestigious institutions among the Arikaras. The annual Medicine Lodge ceremony, in which the different doctors' societies competed against each other in extraordinary feats of legerdemain, became one of the most awe-inspiring ceremonies among the Arikaras. It also survived longer than all other great Arikara ceremonies.

In fact, the doctors' societies were fully integrated into the Mother Corn, or Cedar Tree, Ceremony, described by various scholars. In July 1924, segments of the ceremony were even recorded on film.[62] Only two years earlier, a destructive sudden hailstorm had caused a premature end to the ceremony after an

Arikara ledger drawings depicting a doctors' society dance around a sacred cedar tree (a manifestation of Mother Corn), circa 1876. The dancers make offerings of furs and sage grass. Courtesy Smithsonian Institution, NAA MS 154,064B (INV 08510631 and 08510632).

error was made in the proceedings. Still, the Arikara elders were determined to have this important ceremony recorded. In July 1924, Melvin Gilmore returned to record the ceremony on film. The most sacred parts of the ceremony were not filmed in order not to offend the sacred powers.[63]

This time the ceremony went off without incident. Many of the performers were elderly men who still adhered strongly to their Native beliefs, despite the fact that all of them were also affiliated with one of the Christian churches on the reservation. Strieby Horn, for example, was a lay reader in the Episcopal Church but also an expert on the sacred plants used in the ceremonies.[64]

In 2005 Loren Yellow Bird, an Arikara scholar and a National Park Service ranger and American Indian interpreter at Fort Union National Park, discovered the film at the National Museum of the American Indian in New York and reintroduced it to the people at the Fort Berthold Indian Reservation. For the first time in more than eighty years, people saw their ancestors reenact episodes from the Arikara creation story. Although the recording was rather blurry and in a strange emerald-green color due to the wear of time, the film took its viewers back not just to 1924 when it was filmed but to the time when Whirlwind came to punish the people. With lumps growing in throats, modern-day Arikaras watched as the doctors' societies danced around the Sacred Cedar Tree and Grandfather Rock to thank them for rescuing the people. Thanks to these Arikara reenactors and the elders who shared their traditions with Dorsey, the story of the Arikaras shall never be forgotten.

CONCLUSION

The smallpox epidemics of the 1700s were traumatic events in Arikara history. Occurring only shortly after the Arikaras separated from the Pawnees, and while the Arikaras were still in the process of establishing a national identity, the epidemics hit with terrible force. It is not surprising that the Arikaras came to regard this as an event of great cosmogonic significance.

The great smallpox scourge of 1780–81 especially was a disaster of cosmic proportions. The Arikaras attributed it to supernatural causes, possibly as a punishment for religious declension among the people. This and other epidemics were of such scale and intensity that they could be represented only symbolically to reflect their cosmological nature. Hence they appear as mysterious powers: as Whirlwind, ravenous bears, or vicious snakes seeking to avenge human insults.

However, as Arikara oral tradition shows, the sacred powers also offered hope. They provided the Arikaras with medical specialists who could treat these maladies. Eventually these doctors, though never quite overshadowing the ceremonies and sacred objects associated with corn horticulture and subsistence, became increasingly important in Arikara social and sacred affairs.

THREE

"The Spiders Who Recovered the Chief's Grandson"

A Wichita Tale of Encounters with the Spanish and French in Texas

> When his chance came the Coyote made a quick dash, and took the child down from the pole, saying: "Spider-Man has come!"[1]
>
> Ahahe, Wichita storyteller, circa 1904

One hundred and fifty miles northwest of San Antonio lies the town of Menard, Texas. It is a small and sleepy community surrounded by low hills in the distance. The hills are covered with rocks, dry grass, and patches of brush. The San Sabá River meanders lazily through the landscape. A few miles east of the town stands a gray stone marker in front of a farmer's field. The marker bears the following inscription:

Site of
Mission Santa Cruz
De San Saba
Founded among the Lipan Apache
Indians by Franciscan Missionaries
in 1757 through the financial aid
of the Count of Regla. Sacked and
left in ruins by the Comanches
in 1758. Here perished Padres
Alonso Giraldo de Terreros and
José Santiesteban, martyrs to the
Christian Cause.

The marker refers to the tragic events that occurred here on March 16, 1758, when a large force of Comanche and Wichita Indians attacked San

Sabá Mission, killing two friars and two guards while wounding numerous others before burning the wooden buildings and its stockade to the ground.

The inscription on the marker tells only one side of the story. To the Spanish, the missionaries who went there under the banner of Our Lady of Refuge to convert Apache Indians were martyred in a treacherous attack by Indian villains armed with guns provided by manipulative and conspiratorial Frenchmen.

In 1903, however, Wichita storyteller Ahahe told interpreter Burgess Hunt a very different story of the events at San Sabá. According to Wichita oral tradition, the padres were servants of an evil witch-woman abductor, who enslaved their people, tortured them, and forced them to bow to an alien god. Led by a mysterious hero named Coyote and armed with tools provided by a new powerful ally called Spider-Man, the Wichitas defeated and destroyed the witch's people. To the Wichitas, this was not a massacre but a glorious victory over the forces of evil. To the Wichitas, *they* were victims and the padres were the villains.

The two traditions could not be more different in both perspective and the way in which the story was remembered. To many non-Native ears, the Wichita story is filled with strange figures and seemingly bizarre events that would puzzle most mainstream historians today. Indeed, if not for a new reading of Ahahe's account, the Wichita view might have never been discovered. Ahahe's account presents an authentic, if unconventional to non-Native ears, history of the destruction of San Sabá Mission.

AN EXPLODING TORTURE POLE

The Wichitas are one of the original Plains Indian tribes in North America. When Francisco Vázquez de Coronado contacted them in 1541, the Wichitas occupied a territory stretching from central Kansas to northern Texas. They subsisted on corn horticulture, supplemented by the bison hunt, and lived in characteristic grass dwellings shaped like giant beehives. Scholars estimate that their population was large at the time of contact, indicating a high standard of living. Early French and Spanish sources described the Wichitas as having a darker complexion than other tribes and noted that they practiced the art of tattooing. For these reasons, the Europeans often called the Wichitas "Black Pawnees" or "Tattooed Pawnees."[2]

The Wichitas had a rich oral tradition. In the early 1900s, Wichita interpreter Burgess Hunt collected sixty, mostly lengthy stories for George Dorsey, who published them in his book *The Mythology of the Wichita* (1904). Dorsey organized the stories into four eras. The first era (one story) was the period of creation. The second era, containing fifty-five stories (including the one discussed in this chapter), was the period in which the world was transformed to its current shape. The third era, containing four stories, pertained to the present. The Wichitas also believed that the world would come to an end in the fourth era, before the cycle of life would begin again. Dorsey treated these stories exclusively as myths; he did not consider any of them to be historical accounts.

Still, it seems likely that many of the stories were based on actual historical events and subsequently slipped into myth. But in the absence of clear markers, it is hard to place these stories at a specific moment in time. However, the story "The Spiders Who Recovered the Chief's Grandson" offers a promising lead. The story, told by Ahahe, tells how Coyote rescues a child who had been kidnapped by an evil woman. It contains an intriguing passage that serves as a starting point for further inquiry. The passage deals with the moment Coyote liberates the child from a mysterious torture pole:

> Then [the pole] exploded, and he could hear thundering and something like a streak of lightning coming near him, but he still went on at full speed. This was the last thing to escape. The things that flew by him were small stones, that are said to strike things when we say "lightning has struck" anything.[3]

It does not require much imagination to recognize in the torture pole a cannon. This would mean that the events described in Ahahe's story took place in the post-contact era. If so, perhaps this myth was documented in Spanish or French sources. While it is true that American Indian storytellers sometimes updated technologies to keep stories that originated before contact relevant, it nevertheless remains worthwhile to investigate whether Ahahe's account indeed refers to a post-contact historical event.

The search for the event described in Ahahe's account took me across time, beginning with Coronado's expedition in 1540 and deep into the eighteenth century. Fortunately, thanks to the diligent record-keeping practices of Spanish colonial administrators, it did not take me long to discover that the event described by Ahahe was a well-known attack on the Spanish mission of Santa Cruz de San Sabá in Texas by a combined force of Wichita, Comanche, and other Indians in 1758.

Even though Ahahe's account contains many fantastic figures, including the evil old woman, Spider-Woman, Spider-Man, Coyote, and four "headless men," all of these are based on very real historical characters and can be explained accordingly. Apart from a Wichita hero (Coyote), Ahahe's story features two powerful European forces: Spain—represented by the old "witch" woman—and France—represented by Spider-Man. In addition, Ahahe's account not only adds new details but also deepens our understanding of the San Sabá massacre, as the event became known among whites. Of course, to the Wichitas this was a tale of redemption and victory, but it also reveals the trauma caused by the Indian slave trade, of which the Wichitas were one of the principal victims.

"HE TOLD EVERYTHING THAT TOOK PLACE": THE TRADITION AS TOLD BY AHAHE

The story of the spiders, Coyote, and the abducted child was told by Ahahe, a member of the Waco branch of the Wichita tribe. We know virtually nothing about Ahahe. He must have been a prolific storyteller, because he contributed no less than sixteen of the sixty stories in Dorsey's collection. This particular story was recorded between 1901 and 1904, when Dorsey was working with interpreter Burgess Hunt. Dorsey described Hunt as "a well-educated Wichita of full blood."[4]

Like the other Caddoan tribes discussed in this book, the Wichitas had suffered tremendously in previous centuries as a result of diseases, warfare, removal, economic dislocation, and forced cultural transformation. The tribe itself was made up of the remnants of several other tribes, including the Wacos and Kitsais. In 1874 the census rolls of the Bureau of Indian Affairs listed the total number of Wichitas at 671. By 1885 this number had dropped to 448. The low point was 1896, when there were only 365 Wichitas left. We will never know how many oral traditions passed away with their owners. Fortunately, Wichita population numbers began to recover around the turn of the twentieth century. In 1903, when Hunt began to collect stories for Dorsey, the total was up to 433, although this also included a number of Delaware Indians.[5] Because Ahahe's identity is unknown, it is hard to say how these developments affected him. Perhaps the story of Coyote's rescue of the child from the witch-woman's people not merely entertained the people but also gave them the courage to face day-to-day challenges.

Ahahe's account is too long to be included here. Therefore, only a short summary is given.[6]

At the beginning of the story, the Wichita people were divided into two communities separated by a street. One day, the daughter of the west village chief and the son of the east village chief made up their minds to meet each other. They met in the middle of the street and decided to get married so that the people would be united. The girl moved into her husband's parent's lodge and eventually gave birth to a boy. The people were happy and took turns caring for the child. One morning, a little old woman took the child. Instead of returning the child, she disappeared underground with him. The people were grief stricken. The boy's grandfather promised to make a chief of the man who would find and return the child. An old woman, Spider-Woman, searched for the child and discovered a watery place where the witch-woman had disappeared into the ground. Spider-Woman followed the underground trail, but she could not recover the child because the witch-woman was too powerful for her. Disappointed and saddened after this failed attempt to retrieve the child, the people left to go on the tribal hunt.

While the people were away on their hunt, Coyote stayed behind. One day he met a curious stranger named Spider-Man, who was also known as Moving Fire. This man was very handsome. He wore a beautiful robe that had buttons shaped like arrows. Admiring Spider-Man's appearance, Coyote said that he wanted to look like him. Spider-Man threw Coyote into the water, and Coyote came out looking like Spider-Man. Spider-Man also gave Coyote a stick that magically produced meat. Spider-Man now told Coyote to take his magic stick and rescue the boy, who was being scorched to death by the evil woman's people. He told Coyote that he would encounter four headless men during his march while searching for the child. "The four Headless-Men," Ahahe explained, "were a sort of guard for the people who had the child, and since the little old woman had such guards, it was certain that she was famous."[7] Spider-Man told Coyote that "if he was a brave man these four dangerous men would not scare him."[8]

Coyote went on his way, and after a long journey he met the four headless men. Each time he met one, Coyote stood his ground and overpowered him. Finally, he arrived at the old woman's village. There he shot his four arrows into the four directions. Where his arrows struck, a fire started. The evil people, who had been slowly burning the child to death on a strange-looking pole, scattered in fear when they saw that Spider-Man had come. Taking advantage of the panic and confusion, Coyote grabbed the child and ran away. As he was running, there was a blast like thunder and lightning and little stones flew by him, but Coyote and the child escaped unharmed.

On his return journey, he made the headless men take turns carrying the child. Each time one of the headless men gave out, Coyote killed him by clubbing him over the head (a strange contradiction) until all four were dead.

After Coyote arrived home, Spider-Man took the child, threw it in the water, and called it back up. Spider-Man had given Coyote great powers, but he had warned Coyote not to have intercourse with women or his powers would disappear.

When the people returned from their hunt, they were overjoyed at the return of the child. The chief was so glad to see his grandson alive and well that he made Coyote a chief. Everyone respected Coyote because of the special powers that Spider-Man had given him. Women took an interest in him and wanted to marry him, but mindful of Spider-Man's warnings, Coyote always resisted the temptation. Yet one day Coyote violated the taboo and slept with Woman-Who-Wears-Shell-Rattles. Upon waking up, Coyote discovered that he had been transformed into an actual coyote, and he ran away into the woods.

Ahahe ended his account in an almost formulaic manner: After Coyote's transformation, the old village chief told his people that they could turn into any animal they wished. Some people did choose to become animals, but others, including the chief, remained human beings.

"THERE WAS SADNESS AMONG THE PEOPLE": CAPTIVITY AND SLAVERY

Ahahe's story is basically a tale of abduction and redemption. We shall soon see how this story ties into the attack on the mission of San Sabá in 1758. First, however, it might be useful to discuss the effects of the Indian slave trade on the Wichita Indians.

Slavery had existed among Plains tribes long before the arrival of Europeans. Tribes, including the Wichitas, raided neighboring peoples to obtain captives for cultural purposes: to replace deceased relatives or to perform ceremonial rites. Many of these captives were eventually adopted into the community. They married and founded families within their adoptive tribes. Although this form of slavery was not uncommon, it appears to have been relatively small scale.[9]

The arrival of the Spanish and French changed this situation. Their appearance had major repercussions for the Wichitas and their Caddoan relatives to the north and south. The Spanish introduced horses to the tribes southwest of the Caddoans, while the French introduced guns to the tribes in the east. These objects triggered a frenzied quest among Indian tribes in these regions for more slaves to pay for these powerful objects. The unlucky Caddoan tribes were caught in the middle between the horse and gun frontiers. Mounted on horses obtained from the Spanish through trading or raiding, the Apaches especially raided Caddoan tribes for slaves. The Apaches then exchanged their captives at Spanish markets for more horses. Meanwhile, the Osages to the east of the Caddoans raided the Caddoan tribes for slaves with guns they had obtained from French traders.[10]

As a result of the European presence, the volume of the slave trade increased dramatically. Historian James Brooks estimates that by the late 1600s, 21 percent of the total population in New Mexico consisted of non-Pueblo slaves. A large number of these were Wichita.[11] By 1700 the volume of trade in Caddoan slaves was so large that French officials in Quebec used the name Panis (those related to the Caddoan language family) for any kind of Indian slave captured west of the Missouri River.[12]

In the 1630s, New Mexico governor Francisco de la Mora y Ceballos issued numerous permits to enslave Indian boys and girls. A Franciscan critic of the governor protested that such children were placed into perpetual slavery "as if they were calves and colts." Franciscan monks, however, eagerly participated in the trade "but cloaked their commerce in the notion that Christian charity required the redemption of young captives from the heathen."[13]

The treatment of Indian slaves among the Spanish varied from owner to owner. Some owners treated them no better than galley slaves "and literally work them to death or force young women into concubinage." Other owners shipped their slaves south to work as laborers or presented them as gifts to influential patrons in Mexico. A few fortunate slaves were adopted by their masters into (subordinate) fictive kinship relations. "In most cases," Brooks speculates, "slaves' lives probably reflected some middle range between these two extremes."[14]

Regardless of the treatment they received, enslavement was a traumatic experience for both the slave and his or her relatives back home. Although the Wichitas also seized enemies to trade away as slaves, they more often were victims rather than beneficiaries of the trade. This situation changed dramatically between 1700 and 1750, when the Wichitas established diplomatic relations with the French and the Comanches. It was this alliance that turned them from slave victims into slave traders.[15] Indeed, it is this transformation from victim to victor that is told in the story of Coyote and the evil witch.

"SINCE THE LITTLE OLD WOMAN HAD SUCH GUARDS, IT WAS CERTAIN THAT SHE WAS FAMOUS": ANALYZING THE STORY

Ahahe's account is, in effect, a story of abduction and rescue. It is possible to break this story down into its essential components. Doing this will help us analyze the story and find possible links to an actual historic event:

1. The tribe is divided into two villages by a street.
2. The son of the east village chief and the daughter of the west village chief secretly marry each other and have a child.
3. The people are happy with the child and look after the child lovingly.
4. One day the child is abducted by an old woman with a cane, who disappears into the mud.
5. Spider-Woman finds the trail of the old woman, but she is forced back by the old woman, whose powers are too strong for her.
6. The people go on a buffalo hunt to forget their sorrows over losing the child.
7. Coyote remains behind. He is ugly, but Spider-Man turns him into a handsome man.
8. Spider-Man gives Coyote certain powers, including a stick that magically produces meat and four arrows that cause fire.
9. Meanwhile, the old woman's evil people are torturing the child, burning him while he's tied to a pole.
10. Spider-Man urges Coyote to rescue the child, but he must forever give up women to keep his power.
11. Coyote sets out and encounters four headless men, who are guarding the old woman's people. Ahahe suspects that these people were famous. Each headless man tries to block Coyote's path and uses abusive language.
12. Coyote overcomes the men, and their feet are stuck to the earth. Then he sets fire to the village from four directions.
13. Coyote rushes in to rescue the boy. When the witch's people see him, they think he is Spider-Man. They panic. Coyote rescues the child from the pole.
14. The pole explodes, and little stones fly by Coyote like lightning.
15. After making his escape, Coyote makes the headless men take turns carrying the child. When they are exhausted, Coyote kills them.
16. Coyote returns with the child, and Spider-Man turns one of Coyote's own children into an exact copy of the chief's grandson.
17. The people return from their hunt, still mourning the loss of the child. But they are happy when Coyote shows them the child. The chief now makes Coyote a chief as well.
18. Coyote breaks his vow and marries a woman and subsequently loses his power. He turns into an actual coyote and runs away.
19. The people divide again into three groups: air animals, wild (land) animals, and the chief's own people.

The first part of the account (items 1 to 3) tells the story of the unification of the different Wichita groups or of the creation of an alliance between the Wichitas and another tribe. The child that resulted from the marriage of the eastern chief's son and the western chief's daughter symbolized this unification. The people treasured the unity and thus caringly and lovingly looked after the child. But this perfection came to an end when the child disappeared mysteriously. The implication is that the recently accomplished tribal unity was threatened.[16]

This interpretation is based on fact. Several stories in Dorsey's collection talk about the unification of two communities that lived on opposite sides of a "street." Sometimes the orientation of this street is north–south; at other times it is east–west. There is actual historical evidence for such a division. When Spanish priest Fray Joseph de Calahorra of Nacogdoches, Texas, visited the Tawakoni and Iscani villages on the Sabine River in 1760, he wrote that a "street" separated these two groups.[17]

The abduction of the child (item 4) was a traumatic event. It is possible that the abducted child of the story represented more children, some of whom might have been the offspring of intermarriage between the different Wichita bands. After all, as mentioned before, the Wichitas were the target of slave raids by the Osages, the Lipan Apaches, and the Comanches. The Osages raided the Wichitas to exchange slaves for guns at French markets in Louisiana and the Illinois country. The Apaches and Comanches exchanged their Wichita slaves for horses at Spanish markets in New Mexico. The child represents the loss of children and other loved ones (especially young women of childbearing age) in such raids.

The old woman (items 4 and 11) is intriguing. Whom does she represent? There are multiple possibilities, but the most likely option is that she represents the Spanish. After all, the Spanish were the main buyers of Wichita slaves. In addition, from the Wichita perspective, the Spanish were also associated with the Apaches. The witch-woman's cane may represent a gun, a lance, or a religious staff. At first I believed that she was a representation of the Virgin of Guadalupe, who had replaced Santiago Matamoros as patron saint of the Spanish in the Americas. But as we shall see later, she was in fact another type of Madonna.

It is difficult to determine whom the Spider-Woman (item 5) may represent. She discovered that the old woman disappeared into the mud. Perhaps this "mud" was a swamp, river, or spring. What is also significant is that Spider-Woman's powers were not sufficient to overcome the witch-woman.

After the tribe goes on a collective buffalo hunt to forget its sorrows, the story introduces two characters: Coyote and Spider-Man (items 6 to 8). Coyote, of course, usually appears in Wichita stories as a trickster figure, who can be both heroic and a charlatan. Indeed, in this account he appears in both forms. However, elements in this story set this particular Coyote apart from the usual trickster type. In this story, Coyote appears far more human-like. While it is tempting to see this account as simply another trickster tale, one must consider that this character may have been based on a historical human figure.

This human Coyote is described as being ugly. This was a traditional way of saying that he was poor, although the description could also apply to a foreign Indian. In any event, Coyote was a person of low social status or a stranger. He was transformed by Spider-Man. Spider-Man had powerful qualities. In this regard, Spider-Man's other name, Moving Fire, is intriguing, because it may refer to someone who possessed one or more guns. If the old woman abductor was Spanish, perhaps Spider-Man was French. After all, the French maintained peaceful relations with the Wichitas after Jean Baptiste Benard de la Harpe first visited them in 1719. Also significant is the fact the Spider-Man did not go on the warpath against the old woman's people himself. Instead, Spider-Man turned Coyote into an image of himself by dipping him into the water. Perhaps this was a form of baptism or some other form of transformation. More importantly, Spider-Man was dressed differently: he wore a robe that had an "arrow for a button." This sounds much like an eighteenth-century frock coat with "fish-bone" button design, made famous in the *Pirates of the Caribbean* movies. He dressed Coyote in the same outfit. In other words, Spider-Man transformed Coyote into a Frenchman.

Spider-Man also gave Coyote a stick that magically produced meat. Clearly this was a gun. With this magical stick, Coyote provided meat for his family. Later he would use it in his battle against the old woman's people. The four "arrows" may also be guns or, because they were used to set the grass and the village on fire, some other fire-making tools: fuses, matches, or something similar.

Being captured from family and loved ones was traumatic, but the story also makes clear that enslavement was a form of torture (items 9 and 10). This is symbolized by the fact that the old woman's evil people were slowly burning the child to death. "The people were scorching the child every night, and were making all sorts of fun," Ahahe tells us.[18] To be sure, many American Indian tribes practiced pole torture, but burning at the stake was also a distinctly common form of execution among the Spanish. Sometimes gunpowder was used as a fuel, although this may have been a scarce commodity on the frontier, not to be wasted unnecessarily. In fact, the Spanish had invented several ingenious and cruel forms of pole tortures. Of course, flogging was one of these. Hanging, either by the neck or by some other part of the body, was another. The Spanish had also pioneered garroting, which they sometimes combined with burning. Garroting involved tying someone to a pole and then slowly strangling the victim to death by a metal cord or a rope attached to a stick or lever at the back of the pole, which tightened the rope when it was turned. In more mechanically advanced designs, the stick was also attached to a kind of screw that would drill itself into the victim's neck vertebrae. Although crucifixion was another possibility, it seems unlikely that the Spanish used this method. However, the Spanish did introduce sculpted images of a crucified Jesus, which might have caused the Wichitas to associate them with Spanish pole tortures. In any case, the Spanish Crown did not outlaw torture until 1790, and even then it likely continued on the North American frontier for much longer.[19]

Because the child faced a slow and agonizing death, Spider-Man urged Coyote to make haste with his rescue. Spider-Man also explained that Coyote could succeed only if he observed his religious vow to abstain from women. In fact, Coyote told his wife that she would no longer be his spouse but rather his sister. Sexual abstinence was common practice among men searching for and maintaining their spiritual power. As a side note, some American Indians believed that Catholic priests were storing up spiritual power through their vows of celibacy.

It is difficult to establish the exact identity of the four headless men (items 11 and 12). Initially I believed that the headless men represented the different enemies of the Wichitas: Osages, Apaches, Comanches, and Spanish. Interestingly, all of these enemies occupied different directions, much like the four headless men in the story. The Osages threatened the Wichitas from the northeast, the Apaches from the southwest, the Comanches from the west, and the Spanish from further southwest. However, as we see later, the headless men probably stood for monks sporting tonsures (shaved crowns of heads), which was typical of the Franciscan order. They were, then, *hair*less rather than *head*less.

Coyote's mysterious appearance caused panic among the evil people who were holding the child (items 13 and 14). Anxiety caused by the supposed French association with American Indian tribes was a recurrent theme on the Spanish colonial borderlands. Rumors of French interference and agitation among the Indians of the plains dated back to the mid-1690s. The specter of the French caused great concerns at the colonial court at Mexico City, which sent out expeditions to intercept trespassing Frenchmen. Perhaps the most famous of such expeditions was the Villasur expedition of 1720, when Captain Pedro de Villasur's command was ambushed and routed by the Pawnee Indians. Spanish survivors erroneously reported that a large number of Frenchmen had been among the Pawnee attackers. Although many scholars believe that the stories of Frenchmen at this battle were probably a face-saving device, used to avoid Spanish embarrassment for having lost to supposed "primitive" Natives, the fact remains that French *coureurs de bois* did venture deep into hitherto unexplored territories. The idea that they had contacted and perhaps established temporary presence with these Indians was not so farfetched. Even if there were no Frenchmen present, it is quite possible that their trade goods, including guns and coats, had fallen into Wichita hands. In any event, the sudden appearance of foreigners would have been cause for panic.[20]

We return once again to the mysterious pole to which the witch's people had tied the child. Spider-Man had instructed Coyote that this pole was dangerous and that when Coyote got the child, "he should run hard, for something would explode, so that if he made any movement in dodging it he would be hit by the explosion of the thing that was hid under the pole that the child was hung on."[21] Indeed, as mentioned above, this pole was likely a cannon. The small stones may have been grapeshot, canister shot, or simply gravel, with which cannons were sometimes loaded. Ahahe said that the stones were "like lightning," but to modern-day ears, the weapon sounds like a cannon. Indeed, the Spanish were the first to introduce cannons into the Americas, and Spanish settlers used cannons to defend their settlements. Depending on the time period, various cannons could be meant. Regardless of the type of cannons used by the Spanish, the fact that the evil people had a pole that flashed like lightning and shot little round stones can safely be viewed as evidence—a smoking gun, if you will—linking this story at least to post-Columbian European contact.

After escaping from the evil woman's town or camp, Coyote forced the headless men to carry the child (item 15). Here Coyote was in fact enslaving enemies himself. In revenge, Coyote executed the headless men after they had served their purpose. The fact that these men were headless may seem puzzling until one considers that the Wichitas sometimes decapitated their enemies after death. Perhaps this is what was meant by the term "headless men." Rather than "headless men," they were more accurately "soon to be headless men."

The next passages continue the story of Coyote's rise from a low social status to a position of prominence (items 16 and 17). It is not just Coyote himself who is raised up the social ladder, but his family, most notably one of his sons, as well. In fact, Spider-Man symbolizes this social rise by dipping Coyote's son into water, thus transforming him. Again, one is tempted to view this as a kind of baptism, but this interpretation does not apply because Coyote's son assumes the likeness of the chief's grandson, not a Frenchman. It seems more plausible that the chief adopted Coyote's son as his own grandson.

Coyote's political and social rise ends when he violates the taboo imposed by Spider-Man (item 18). This sounds much like common Coyote stories in which Coyote's sexual appetites and carelessness prompt him to throw his powers away. Here, the basic theme is that when people turn away from their religious responsibilities and pursue selfish interests and self-gratifying pleasures, they lose their powers. Woman-who-wears-Shell-Rattles represents the temptation that led Coyote astray from his religious observances. In other words, he has sinned. In punishment, Coyote is turned back into his actual form. Literally, he is a coyote, but symbolically, he has returned to his previous, lowly status. Interestingly, Woman-who-wears-Shell-Rattles is a common character in the oral traditions of southeastern Indians. Perhaps she represents a tribe that lured Coyote away from the Wichita alliance. In any case, this episode raises the interesting possibility that the Wichitas applied the name of the trickster to the Wichita–Comanche hero because they shared thematic parallels. This would also explain why I was unable to find any evidence of a Comanche war leader by the name of Coyote in French and Spanish sources.

At the end of the story, the people again divide themselves into three groups (item 19). Some turn into birds while others transform into land animals, which reminds scholars of the division of communities into sky and earth moieties. However, the Wichitas did not have a clan and moiety system. Besides, there is also a third group, which consists of humans proper. It is not possible to link the two animal groups to any of the Wichita bands, so this part of the tradition remains a mystery.

So far the interpretations; what about the evidence?

"THEY RESORTED TO THEIR FALSE AND TREACHEROUS PROFESSIONS OF FRIENDSHIP": THE WICHITA INDIANS AND THE SAN SABÁ MASSACRE OF 1758

The above assumptions are, of course, speculation only. Confirming the link between the oral tradition and an actual historical event requires evidence. Fortunately, Spanish colonial sources offer many opportunities to look.

My investigation started with the conquistadors, beginning with Francisco Vázquez de Coronado (1540) and including every other Spaniard known to have contacted the Wichitas: Father Agustín Rodríguez (1581), Antonio de Espejo (1582), Gaspar Castaño de Sosa (1590), Francisco Leyva de Bonilla (1593), and Don Juan de Oñate (1601). However, none of these men had contact with the Wichitas that resembled the events described in the Wichita tradition.[22]

Because none of the above scenarios presented a convincing case for a link with the Coyote story, I was about to throw in the towel. After all, one now enters the relatively recent past, because the next noteworthy incident occurred on March 16, 1758—more than a century and a half after Oñate's expedition—and involved the attack by a combined force of Wichita, Tonkawa, Bidai, Comanche, and other Indians against the Spanish–Apache mission at Santa Cruz de San Sabá in present-day central Texas. The time span for such an important event to be turned into myth seemed too short to me at the time. Still, Spanish colonial sources on the San Sabá Massacre soon provided many parallels to the Coyote story, making it highly probable that this was indeed the event described by Ahahe.[23]

In the spring of 1757, Franciscan missionaries established the mission of Santa Cruz de San Sabá, near present-day Menard, Texas. The mission's purpose, in addition to converting Natives, was to make peace with the Apaches and so prevent French expansion into the region. Father President Alonso Giraldo de Terreros led the mission. Four friars assisted Terreros, although at the time of the attack, one of these was absent.

Apart from the friars, nine families of Tlascaltecan Indians served as instructors of the neophytes. According to Father Miguel Molina, one of the survivors of the massacre, some Apache women and children were also at the mission at the time of the attack. The mission complex itself consisted of several buildings, including a church, the friars' quarters, storerooms, and stables. Each building was made out of logs and had a tile roof. A stockade of wood protected the complex. A large gate, secured by heavy bars, was the only entrance. To complete the defense, the mission had two light cannons.[24]

At the same time, Spanish troops under Colonel Don Diego Ortiz de Parrilla built a presidio four miles away, on the opposite side of the river. The presidio housed between 300 and 400 people, including 237 women and children. Effectively, however, there were rarely more than thirty or forty soldiers guarding the presidio.[25] Their commander, Colonel Parrilla, was an able man with experience in the North African wars, as well as several Indian wars in the Spanish borderlands. He was skeptical of the undertaking, believing that the Apaches were not sincere in their pledge to make peace. Still, as a good officer, he carried out his duties diligently.

Periodically, Apache groups, especially the Lipan Apaches, stopped by the mission to ask for supplies. Despite professions of their willingness to settle near the mission and become Christians, the Apaches never stayed long enough to show that they were truly committed to the Spanish plan. However, the Spanish decision to reach out to the Apaches angered the Taovayas and the other Wichita bands that had suffered Lipan Apache slave raids for more than a century. In fact, in the weeks and months before the Wichita–Comanche attack against the mission, the Apaches had staged several raids against the Wichitas.

In the weeks before the attack, Apache visitors warned the friars and Colonel Parrilla of the presence of a large combined force of Comanches, Wichitas, and other Indians nearby. In March 1758, Norteño Indians (this was the name Parrilla gave to the "wild tribes" of northern Texas, including the Wichitas) stole sixty-two horses from the mission. Although a detachment of fifteen soldiers gave chase, they quickly returned because they feared they might be lured into an ambush. On March 9, the Indians attacked four Spanish prospectors. Although wounded, all four managed to reach the safety of the presidio. News of these incidents alarmed Colonel Parrilla, who made several attempts—the last on March 15—to persuade Father Terreros to give up his mission post and seek shelter in the presidio. Father Terreros refused. He was unwilling to leave valuable religious items behind. He also believed he was safer in the mission because it had ample firepower and was smaller than the presidio, and therefore was more defensible. Just in case, Parrilla sent some additional soldiers as well as an extra supply of ammunition and powder.[26] Robert S. Weddle, historian of the battle, summed up the different attitudes between Parrilla and Father Terreros. "Parrilla, in this time of crisis, put his trust in armed might," Weddle wrote, while the "missionaries put their trust in God."[27]

The attack took place just after dawn on March 16. Father Terreros had just finished leading Mass and Father Santiesteban was still inside the church building. Several mission workers had left the stockade that morning. Among these was Juan Leal, a fifty-year-old mission guard. He had come to the Americas when he was twenty-five. He was one of the first to meet the Indians. When he tried to hide by the river, the Indians discovered him. Two Indians began beating him, but another stopped them. Leal also saw one of the Indian mission women, who had been stripped naked by the Indians. Only later did Leal realize that the Indians had spared their lives because they hoped to enter the stockade under a guise of peace.[28]

The clamor had alarmed the people inside the stockade. They hastily closed the gate and prepared to defend themselves. The Indians marched up to the stockade and assured the defenders that they had come in peace. They said they were looking only for Apaches who had committed crimes against their people recently. Two defenders, Ascencio Cadena and the son of soldier Juan Antonio Gutíerrez, recognized the Indians as belonging to peaceful tribes. They assured Father Terreros that it was safe. Terreros then ordered the defenders to open the gate.[29]

Immediately, the plaza in front of the church filled with hundreds of Indians. Although many of the Indians were armed with firearms, swords, and sabers, they shook hands with the missionaries. Only the younger Indians were carrying the traditional bows and arrows. The priests brought out tobacco and began to distribute it among the Indians. Father Molina spotted a big Comanche chief, still mounted on his horse, whose face "did not betray friendliness," even after Molina gave him four bundles of tobacco. This chief was dressed in a French uniform.

Several Indians now started pilfering the mission for loot. At this time, the wounded Leal also arrived. At this point Terreros probably realized that the Indians had come with bad intentions. It was too late now. A "Tejas" chief approached him and demanded that Terreros write a letter of security so that they could present it at the presidio. Terreros wrote the letter and the Tejas chief rode off, only to return after a little while, claiming that his group had been fired at from the presidio. He demanded that Terreros go with him. Terreros and a soldier named Joseph Garcia mounted their horses to ride with the Indians. Just outside the stockade, however, both were shot out of the saddle by an Indian volley.[30]

Now a fierce battle broke out. In the confusion, several of the mission personnel were wounded or killed. The Indians also began to shoot the livestock. Father Molina and several others found refuge in Father Terreros's quarters. Juan Leal and others found refuge in the church, where they mounted one of the light cannons on some boxes, pointing toward one of the entrances, in case the Indians broke through the door.[31] The Indians, however, responded by setting fire to the buildings.

Meanwhile, Colonel Parrilla sent nine soldiers to assist the defenders at the mission. They soon ran into the Indians, who killed two soldiers and wounded another. The wounded man was Joseph Vazquez. Believing Vazquez was dead, the Indians tossed him over the stockade into the burning mission. Miraculously, Vazquez received only minor burns and crawled to safety in the office, where Father Molina and several others had ensconced themselves. He managed to stay undetected because the Indians were too busy looting the mission.

Later that day, the Indians made an attempt to attack the presidio. They set fire to the grass to lure the soldiers out of the fort and into an ambush. Colonel Parrilla, however, refused to be drawn into the trap. Apparently, the Indians withdrew from the presidio and headed back to the mission.

Toward darkness, Parrilla sent out fourteen more soldiers to investigate the situation. These men observed the burning mission from a distance, but they soon were detected by the Indian dogs, whose angry barks alerted the Indians. Fearing an attack from the presidio, Indians rushed from the mission toward the river valley, where they suspected the soldiers to be. Because of this sudden diversion, Father Molina, Joseph Vazquez, and several others managed to escape from the mission and run away. One man, Juan Antonio Gutíerrez, was wounded in the hip and was left behind. The soldiers found his charred remains several days later. The Indians spotted Molina and the other escapees and shot at them. Vazquez once again lost consciousness, but when he woke up later, he set out on foot and arrived days later in San Antonio. Molina and the others, however, reached the presidio in safety after a long and arduous march.[32]

Not until March 20, four days after the attack, did Colonel Parrilla dare to leave the presidio to investigate the mission. His soldiers found the bodies of the slain men, several of whom were entirely charred, while others had been only partially burned. They did not find the decapitated body of Father Santiesteban until March 24. When they went looking for the head, they discovered it inside the remains of the mission.

Although the San Sabá Massacre seems a small affair, it was a significant event in the history of the Spanish borderlands. When news of the attack spread, panic broke out at the other missions and settlements. Rumors spread that the presidio of San Luis de las Amarillas had been destroyed as well. Surrounding settlements refused to send troops to assist Parrilla's garrison. For months, the fear of an all-out Comanche–Wichita uprising kept administrators in Mexico City and the Spanish Provincias Internas in a state of emergency.[33]

If the massacre at San Sabá shook New Spain on its foundations, would it not be logical for such an important event to be recorded by Wichita historians as well? I am convinced that the Wichitas indeed recorded the event in their oral traditions; the Coyote story suggests that the Wichitas considered this event of great importance as well. Indeed, the Coyote story shines additional light on the San Sabá tragedy.

"[THEY] WERE SURPRISED TO SEE SUCH A WONDERFUL MAN AS THIS": CONNECTING THE WICHITA TRADITION TO SAN SABÁ

It is now possible to connect the two stories. Despite some discrepancies, which I address later, the parallels between the Wichita tradition and the events at San Sabá Mission are striking.

The attempts by the Spanish to draw the Apaches into a friendly alliance alarmed the Wichitas. The Apaches had been preying on the Wichitas for slaves for more than a century. Spanish peace overtures with the Apaches prompted the Wichitas to consider them to be enemies as well. Although the real-life Coyote said "that they had no intention other than to fight Apaches," his men clearly had come to send a message. The Coyote tradition implies that the Wichitas had recently lost some of their people to the Apaches, and they held the Spanish accountable. Father Molina was deceiving the Wichitas when he denied that there were any Apaches on the mission premises. We "had managed to shelter and conceal [the Apache women and children] in the quarters of the Father President, the entrance to which was protected by a constant guard of soldiers," Molina later reported.[34]

The Wichita story also confirms the creation of an alliance between the Wichitas and the Comanches as symbolized in the beginning of the myth by the two separated villages that were united through the marriage of the son and the daughter of the opposing chiefs. Intermarriage was a common way for tribes to establish and solidify diplomatic relations. Both sides benefited from the alliance. The Wichitas gained a powerful ally against the Apaches and could capitalize on their role as trade middlemen between the French and the Comanches. Meanwhile, the alliance with the Wichitas allowed the Comanches to tap into the newly established gun trade with the French.[35]

It was this alliance that alarmed the Apaches, who stepped up their raids against the Wichitas to drive a wedge between the two new allies. Simultaneously, the Apaches hoped that they could draw the Spanish into the war against the Wichitas and Comanches. The construction of San Sabá encouraged them in this regard. According to historian William Dunn, the Apaches intentionally fueled Wichita anger over a supposed Spanish–Apache alliance by leaving Spanish objects (such as shoes and articles of clothing) at sites they had raided.[36]

The Destruction of Mission San Sabá in the Province of Texas and the Martyrdom of the Fathers Alonso de Terreros, Joseph Santiesteban, probably by José de Páez, circa 1765. Depicted are Father Santiesteban (*right*) as a "headless man" and Father Terreros (*left*) with scalp marks around his head. Coyote, dressed in the robe given to him by Spider-Man, appears in several scenes but is most prominent in the lower right corner. In the center of the painting the Wichitas take revenge on the painting of the "witch-woman" holding the child. © D. R. Museo Nacional de Arte/Instituto Nacional de Ballas Artes y Literatura, 2017.

Official Spanish records were most helpful in confirming the identity of several of the characters in the story. Yet it was an unexpected and unconventional source that proved to be particularly instructive. Shortly after the massacre, Pedro Romero de Terreros, cousin of Father Terreros and financier of the mission, commissioned renowned artist Miguel Cabrera to commemorate the event in a painting. Cabrera left the job to one of his students, most likely José de Páez. The painting is titled *The Destruction of Mission San Sabá* and is now housed in Mexico City. It depicts various events of the massacre that confirm many of the details in the Wichita story. It depicts, among other things, "Coyote" in his French frock coat, several "headless men," and even the "Witch Woman."

The painting also relates the ordeal of Juan Leal, the surrounding of the stockade by well-armed Indians, the entrance into the stockade by the Indians, the murder of Father Terreros, the burning of the mission, the murder of Father Santiesteban, the miraculous escape by Joseph Vazquez, and numerous other episodes. Each of these is marked by a letter with a corresponding written description at the bottom of the painting.[37]

Perhaps the most striking character in the painting, apart from Father Terreros and Father Santiesteban, is the leader of the Indian fighting force. He appears in several scenes. His most striking feature is the fact that he wears a French frock coat. However, he was not French. The written Spanish sources that the artist relied upon to compose his canvas state that he was a Comanche Indian. These two facts correspond perfectly with the Wichita story. Ahahe, the storyteller, implied that Coyote was not a Wichita Indian at all but a "stranger" who, after meeting Spider-Man, was transformed into a "handsome man." His transformation included a robe with arrow-shaped buttons. Spider-Man also gave him a magical stick, or more precisely a gun, which made him not only more handsome but also more powerful. He in effect became a Frenchman.

Dressed in his French frock coat, this Comanche chief led his Wichita–Comanche warriors to San Sabá and tricked Father Terreros into opening the gates to the mission. Father Molina described him in his account: "He was a Comanche, according to the barbarians themselves, and worthy of respect. His dress and his red jacket were well-decorated, after the manner of French uniforms, and he was fully armed. His face was hideous and extremely grave."[38]

Based on this description of the Comanche chief, it is safe to conclude that this was the real-life Coyote from the Wichita myth. A search to find possible references to a chief by the name of Coyote in sources on Comanche history was unsuccessful. Nor was I able to find a story similar to the Wichita myth in Comanche oral tradition.[39] It seems more plausible that the name Coyote refers to his cunning ways (he was, after all, the mastermind behind the attack on the mission post) or the fact that his behavior at the end of the tradition mimicked that of the typical mischievous and lustful Coyote trickster of Wichita tradition. The only apparent discrepancy is that the Wichita account implies that Coyote acted by himself, when in reality he had many men to support him in the attack. But this fact does not significantly change the basic narrative of the history.

The positive identification of Coyote with the Comanche chief in the San Sabá painting and the Spanish sources now also allows us to confirm that Spider-Man (aka Moving Fire) had to be a Frenchman. Until La Harpe's visit in 1719, the French had not played a direct role in Wichita history. The French presence was felt only indirectly, though negatively, because they supplied guns to the Osages, who raided the Wichitas for slaves. After 1719, however, the French also began to supply the Wichitas with guns. Therefore it is possible to associate the French with Spider-Man, who gave Coyote the magic items with which he defeated the evil people. In fact, the attack against San Sabá was the first time the Wichitas ever used these weapons on such a massive scale. We know this from the deposition of Juan Cortinas, ensign in the Spanish presidio of San Luis de las Amarillas. Although the presidio was four miles away from San Sabá, Cortinas heard the gunfire and saw the Indians as they attacked the mission. Cortinas had served on New Spain's northern frontier for forty years and had never known the Indians to possess such dramatic firepower. Cortinas's deposition described his anxiety at the knowledge that the Indians were now armed with guns. In his years of service, Cortinas "had never known hostile Indians to use weapons other than bows and arrows, with some pikes and wooden cudgels or clubs." Because of their superior firepower, the Spanish had held "a great advantage over the barbarians." Now the playing field had changed. The attack against San Sabá was "the only instance he had ever seen or heard of in which the heathen Indians, because of their great numbers and ample supply of firearms, had been able to perpetrate so bold an outrage."[40]

Cortinas's claim is upheld by other sources. Servant Joseph Gutiérrez testified that the Indians had "French firearms, bullet pouches, and very large powder horns." Mission guard Juan Leal added that the Indians "had helmets, and many had leather jerkins, or breastplates like those of the French." Father Molina estimated that there were two thousand enemy Indians, about half of whom owned firearms. Sergeant Joseph Antonio Flores told Colonel Parrilla that "he and his soldiers would have put up a stronger resistance if the enemy had been armed only with bows and arrows, for the Spaniards were accustomed to fighting Indians armed with less powerful weapons [than muskets] . . . but they were helpless against the accurate musket fire of the Indian barbarians." Colonel Parrilla himself emphasized this matter in his correspondence with his superiors. "It is now evident," Parrilla reported, "that the Indians have been trained in the skillful use of firearms and are thoroughly experienced in making war with the greatest sagacity and cunning." He added, "For these reasons their forces must now be considered stronger than those of the Presidio."[41]

Juan Leal clarified that "the French supplied them [the hostiles] with things of that sort in exchange for horses, mules, and the meat, hides, and fat of buffalo and bear, and the skins of deer, which the Indians take in great numbers in the open country." This observation neatly matches the role of the "stick" that Spider-Man gave to Coyote. This stick, or rather gun, miraculously produced meat.[42]

Although Molina, Parrilla, and others may have overestimated the number of Indians and the amount of weapons they carried, the fact that the Indians had such weapons at all was terrifying. In a letter to the marqués de las Amarillas, Parrilla repeated this concern. "But the heathen of the north are innumerable and [they are] rich," Parrilla wrote. "They enjoy the protection and commerce of the French; they dress well, breed horses, handle firearms with the greatest skill, and obtain ample supplies of meat from the animals they call *cíbolos* [buffalo]." As a result of their trade with the French and with Spanish smugglers, these Indians had "picked up a great deal of knowledge and understanding," which made them "far superior to the Indians of other parts of these Kingdoms."[43]

The panic caused by the appearance of these Indians is captured in the Coyote myth. Ahahe describes the panic as follows:

> They believed that Spider-Man was the only man who had great powers; and if he should ever try to get the child he would be successful; and this is the reason why the people at the village would say: "Spider-Man has come," and run to their lodges. When his chance came the Coyote made a quick dash, and took the child down from the pole, saying: "Spider-Man has come!"[44]

Although the official Spanish documents do not offer any clues to the identity of the witch-woman abductor, the painting offers a key piece of the puzzle. There are, in fact, two possibilities. The first of these is that the Wichitas confused Father Terreros and Father Santiesteban with the old woman of the story. After all, the fathers wore robes that resembled Wichita women's clothing. Furthermore, because friars refused to fight, Indians sometimes viewed them as "women" or as "woman-hearted." However, the painting also depicts an actual woman in the form of a painted Madonna. Her portrait appears in the very center of the painting in a scene marked by the letter *O*. The written caption at the bottom of the painting reads: "The outrages and desecrations that were performed upon the holy images and the destruction of the divine banner of Nuestra Señora de Refugio, the patroness and protector of the Mission." In the scene, some Indians hold up the image of the Lady of Refuge while others shoot their guns and arrows at her.[45]

The presence of this banner is confirmed in the "Inventory of Supplies in Mexico for the Mission Santa Cruz de San Sabá." It is listed under "painting on linen of the Divina Pastora for P. Pres." In fact, the inventory lists two paintings; there was one of "San Fernando for Padre Santiesteban." Both of these were kept in a large box, but we do not know what happened to the paintings. Perhaps they both perished in the fire, but the Wichita tradition implies that the Wichitas carried them home as spoils of war.[46]

This, then, appears to be the "little old woman" mentioned in the story. Note Ahahe's description: "The four Headless-Men were a sort of guard for the people who had the child, and since the little old woman had such guards, *it was certain that she was famous*" (emphasis mine).[47] In other words, because the Spanish treated this object with such reverence, the Indians believed that she was their leader. Furthermore, Spanish missionaries had been converting (that is, enslaving) Indians in her name. It is not hard to see, then, why she features so prominently in the story. Also noteworthy is the fact that the Indians exact revenge on her by shooting their weapons at her image.

It is difficult to see the exact details of the banner of Our Lady of Refuge in the painting of the massacre. Typically, however, the virgin is depicted holding the infant Jesus in her hands. In fact, José de Páez (1720–1790), the assumed painter of *The Destruction of Mission San Sabá*, painted several of these portraits in his career.[48] The pose of the Madonna holding the child probably reinforced the Indians' idea of an "old woman" who stole infant children. It may also explain the wrath that the Indians displayed toward the image.

The fact that the woman and child were on a banner may also explain the reference to the child attached to a pole in the story, or that the woman was walking with a "cane." Suspended from the top of poles, such banners were often carried in ceremonial processions. The story implies that Coyote took the banner from the pole and carried it home. Once there, Coyote and the Wichitas showed the portrait to Spider-Man, who threw it into the water, after which the child floated up to the surface. If this explanation is correct, the Wichita story adds new details to this part of the San Sabá story.

The portrait of Our Lady of Refuge illustrates the iconographic confusion between American Indians and Europeans. To the Spanish, she was a saint. The Wichitas, in contrast, saw in her an evil witch who abducted children.

The painting and the Spanish records also confirm the presence of the "headless men" in the story. Indeed, Father Santiesteban was *decapitated* by the attackers. Ahahe described it thus: "On his way home the Coyote came to the last Headless-Man that he had met, and he made him carry the child on his back until he gave out, then took his bow and struck him on the head [!], killing him instantly."[49] Ahahe also explained how each Headless Man had begged to be released without harm.

Father Maria Ano de los Dolores reported later that "the Indians disrobed the fathers, leaving the bodies on the ground, with their undergarments and sandals."[50] Interestingly, Father Santiesteban's decapitated corpse was not found until March 24, eight days after the massacre. His charred corpse was found among the ashes of the mission. His head, however, was found in a different location: the mission's storehouse.[51] "They buried him in the cemetery," Parrilla reported, "as had been done with the Reverend Father President."[52]

The decapitation of Father Santiesteban was apparently worthy of note by an Indian artist who commemorated this event in a rock carving near present-day Paint Rock, Texas. In his masterful history of the massacre and the Spanish punitive expedition that followed, historian Robert S. Weddle published an image of the pictograph. It depicts not only the headless priest but also other episodes from the massacre, such as the surrounding of the stockade, the (partial) surrounding of the presidio, and the slaughter of the livestock.[53]

With a little imagination one might distinguish a second decapitated victim in the mission. When soldiers investigated the mission four days after the massacre, they found that many of the sacred objects had been smashed and destroyed. Among these was a statue of Saint Francis of Assisi, the founder of the Franciscan order. Sergeant Joseph Antonio Flores discovered that the "effigy of the Holy Saint Francis had been overturned and the head severed from the body."[54]

It is important to point out that Ahahe's account suggests that the headless men might not have been truly headless at all. One was killed after being clubbed *over the head.* This suggests that these men lost their heads or scalps after they were killed. Indeed, several defenders were scalped that day. Apart from Father Santiesteban, who lost his entire head, Father Terreros was scalped, as were Juan Antonio Gutiérrez, mission administrator and *mayordomo,* and soldier Joseph García. An interesting detail is that the Indians also tore out Gutiérrez's eyes, which may be a further indication that he was, if not entirely headless, at least sightless.[55]

There were Spanish troops at the mission when the Indians attacked. In fact, apart from friars Alonso Giraldo de Terreros and José de Santiesteban and several other mission dwellers, four soldiers were killed in the fight. Three more died from their injuries a few days later, and six other soldiers were wounded in action. The soldiers defended themselves well. Before the mission was completely razed by fire, the soldiers and guards reportedly killed seventeen of the attackers.[56] This may also support Coyote's claim that bullets were flying all around him when he was carrying the child (or rather the banner of Our Lady of Refuge) away from the enemy camp.

Sergeant Joseph Antonio Flores stated that all the men in the mission "were armed, and the Father President kept a reserve supply of weapons in addition to those the resident Indians had for their own use."[57]

In addition, there were two cannons and a supply of ammunition in the mission. One of the men in charge of the cannons was Andrés de Villareal, who was wounded by a musket shot in the arm when he tried to close the gate at the beginning of the fight.[58] Twenty-two-year-old servant (and survivor) Joseph Gutiérrez stated that the gestures of peace and friendship at the beginning of the episode came only "because they found [the Spaniards] inclined to resist, the gates of the stockade closed and the *cannon loaded and trained* [emphasis mine]."[59] The presence of these light cannons at the mission corresponds perfectly with the presence of a pole that exploded in the Coyote myth.

The Spanish sources confirm that the Wichitas and Comanches surrounded the mission and set fire to the mission buildings during their attack. This corresponds well with Ahahe's account, in which Coyote shot his arrows into the four directions, thus surrounding the enemy camp with fire. Ahahe explains: "The Coyote left the village, burning up the evil ones who had stolen the child."[60] Sergeant Joseph Antonio Flores, a member of the scouting party sent out by Parrilla at dusk, described the scene at the mission: "He could see the road for almost three quarters of a league crowded with hostile Indians, and the mission stockade completely surrounded by Indians firing their muskets."[61]

The fire destroyed most of the mission and its supporting structures, although several Spaniards found temporary refuge inside Father Terreros's room until they were able to escape. The charred remains of several of the dead and wounded defenders were found there later. From his hideout across the river, Sergeant Flores saw that the entire mission was on fire. The fire was "giving off a strong, bright light, which was to the advantage of the enemy Indians," he told Colonel Parrilla later.[62]

The Indians used a similar tactic during their short-lived attack against the presidio. Sergeant Flores testified that the Indians set fires "as closely as possible to the Presidio" to "lure the garrison out into the open, with the evil design of finishing them off."[63] Other witnesses confirmed Sergeant Flores's statement. But they also noted that the Indians had flanked the presidio only on the west, north, and south. Because they had left open the approach from the east, refugees were able to make their entry from that direction. "The enemy had not occupied it, because the river, the ravines, the springs of water, and other obstacles would be to their advantage if they should make an assault."[64] Perhaps the Indians thought that the gap in the offensive line would also entice the garrison to make a break for safety, after which they could be slaughtered in the chase.

To Parrilla's relief, the Indians did not attack the presidio at dawn. He believed they did not because of the "discharge of a cannon, the beating of drums, and the bugle calls [that] were evidently understood by the enemy as demonstrations of our confidence and security."[65]

Historians have suggested that Parrilla's claim to his superiors in Mexico City that the French had encouraged the Indians to attack was merely a face-saving matter. However, the Wichita story makes clear that Parrilla was correct. These historians also claim that the defenders inflated the number of Indians to justify Parrilla's reluctance to ride out in defense of the missionaries. Most Spaniards later testified that there were some two thousand warriors in the attack; about half of them reportedly had guns. The numbers seem very high indeed, possibly caused by the natural tendency in high-stress situations to see enemies everywhere. Still, the number of warriors was high, and Parrilla's reluctance to set out with his relatively small command was undoubtedly prudent.

DISCREPANCIES

Despite the similarities between the Wichita and Spanish accounts of the events at San Sabá, there are also some minor discrepancies.

First, instead of only Coyote attacking, this was a major attack by multiple tribes. Furthermore, it does not appear that the Wichita tribe was out hunting buffalo, as the tradition suggests, but that they were involved in the attack. In addition, Ahahe makes no mention of Indians killed in the attack. According to Joseph Vazquez, who miraculously survived the massacre and strolled into San Antonio days later, seventeen enemy Indians had been killed: "three on the road to the Presidio, five by the soldier Joseph de los Santos firing through loopholes, six by the servant Nicolás, and three by Juan Antonio Gutiérrez."[66]

Second, there is no mention of Wichita captive children at the post, even though the sources do mention that eight (probably Apache) children escaped from the mission during the attack. In other words, there was no rescue of a Wichita or Comanche child. There was, however, revenge. By taking the scalps of their enemies, the attackers had, symbolically, reclaimed the life they had lost earlier. Another possibility is that the Indians took the holy image of the Madonna and child with them, thus metaphorically returning home with the child. But this is of course speculation.

Finally, despite the presence of two cannons, none of the Spanish accounts mention that they were fired during the battle. The Wichita story is the only evidence that a cannon was indeed fired during the attack.

The discrepancies do not fundamentally undermine the argument of this chapter: that Ahahe's story is in fact a Wichita account of the San Sabá Massacre. There are more similarities than differences between the Wichita and the Spanish versions of what happened. One should also consider that there are discrepancies among the Spanish accounts as well. Dismissing the Wichita tradition because it does not correspond entirely with the Spanish sources would hamper our understanding of what led up to the events at San Sabá and prevent us from recognizing the unique perspective that the Wichita account offers. Although the language of the Wichita oral tradition may appear strange to historians who are more familiar with conventional written sources, there is much that we can learn from these accounts.

CONCLUSION

If the capture of children was traumatic for the Wichita people, the San Sabá Massacre was likewise a traumatic event that sent shock waves throughout New Spain. It signified a momentous shift in the balance of power on the southern plains. This time, the balance swung in favor of the Comanche Indians and their Wichita allies. The fact that these Indians were now armed with guns supplied by the French forced colonial administrators in Mexico City to reevaluate their Indian policy along the northern frontier.[67]

The oral tradition shows that this event was important to the Wichitas too, because it marked a break with their own national trauma: the slave trade. At San Sabá, the Wichitas and their allies not only destroyed the Spanish dream of an alliance with the Apaches, but they exacted revenge on both the injustice of slavery *and* the forced Christian conversion attempts that had been imposed on them for almost two centuries. This revenge expressed itself in the intensity with which the Wichita warriors treated the friars and their sacred objects.

The Coyote myth also sheds new evidence on the role of the French in this event. Spanish concerns of French manipulations may not have been as far-fetched as is sometimes suggested by historians. Clearly, the Wichitas and Comanches were not easily manipulated; they based their actions on rational considerations of their own. In short, the decision to attack the mission at

San Sabá was entirely their own. Still, the Coyote myth explains that the French actively encouraged the Wichitas and Comanches not only verbally but materially as well.

The story of Coyote and the Spider-Man also shows that American Indian oral traditions contain valuable information. That is a fact that many American Indians have always understood. Rather than questioning the authenticity of these traditions, historians ought to study the language of myths to unlock their secrets.

FOUR

Death of the Flint Monster

A Skiri Pawnee Story of Post-Contact Warfare

The boy went to the animal, and it did not look like any animal he had ever seen, for this animal was clothed with flints all over. The flint flakes looked like fish scales, but they were really flint. The boy cut off the paw, and tied the paw upon the forked stick.

From "Death of the Flint-Monster: Origin of Birds," told by Curly-Head (1904)[1]

Historians have addressed the revolutionary impact of horses and guns on Plains Indian warfare but have not attributed the same significance to metal weapons technologies.[2] The Skiri story of the Flint Monster illustrates the impact of these weapons. In this story, narrated by a Skiri named Curly-Head, a monster drags people away into captivity and death, until a young hero destroys him with the help of a magical willow stick. The man-abducting monster wears a garment covered with pieces of "flint" shaped like "fish-scales." After killing the monster, the hero displays the monster's paw on a pole.

George Dorsey believed that this particular story was a cosmogonic myth because it also related the creation of birds. Indeed, he included the story almost immediately after the Skiri creation stories, suggesting that the Flint Monster story took place in deep time. Because stories of stone-covered monsters and heroes who take the limbs or other body parts of the monsters are quite common, folklorists may simply view this as an archetypal story in which a hero goes on a difficult journey into dangerous territory, where he confronts—and defeats—evil, thereby establishing civilization and human domination over the forces of nature. Such culture heroes created order where there was once chaos. Literary scholars, in contrast, might recognize interesting parallels with the Beowulf legend, in which the hero also arrived in a community terrorized by a monster that carried away people during feasts. Just like Wonderful Boy in the Skiri story, Beowulf has to overcome many challenges before he finally defeats the monster. Also like Beowulf, the hero in the Pawnee story takes the arm of the monster.

But is this myth truly a cosmogonic vision, an archetypal hero epic, or perhaps even a Pawnee version of the Beowulf myth? This chapter argues that it is none of these. It contends instead that Curly-Head's story is most likely based on an actual historical event. The Flint Monster was an enemy, dressed in a coat of mail, who terrorized the Pawnee people. A look at the historical record shows that there was not one but *many* Flint Monsters in Pawnee history. Although I was unable to link the Flint Monster from Curly-Head's tradition conclusively to a specific armor-wearing man, the preponderance of Flint Monsters leaves the possibility that there was one whose existence was not recorded in colonial sources. In that case, Curly-Head's story is the only source in existence describing this event.

Based on the aforementioned, I hypothesize that the Flint Monster was most likely an armor-wearing Spaniard or Apache Indian who, mounted on a horse, terrorized the Skiri Pawnees, carrying off men, women, and children to be sold into slavery on Spanish markets in New Mexico. This was during a time when the Pawnees did not possess guns or many horses themselves: the late 1600s or early 1700s. The hero of the story, simply called "wonderful boy," may have been a French *coureur de bois* who, armed with a gun, slew the armor-wearing enemy and returned with the man's gauntlet as a trophy of war.[3]

Although I am able to *explain* many of the mysterious events in the story, I am ultimately unable to *prove* conclusively that the Flint Monster was an Apache and that Wonderful Boy was a *coureur de bois*. Still, I hope the following analysis will prompt fellow historians to at least consider the possibility of the events transpiring as they are sketched in this chapter. What is beyond any doubt after analyzing this story, however, is the fact that metal weapons had a significant impact on Plains Indian warfare.

"NOW YOU MUST LISTEN, SO THAT YOU CAN LEARN THE STORY": THE TRADITION

Little information exists on Curly-Head, the Skiri Pawnee narrator of the story. The name Curly-Head does not appear in Pawnee census records between 1887 and 1901.[4] At least two men named Curly (listed as "Buck-scud-dy" or

"Buck scoddy") served with Major Frank North's famous Pawnee Battalion between 1865 and 1869. They would have been between sixty and sixty-five years old when Murie recorded the story of the Flint Monster. Whoever he was, Curly-Head contributed at least four stories to Dorsey's *Traditions of the Skidi Pawnee*.[5]

Curly-Head placed his tradition a long time ago, when only people and certain animals lived on earth. There were no birds. The people were divided into eastern and a western villages. Between these villages lived Wonderful Boy and his sister. They were children of the sun. The boy often traveled through the country. One day he told his sister about a mysterious animal in the south that comes up to carry people away. "I know that I ought to go," the boy said, "for I have wondered if this animal could carry me away as he does the other people." Then his sister made "twin balls . . . connected by a string" and a "shinny ball of large size" on which they would travel to the south land.

Leaving their tepee behind, they set out together. When his sister became tired, Wonderful Boy took the magic balls from his bundle. Standing on the balls, they traveled along effortlessly. Whenever they stopped to camp, the boy magically conjured up the tepee and everything else they had left behind.

And so they traveled for many days, until they arrived at one of the villages. There Coyote-Man came to visit them. Wonderful Boy gave Coyote-Man meat for his hungry children. Then Coyote-Man went to the chief's lodge to tell the chief that Wonderful Boy had come and arranged a meeting between the two. The chief followed Coyote-Man to Wonderful Boy's tepee, where they were treated to a meal. The chief was pleased with Wonderful Boy, and the people were happy.

While living among the people, Wonderful Boy waited to see when the mysterious animal would come and carry someone away. After a successful war party returned and the people celebrated at night, the mysterious animal snuck in and carried off one of the warrior leaders. Then he escaped.

Wonderful Boy now invited a young man to go on the warpath with him. They brought back many scalps, and the people celebrated deep into the night. But early the next morning, the monster carried off one of the dancers. When he learned about the abduction, Wonderful Boy was angry and frustrated. He went into the timber, where he thought about what to do. He cut down a forked willow tree and took the forked stick to his tepee. He placed the forked stick in the ground next to his bed. Then he invited all the girls to dress up and meet him while he was resting on the bed. Each girl had to guess what the purpose of the forked stick was. Wonderful Boy had determined that the girl who knew what the stick was for should become his wife. Girls came, but none guessed what the stick was for.

In the village was a family that had an "ugly looking girl." Her hair was "bushy" because she did not own a hairbrush. She also had nasty sores, and "[m]atter was running down the sides of her neck." Her sisters were pretty, but the ugly girl wanted to see Wonderful Boy. Her father was reluctant, but the girl begged him, and after she had washed and painted herself, at last the father agreed. "Now you must listen," the father told his daughter, "so that you can learn the story, and tell the story to the boy." The father told her exactly what Wonderful Boy wanted to hear: that Wonderful Boy and his sister had lived between the two villages; that the boy had wondered if the monstrous animal could carry him away; that he had instructed his sister to make double balls and a shinny ball; how they had traveled and how he had made a tepee; how they had found the village; how they had met Coyote-Man; how the young man had found the forked stick; how he intended to kill the animal; how he was to place the animal's paw upon the forked stick; and, finally, that people were to pass the paw and tell the young man what kind of birds they wanted to be.

The girl memorized the story word for word and joined the line, which now consisted of middle-aged women because all the young girls had passed by. When it was her turn, the girl told Wonderful Boy what her father had told her. As the girl was recounting the story, Wonderful Boy was imitating her, trying to get her to lose her story. But the girl went on until she finished the story. As soon as the girl was done, Wonderful Boy invited her into his tepee, and his sister used ointment to cure the girl of her sores. And so she "became a beautiful woman, and the wife of the young man."

The young man went on the warpath with his forked stick in search of the animal. He told his wife to "stay in the tipi, never going out." He instructed his sister to look toward the dawn every morning. If she saw red streaks in the sky, she would know that he was dead. But if she saw blue streaks, she would know that he had been victorious.

Wonderful Boy traveled south until he came to two animal trails (with a hollow between them) that led east–west. He decided not to follow these paths but to continue farther south. He came to a new, fresh path with "dust falling on the sides of the hollow." He followed this path and saw that "even rocks were cut where the animal had gone." The grass was burned, and the ground was red and seemed to be baked. From a hill, Wonderful Boy saw the animal coming. The animal told Wonderful Boy to leave because this was his place.

But the boy pressed ahead anyway. As he did, the animal began to recount the story of the boy's travels. When he was done telling the story, the boy pulled out the magic stick, which he was carrying on his back. When he aimed the stick at the animal, it fell down. As it fell over, the boy shot the animal under the arm with his bow and arrow. He had killed the animal, which did not resemble any animal he had seen before because it was "clothed with flints all over." Upon further examination, the boy saw that the flint flakes "looked like fish scales, but they were really flint." The boy "cut off the paw, and tied the paw upon the forked stick." Then he started the journey back home.

The next day, Wonderful Boy's sister saw blue streaks in the sky and told Coyote-Man and the chief that her brother had killed the animal. A little later, Wonderful Boy arrived, carrying the forked stick with the paw attached to it. He told Coyote-Man and the chief that the next day all families should come to see the animal's paw and decide what they desired to be. The following day, each family passed by the paw and said what kind of animal or being they wanted to be. The chief's family came first and wished that they might remain people. Other families wanted to turn into birds or other animals. Coyote-Man's family wished to be coyotes. When his wife's people came, Wonderful Boy told them they would be owls, "for you found out my thought, but my wife will stay with me." After each family had passed the paw and had been transformed, Wonderful Boy told his sister and wife to go with him into the timber, where the boy turned into a red bird with black streaks running down from the eyes, and the two girls became brown birds with black streaks running down from the eyes.

"THE FLINT FLAKES LOOKED LIKE FISH SCALES, BUT THEY WERE REALLY FLINT": MAIL ARMOR

Although the Flint Monster of Skiri tradition is unique in Plains Indian oral literature, there were "stone coat" monster traditions among the Senecas, the Cherokees, and certain southwestern tribes (see chapter 5). Colonial sources confirm that there were many different Flint Monsters on the plains between 1542 and 1852; several of them fought the Pawnees at some point.[6] They included a Cheyenne Indian named Alights on the Cloud, who died in battle with the Pawnees in 1852; a Comanche chief named Iron Shirt, who sustained fatal wounds in a battle with the Pawnees in 1793; and a number of Spanish conquistadors who may have engaged the Pawnees between 1541 and 1601. The colonial sources may not be complete, however. The name Flint Monster could also refer to an Apache or Navajo Indian who regularly attacked

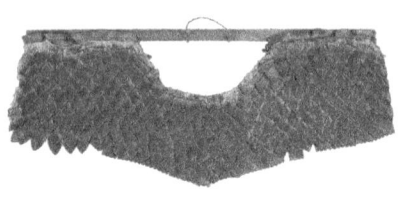 

Part of a scale mailed cape (*left*) and detail (*right*), obtained by Lieutenant John G. Bourke in the nineteenth century. The artifact was manufactured between 1600 and 1750. Courtesy Nebraska State Historical Society, Lincoln, collection number 11220–1.

Pawnee settlements in search of plunder and slaves in the sixteenth and seventeenth centuries.

Clearly, mail armor was not rare on the plains. Europeans, the Spanish especially, imported such armor on a relatively large scale. Chain mail had been in use in Europe since late antiquity and was widespread by the time of Charlemagne. Although full plated armor became more significant as a result of the invention of the longbow in the fourteenth century, chain mail continued to be used in Europe. The most common form of chain mail was the "byrnie" or "hauberk," a vest with or without sleeves. Hauberks usually extended to the knees. Arm guards and gauntlets also appeared in the age of Charlemagne. Eventually, armor designers combined chain mail with textiles. Chain/textile garments were variously called pourpoints, aketons, or gambesons, even though there were no significant differences between the three.[7] Gauntlet designs gradually became more intricate and larger, until they resembled the "paw" described in the Pawnee story.[8]

Scale or lamellar armor was also worn in Europe during the Middle Ages, but it was less common than chain mail.[9] Still, archaeological evidence shows that scale mail shirts existed in North America. In the 1870s, frontier army officer and anthropologist John Gregory Bourke obtained some scale armor found in Southwest Texas, where it reportedly had been removed from a buried skeleton. Several parts of the armor had been stolen, but a helmet and a scale mail gorget remained. These objects eventually ended up in the collection of the Nebraska State Historical Society in Lincoln. The gorget perfectly fits the description of the Flint Monster's skin in Curly-Head's story. Carbon 14 dating revealed that the gorget was made sometime between 1665 and

1952, but since Bourke obtained it in the 1870s, the former date seems plausible. Could this armor have belonged to the Flint Monster? Were there many more such protective garments around at the time? Similar scales were found at a site near the town of Aztec, New Mexico, in 1922. Clearly, these finds confirm the existence of scale mail on the southern plains and in the American Southwest. It is unclear where they were made and who made them.[10]

By the sixteenth century, the gambeson (a protective garment made of fabric) was generally no longer used for protection, but it was still worn for comfort. And in some cases it had mail attached to protect the neck, armpits, elbow joints, thighs, and groin.[11] According to the Pawnee tradition, the Skiri hero shot the Flint Monster under the arm, which might indicate that the monster instead wore a chain mail cuirass (a sleeveless vest that extended to the waist), which left it vulnerable under the armpit.[12]

Because full plate armor was significantly more expensive than chain mail, ordinary troops continued to wear the latter.[13] Even more expensive was horse armor. Horse armor consisted of various parts, which, to allow greater flexibility on the battlefield, were not always used together. A shaffron protected the horse's head; a crinet protected the neck; a peytral protected the chest; a crupper protected the hind parts; and flanchards, which hung down from the saddle, protected the sides.[14]

Spanish conquistadors such as Coronado and De Soto introduced chain mail to the American Southeast and Southwest, but it is unclear how many armor smiths settled in the Americas at this time. I have found the name of only one; armor maker Juan Ramirez accompanied Spanish forces to Mexico, where he was active in 1590.[15] He may have been a busy man, because chain mail offered adequate protection against Native bows and arrows. Stone arrowheads were usually not strong enough to penetrate steel. Steel arrowheads did better, but these were available in limited numbers only.

In 1584 Spanish conquistador and chronicler Baltasar Obregón wrote about the use of mail armor in New Mexico: "It is essential to carry good coats-of-mail of medium mesh, for if it is very fine it is destroyed by rust, and arrows pierce it more readily than if it is coarser." According to Obregón, "the mesh should not be too small or too large but medium, because that resists the force of the arrow more effectively." An additional advantage was that it did "not need to be cleaned, which is not the case with the fine mesh."[16]

Chain mail also had major disadvantages: it was expensive, cumbersome, and uncomfortable. Chain mail was heavy and restricted the wearer's freedom of movement. In hot and damp climates, it was extremely uncomfortable.

Finally, it did not always provide adequate protection. Arrows without stone or metal tips may actually have been more dangerous because they would splinter upon impact and thus cause multiple bloody wounds as splinters penetrated the mail and subsequently the skin. This last danger could be prevented by wearing a thick leather gambeson underneath the mail.

Chain mail did not protect the wearer's face; nor was it effective enough against gunfire to warrant the lack of freedom and agility that was so important in combat. By the mid-1600s, the Spanish had stopped using chain mail. However, because the Spanish banned the sale of guns to American Indians, individual soldiers may have used chain mail longer because it afforded some protection against traditional Native weapons.

American Indians continued to use mail armor long after the Spanish had abandoned it. Until Spanish arrival, Plains Indians used leather armor. After the Spanish arrived, many Indians adopted mail armor. Many Spanish coats of mail apparently ended up in American Indian hands. Spanish settlements in the American Southwest, such as Santa Fe, were probably the main source of chain mail on the Great Plains. Ethnologist George Bird Grinnell observed that the names Iron Shirt and Iron Jacket were quite common among Plains Indians.[17]

Plains Indians often attributed great power to such shirts. Like guns and other items of warfare, armor was effective not merely because of its material qualities but also because of its spiritual properties. As a rule, what made a weapon effective was the sacred power or "medicine" behind it. In any case, coats of mail were not at all rare on the Great Plains. However, this fact poses a problem: If coats of mail were not rare, why would Skiri storytellers describe them in such vague terms?

Coats of mail found their way into Indian hands through trade or as spoils of war. Perhaps the most famous blacksmith and armor maker on the southern plains was the French–Spanish frontiersman Pedro Vial. Before Vial became famous for discovering the route from Santa Fe to Saint Louis, he was a blacksmith, armor maker, and gunsmith by training.[18] Vial was born in Lyon, France, but migrated to America, where his skills as a blacksmith were highly appreciated. His early exploits are little known, but apparently he lived and traded among various Plains Indian tribes, especially the Taovaya Wichitas. Perhaps because of his skills as a blacksmith, these Indians believed he had great supernatural powers. In 1779 he visited Natchitoches and New Orleans. In 1784 he traveled to San Antonio with a Taovaya delegation. Governor Domingo Cabello y Robles of Texas pardoned him for living among the Indians without

Spanish permission, and Vial established "a smithy and soon proved himself a skilled armorer, locksmith, and silversmith, as well as a good blacksmith and an exceptionally alert and intelligent citizen [who] spoke Comanche and Taovayas as well as Spanish and French."[19]

"THERE IS AN ANIMAL FAR IN THE SOUTHERN COUNTRY, THAT COMES UP AND CARRIES PEOPLE AWAY": FLINT MONSTERS IN PAWNEE HISTORY

Because so many Plains tribes adopted chain mail armor, the identity of the Flint Monster remains uncertain. There are several possible alternatives. Perhaps the Flint Monster of the Pawnee tradition was a conquistador, but there are also examples of Apache, Comanche, and Cheyenne Flint Monsters.

Several Spanish conquistadors met the Pawnees. The first and most famous of these was Captain Francisco Vázquez de Coronado, who entered Pawnee territory in 1540.[20] Coronado's "Muster Roll of the Expedition," compiled at Compostela on February 22, 1540, shows that of the 289 men in the expedition, 61 wore chain mail.[21] Perhaps even more intriguing is the fact that at least two expedition members wore an armored gauntlet (the "paw" in the story). García del Castillo took "five horses, an elk hide jacket, a chain mail vest, [and] a gauntlet" with him. Juan Pérez de Vergara took "seven horses, a mule, a jacket and breeches of chain mail, a beaver, a sallet, a gauntlet, native arms and armor, two arquebuses, and a crossbow."[22] Luckily for Castillo and Vergara, but unfortunately for the scholar seeking to connect Curly-Head's account to Coronado, both men survived the expedition. Neither lost his life, or an arm, although one or both may have lost his gauntlet during a violent storm while camping on the plains near present-day Floydada, Texas. A Texas farmer discovered a mail gauntlet there in the 1950s.

There are several reasons why the Coronado expedition was not the event described by Curly-Head. To be sure, Coronado had a Pawnee guide, nicknamed El Turco, who was executed for misleading Coronado and for supposedly inciting the Quivira (Wichita) and Arahey (Pawnee) Indians into a rebellion against the Spanish. But beyond this, the saga of Coronado's expedition does not share any similarities with the Skiri story. The subsequent murder of Franciscan friar Juan de Padilla, who returned to spread the Gospel among the Wichitas, does not match the story either, for Padilla took with him only "sheep, mules, one horse, vestments, and other small items." He had no armor with him. We do not know the exact circumstances of his death (it may have been in retaliation for the death of El Turco),[23] but it is highly unlikely that he was the Flint Monster killed by Wonderful Boy in Curly-Head's tradition.

It is difficult to connect the next conquistadors who may have contacted the Pawnees to the Flint Monster story either. Half a century after Coronado's *entrada,* two Spanish adventurers, Francisco de Leyva de Bonilla and Gutierrez de Humaña, led an unauthorized expedition deep into Kansas in search of gold or slaves.[24] Some thirty men accompanied the expedition. No existing documents list what these men carried with them, but it is safe to assume that chain mail was again part of the equipment.[25] The Leyva–Humaña expedition eventually arrived in Wichita territory. The Wichitas welcomed the captains, but because there was no trace of gold anywhere, the expedition continued its march northward. The journey ended at a wide and deep river, possibly the Arkansas River, where tensions between the two captains resulted in Humaña stabbing and killing Leyva. In the consternation, five Indian slaves escaped toward the great river. Only one of them, Jusepe Guttiérrez (from Culhuacán, Mexico), eventually made it back to Spanish territory. Humaña returned to the Wichitas. There he must have offended his hosts, because all men in the expedition were massacred. According to Indian sources (who spoke with Don Juan de Oñate when he visited the area eight years later), the Spaniards "had been burned to death in a prairie fire set by Indians." According to the same sources, only one man survived, but his legs were burned badly. This crippled survivor was held prisoner by the Wichitas.[26]

The details of this expedition are too obscure to allow for a positive identification of Humaña with Curly-Head's story of the Flint Monster. For example, it is not at all clear that the Pawnees were even near the Wichitas at this time. It is remotely possible that Curly-Head's story pertained to this event, but without further evidence, this remains speculation. However, archaeologist Waldo Wedel noted that the expedition's "near-total destruction would have provided the Indians with Spanish arms, armor, and other gear in substantially more generous amounts than they could have acquired by trade, theft, or otherwise from the legitimate expeditions that returned to their home quarters without recorded loss of men or material while on the buffalo plains." In short, this may have been how subsequent Flint Monsters acquired chain mail armor.[27]

No convincing evidence links Oñate's 1601 expedition into Texas, Oklahoma, and Kansas to Curly-Head's account either. In 1598 Oñate had established the colony of New Mexico, which he had acquired with much violence and brutality. Even though slavery had been forbidden by the Spanish Colonization Law in 1573, slavery quickly became one of the colony's most important economic pillars.[28]

In 1601 Oñate led an expedition in search of Quivira, the legendary city of gold. During this expedition, Oñate befriended the Escanjaques tribe (probably Lipan Apaches), who lived in tepees, used dog travois, and were fierce enemies of the Rayado (Wichita) Indians, who had a major settlement in south-central Kansas. Although the Rayado Indians were friendly, Oñate nevertheless seized a few of them and put them in chains so he could use them as guides. Oñate also showed his treacherous nature when he arrested a chief who came with a peace delegation. In fact, Oñate's actions terrified the "Rayades," who abandoned their village. The Escanjaques immediately proceeded to plunder and burn the village. They turned against the Spanish, who refused to press on against the Rayados. Oñate's lieutenant Vicente de Zaldívar dispersed the Escanjaques using harquebuses and swords, killing several Indians. In late September, without contacting the Rayados again, Oñate turned his expedition back home. He arrived back in San Gabriel in late November 1601.[29]

Other than the apparent hostility between Oñate and the "Quivirans," there is not much evidence linking the expedition to the Flint Monster myth. Once again, it seems unlikely that Skiri Pawnee Indians were near these events. Furthermore, Oñate was not defeated, although he did leave the area, never to return.

If the Flint Monster was not a Spanish conquistador, could he have been Indian instead? Perhaps he was a Comanche. After all, the Comanches considered coats of mail and other Spanish gifts, such as silver-headed staffs and flags, to be symbols of power and authority.[30] In 1785 Governor Cabello sent Pedro Vial on a diplomatic mission to make peace with the Comanches. Vial met a Kotsoteka Comanche chief named Camisa de Hierro (Iron Shirt),[31] who was dressed in a *cota de maya* (coat of mail) that he reportedly had taken from an Apache *capitán* (chief). Iron Shirt was one of the most powerful leaders of the Texas branch of Comanches.

Incidentally, when Vial met the Comanches in 1785, he noted that smallpox had just raged among them. This would correspond with the neck sores that Wonderful Boy's wife suffered from in Curly-Head's story. The smallpox epidemic may have been an additional reason for warfare between the Pawnees and Comanches, as captives were needed to replace losses as a result of the disease. "They asked us if we brought some illness that would bring death to their nation, since smallpox had struck them as a result of some Frenchmen having entered their rancherías from La Zarca," Vial wrote in his diary. He added that "[t]wo-thirds of them had died" from this dreaded disease.[32]

Although Spanish forces under Don José Menchaca killed the Kotsoteka Comanche chief in 1786 (therefore he could not be the Flint Monster of the Skiri tradition), his name may have passed on to another Kotsoteka Comanche chief whose real name was Ecueracapa or Contatanacapara. This man, now known as Cota de Malla, met New Mexico governor Juan Bautista de Anza in 1786. He also fought bloody wars with the Pawnees in the 1780s and 1790s. In 1790 he joined Spanish commander Juan de Dios Peña in a campaign against the Pawnees. Two years later, his Comanches attacked three small Pawnee *rancherías* (towns) and killed a *capitán* and four warriors. They also captured four women and nine children.[33]

Although Ecueracapa was mostly successful in these battles, the Pawnees delivered a crushing blow against him in 1793. During a battle, the Pawnees killed his highest officer (a man named Hachaxas) and mortally wounded Ecueracapa himself. He died later that fall. We do not know what kind of wounds he sustained or if he or Hachaxas lost any armor in this fight.[34] What is certain is that Ecueracapa's successor, Encanguané (Red Fox), decided to make peace with the Pawnees. With the help of Pedro Vial, Red Fox negotiated a peace that was beneficial to both sides. Vial "delivered a medal, a complete suit of clothes and other things to the [Pawnee] Chief." The peace ended a war that had raged for more than a decade. Apart from lives lost, both sides had also raided each other for captives. Both sides now engaged heavily in trade. Although violent incidents sometimes interrupted the peace, the Comanche–Pawnee connection endured into the 1840s.[35]

Although the death and succession of Ecueracapa were of great historical significance for the Pawnees—and worthy of preservation in tribal oral tradition—the story does not quite match Curly-Head's account of the Flint Monster. Although Ecueracapa fit the description of a human-stealing enemy in a chain mail shirt, who was defeated by the Pawnees in battle and whose death forced the Comanches to peace, there is a major discrepancy: Ecueracapa did not die right away but several months later. Furthermore, the historical record does not state that he lost an armored gauntlet or any other piece of armor. Consequently, it is impossible to confirm the connection between Ecueracapa and the Flint Monster from Pawnee lore.

Perhaps the Flint Monster of Pawnee tradition was not a Comanche but a Cheyenne Indian. Sources identify several Cheyennes named Iron Shirt in the nineteenth century.[36] But the most famous of the armor-wearing Cheyennes

Detail from a Kiowa winter count calendar depicting Cheyenne warrior Alights on the Cloud in his iron shirt. He was killed in battle by Pawnees in 1852. From Mooney, "Calendar History of the Kiowa Indians."

was Alights on the Cloud. This man met his death in battle, while wearing his armored suit, at the hands of the Pawnees in 1852. His story has been well-known ever since George Bird Grinnell published it in *The Fighting Cheyennes* in 1915.[37]

According to Grinnell, Alights on the Cloud received the shirt from his uncle Medicine Water shortly before a fight with Delaware Indian trappers in 1844. He wore a red blanket over his iron shirt. He rode out and drew fire from the Delawares, who emptied their guns at him. Before the Delawares could reload, the Cheyennes charged and killed all of them. Some of the fallen Delawares still had their ramrods in their guns. This battle established Alights on the Cloud's reputation as a great warrior. According to Grinnell, "His feats of daring, while protected by the iron shirt, had given to the people generally an impression that he possessed spiritual power and was invulnerable."[38]

In the summer of 1852, Alights on the Cloud joined a war expedition against the Pawnees. The expedition consisted allegedly of Arapahos, Sioux, (Plains) Apaches, and Kiowas, as well as 230 Cheyennes. The Pawnees were out on their annual buffalo hunt, but they had seen signs of the enemy and were prepared for battle. Alights on the Cloud distinguished himself in battle by touching a Pawnee in a chase. When the Pawnees saw what was going on, they rode out to meet the attackers. Now it was their turn to charge Alights on the Cloud. But their arrows could not pierce his armor. When the Cheyennes counterattacked, the roles reversed once again. Alights on the Cloud chased a young Pawnee warrior, approaching him from the left. But the young Pawnee, who was left-handed, turned toward Alights on a Cloud with his bow and fired his arrow, which hit the Cheyenne in the right eye, killing him instantly. When Alights on the Cloud's brother Ear Ring learned of his brother's death, he determined to fight to the death as well. Several more brave Cheyennes fought to the death that day. The Pawnees cut them all up and took the iron shirt. When the battle ended, the Cheyennes had lost their best warriors. In mourning, "They all cried, and cut themselves with knives, and cut their hair and the tails of their horses."[39]

Grinnell also obtained information on the battle from the Pawnees. Although Grinnell's Pawnee source stated that a Pitahawirata killed Alights on the Cloud, most other Pawnee sources indicate that he was a Skiri. This man possessed four sacred arrows that were passed down from generation to generation.[40]

According to Eagle Chief, one of Grinnell's sources, the Skiris traveled south that summer to hunt buffalo on the Republican River. During an enemy attack, a Skiri named Kō'kā'kā was killed there, together with his wife and child. The next day the Skiris joined the three South Band Pawnees at Beaver Creek. While hunting together, they were again attacked. A Pawnee named Wearing Horns was killed, and another Pawnee, Crooked Hand, broke his leg. The people waited a few days before moving southeast. There, Sioux attacked them and killed a Skiri chief named Dusty Chief. The rapid succession of these deaths sounds similar to the terror inflicted by the Flint Monster in Curly-Head's tradition.

The next day, Kaw or Osage Indians attacked the Pawnees. This attack, apparently designed to stampede the horse herd to immobilize the Pawnees, failed. The day after this attack, the Pawnees continued their journey southeast. They were alarmed at the frequency of attacks and the fact that so many different tribes were attacking them. The worst was yet to come, however, for on that day, the Cheyennes, Arapahos, Comanches, and Kiowas attacked them. The fight started at 8 A.M. and lasted all morning. The battle line was reportedly a mile and a half long. After a short lull in the fight at noon, the battle resumed in the afternoon. Eagle Chief spotted a warrior holding a saber. This was Alights on the Cloud. According to Eagle Chief, he rode "one of the largest horses they had ever seen." This man kept riding out in front of the Cheyenne line and frequently charged the Pawnees. Eagle Chief noticed that the iron shirt restricted his movements. "He could not bend over, but sat straight up on his horse," Eagle Chief recalled. The Pawnees were frightened, and whenever this "terrible man" came close, they would fall back.

Only one warrior, Carrying the Shield in Front, decided to stand and challenge Iron Shirt. According to Eagle Chief, Iron Shirt rode up to kill Carrying the Shield in Front. When he was within striking distance with his saber, "Carrying the Shield in Front shot him with an arrow, and it struck Iron Shirt in the eye, and he fell off his horse in front of the Pawnee." As soon as he fell, "all the Pawnees rushed forward to where Carrying the Shield in Front was and cut Iron Shirt open." Although the Cheyennes made a fierce charge to recover Iron Shirt, the Pawnees held them off. The Pawnees quickly "cut the shirt in small pieces and carried them away." They also scalped the man. It might be important to note here that scalping sometimes included removing hands or other body parts. In any event, according to Eagle Chief, the iron shirt reached "to his knees and to his elbows, and covered him in front and around his neck."[41]

Tom Morgan, Carrying the Shield in Front's son, provided Grinnell with additional details about the duel. According to Morgan, Carrying the Shield in Front killed Alights on the Cloud with one of the sacred arrows—the white one. "Carrying the Shield in Front rode out in front of the line," Morgan said, "dismounted, and let his horse go free," thus challenging Alights on the Cloud to a duel. When Alights on the Cloud rode up, the Pawnees warned Carrying the Shield in Front. He bravely stood his ground. "If he possesses great power I shall not kill him," Carrying the Shield in Front said. "If he does not possess this great power perhaps I shall kill him." When Alights on the Cloud came close, Carrying the Shield in Front aimed and fired his arrow, which struck Alights on the Cloud in the right eye, killing him instantly.[42]

This battle has become one of the most celebrated events in Pawnee history. Stories about this battle were told, and Pawnee composers commemorated the event in a song. In her book *Pawnee Music* (1929), Frances Densmore published the lyrics of this song:

Wē ra tsa	Now he lies yonder
Wē ra tsa	Now he lies yonder
Wē ra tsa	Now he lies yonder
Wē ra tsa	Now he lies yonder
Wē ra tsa	Now he lies yonder
Wē ra tsa	Now he lies yonder
Pa-pi-tsi-su ruks tax kā-si-u	He who has on a metal shirt
Ra rū-te ra-kū ru tsiks ta is-ti ra pa-pi-tsi-su ruks tax ka-si-u.	The protection in which he trusted is set aside.[43]

Wichita Blaine, one of Densmore's Pawnee sources, provided important additional information. According to Blaine, the Cheyenne warrior's name was Touching Cloud and he had employed "a Mexican" who had made the shirt. This man had cut round disks from the thin frying pans used at that time and sowed these disks on a shirt and cap, the pieces "overlapping as in old-world armor." During the battle, "Touching Cloud felt so secure that he rode directly among the Pawnee." However, his arms were so "stiffened by the metal disks on his sleeves that he could use no weapon except a sword." Still, his sword-yielding skills "drove the Pawnee back to their village." Only Carrying the Shield dared to stand up against him. Carrying the Shield took the red sacred arrows that his father had once given him. His father had said, "Use this arrow when you are in great danger and it will save your life." It was this arrow that killed the armored Cheyenne warrior. After they had counted coup on his body, they "found that he wore, concealed beneath his out raiment, the metal-covered shirt made for him by the Mexican." Henceforth, the Pawnees remembered the fallen Cheyenne as Iron Shirt.[44]

Kiowa historians recorded the death of this Cheyenne Flint Monster on their winter counts that year. They depicted Alights on the Cloud in his peculiar "coat of mail." The picture shows the fish scale design that the Skiri myth describes. Although scale armor had been known in Europe, it had been particularly popular in the East among the Ottomans and in India. It is possible that the maker of this scale-armored shirt had been inspired by such occidental examples.[45]

There are several parallels between the tradition published by Dorsey and the accounts recorded by Grinnell, Densmore, and others. First, the Skiris were traveling south, as the tradition indicates. Second, they united with the South Band Pawnees, who were on their summer hunt and traveling with their tepees. Third, while traveling farther south, they suffered several attacks in which they lost prominent individual warriors: Kō'kā'kā, Wearing Horns, and Dusty Chief. Fourth, the man in the iron shirt not only rode the largest horse the Pawnees had ever seen, but he also had a terrifying—monstrous—appearance. Fifth, despite an earlier statement by Grinnell, Eagle Chief and Tom Morgan make it clear that the Pawnees who killed the man in the iron shirt was a Skiri, which corresponds with the fact that the Flint Monster story was a Skiri tradition.[46] Sixth, this Skiri used a special kind of "sacred arrow" (paralleling the forked willow stick) to overpower the man in the iron shirt. Seventh, after the man in the iron shirt had fallen from his horse in front of his victor, the Pawnees scalped the man and cut up his shirt. Apart from his scalp, they may have also cut off his hands. They undoubtedly would have carried these trophies away on scalp poles, as Curly-Head's account suggests. Finally, the attacking Indians retreated in defeat.

But there are also several discrepancies. First, the Cheyennes were on the offensive rather than moving away from the Pawnees. Second, the implication is that Wonderful Boy was alone. Although Carrying the Shield in Front was dismounted and facing Alights on the Cloud by himself, he was hardly alone that day. Third, Grinnell's account is missing several elements, such as the stripes in the sky. Perhaps most troubling of all, however, is the fact that Wonderful Boy of Curly-Head's story was not Pawnee but a "child of the Sun." Furthermore, if the story of Carrying the Shield was so well remembered, why would Curly-Head's version be so different in character and details?

The answer can be only that these stories relate two different events.

PAWNEE BATTLES WITH THE APACHES AND NAVAJOS

Rather than a relatively recent event, such as Alights on the Cloud's death, Curly-Head's account implies that it took place in the distant past, when there were people and other animals "but no birds." In addition, Curly-Head does not mention horses, although the speed with which the Flint Monster traveled and the trails he left imply that he might have been mounted. Although the Pawnees were familiar with horses since the Coronado expedition, they did not acquire horses in any significant number until the early 1700s. When Claude-Charles Du Tisné visited two Pawnee villages in 1719, he counted three hundred horses among them.[47]

According to Curly-Head, the people were divided into two villages: one located in the east and the other in the west. This division is typical of the Skiri Pawnees, who referred to their South Band relatives (Chawi, Kitkehahki, and Pitahawirata) collectively as *tuha·wit* (east village).[48]

The story also indicates that the animal lived in the south and occasionally traveled north to carry off people. Therefore the animal was most likely Spanish (or Mexican) or an Indian from the southern plains. The most likely candidates for these Indians are the Athapascan Apaches and Navajos. Both tribes had access to Spanish horses and metal weapons, including coats of mail, which they obtained at slave markets at Taos and Santa Fe. Indeed, access to these strategically important resources made the Apaches for several decades one of the most powerful tribes on the southern and western plains.

Long before the Cheyennes and Comanches, the Apaches posed the greatest military threat to the Pawnees. The Apaches had moved from western Canada to the western plains in the seventeenth century. Here they came in contact with the Spanish in New Mexico, from whom they acquired chain mail. They were also among the first Indians to adopt horses. To pay for these new technologies, they raided the Pawnees for captives. In the late 1600s and early 1700s, the Apaches dominated the sedentary tribes and expanded into eastern Colorado, northeastern New Mexico, and the western parts of Nebraska and Kansas. The Spanish distinguished between different Apache groups: Padoucas,[49] Cuartelejos, Palomas, Jicarillas, Faraons, Sierra Blancas, Carlanas, Natagés, and Llaneros. Unlike the majority of Apache bands, the group that eventually came to be called Plains or Kiowa Apaches adopted an exclusively nomadic lifestyle based on the buffalo hunt. The Pawnees called this group the "Gattacka," or a variation of that name.[50]

Taking advantage of their horse and armor technologies, the Apaches harassed not only the Pawnees but other Plains Indian tribes as well. The famous Segesser I painting illustrates how Athapascan warriors (either Apache or Navajo) used horses and armor to their tactical advantage against a group of tepee-dwelling Plains Indians who still used dogs for transportation. The attackers wore armor that not only covered their bodies, but part of their horses as well. Although leather armor was widespread at this time, it appears that these attackers used a combination of leather and mail armor. Was this armored man–horse combination the Flint Monster of the Skiri myth? The parallels are striking.[51]

Apache slave raids against the Pawnees reached a peak between 1680 and 1695. The Apaches, who were mounted on horses and armed with "metal-pointed lances and Spanish knives and hatchets," waited until February, when cold weather confined the Pawnees in their towns. In surprise attacks, they killed as many men as possible, capturing the women and children. After setting fire to a town, they sometimes moved on to the next one. In this manner they often destroyed several villages before turning homeward in triumph. In May they would sell their slaves to Spanish and Pueblo traders in New Mexico in exchange for more horses and metal weapons, to be used in future raids.[52]

The Navajos, linguistic relatives of the Apaches, also targeted the Pawnees at this time. Navajo war expeditions frequently raided Pawnee towns for slaves to sell in New Mexico. In 1694 the Spanish refused to buy any slaves, and the angry Navajos decapitated all the captives. This incident prompted the Spanish Crown to provide sufficient funds to save other unfortunates from similar fates. However, when the Navajos staged another slave raid in 1697, the Pawnees, reportedly with French assistance, supposedly annihilated four thousand of them. Undoubtedly, the number of casualties was wildly exaggerated. In retaliation, the Navajos destroyed three Pawnee *rancherías* and a fortified place in 1698 and returned the next year laden with spoils, including "slaves, jewels, carbines, cannons, powder flasks, gamellas [metal tubs or boxes], sword belts, waistcoats, shoes, and even small pots of brass."[53]

How firm the French presence among the Pawnees was is unclear. If there were French traders among the Pawnees before 1719 (the date of the first official visit), these were most certainly *coureurs de bois*. Armed with the weapons that these illegal traders provided, the Pawnees attempted to drive the Cuartelejo Apaches out of eastern Colorado in 1706.[54]

It is quite possible, then, that the Flint Monster in the Skiri story was one of the mounted and armored Apaches (or Navajos) who had been raiding the Pawnees for decades. Not until the arrival of French traders did the Pawnees obtain a tool that allowed them to strike back. The tool, of course, was the gun. The Spanish prohibited the sale of guns to Indians, but the French did not.[55] The impact of the gun was clear: now the Apaches came under pressure. In 1719 Governor Antonio Valverde met the Cuartelejo Apaches, who told him that they had fled their settlement after they had been attacked by the French, the Pawnees, and Jumano Indians. The Cuartelejos also reported that the French had established two "pueblos" in Pawnee country—each as large as Taos. The identity of these "pueblos" is uncertain, but the French had a significant presence in Cahokia and Kaskaskia, both quite far removed from Pawnee country. In any event, Valverde's discovery prompted him to send Lieutenant General Pedro de Villasur on an expedition to Pawnee country to inspect the rumors. What happened next is well-known: Villasur's command, which was composed of forty-two soldiers, three settlers, sixty Indian allies, an interpreter, and a priest, was defeated by Pawnees and Otoe allies in August 1720. More than forty men on the Spanish side, including Villasur himself, lost their lives. Perhaps this was the battle in which the Pawnees obtained the iron gauntlet.[56]

When Prince Paul of Wurttemberg visited the Pawnees in the early 1820s, the memories of these conflicts with the Spanish and their Apache allies were still fresh.[57] Paul's host, Chief Schake-ru-leschar, told the prince that "their hate toward the Spaniards and the Mexicans knew no limits." The prince added that the Pawnees waged a "relentless war of extermination" against the peoples "in the eastern Provincias Internas, along the Rio Bravo [Rio Grande] and in Texas."[58] This war with the Spanish, the Mexicans, and their Indian allies went back a long time. Paul suggested that the Pawnees had even captured many trophies from the conquistadors, stretching these conflicts back as far as the mid-1500s. Because the sources do not really confirm Pawnee battles with the conquistadors, it appears that these trophies were captured from other Indians. "The Pawnees are proud of the great damage which they in their time have inflicted upon the descendants of the Spaniards, and that even in the earliest times of the conquest they fought hard battles against the Conquistadores," the prince wrote. He added, "Of the latter they still possess many trophies."[59]

Nor did the slave raids end. Only a few years before Paul's visit, the Pawnees had captured a Spanish boy, whom they intended to sacrifice in the Morning Star ceremony. The Pawnees had captured this boy near Taos. The prince also found a Skiri Pawnee man who, as a boy, had "been captured near the mission of San Antonio and dragged by the Spaniards to the interior of New Spain," where he had been baptized. Although the Spanish had tried to integrate him into their society, this man managed to escape and return to his people.[60]

When the prince visited a Pawnee medicine lodge, a Pawnee priest told him that "the bearded people toward the west near the mountains hate the red people, and since the time of our fathers have driven us out and killed us." The priest added that the Pawnees would "drink their blood and hate them, for our country was toward the evening [in the west]."[61] Then the priest showed him several objects, including Spanish weapons from the sixteenth century. According to the priest, these weapons "had been captured a long time ago in a war which the Pawnees had fought with the Spaniards in the mountains to the west." The priest also "spoke of several Indians of his nation who on their raids had gotten as far as the mouth of the Bravo River," indicating that Pawnee raids into Spanish territories had been common.[62]

The objects the Pawnee priest showed the prince were kept in the medicine lodge, which might indicate that the Pawnees regarded them as objects of power, much like the "paw" of the Flint Monster in the story was treated as an object with mysterious properties.

Although Prince Paul's account does not provide a definitive identification of the Pawnee story with a specific historical event, it is nevertheless clear that Curly-Head's account refers to one of many battles with an armor-wearing Flint Monster. Perhaps an analysis of the Wonderful Boy story may narrow the time period down more specifically.

"THE BOY WAS A WONDERFUL BOY, AND USED TO TRAVEL FAR THROUGH THE COUNTRY": SPECULATIONS ABOUT THE IDENTITY OF THE HERO OF THE STORY

The "child of the sun" may offer clues that allow us to date the events in Curly-Head's story. Establishing his identity would present a significant step into solving the mystery of the story. Who was he? Where did he come from? What was he doing there?

Some folklorists point out that there is little new under the sun (pun intended) with this particular character. "Children of the sun," they say, are not uncommon in Native American stories. Stories in which these characters appear have been recorded from the American Southeast to the American Northwest. Thus, they argue, the answer is simple: he is a mythological or archetypal character, not a historical one.

I am not entirely satisfied with the assumption that the "child of the sun" is merely an archetypal figure. Is it possible to propose an alternative explanation that suggests post-contact figures? It is, but I must forewarn the reader that my explanation is hypothetical. Although this may not be satisfying to some readers, neither is the assumption that he was simply an archetypal figure or common motif that precludes any further investigation.

"Nobody knew of them," said Curly-Head about Wonderful Boy and his sister. In other words, they were not Pawnee. Wonderful Boy himself alludes to his origins at the end of the story. "My father is the Sun," he said. Although this suggests that he was of celestial origin, there might be a more mundane explanation: he was possibly a French *coureur de bois* from Canada. Instead of being a child of a celestial star, perhaps Wonderful Boy meant to say that he was a subject ("child") of King Louis XIV, better known as the Sun King. Louis's crest was a sun emblem, and perhaps Wonderful Boy carried this crest on his journey. Louis XIV ruled from 1643, when he was only five years old, until his death in 1715. This would place the date of the story in the late 1600s and early 1700s.

Curly-Head's own words offer some anecdotal support for the claim that Wonderful Boy was a French traveler. Like *coureurs de bois*, Wonderful Boy "used to travel far through the country." Indeed, Wonderful Boy and his sister traveled a long way to reach the Pawnee country. "For many days they travelled," Curly-Head states. "We have been a long time coming," Wonderful Boy told Coyote-Man upon his arrival in the Skiri village.

The length of the journey is curious, because it would have been far easier for the cosmic sun-father to place the "children of the sun" closer to the Pawnee people. Instead they had to travel by means of the single and double shinny balls. This mode of transportation is a mystery. It should be noted that transportation by shinny balls has been recorded in the oral traditions of other tribes as well.[63] The simplest explanation is that these were corn balls, a mixture of cornmeal, dried fruits, buffalo fat, and ground-up nuts that Pawnee warriors would take along on war expeditions. Packed with nutrients and energy, they would have allowed Wonderful Boy and his sister to travel almost effortlessly. Another option is that the double shinny ball was a cart or wagon, in which the two balls were actually wheels and the string was an axle. Still, this would be a very laborious and time-consuming way to travel from Canada, and not a very satisfying answer either.

There is a third option, although it is speculative. Perhaps the balls refer to a mode of transportation over water. After all, most French voyageurs and *coureurs de bois* traveled by rivers and streams. The peculiar shape of the shinny balls may indicate so-called bull boats rather than canoes. These half-round, ball-shaped vessels, made of wooden frames covered by animal skins, were often tied together (the "string") and gently float downstream. The story says that the boy and his sister were standing on the twin balls as they traveled. Curly-Head added that "the girl did not feel the motion," as one would expect drifting along the stream. Such vessels would also have allowed the two travelers to carry their tent equipment. This would also explain Wonderful Boy "swinging" his "shinny stick" so that they could travel fast. In this case, the shinny stick was likely a paddle.

Of course, there are some issues with this explanation. On the last stretch of the journey, on the Missouri, Platte, and Loup Rivers, Wonderful Boy and his sister would have had to paddle upstream. Furthermore, Curly-Head states that in the evening, Wonderful Boy "stopped the balls" and put them in his sacred bundle, making it unlikely that they were actual bull boats. In any case, as "magical" as this means of transportation was, it was apparently not fast enough to catch up with the Flint Monster, who outran Wonderful Boy's chasing party at a later point in the story, probably because he was traveling on horseback. There is another major problem with this hypothesis: if the Pawnees were familiar with bull boats, why would they speak of magic shinny balls instead? Folklorists might argue that in the process of mythologizing the story and fitting it into traditional storytelling patterns, the Pawnees simply borrowed this motif from other accounts.

Wonderful Boy and his sister seemed to possess other magical qualities as well. For example, they possessed the ability to make fire by breathing upon dry grass and sticks, a feat that greatly impressed the Pawnees. A less spectacular explanation is that they used matches or a lens, with which they caught the rays of the sun to set fire to the grass, thus further fueling the idea that they were related to the sun. Additionally, they treated the ugly girl's sores with a medicine that was apparently unknown to the Pawnees.

Why had they come? Most *coureurs de bois* traveled to the far corners of New France in search of things generally denied to ordinary men in France at this time: riches, freedom, and social status. At first Wonderful Boy simply shared meat with Coyote-Man and the chief. But this *coureur de bois* soon realized that if he wanted to gain respectability with the Skiris, he had to confront the Spanish–Athapascan enemy. Curly-Head explained that Wonderful Boy wondered if the "animal could carry me away as he does the other people." For this reason, Wonderful Boy led a war party against the enemy. His success may have won him the admiration of the Pawnees at first, but when the enemy launched a counterattack and killed his partner war leader, Wonderful Boy's prestige diminished quickly, especially because he was unable to catch up with the escaping Flint Monster. He then solidified his friendship with the Pawnees by marrying into the tribe. Indeed, the entire episode in which the ugly girl has to relate the purpose of his journey has much the character of a negotiation, in which both sides came to an agreement that Wonderful Boy would try to defeat the enemy. At one point in the story, the girl tells Wonderful Boy that he was "to find the animal, kill it, and cut off its paw, so you can place the paw upon the forked stick."

It is at this point that Wonderful Boy introduces his most powerful magic: the "forked willow stick." The nature of the "stick" is strange, but if one substitutes the word with "gun," the story immediately becomes more plausible. The gun was a tool that evened the odds between him and the armored and mounted Flint Monster. Indeed, Wonderful Boy used it to knock the Flint Monster down in the duel before finishing him off with a bow and arrow. Curly-Head's description in this regard is reminiscent of a soldier pointing and shooting his gun. "As he pulled the stick," Curly-Head said, "the animal fell over." Then he administered the coup de grace by shooting an arrow into the man's armpit, thus severing the axillary or brachial artery, which caused the Flint Monster to bleed to death.

So far, all of this is speculation. However, Spanish colonial sources do provide some supportive evidence. For example, Spanish sources from the mid-1690s frequently complain about trespassing French *coureurs de bois* inciting Indians, such as the Pawnees, against the Spanish and their Indian allies. Modern-day historians often dismiss these stories as paranoia, or as convenient ways for Spanish colonial administrators to justify embarrassing Spanish military failures in subjugating the northern frontier. Still, the Spanish sources, although based primarily on rumors passed to them by their Indian allies, should be taken seriously. Even if the Spanish inflated the numbers of Frenchmen in the region, that does not mean there were no Frenchmen at all.

French colonial sources are not very helpful in confirming the presence of *coureurs de bois* among the tribes of the Missouri River at this early stage. After all, *coureurs de bois* were smugglers. As a result, they rarely appear in official records. Still, around 1700, French traveler Pierre-Charles Le Sueur reported that Frenchmen lived with the Panis and Iowa Indians. Because these nations often fought wars with each other, there was a risk that Frenchmen might kill other Frenchmen in these conflicts.[64]

Archaeology might provide additional insights. At the Swan Creek site (39WW7) in present-day Walworth County, South Dakota, much farther up the Missouri River than Wonderful Boy would have been, archaeologists discovered the remains of a forty- to fifty-year-old male with Caucasoid features who had been buried between 1675 and 1725. He may have been the first white man to visit the Arikaras, tribal relatives of the Skiri Pawnees. Like Wonderful Boy, he was most likely a *coureur de bois,* although it is also possible that he was a fugitive from the law or a runaway Spanish slave. Although the archaeological and osteological findings are not conclusive, they nevertheless suggest that Europeans were on the central plains in the late 1600s.[65]

The size of the French presence among the Pawnees is unclear. If there were French traders among the Pawnees before 1719 (the date of the first official visit), they could have impressed the Pawnees with their guns. Indeed, Spanish sources state that the Pawnees had attempted to attack the Cuartelejo Apaches in eastern Colorado in 1706 armed with French guns, but they had to retreat before the battle was well under way. Later that year, Spanish commander Juan de Ulibarri met with the Cuartelejos, who urged him to join them against the Pawnees and the French. Ulibarri declined but promised to return later.[66]

Interestingly, the Cuartelejos told Ulibarri on this occasion that they had killed a white man and woman. The man, they said, was bald, but he apparently wore a red cap. After killing him, the Cuartelejos took his red cap, his powder, and his gun.

Could this man have been the Wonderful Boy of Curly-Head's tradition? The red color of his cap corresponds with the color of the bird of the story. Perhaps this was the traditional Phrygian cap, or *bonnet rouge.* Such caps became famous in Bretagne, France, during the 1675 Révolte des Bonnets Rouges (Red Cap Revolt) against the Sun King, Louis XIV. Indeed, these caps became the unofficial emblem of the French Revolution more than a century later. Perhaps this man was from Brittany. In any case, the dates match up well.[67]

The peculiar shape of the Phrygian cap resembles the feathered tuft on the head of a cardinal. Perhaps this resemblance is coincidental, but the analogy between human and bird is very Pawnee. Perhaps the mysterious end of Curly-Head's account refers to a French *coureur de bois* (Wonderful Boy) returning to New France ("the woods").[68] If this speculation is correct, then he never made it home with his white wife because, as Ulibarri's letter explains, the Padoucas intercepted and killed them.

Here is where any analogy ends. Indeed, there are also important arguments against the hypothesis that the mysterious *coureurs de bois* was Wonderful Boy. The most obvious is the fact that apart from testimony by the Apaches (which they later retracted), colonial sources do not mention a Frenchman and -woman who fit the descriptions. Still, Spanish sources make it clear that Frenchmen were indeed sighted among the Pawnees at least as early as 1706.

While I admit that the above explanation is hypothetical, folklorists have found cases in which historical figures acquired (semi-)divine qualities as stories were retold over the years. In his book *Reading the Fire* (1999), folklorist Jarold Ramsey showed how the Thompson River Indians turned the story of Simon Fraser's expedition into the American Northwest into a mythological account. In 1808 one of the canoes with Fraser's expedition capsized and one man nearly drowned. The event made a great impression on the Thompson River Indians, who had never encountered such people before. Interestingly, the Thompson River Indians remembered the strangers by their *appearance.* A Thompson storyteller named Semalitsa called the expedition leader "Sun" because this man wore a sun emblem on his hat. When Semalitsa recounted the event around 1900, she said, "The Indians applied names to most of the strangers, all taken from some feature of their appearance or from certain marks or emblems on their clothing." Some Thompsons believed these were simply strangers of a different race from far away, but others thought they were the same "beings spoken of in tales of the mythological period, who had taken a notion to travel again over the earth." Ramsey says that the fact that the Thompson River Indians began nicknaming the strangers by their appearances "may suggest in itself that the mythologizing process began on the spot, or very soon after, as 'Sun' and the others began to figure in Native reports and stories of the episode." In short, the event became mythologized not as a result of "the disease of language . . . but rather in this instance the power to hasten the assimilation of Fraser and his company into the Thompson River myth-system." One must remember, Ramsey argues, that "the appearance of the white men among the Indians was here and elsewhere ipso facto a mythic happening, an unprecedented but possibly precedent-setting 'first time,' and the Thompsons seem to have come to terms with it collectively by interpreting it according to their mythological system."[69]

I believe that something similar happened with the stranger in the Pawnee story. The Pawnees may have associated him with the sun because he wore a sun emblem, and they associated him with a cardinal because of his appearance.

(The black streaks from a cardinal's eyes bear a resemblance to a human beard.) Unlike Ramsey, we do not have an emic source to confirm this idea. But as Ramsey's example of the Thompson River Indians suggests, there is precedent for this hypothesis.

CONCLUSION

A look at the historical record shows not one but many Flint Monsters in Pawnee history. But because French and Spanish colonial records are sparse, it is impossible to link Curly-Head's account definitively to a specific event. This does not mean that the events described in Curly-Head's story never took place. Indeed, based on circumstantial and anecdotal evidence, I argue that this event probably took place in the late 1600s or early 1700s. Though this answer is unsatisfying, it is possible that Curly-Head related an event that had escaped French and Spanish chroniclers. Rather than viewing Curly-Head's story as myth, scholars ought to consider that it might be history.

In any event, this chapter shows that metal weapons technologies had a dramatic impact on Plains Indian societies such as the Pawnees before the arrival of the gun. For perhaps four or five decades, metal weapons and armor gave certain American Indian tribes a major advantage over other tribes. During that time period, the Pawnees suffered tremendously at the hands of technologically superior foes, until the French began to supply the Pawnees with an even more powerful technology: firearms.

FIVE

The Old Man with the Iron-Nosed Mask

Caddo Oral Tradition and the De Soto Expedition, 1541–42

> The old man was just about to spear him with the iron nose of the mask he wore, when some unseen power pulled the boy off the log, and the iron nose of the mask caught in the log and held the old man fast.
>
> Story of "The Young Men and the Cannibals" as told by Wing[1]

In 1917 anthropologist Robert Lowie asked why American Indian oral traditions often related insignificant events while important events were not remembered. Of course, what Lowie considered important might not have been the same as what Indian tribes found worthy of remembrance. Still, Lowie's observation has some merit. The Caddo Indians, for example, apparently did not record stories of their first contact with Europeans, even though their first encounter with Spanish conquistadors under Hernando de Soto in 1541 was extremely violent and disruptive. De Soto's men fought several bloody battles with the Caddos; plundered Caddo settlements; enslaved men, women, and children; and tortured or executed anyone who resisted. How could such an event have escaped tribal memory? Was this a case of a historical experience that was too traumatic to be remembered?

Perhaps a more plausible answer is that the event was recorded, but we have been unable to recognize it as such. Perhaps the story continues to live on in tribal oral tradition but in a form that seems hardly recognizable to modern-day historians. This chapter argues that two Caddo stories published by Dorsey may refer to the De Soto expedition. They are "The Young Men and the Cannibals," told by Wing, and "Coyote and the Six Brothers," related by an anonymous Caddo storyteller. Both stories tell of a masked cannibal man who killed his victims with the spiked iron nose of his mysterious mask.

Although these stories provide little that is familiar to De Soto scholars, there are some interesting parallels between this story and the De Soto *entrada*: enslavement, violence, and the intriguing character of a man who speared his victims with the iron "nose" of his mask. If the weapon truly was made of iron as the story suggests, then the story must refer to a post-contact event, since American Indians did not have iron tools until Europeans introduced them. Although it is possible that the "iron" spear was a later addition to the story, it is worthwhile to take a closer look at the story to see if other elements indicate that it indeed refers to the invasion by De Soto and his fellow conquistadors.

Why are these stories so strange and almost unrecognizable? It is possible that the passage of time distorted them beyond recognition. However, one must also remember that the Caddos had no idea who the Spanish were, what part of the world they came from, why they acted as they did, and who had given them horses and strange technologies, both new things to the Caddos. If the Caddo stories seem strange to us now, one can only imagine how strange and puzzling De Soto's band of conquistadors must have looked to the Caddos in 1541.

"THESE INDIANS SHOWED THEMSELVES TO BE SO OBSTINATE . . . THAT IT WAS NECESSARY TO KILL THE MEN WHO WERE CAPABLE OF FIGHTING": THE DE SOTO EXPEDITION IN CADDO COUNTRY

In 1492 the Caddos occupied a territory along the borders of present-day Oklahoma, Texas, Arkansas, and Louisiana. The Caddos were Mound Builders who had been influenced by the great Mississippian civilization. Their villages were centers of trade and cottage industry. Corn was the lifeblood of their civilization. The Caddos were skilled horticulturalists. While the men hunted, the women cultivated corn and other crops in gardens. After the harvest, Caddo women pounded the corn into flour with large pestles and mortars.[2]

Although the Caddo Indians were no strangers to warfare, nothing had prepared them for the confrontation with Spanish conquistadors, who, under command of Hernando de Soto, entered Caddo territory in 1541. De Soto had come to scour the American Southeast in search of riches. Instead of gold, his men found numerous fiercely independent Indian tribes. When these tribes refused to submit themselves to the invading strangers, they soon felt the ironclad fist of war raised against them. When they contacted the Caddos, De Soto's men had already left behind a path of destruction. Like earlier meetings with Indians,

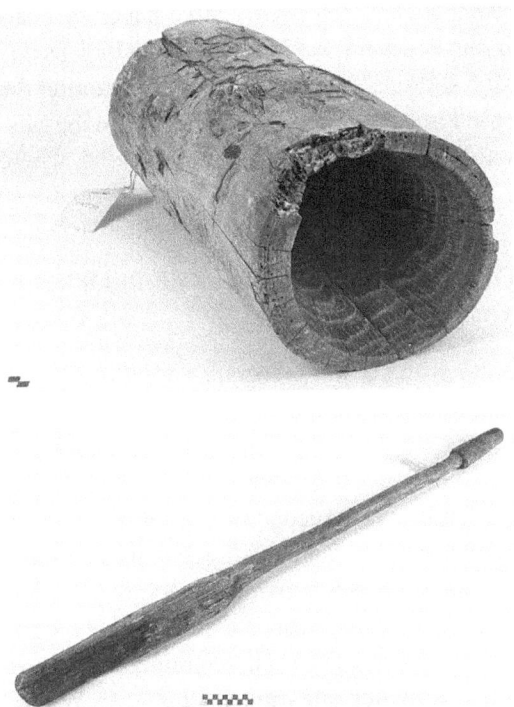

Caddo mortar and pestle for grinding corn, circa 1900. A pestle ("corn mill") was the weapon used by the heroic Caddo defender at Tula and by Coyote in the Caddo tradition of the masked cannibal man. Courtesy the National Museum of the American Indian, catalog numbers 2/2242 and 2/2243.

De Soto's contact with the Caddo Indians is a story of conflict, torture, murder, and enslavement.

In 1539 Hernando de Soto set out with around six hundred men in search of wealth and fortune. Landing in Florida, the expedition marched through Georgia, the Carolinas, Tennessee, Alabama, and Mississippi. Along the way, De Soto fought Native tribes and his men frequently destroyed crops and enslaved men, women, and children.[3]

In 1541 De Soto's campaign reached western Arkansas, the site of several Caddo villages, such as Tula.[4] Caddo contact with the Spanish was not peaceful. The Spanish invasion promptly led to armed conflict and forced the Caddos to abandon Tula. Several more battles followed, until the Caddos submitted themselves to De Soto. In May 1542, De Soto died of disease and his body was interred in the Mississippi River. Luis de Moscoso y Alvarado succeeded him as expedition leader.

On June 5, 1542, Moscoso led the expedition westward into Texas, where he would encounter other Caddo groups. By this time, Moscoso's army had been reduced to about three hundred soldiers, forty to sixty horses, and an unknown number of pigs. Accompanying them were Native slaves who carried supplies. Moscoso's men fought several battles with Caddo Indians and maimed and executed several Caddo people. However, unable to find the coveted riches, in 1542 Moscoso turned his expedition back toward the Mississippi River. There they boarded small boats to return to Mexico, where they arrived in 1543.[5]

"THE BAD PEOPLE MADE SLAVES OF ALL OF THE PEOPLE": CADDO ORAL TRADITIONS

At first glance, Caddo experiences with De Soto's conquistadors do not seem to have been preserved in Caddo traditions. However, two intriguing stories in Dorsey's *Traditions of the Caddo* (1905) mention a "cannibal man" who might fit the description of a conquistador. Dorsey provided the name of the first storyteller only; the identity of the second storyteller is unknown.

The first story, "The Young Men and the Cannibals," was told by a Caddo medicine man named Wing. Although Dorsey provided no additional information about him, anthropologist Elsie Clews Parsons provides some biographical detail in her study *Notes on the Caddo* (1941). According to Parsons, Wing's Caddo name was Tsa'Bisu, which she translated as "Mr. Wing." Apparently he was also known as Dr. Gerrin, and he had achieved fame as a traditional healer who had obtained sacred power from various sources, including a redheaded woodpecker and a buffalo. In one of his stories, Wing explained that there were two kinds of medicine men: "One kind has power to doctor and heal the sick; another has the power to prevent anyone from being hurt or harmed, and can charm away all danger." Wing reportedly belonged to the second group of medicine men, who were regarded as the most powerful of the two because "they can perform their magic without medicine and have power to bewitch people who are afar off, and thus make them lose their minds and not know what they are doing." This ability earned Wing the reputation as a witch. Such medicine men also had a song of death with which they frightened death away from people on their deathbeds. Wing's birth year was not documented, but he died in 1907. In addition to being a powerful medicine man, Wing was apparently also a prolific storyteller because he contributed no less than thirty-two stories to Dorsey's *Traditions of the Caddo*.[6]

Wing may actually have been influenced by Christian ideas, because shortly before his death, he had a vision of a "man with thorns all over his face" who showed him the evil men who had caused a deadly disease among the people.[7]

Although this was clearly a reference to Jesus Christ, it must be pointed out that Wing's account of the masked cannibal man shows no obvious Christian elements. Wing's account is short enough to be presented here in full:

> Ten boys lived with their grandmother. One day the oldest went out to hunt and did not return. The grandmother worried about him, and so the next day one of his brothers went to look for him. He did not return, and so the next brother went out to look for his brothers. He did not return and another went, and so on until the ninth boy went out, leaving his little brother at home with his grandmother. They waited long, but none of the brothers returned and no news came of them. They worried and grieved and became sadder each day, until at last the youngest boy declared that he was going to look for his brothers. His grandmother begged him not to go and leave her alone, for she felt that the same evil fate would befall him that had come to his brothers; but the boy was determined and prepared to go. He went out and prayed for help and put an eagle feather in his hair just before starting, thinking that it might have some hidden power. The boy traveled far, and after a time he saw a tipi. He approached the tipi, and as he went near he heard someone laugh and say: "Another one is coming. Cook some corn and we will soon have the meat." The boy understood the meaning of this, but he was so sad and weary that he thought he would as soon die as live, and so he went on to the tipi. An old man came out of the tipi and said to him: "Are you looking for your nine brothers?" "Yes," the boy answered. Then the man said: "I know where your brothers are and I will put you on the right path to find them, but first you must do some work for me. Lift that big log there and put it on the fire. I will give you four trials, and then if you can not do it you must lie down upon the log and let me lift it."
>
> The boy did not believe anything the man said, but thought he would try to lift the log and see if some power would not come to his aid in answer to his prayers. He tried four times, but could not move the log; then he lay down upon it. The old man was just about to spear him with the iron nose of the mask he wore, when some unseen power pulled the boy off the log, and the iron nose of the mask caught in the log and held the old man fast. A voice said to the boy: "Run to the tipi and take the pounder away from the woman who is pounding corn, bring it here, and beat the old man to death." The boy obeyed, and when the old man was dead, the voice said: "Gather up all of your brothers' bones. I will help

you, for I know the bones of each boy, and put them in nine piles." A strange man, the possessor of the voice, appeared and helped the boy gather up the bones. When they had them all piled up the man said: "Put your robe over them, shoot an arrow up in the sky, then cry: 'Look out, brothers, the arrow will hit you!'" The boy obeyed, and as he cried "Look out, brothers, the arrow will hit you!" his brothers jumped out from under the robe. The man then told them to burn the tipi with the man and his wife in it and to scatter the ashes. After they had done all that, the man said: "Return now to your grandmother. I am the Sun and I have helped you destroy the cannibals." Then he disappeared. The brothers all returned to their grandmother, who had almost grieved herself to death. They told their story, and the youngest boy told how the Sun had taken pity on him and helped him; and from that time all the people knew that the Sun was their friend and always willing to help them in times of trouble.[8]

At first glance, there appears nothing in this story to connect it to the De Soto expedition. Fortunately, a second account, "Coyote and the Six Brothers," provides more details. *Un*fortunately, the name of the storyteller of this account is unknown. This version too features a cannibal man with an iron-nosed mask, but it provides an alternative and more detailed ending. In addition to a different ending, there are other differences: instead of ten brothers, there are seven, and perhaps more striking, the hero is not Sun but a character named Coyote. Because the identity of the second storyteller is unknown, it is impossible to account for these differences. Still, the similarities between the stories implies that these are different versions of the same event.

In the second version, an old woman had seven sons. Six of them disappeared. Only their dogs returned. When the youngest son wanted to look for his brothers, his mother forbade him to go. However, while out hunting for raccoons in a forest one day, the boy met a witch-woman who aimed to kill him. He managed to escape from her and return home. That night Coyote appeared to him in a dream. Coyote told him that his brothers were not dead "but were with some bad people who made them work so hard that they would soon die if they did not get away." Coyote promised to help the youngest boy rescue his brothers. When the boy told his mother about the dream the next morning, she encouraged him to do as Coyote had instructed him. That day the boy met Coyote and Flying Squirrel. Flying Squirrel had been captured by the bad people and had to work for them as a slave.

At this point, we shall let the Caddo storyteller finish the tale in his "own" words:

> Squirrel told him that the bad people made slaves of all of the people that they could catch alive, and that they ate all that they killed. Coyote asked about the six brothers, and Squirrel told Coyote that they were slaves like himself and could not get away, but had to work. Coyote said that he would like to help them, and that he thought he could, for he was very cunning and had a good deal of power. Squirrel told Coyote if he could only find some way to kill the wicked chief that there would be no more trouble. Coyote said that he thought he could plan to kill him if he could only get to him, but that he lived across the river and had no way of getting across. Flying Squirrel said that he would take him across if he thought he could hold on to his tail as he flew. Coyote said that he could, and so they started. When they were almost to the other bank Coyote let go Squirrel's tail and fell into the water. He hid in the tall grass until he thought of a plan. When he had made up his mind what he was going to do, he turned into a nice, new corn mill, and floated out on the water where he would be in plain sight. Soon a woman came down to the river to get some water. She saw the mill and tried to get it, but could not. She ran back and told the chief about the nice, new mill, and asked him to get it for her. He told her that he was afraid it was Coyote, or someone trying to play a trick on them, but the woman said that it could not be anything but a fine corn mill and that she wanted it. The chief sent someone to get it, and then all of the women came to pound their corn in the new mill. They used it for several days, and all thought it was the best mill they had ever had. One day someone put some fine sweet corn in it, and after she had ground a little while all of her corn was gone. She ran to the chief and told him. He said that the corn mill was Coyote, as he had feared, and he told the people to bring it to him. They brought it, and he placed it on the big log where he always speared people with his long, spiked nose. He raised his head high, then dropped it, and his nose stuck in the log so that he could not get loose. The corn mill had rolled off the log and turned into Coyote. He grabbed the chief by the head and held him there while he called all the slaves to come and kill him. With the others came the six brothers. After they had killed the chief, Coyote told all that they were free, and to go to their homes. The six brothers

returned to their home, and ever after that whenever they killed any game they always left some for Coyote.⁹

Like the previous story, this one does not seem to have any clear links to a known historical event. There seem to be too many fantastic elements to make this a plausible history. Apart from the cannibal man, there are witches, a flying squirrel, and finally Coyote, who transforms himself into a corn mill. Indeed, there are very few clues with which to start the investigation into the historical basis of the story.

Still, the Caddo stories of the masked cannibal show some intriguing parallels with the De Soto expedition. Indeed, the iron-nosed mask may actually be either a type of helmet or an iron-tipped lance that De Soto or some of his officers carried. If so, this would make the De Soto expedition the most likely candidate, not only because this was the first contact but also because it would be another century before Europeans returned to the region. By that time, both spears and helmets had become obsolete and iron objects had become more common as they reached the Caddos through intertribal trade routes. In addition, the time span between first and second contact with whites provided ample time to transform a historic encounter into myth.¹⁰

A quick overview of the types of monsters in the Caddo stories shows a great diversity: cannibals, witches, ghosts, and monstrous animals, including snake-tongued squirrels, murderous bears, as well as a snakelike water monster. Compared to the traditions of the other Caddoan tribes, the Caddo storytellers made more references to cannibal monsters. Of these monsters, the masked cannibal with his sharp or long, spiked nose is the most intriguing. He is also distinct in American Indian monster iconography, appearing only in the Caddo traditions.

Although my interpretation that the iron-masked cannibal man may have represented Hernando de Soto; his successor, Luis de Moscoso y Alvarado; or one of De Soto's captains is conjectural, I nevertheless believe that a case can be made that the stories refer to the encounter between the Caddos and the De Soto expedition. If so, this story would provide a unique account of De Soto's infamous expedition from an American Indian perspective.

ARMORED MONSTERS IN OTHER AMERICAN INDIAN ORAL TRADITIONS

If the assumption that the mask is indeed a helmet is correct, it is only proper to point out that the Caddo story is not the only Indian tradition featuring an armor-wearing cannibal man. Chapter 4 discussed an armor-wearing Flint Monster in Pawnee tradition. Similar monsters can be found in other American Indian traditions as well. Frank G. Speck observed that there were many armored monsters in southeastern traditions. "Stories of monsters clad in bone, stone, metal or scales are very characteristic of the region," Speck wrote. "The monster is usually a cannibal, and is finally slain by persons or beings who have learned the secret of its only vulnerable spot." Speck concluded that the tribe's culture hero often appeared as the slayer of the monster.[11]

Likewise, James Mooney recorded stories featuring so-called Stone Coat people among the Cherokees. In one of these, titled "Nûñ'yunu'wï, The Stone Man," a lone hunter spotted a mysterious-looking man in the mountains. The man carried a strange stick that led him in the direction of the Cherokee hunting camp. The frightened hunter reported what he saw to his comrades, and a medicine man said that this mysterious old man was "a wicked cannibal monster called Nûñ'yunu'wï, 'Dressed in Stone.'" This monster was always on the lookout to kill and eat humans. According to the medicine man, "[I]t was nearly as hard to kill him, because his whole body was covered with a skin of solid rock." In the story, the Cherokees weakened the monster with the menstrual blood of seven women. Then they killed him by driving seven wooden stakes through his body and burning him to ashes. As he burned to death, the monster told the Cherokees of medicines that were effective against all kinds of diseases.[12]

Such stone-coated monsters are not limited to the Southeast. The Seneca Indians of New York, for example, tell stories of a race of Géno^{N}skwa, or "Stone Coats." They are also called "Ice and Cold Weather" people. The Stone Coat people were actually not made of stone but wore "stone" garments that sound much like armor. In one story, a boy hero defeated several enemies who wore "medicine shields" (helmets) before their faces. These "shields" were capable of warding off arrows. In another story, a Seneca warrior spotted the "stone clothing" of a Stone Coat chief "leaning against a tree." In this story, the Stone Coats were defeated with the help of Háweniyo, the Great Spirit, who explained that the Stone Coat people were of a mysterious origin: "I did not make the Stone Coats," Háweniyo said, "some one else made them." In another story, a female Stone Coat fell into the water and the weight of the garment caused her to drown. In addition to "stone coats," these strangers possessed a mysterious and powerful "finger" that, like a compass, pointed the person in the right direction.[13]

The puzzling fact about the Géno^{N}skwa is that they present many contradictions: sometimes there is a single god; other times there is a complete "tribe" of Stone Coat people. According to most stories, these people lived in the north, but in others they lived in the south, and in one story the Senecas pushed them west. In several stories they are distinctly humanlike, while in others they are supernatural giants. In some Seneca stories they are cannibals; in others they intermarry with Seneca heroes. In most stories Stone Coats are associated with winter, but in others they are associated with bears and the Cherokee Indians. Although they are generally hostile to the Seneca people, there are also stories of intermarriage between Seneca men and Stone Coat women. Indeed, in one story, a young man who once belonged to the Stone Coat people himself becomes a Seneca chief.[14]

Some scholars see in the Stone Coat people an Iroquois version of Witiko/Windigo of Algonkian tradition, while certain cryptozoologists believe they are stone-skinned versions of Bigfoot. In my opinion, the most plausible explanation is that they were most likely armor-wearing invaders who supposedly possessed "supernatural qualities" through their powerful objects and their association with the sacred powers of winter. Thus, rather than seeing the Stone Coat people strictly as supernatural beings, I am inclined to think of most of them as Europeans. Even the "bear" in one of the Seneca stories may have been a reference to the bearded strangers. This last observation, of course, is pure speculation.

There are several references to stone-covered monsters in the Southwest. Matilda Coxe Stevenson recorded a story among the Sia Pueblos of the Southwest of a mysterious wolf that wore a protective "shirt of stone which could be penetrated only at certain points."[15] Morris Opler published two Jicarilla Apache stories in which several culture heroes received protective garments made of "flint."[16] In another Apache story, also collected and published by Opler, Talking Hactcin gave flint stone garments to Bear Hactcin. For this reason, bears have nails and teeth of "flint." In this case, however, the flint garments would prevent the bear from attacking and stealing humans. Talking Hactcin gave the bear these garments with a warning: "If you disobey what I tell you," Talking Hactcin said, "if you hurt the people and make them sick, I will punish you severely with the clothes which I have given you."[17] If these garments are indeed armor of European make (admittedly a speculation) then this story illustrates that the Apaches attributed to them not merely power in warfare but power in different realms as well.

In short, references to armored monsters are quite widespread in American Indian lore. However, the Caddo traditions are unique because the monsters were wearing masks with spiked noses.

DO THE CADDO TRADITIONS REFER TO THE LONG-NOSED MASKETTES AND THE MYTH OF THE TWINS?

Perhaps the Caddo stories connect the iron-nosed masked cannibal with the long-nosed maskettes that archaeologists have discovered in various sites all over the American East. These maskettes date to Mississippian times. Some are small, with either a long- or short-nosed face. These "masks" were made from bone, copper, or shell. It appears that quite a few of them were ear ornaments. In addition, there are also rock carvings and other pictographs of long-nosed figures, as well as a small statuette that depicts long-nose-faced ear ornaments. One of the small maskettes was found in Gahagan Mound, Louisiana, in the southeastern corner of Caddo territory.[18]

Archaeologists have proposed two major theories on the meaning of these maskettes. Some believe they represent the Aztec deity Yacatecuhtli, patron saint of the *pochteca*, as the Aztec merchant class was called. These scholars argue that the *pochteca* introduced this cult into the region, together with other Mesoamerican objects and ideas.[19]

Others scholars see a link between the maskettes and widespread American Indian oral traditions of two mythical twins or the Red Horn myth of the Winnebagos and Iowas. These scholars argue that the long nose was part of an adoption ceremony among the Mississippian culture, the pre-Columbian civilization that influenced the Caddos as well. According to these myths, a mysterious boy (an "afterbirth-boy" who had been thrown into a river when his mother was murdered) was adopted by his father and twin brother. Afterbirth-boy's long nose was cut to look more like a human nose.[20]

There is a Caddo version of this twin hero myth. According to this version, Water Monster killed the wife of Medicine Man. Medicine Man and his son mourned for her for six days. Later, Medicine Man's son met a strange boy who said he was his brother. The boy came from the water and always disappeared before the father came home. One day the son told his father about the strange boy. Medicine Man planned to capture the strange boy by hiding inside the house as a fly, then by hiding in the fire, and so on. Six times they tried before they finally captured the mysterious boy by "tying up his hair." They held him for six days, and Medicine Man cut his nose so it looked more like a human nose. Medicine Man told the boys not to go near the timber where some monstrous snake-tongued squirrels lived. But the boys went anyway, and one of the squirrels captured the younger brother and took him into the hole. The brother returned home and told his father what had happened. Medicine Man then heated up some stones and threw them into the hole.²¹ The squirrel came out of the hole and dropped to the ground dead. Medicine Man then cut open its stomach and there found the mysterious boy, who was still alive. They washed him in the river and went home. One day the mysterious boy made a black arrow and a blue arrow and a wheel. The boys rolled the wheel and chased it but could not catch up. While resting, the mysterious boy put a pecan into the ground. As the boys prayed, the nut began to sprout and quickly grew up into the sky. The mysterious boy told his brother that he would climb up the tree and that one by one his bones would drop down to earth. The boy would have to stare at the ground at all times. The skull would fall last. When it did, his brother would have to collect the bones, put them in a pile, cover them with a buffalo calf's hide, shoot the black arrow at the pile with all force, and tell the pile of bones to get out of the way. The brother did so, and soon the mysterious boy was restored to life. Now it was his brother's turn. As he climbed, his bones fell to the ground until he heard the mysterious boy warn him to step aside because the arrow was coming his way. He did so and was turned into a boy again, but now he had the mysterious boy's power. Each brother now had power. One had the power of thunder and the other of lightning. They continued their journey and came upon a large lake, which they crossed with help from a forked tree. As they were crossing, they saw an old man coming toward the lake. "We must kill this man, because we know he is a bad man; he is a cannibal," said Lightning Boy, whose tongue was the shape of lightning. They killed the man and then found the cannibal people, and they killed these as well. They found the bones of Medicine Man's wife, piled them together, covered them with the buffalo calf robe, shot at the pile, and restored her to life. Then they went home and lived happily for many years. When Medicine Man and his wife finally died, the two boys were lonely and went up into the sky, where they are lightning and thunder. These were the boys who had killed the monsters on earth.²²

Although the myth of the twin heroes is widespread and long-nosed maskettes have been found around all over the eastern United States, it is difficult to apply the adoption theory to the story of the "iron-nosed masked cannibal man." Although there are a few similarities with the masked cannibal stories (the presence of cannibals and squirrels, and restoring people to life by shooting at their robe-covered bones), there are also major differences. First, the "snake-tongued squirrels" in this story are monsters rather than victims. Second, the cannibal people are not wearing the distinct masks with which they killed their victims. Third, the mysterious long-nosed twin hero was a *slayer* of monsters rather than a monster himself. In contrast, the long-nosed man in the stories discussed in this chapter was a man-spearing cannibal. Furthermore, unlike the hero twin, the cannibal man himself was slain. Lastly, in the Red Horn stories the trickster is mischievous, whereas in the cannibal story he is a hero who earned the appreciation of the Caddo people, who honored him ever after by leaving behind meat for him in the field.

Thus it seems unlikely that the iron-nosed cannibal man had anything to do with the Red Horn myth and the long-nosed god maskettes. The fact that this particular cannibal wore a mask with a "nose" made of *iron* makes it possible to date this story after, or perhaps *during*, first contact, because iron was not used among the Caddo Indians until Europeans introduced it. Although iron objects could have found their way to the Caddos from Mexico through existing Indian trade networks, the historical record allows us to pinpoint a more specific date when the "Stone Age" Caddos encountered iron. The encounter between stone and iron took place in 1541, when Spanish conquistadors under Hernando de Soto entered Caddo territory.

CONNECTING THE DE SOTO EXPEDITION TO THE IRON-NOSED CANNIBAL TRADITION

The arrival of the Spanish undoubtedly made a great impression on the Indian tribes they encountered. Apart from their odd appearance, metal weapons, horses, conduct in battle, and the enslavement of Native people, the Spanish may have introduced infectious diseases among the Indian population at this time. Finally, the Spanish expedition would destabilize the region. As one historian wrote: "Political hierarchies were toppled, alliances broken, and trading routes disrupted."[23] Indeed, in the wake of the De Soto expedition, tribes rose and fell from power due to warfare and diseases, and new confederacies, including the Creeks and others, came into being.

Apart from arriving with helmets and steel weapons (the "iron-nosed mask") the Spanish also enslaved many of the Indians they encountered on the expedition. The second Caddo story refers to people, including Flying Squirrel, who were forced to work for the Spanish as slaves and forced to carry supplies and do chores around camp. De Soto's men also captured Indian people for information, and frequently used torture to extract that information from them. According to the sources, by 1541 De Soto may have had as many as five hundred Native slaves, who served as bearers, servants, and concubines. Perhaps female slaves were allowed to keep their children so that they would be more cooperative. Indians who resisted, however, were killed.[24]

The identities of the slaves in the Caddo story are uncertain—except for the Caddo brothers. (Although "brothers" could also refer to allied or friendly tribes.) The identity of only one other slave is known. It is Flying Squirrel, an anthropomorphic animal who has both human (speech) and animal (a tail) features. If one assumes that Flying Squirrel is not a magical animal but, like Coyote, a real person, it might be possible to ascertain his tribal identity.[25]

References to flying squirrels in southeastern Indian ethnography and lore are rare. Flying Squirrel may have been a personal name, to which the Caddo storytellers later attributed supernatural qualities. After all, the name Squirrel was not uncommon among southeastern Indians. Indeed, a Caddo named Squirrel traveled to meet with Ghost Dance messiah Wovoka in the fall of 1891.[26] A Chickasaw chieftain by the name of Squirrel King rose to prominence in the mid-1700s. There are also a few references to squirrels in southeastern myths. A Cherokee story recorded by ethnologist James Mooney tells how Flying Squirrel and Bat joined the birds in a Cherokee ball game against the four-legged mammals, led by Bear, Terrapin, and Deer. Receiving the gifts of flight, Flying Squirrel and Bat helped secure victory for the birds against their more powerful opponents. In their honor, Cherokee ballplayers invoked the names of Bat and Flying Squirrel during the ball game.[27] While it is true that the Cherokees met De Soto in several unfriendly encounters in 1540, the evidence linking them conclusively to Flying Squirrel is thin. The idea of a strong and swift Cherokee athlete capable of great feats of strength and endurance may be intriguing but cannot be supported by firm evidence.[28]

A slightly stronger—but nevertheless problematic—possibility is that Flying Squirrel was actually a Chickasaw Indian. The Chickasaws had numerous clans, many now extinct, one of which was the Iksa' Fáni' (Squirrel Clan). When ethnographers collected information on the Chickasaw clan system, they were told that the Squirrel Clan belonged to the "Spanish" moiety, but this association may be purely coincidental. Chickasaw clans were totemic, meaning they were animal based or, rather, based on an ancestor's vision of an animal spirit. According to Robert Brightman and Pamela Wallace, "Eating the clan animal was not proscribed, but members of the clan attempted to foster respect for the species and recited laudatory tales about it."[29] De Soto stopped at several Chickasaw settlements in present-day northern Mississippi. Indeed, they were in effect neighbors of the Caddo. But the presence of the Squirrel Clan may not be enough to connect, with certainty, Flying Squirrel of the story to the Chickasaw Indians, who lived quite a distance from the Caddos.

Although the Spanish enslaved Native people, less obvious is the idea that they would have eaten those Indians they killed. Although the food supply was somewhat problematic by the time De Soto's men reached Caddo territory, it does not appear that the Spanish actually reached the point of starvation, which would have forced them to consume the flesh of their Native slaves.[30]

Perhaps the reference to cannibalism should be taken not literally but figuratively. It was not uncommon for tribes to accuse enemies of such atrocities. The Tonkawas, for example, were once, rightly or wrongly, accused and scorned for supposedly practicing anthropophagy. Spanish behavior may have fed speculations of cannibalism because the Spanish were responsible for many cruel and unnecessary deaths. De Soto's campaign seemed to devour the people it encountered. On several occasions, De Soto and Moscoso cut off noses, hands, or arms of prisoners before releasing them to impress other resisting Indians.[31] Their cruelty even made some expedition members shudder. One of these witnesses described the massacre of non-Caddo Guachoya Indians in southeastern Arkansas by men under command of Captain Nuño de Tobar. "The captain had ordered that no male Indian's life should be spared," Nuño de Tobar wrote. "The cries of the women and little children were so loud that they deafened the ears of those who pursued them." The Spaniards killed around one hundred Indians and wounded many others with their lances. They let the wounded go "in order that they might strike terror into those who did not happen to be there."[32]

The Caddos also experienced De Soto's brutality at Tula. When De Soto arrived at Tula with cavalry and fifty foot soldiers, fifteen to twenty Indians tried to stop them, but the Spanish cavalry ran them down. The Tulans killed one horse and wounded several others. Indeed, Caddo resistance was so fierce that De Soto had to retreat. A few days later, De Soto returned with reinforcements but found Tula abandoned. After he moved into the settlement, however, the Tulans came back with their army and attacked. De Soto's men reportedly slaughtered many Tulans. To send a message to the Caddo resisters, De Soto ordered his men to cut off the noses and right hands of six prisoners. Faced with this brutality, the Tulans moved to make peace, perhaps because De Soto held more captives who might suffer the same torture. The Tulans provided De Soto with buffalo robes, which the Spanish accepted gratefully, as it was cold at this time of year. The Tula cacique then subjected himself to De Soto.[33]

This did not end the violent treatment of the Caddo people. After De Soto's death on May 21, 1542, Luis de Moscoso took over and turned the expedition westward again. Traveling through Caddo country in southern Arkansas and eastern Texas, Moscoso fought a number of battles with the Caddo Indians there. After one battle, Moscoso ordered his men to cut off the nostrils and right arm of one chief and to send him to the chief of the Naguatex as a warning. When the Naguatex refused to surrender to the Spanish Moscoso sent two of his captains in different directions to burn Caddo towns and to capture and enslave people. The chronicles also document how Moscoso, while continuing his march, became unhappy with two of his Indian guides and hung them from a tree. Interestingly, both Caddo accounts note how the cannibal killed some of his victims by attaching them to a tree or log.[34]

Moscoso also fought a bloody battle with the "Aays" (Hais or Eyeish) Indians, neighbors of the Caddos, and reportedly did "great damage to the Indians." After traveling farther into Texas, Moscoso once again became unhappy with an Indian guide and had him tortured and thrown to the dogs. These were probably specially bred war hounds—mastiffs or similar breeds—which were infamous for tearing up Moors during the Reconquista.[35] Finally, in October 1542, Moscoso turned his men around and followed the same route back through Caddo country toward the Mississippi River.[36]

Other distinct elements of the De Soto expedition have no apparent place in the Caddo tradition. For example, De Soto's men introduced horses into the region, and even though the Caddos had never seen these animals before, the stories do not make any references to them. To be sure, there are references to dogs in the second story, and it is possible that these were horses. According to linguist and Caddo expert Wallace Chafe, the root of the Caddo word for horse (*di:tamah*) derives from their word for dog (*di'tsi'*). The particle *-tsi'* is a diminutive suffix, often used in animal names.[37] It is not clear what *-tamah* means. Perhaps it stands for "big" or even "sacred" or "holy," as with the Lakota word for horse, which translates as "holy dog." However, while it is possible that the "dogs" in the second story were horses, this seems unlikely because these were killed by the strange witch before the youngest brother and Coyote encountered the cannibal man. The absence of horses from the story does present a puzzling problem for my interpretation.[38]

According to the story, the cannibal lived in a tent. Although this could be a reference to the Plains Indian tepee, the use of tents was probably widespread among almost all tribes in this region. Indeed, the Caddo had tents. There is only one reference to De Soto having a tent in the Spanish sources. However, it seems likely that the Spanish brought tents on their expedition or used ship sails as tent covers. It appears that the Spanish lost some of these tents during Indian attacks, which would explain the frequent occasions on which De Soto's men forcefully evicted Indian families from their homes to make room for the conquistadors.[39]

The most distinctive feature of the monster in this story remains his mask. The long-nosed iron mask could refer to armor (including helmets and shields) worn by the Spanish expedition members. But to my knowledge, inventories of the De Soto expedition no longer exist. One source states that when De Soto recruited men for his expedition in Spain, most brought their own armor. The

Portuguese men were "armed with very excellent armor," but the Castilians "wore poor and rusty coats of mail, and all [wore] helmets and carried worthless and poor lances."[40]

In fact, De Soto's expedition may have been one of the last in which men wore armor. Heat made body armor uncomfortable, and the weight added further discomfort and could even pose danger: eleven of De Soto's men drowned after Indians overturned their canoe in a battle on the Mississippi River. The coats of mail of infantrymen probably offered relatively little protection against the longbows of the Indians because the chains would have caused reed arrows to split into long, sharp, and deadly splinters upon impact. One source even stated that the coats of mail provided better service as sieves, with which the men sifted the flour they ground up with their mortars and pestles. This interesting fact provides yet another intriguing link with the Caddo story in which Coyote turned himself into a corn mill that the cannibals needed to process their corn. The chronicles make clear that the Spanish forced their slaves to process flour for them.[41]

Spanish helmets probably included morions, celadas, and burgonets. From the inventory of the concurrent Coronado expedition, we know that Coronado's cavalry carried twenty morion-style helmets and seven burgonet-style helmets. At least two of Coronado's infantrymen wore burgonets. Usually, only officers owned burgonets, because they were very expensive. As the Caddo stories indicate, the "chief" wore this item. This could mean either De Soto or Moscoso, but one of the other captains could be a possibility. Sometimes these helmets were decorated and shaped in the most fantastic designs. The Museo Nacional del Prado in Madrid, Spain, has several burgonets that once belonged to Emperor Charles V, a contemporary of De Soto. Several of these are shaped like the heads of monsters. Importantly, some burgonets had visors shaped like sharp beaks that could be easily mistaken for noses.[42]

Another explanation for the iron-nosed mask is horse armor. At this time, horse armor was used in Spain. The Royal Armory at the Prado Museum displays several pieces that date to the early 1500s. Apart from breastplates (peytrals), hind protection (cruppers), and neck protection (crinets), horse armor included the shaffron, a kind of mask used to protect a horse's head. Not only were these masks elongated to fit the shape of the horse's head, but after 1400 they often also included a sharp spike on top, much like the horn of a unicorn, that could inflict serious wounds upon enemies.[43] From the accounts of the De Soto expedition, we know that horses were used to trample and break through enemy lines and run down Caddo warriors. It is not hard to imagine the terror inflicted upon the Indians by a horse with a spiked mask.

There are several problems with this theory. Horse armor of the above kind was even more expensive than a man's armor.[44] Only a handful of men could have afforded it. It is uncertain if De Soto brought any horse armor along. The muster and inventory lists of Coronado's concurrent expedition do not mention horse armor. Still, De Soto's horses may have worn not full metal armor (bards) but leather armor. However, it is possible that some wore the iron-spiked shaffrons that may have horrified the Indians. But even so, as mentioned earlier, the Caddo story does not mention horses, which would make helmets more likely candidates for the spiked masks.

Another possibility is that the long spiked nose of the mask refers to the weapons that De Soto and his men carried. De Soto's expedition consisted of crossbowmen, sword- and musket-carrying infantrymen, and lance-carrying horse soldiers.[45] The crossbow was a powerful weapon. At this time, crossbows were highly accurate and lethal at sixty to seventy yards. At a 45-degree angle, a crossbow could shoot a projectile 350 yards, making it an efficient defensive weapon. Loading and firing was time-consuming and required the help of a mechanism to bend the bow. The Indian longbow matched and may have even outperformed the crossbow in battle because of its higher rate of fire. Still, the range and awesome striking power of the crossbow must have impressed the Indians.[46]

Infantrymen, the so-called targeteers, may have carried muskets or harquebuses, but by the time they reached Caddo territory they had almost exhausted their supply of powder and balls. Hence they relied on swords. A few soldiers may have also carried a halberd, a long stick with an ax-shaped blade, an opposite "beak," and a sharp steel point emerging from the center. Soldiers also carried shields, usually round or oval in shape.[47]

Perhaps the most efficient weapon was the cavalryman's lance. According to one scholar, the Spanish "introduced the lance to America and it became, indeed, their trademark."[48] From horseback, this would have been a formidable weapon. De Soto prided himself on his skill with the lance and according to some sources enjoyed displaying this skill by spearing human targets.[49] In fact, it appears that most Indians were killed by spear-carrying horsemen.

"HE WENT OUT TO MEET HIM WITH ALL FEROCITY AND BOLDNESS": COYOTE FACES THE CANNIBAL MONSTER AND A CADDO HERO FACES A CONQUISTADOR

One of the more spectacular episodes in the Caddo tradition is the dramatic escape of the Caddos from the masked cannibal monster. In Wing's story, the cannibal is killed by a corn pounder, a medium-length pestle with which Caddo women pounded corn. In the second story, Coyote transformed himself into a "corn mill," which also refers to the long pestle and mortar with which the Caddos turned corn into flour.[50]

Interestingly, Garcilaso de la Vega's account of the battle at Tula refers to a Caddo man who, armed with such a corn pestle, successfully defended himself against a Spanish lancer. In a subsequent battle, other Caddos, possibly inspired by this real-life "Coyote" warrior, carried similar clubs against the Spanish. These references in Garcilaso appear to confirm that the Caddo stories indeed refer to the De Soto expedition. Garcilaso's account, then, provides a description of the hero (Coyote) of the Caddo tradition, as well as the name of the iron-masked cannibal. Perhaps the Spanish monster was Juan Páez, a native of Usagre who was De Soto's captain of crossbowmen.

The encounter between the Caddo warrior and Juan Páez took place during the first battle at Tula. Garcilaso describes the event in his history:

> Though he had no skill in horsemanship, but rather was awkward and heavy, he wished to fight on horseback, and going out in the last stages of the battle, he encountered an Indian who, though he was retreating, was still fighting. Juan Páez attacked him, and without aptitude, skill, or dexterity, for he did not have them, he threw a lance at him. The Indian jumped aside and warded off the lance with a piece of a pike more than a fathom long, which he carried as a weapon. Grasping it with both hands, he gave Juan Páez a blow to the mouth that broke all his teeth, leaving him choking, and made his escape safely.[51]

The parallels with the Caddo tradition are obvious: Páez tried to spear Coyote but missed. Coyote next gave Páez a blow to the face that disabled the captain and knocked him out. The weapon this warrior used to knock down Páez was a "piece of pike more than a fathom long." A fathom equals six feet (1.8288 meters). Was this the pounder from the Caddo story? Consider what happened next.

The action of the Caddo hero—Coyote—against Páez inspired the Caddos into a spirited resistance that forced De Soto to leave Tula after the battle. As he was taking his wounded men back to camp, De Soto "was amazed at the obstinacy and temerity with which those Indians fought, and at the fact that the women had the same spirit and ferocity."[52] The next day De Soto returned with his entire army to strike again. However, the town was empty. The Tulans had abandoned their town, even though some of their spies were keeping watch on Spanish movements. De Soto sent out patrols to bring in captives for questioning, but whenever the cavalrymen found Tulans, they "immediately fell down on the ground and said, 'Either kill me or leave me here.'" The Tulans refused to answer their interrogators and resisted when the Spanish tried to carry them away. Because of their "obstinacy," Garcilaso wrote, "the Castilians were forced to kill them all."[53]

At this point in his narrative, Garcilaso paused to report that the Caddo men and women were handsome, graceful, and well proportioned in person but that they had "ugly faces" because "they deform themselves by deliberate distortion of themselves." According to Garcilaso, the Caddos elongated their skulls (a custom that archaeologists date to at least A.D. 1000) and practiced the art of tattooing: "Their heads are incredibly long and tapering on top, being thus artificially by binding them up from birth to the age of nine or ten years. They prick their faces with flint needles, especially the lips, inside and out, and color them black, thereby making themselves extremely and abominably ugly."[54]

More important for the purposes of this chapter, Garcilaso mentions that the Indians carried the same strange, fathom-long clubs into battle that the Caddo hero had carried in his duel with Juan Páez. When the Tulans launched a dawn counterattack to dislodge De Soto from their town a few days after the duel, they carried short sticks. Attacking the camp from three sides, the Caddos engaged the Spanish in a desperate battle. To avoid accidentally wounding their own comrades in the darkness, the Spaniards cried out the name of Saint James. According to Garcilaso, the Tulans called out the name of their province for the same reason. Many Tulans, Garcilaso recounts,

> carried clubs made of pieces of pikes two or three varas[55] long, a new thing for the Spaniards. The reason for it was that the Indian who had broken Captain Juan Páez's teeth two days before had told his people of the lucky stroke he had made with his club. It appearing to them that good fortune lay in the kind of weapon and not in its skillful use (because the Indians generally are great believers in omens), that night they brought many clubs and gave mighty blows with them to many of the soldiers, particularly to a certain Juan de Baeza, who was one of the halberdiers of the general's guard. That night he happened to find himself with a sword and a shield between two Indians with their clubs. One of them broke his shield to pieces with the first stroke, and the other gave him another blow on the shoulders so hard that it knocked him down, and he would have finished killing him if his companions had

not come to his rescue. In this manner many other valiant exploits took place, which, because they were blows with sticks, the soldiers laughed about afterward, comparing their experiences. It was a very good thing for them that they were sticks and not arrows, which would have done more damage.[56]

Ultimately, De Soto's horse soldiers cleared the town of Indians, spearing many of them to death. "The battle ended at sunrise," wrote Garcilaso, "and the Spaniards, without pursuing the enemy, assembled in the pueblo to tend the wounded, who were numerous, though only four were killed."[57]

The reference to the clubs is significant because it is a reference to the corn mill Coyote used to defeat the cannibal man in the story. The term "corn mill" is awkward. As mentioned above, the Caddos used pestles and mortars to ground corn into flour. It seems reasonable to assume that the term "corn mill" is either an imperfect translation or a reference to a new technology that had replaced the traditional mortar and pestle by the early 1900s, when the story was recorded. Thus, rather than referring to an obsolete and possibly forgotten technology, the storyteller perhaps had Coyote use the by then more common corn mill in the story.

Garcilaso's chronicle may also give a clue as to what happened to the Caddo hero—Coyote in the Caddo tradition—after the great Battle of Tula. This man encountered four of De Soto's soldiers looting the field after the battle. The conquistadors discovered him in some nearby brush. They attacked him but were greatly surprised by the Tulan's valor. The Tulan carried Juan Páez's battle-ax, implying that he was indeed the hero who had defeated Páez in the duel. This man severely wounded two of the foot soldiers, Juan de Carranza and Diego de Godoy, with the ax and also wounded the horse of the third man, Francisco de Salazar, before turning against the fourth Spaniard, Gonzalo Silvestre. In an interesting reversal of the Caddo story, the Tulan's blow glanced off Silvestre's shield "and did not break through it, and because of the great force of the blow, it did not stop until it hit the ground." With his sword, Silvestre struck at the Tulan, wounding him on the forehead, face, and breast and severing the man's left hand. Still the Tulan lunged at him with the ax, but Silvestre warded off the blow with his shield and slashed at the brave Tulan, nearly cutting him in two.[58]

The Spaniards were so impressed with the bravery of this Caddo hero that in Garcilaso's account he acquires near *superhuman* qualities, whereas in the Caddo story he has *supernatural* qualities. If this warrior was indeed the same as the Caddo hero—Coyote—who had struck down Páez earlier, both accounts consider him an extraordinary man. According to Garcilaso, after Gonzalo Silvestre had struck the lethal blow with his sword, "the Indian remained standing and said to the Spaniard, 'Peace be with you!'" before he fell dead in two pieces. Critical readers will find this dramatic description quite implausible. Indeed, historians often charge Garcilaso with literary embellishments that discredit him as a reliable historical source. However, one may also see this embellishment as a means to illustrate an extraordinary man. In this sense, both the Caddo tradition and Garcilaso use similar embellishments. Both accounts, Spanish and Caddo, are examples of premodern historical genres.[59]

THE MEANING OF THE MYTH

Scholars will quickly point out that Garcilaso's account is the least reliable of all the memoirs of the expedition because Garcilaso was not an expedition member. In fact, he was born in 1539, the year the expedition set out, and he completed his history in 1599. (It was published in 1605.) Many scholars claim that his account contains more fiction than fact, as well as numerous embellishments to satisfy the literary tastes of his audience.[60]

Still, Garcilaso based his account on information furnished by a veteran of the expedition, Gonzalo Silvestre, the slayer of the Caddo hero, as well as other oral and written sources. Some scholars (myself included) believe that, despite occasional embellishments, Garcilaso's account is indeed reliable in rough outlines and that his embellishments were the result of memorating certain events over the course of years. Memoration is the process of relating a personal experience from memory. In the process of remembering or sharing experiences, memories are subject to subtle changes. Memory often turns small things into bigger ones. Thus memoration can exaggerate the intensity of an experienced moment, but it does not deny the event that was experienced.[61]

In my opinion, Garcilaso's description of the events at Tula has interesting parallels with events described in the Caddo myth. These parallels include the physical appearance of the Spaniards with their iron "masks" or helmets; the presence of shock weapons (the "iron nose") such as lances, swords, halberds, and crossbows; the Spanish use of coats of mail to sift flour (according to the story, the cannibal people needed tools to make flour); the enslavement of Indian people; Spanish methods of torture and execution of opposing Indians; fierce resistance by the Caddos; the armed struggle between the lone Caddo ("Coyote") and Captain Juan Páez (the "Cannibal chief"), in which Páez was struck down by what appears to be a corn pestle; the subsequent use of strange clubs (corn pestles) by the Caddo during their counterattack against the Spanish occupiers of Tula; the courageous resistance by one Caddo in the brush, which won him the praise of the Spanish; and, finally, like the cannibal man in the stories, the Spanish conquistadors leaving Caddo territory.

Of course, there are also important discrepancies. The cannibal chief was not killed; Páez was merely wounded. Rather than being victorious, the brave Tulan was killed in a subsequent fight with four Spanish soldiers. Finally, the remaining Tulans did not defeat the cannibals but surrendered instead, even though, as pointed out above, the Spanish did abandon the area for nearly a century shortly afterward.

Although these facts are problematic, the parallels are also striking. It is likely that the Caddo story of their encounter with the De Soto expedition underwent some changes, but it is impossible to reconstruct the evolution of the story into myth. Although preliterate societies often take great care in preserving stories and passing them on accurately, changes may nevertheless have taken place over time. It is important to note that not only did the Spanish disappear from the Caddo radar screen for nearly a century after De Soto, but the time span between the De Soto expedition and Dorsey's recording of the story covers some 360 years. In addition, by the time Dorsey recorded these traditions, Caddo population numbers had dropped so dramatically that few Caddos familiar with these oral traditions remained. Perhaps the surviving text is a composite of several different stories, or merely a fragment of the original.

Still, rather than being distorted by time and distance, it is possible that the story may have transformed into myth much earlier. One must not forget that the unexpected encounter with the Spanish caused a kind of paradigm shift among the Caddos and other tribes, much like Columbus's Iberian discovery of the Americas caused a similar paradigm shift in Europe. The traditional view of the universe was no longer accurate. It took Europeans some time to adjust to this new image of the world. Folklorist George Lankford observed:

> In the sixteenth century the well-ordered Middle World of the Native Americans was profoundly disturbed by the arrival of previously unknown people, the Europeans and Africans. Over the next four centuries, their unusual appearance, their technological power, their alien understandings of the world, and the devastation they caused—all these required some sort of explanation. The body of mythology expanded to accommodate explanations, as well as attitudes toward them.[62]

Perhaps something similar happened to the Caddos. To make sense of the events that befell them between 1541 and 1542, the Caddos sought to fit them into their cosmology. Unfamiliar with Europeans, European-made weapons systems, horses, iron tools, and European attitudes of imperialism, ethnocentrism, militarism, and aggression, the Caddos had to invent language to explain these new things. Thus horses became "sacred dogs," Spanish conquistadors became "cannibals," and Spanish helmets and weapons became "iron-nosed masks." Incidentally, masks also symbolized the duplicitous nature of the strangers: they were two-faced, being at once both human and monstrous.

In the process of incorporating the traumatic experience of European contact into the Caddo paradigm, the story evolved from history into a timeless myth. So the story took on themes that reinforced traditional moral lessons and values. The myth of the cannibal man with the iron-nosed mask taught young Caddos to be brave, to be loyal toward siblings, to not fear death, and, above all, to place their trust in the sacred powers. In both stories, divine support offered solace and resolution. Indeed, in the first story the people murdered were in fact restored to life by Sun. In the second story, Coyote came to the rescue by fooling the cannibals. To put it simply: to be successful and victorious, one must have *faith*.

This basic message reaffirmed the validity of Caddo religious beliefs. This validity of Caddo religion is symbolized at another level by the pounder or corn mill with which the hero of the stories defeated the cannibals. The pounder, an object associated with the essential life-giving powers of corn, symbolized traditional Caddo culture, whereas the "iron-nosed mask" symbolized the weapons, tools, and imperialistic attitudes of the Spanish invaders. Interestingly, in this battle of traditional versus new, tradition won.

CONCLUSION

It is strange that, at first glance, no Caddo accounts of their contact with the De Soto expedition survived in Caddo oral tradition. This is even more remarkable when one considers that De Soto's men killed many Caddos; enslaved many others; introduced technologies such as horses, weapons, and metal tools into the region; and may have introduced diseases, as well as general political instability.

However, this chapter argues that at least two Caddo stories may refer to the Caddo encounter with the De Soto expedition. Despite some discrepancies, the evidence presented here describes what might be a highly memorated version of this important historical event.

Interestingly, the Caddo view of De Soto's conquistadors as cannibals mirrors European accounts and representations depicting American Indians in the same way. Accounts by Jacques LeMoyne, popularized by the even more famous etchings of Theodore de Bry, engrained the image of cannibalistic American Indians into the European mind. Modern scholars often explain these depictions as resulting from European ethnocentrism and racism, designed to highlight the supposed "savagery" of the American Indian to justify European conquest and enslavement of American Indian peoples. As the Caddo stories show, the Caddos used the same image to characterize and describe Europeans. In short, Europeans and Caddos used a strikingly similar metaphor—the cannibal—to show the supposed inhumanity of the other.

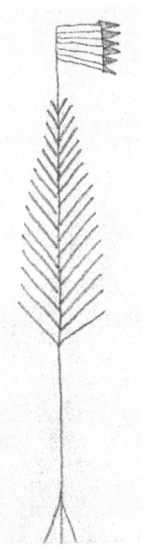

Part III
Oral Traditions and Ethnohistorical Analysis

SIX

From "Monster" to Savior

Scalped Men, Pahukatawa, and the Pawnee Trauma of Genocide

> Pahukatawa was the greatest prophet the Pawnee ever had. When they were hungry, he brought buffalo to them; when the enemy was coming to attack them, he notified the people. When disease was approaching their village, Pahukatawa told the people what to do to keep it away.
>
> James R. Murie, no date[1]

So far, the monsters discussed in this book resulted from direct European contact: Whirlwind of the Arikaras was a metaphor for diseases introduced by Europeans; the child-snatching witch-woman represented Spanish missionaries who bought Wichita children from their Apache captors; the Flint Monster that terrorized the Pawnees was a man in European mail armor; and the masked cannibal of Caddo tradition was a member of the De Soto–Moscoso expedition. However, one category of monsters, the so-called scalped men, were only indirectly related to European contact. Perhaps the word "monster" is too strong, because the scalped men were people who had survived mutilation in warfare. The Caddoan peoples believed that these individuals (who could be female or male) had died and were then restored to life by some mysterious power. Consequently, they were no longer human, and the Pawnees and Arikaras believed they were potentially dangerous beings.

Although all Caddoan nations told scalped men stories, these traditions seem to have proliferated among the Pawnees and Arikaras. Stories of a Skiri Pawnee man who returned from the dead after he was killed by a Lakota war party also abound among the Pawnees and Arikaras. His name was Pahukatawa, and he became the greatest prophet the Pawnees ever had. He was, in effect, the ultimate scalped man. Rather than a terrifying spirit, Pahukatawa sought to protect his people. He not only helped them fight off diseases, but, perhaps more importantly, assisted them against their enemies, particularly the Lakotas and the Cheyennes, who sought their annihilation.

It was genocidal warfare with the Lakotas and Cheyennes that led to the rise of the Pawnee prophet. White expansion, together with the opportunities posed by horses and guns, had driven the Lakotas and Cheyennes into Pawnee territory, making conflict inevitable. When the war took on genocidal features in the early 1800s, it caused a great spiritual crisis among the Pawnees. First affected were the Skiris, who until then had put their trust in Morning Star, the great cosmic warrior, for protection. When Morning Star no longer seemed to provide sufficient security, some Skiris searched for new ways to defend themselves. Two Skiri chiefs—Man Chief and Knife Chief—took the controversial step of abolishing the Skiri practice of sacrificing a human captive to Morning Star in the futile hope of obtaining the support of the United States. Their actions, however, only angered Skiris who remained faithful to the Morning Star ceremony. In addition, the Skiris and their South Band neighbors invited Christian missionaries among them in the 1830s, possibly in another attempt to placate the United States but more likely to gain some additional spiritual advantage against their enemies. But not even the presence of these missionaries stopped the Lakotas and Cheyennes, who in fact intensified their attacks against the Pawnees. Faced with annihilation, the Pawnee people became increasingly desperate.

It was in this atmosphere of desperation that Pahukatawa returned from the dead. His return inspired hope in many Pawnees, although "traditionalist Skiris" (for lack of a better term) questioned his existence and accused him of being a false prophet. Only gradually did Pahukatawa gain ground among the Skiris. Eventually he was revered among the other Pawnee bands as well, for saving the people from annihilation at the hands of their enemies.

Still, Pahukatawa remained controversial in some quarters, and he left the Pawnees after feeling slighted by them. Some sources claim that he went to live with the Arikaras, while others maintain that he ascended into the heavens, where he became a star. In the 1890s, however, Pahukatawa once again returned. This time it was not genocidal warfare that prompted his appearance but the ethnocidal policies of the United States government aimed at destroying Pawnee culture. Once again, Pahukatawa offered comfort and solace when the Pawnee people were under threat.

Both Pahukatawa and the scalped people remain mysterious, complex, and ambiguous figures. They are simultaneously sources of reverence and fear. Like the characters in previous chapters, they were once historical humans who transformed into sacred powers. Modern-day Pawnees continue to view them as truly powerful beings. Indeed, for many Pawnees today, Pahukatawa stands next to Jesus and Morning Star in the constellation of sacred powers.

"THEY WERE ALL FRIGHTENED, FOR THESE PEOPLE WERE ALL SCALPED-MEN": SCALPED MEN STORIES

There are many references to scalped men in Pawnee and Arikara traditions. Scalped men were people who, while "dead" (probably unconscious), had been scalped, lost a limb, or been otherwise mutilated in battle. The Pawnees and Arikaras believed that these men had died and that some mysterious sacred power had restored them back to life. In the process of restoration, these people were imbued with power as well. Because they were no longer truly human (the Pawnees considered them "ruined"), they were forced to live away from the Pawnee towns.[2] Some took up residence in caves along riverbanks or dugouts in hillsides. Because the Pawnees might kill a scalped person upon discovery, these people lived a lonely existence. Sometimes, however, they would sneak into town at night to secretly look at relatives or loved ones.[3]

Contrary to a popular myth, scalping existed in North America long before the arrival of Europeans.[4] Near Crow Creek, South Dakota, archaeologists discovered a mass grave dating to circa 1325 that contained the remains of 486 slain individuals, most of whom had been scalped or otherwise mutilated after a terrible battle. The Crow Creek example shows that Plains Indian warfare could reach high levels of violence in certain high-stress situations—in this case a drought that had diminished food resources—resulting in many cases of scalping and mutilation.[5]

In the seventeenth and eighteenth centuries, the Pawnees faced a new threat with the arrival of the Lakotas and Cheyennes. These newcomers competed with the Pawnees for food resources, such as the bison, and trade privileges with Euro-Americans. Warfare sharply increased and with it the number of scalping survivors upon which the Pawnee traditions are based.

Scalped men among the Pawnees (*kicahúruksu*) and the Arikaras (*tshuníxu'*) often wore caps made of wolf or coyote skin to protect their scarred heads against infections such as septicemia, meningitis, and necrosis. Armed with supernatural power, they were often excellent thieves, hunters, or warriors. In some stories they were terrifying spirits who stole or destroyed property. In many stories, they tried to capture women to keep them company. Typical of such stories was the following Pawnee tradition, "Scalped-Man Loses His Wife," which Dorsey published in 1904:

Scalped-Man had a den alongside of a creek; and one day he thought, "I will go and hunt a woman, so she can live with me." So Scalped-Man went toward the village, and he saw a young girl coming from the village. He sat down until she came close to him. He jumped up and seized her. The girl tried to get away, but he carried her off. She saw that it was no use to resist, so she told Scalped-Man to put her down, for she would go with him.

Now they came to the stream where Scalped-Man had his den; and Scalped-Man was calling the girl all kinds of pet names. They came to the creek and the girl said: "Where are we going?" Scalped-Man said: "We are going to my home. You are to be my wife." "Well," said the girl, "if I am to be your wife, you must first wash all those sores from your head; then I can live with you. Dive and rub your head under the water, so that the scales will come off. I will sit here on the bank and wait for you." This Scalped-Man agreed to do. He went down and jumped into the creek and dived. He did not stay long, and came up again, and said: "Yes, there she is." "Yes," said the girl, "you did not stay long." So he dived again, this time staying longer, and he came up. "Yes, she is there still," said he. "You do not stay under the water long enough to get off those scales," said the girl; "the sores need much water so that they will get well soaked, and will drop off." He dived and stayed for a long time. When he rose, he saw her still sitting there. "Good," he said, "you are a good girl." "Well," said the girl, "stay longer this time, and when you come up we will go to your home." "Very well," he said; so he dived, and as he went under the water the girl got up and ran as fast as she could for her home. About halfway she fell in with some hunters, and she told them about Scalped-Man. They took her home.

Now when Scalped-Man came up from the water she was gone. He ran out of the water to the place where the girl had sat, and knelt down and said: "Here is where she sat." He felt of the place and rolled over, then stood up and cried, and said: "Only for the sore head." He kept on saying this, and after a time came upon the hunters, and saw the girl among them. He shrieked for her and said: "Come! the scabs are off." But the girl would not go back.[6]

The Pawnees found scalped people so terrifying that they might kill them when they found them. This fact likewise made scalped people fearful of the living. In 1861 the Pawnees reportedly killed a female who had been scalped by the Lakotas and nursed back to health by an agency teacher.[7]

Because they shunned and sometimes killed scalped people, the Pawnees had a "deep-seated, superstitious prejudice against maiming of any kind" and refused to have limbs amputated when this was recommended by white doctors. In most cases, Pawnee doctors were able to save the infected limbs. The prohibition against amputation did not apply to maiming (such as cutting off the tip of a little finger) for sacrificial purposes.[8]

Although scalped men, such as the one in the above story, sometimes caused terror, they could be benefactors as well. Occasionally a scalped man bestowed sacred power upon worthy men who had overcome their fears and confronted him. Anthropologist Gene Weltfish recorded the following story by William Riding In, which covers both the theme of mutual dread and the fact that scalped men were potential sources of sacred power:

> A warrior was coming home alone at the close of the day. He came to a stream and saw human footprints. He decided to follow them. They led to the edge of a cliff where they ended. He pushed apart the vines that hung over the cliff and since it was dark he decided to go inside and there he suddenly found himself in a large room where a fire was burning. There were people sitting around the fire telling stories. Near the door there was a large pile of wood and here he decided to sit down. As he sat there he was able to observe the people more closely. They told of incidents that had happened during the day and they would all laugh at each other's stories. The warrior could now see the different people,—one had a peg leg, and one a wooden arm and another was completely bald and still another had only one hair on his head which would wave back and forth. One of them had no ears, and another no hair. The leader ordered his apprentice to get some wood for a fire so that the fire would burn up high. When the apprentice got to the woodpile he thought he saw someone sitting there. He stopped for he was frightened. He knew that all were present and that this must be a stranger. He told the leader that he suspected there was a human being on the wood pile and the leader ordered him to investigate more thoroughly. They were all frightened, for these people were all Scalped-Men. The warrior suddenly spoke to them and asked them to help him. But they were all so frightened that they crowded around the entrance trying to get out. And so his request for help remained unanswered. Then he went outside and he could hear what the men were saying. They said, "He didn't see my head, but he did see yours, One-Hair." Then the warrior approached them again and again asked for their help and blessing,

but this time they were so frightened that each of them wandered off in a different direction. That's all.⁹

How can one explain the strange ambiguity between scalped men as monstrous, fear-inspiring beings and scalped man as bestowers of sacred power? Analyzing different scalped men stories, linguist Douglas R. Parks argued that the character of the scalped man in Pawnee and Arikara folklore evolved over time. Parks distinguished between three types of scalped men stories. In some, scalped men appear in quasi-comical roles to warn listeners and teach young audiences moral values. However, in most traditions they appear as mischievous and terrifying spirits who steal women and objects. In a third category, however, they bestow spiritual power upon worthy individuals, guaranteeing them success in hunting, healing, and warfare. According to Parks, this category signified the transformation of scalped men from boogeymen into powerful but benign spirits who played important cosmological roles. Pahukatawa would follow a similar path. Like the scalped men, he was a real historical character who eventually rose up to become an important member in the pantheon of Pawnee sacred powers.¹⁰

The transformation of scalped men from actual historical individuals into mythological or supernatural characters was further exemplified by their inclusion in the annual Medicine Lodge ceremony of the Pawnees. During this multiweek festival, doctors from various medicine societies competed with each other in sleight of hand performances. On two nights, however, the "dance of the scalped ones" was performed. The dancers had daubed their heads with mud to create the appearance of having been scalped. Careful attention was paid to creating an eerie and suspenseful mood. The drumbeat was irregular, adding to the weirdness of the event, and the song of the scalped men was highly unusual as well. Lured by the music, the dancers emerged from the entrance of the medicine lodge as if emerging from underground caves. They moved erratically to signify their otherworldly nature. Several times they emerged from the "cave" only to run back in, together with the musicians, whenever the music stopped. They repeated this four times. The fourth time, the dancers and drummers would fall down, kicking over their water drums. Then the dancers got up and looked around in a dazed state before running back into the lodge one last time.¹¹

Although Gene Weltfish contended that the dance was performed for entertainment purposes only, I believe it shows the growing importance of the scalped man in Pawnee cosmology. It confirms Parks's finding that the scalped man evolved from a historical character into a mythological or supernatural one.

This transformation was possible because Pawnee religion was flexible. It was open to new ideas. Indeed, it did not owe its existence to a single revelation but was based on the visions of numerous individuals.[12] New visions occurred with regularity (possibly induced by social or political stress), thus allowing Pawnee religion to evolve. Visions may also explain religious differences between the Skiris and the South Band Pawnees (Chawi, Kitkehahki, and Pitahawirata). New visions added to a deeper understanding of the sacred and frequently resulted in additions to the Pawnee ceremonial repertoire.[13] Thus, although the Pawnees had a reputation for being very conservative in their religious observances, it was possible for new revelations and practices to take hold among the people.

At its core, Pawnee religion was based on belief in an all-powerful creative force called Tiiraawaahat (The [Expanse of the] Heavens), who the Pawnees addressed as Atius (Father). Pawnee cosmology further consisted of celestial and terrestrial powers. Celestial powers (stars, the moon, the sun, thunder, lightning, and so on) were the most powerful. They had been created directly by Tiiraawaahat, and they governed the passing of the seasons, the arrival of rain, the planting and harvesting of crops, the arrival of bison and other animals, and other forces relevant to creation and subsistence. Among the Skiri Pawnees the most important celestial powers were Evening Star, who controlled subsistence (farming) and procreation, and Morning Star, who acted as a protector (in warfare) and provider (hunter) for the people.[14]

Interestingly, the Skiri Pawnees and the closely related Arikaras periodically sacrificed scalps through burning in the "New Fire Ceremony."[15] Scalps represented the life force—but not the soul—of a person, and a scalp could be burned to restore sacred powers. As the smoke of the sacrifice rose to the heavens, it revitalized the creative properties of the sacred powers. Thus, while the soul was immortal, the life force could be "recycled." The life force could be captured not only in the form of scalps but through bones, the skull, skin, blood, and other tissue as well.[16]

Perhaps the most spectacular (and often overemphasized) sacrifice was the offering of a captive during the Morning Star ceremony. The ceremony was based on the story of Morning Star's marriage to Evening Star and the subsequent creation of the Skiri people. Morning Star demanded the occasional sacrifice of a human captive to remember his efforts to create humankind. The ceremony was held irregularly, and sometimes years passed between performances. These blood sacrifices were intended to *sustain* life rather than destroy it. Death was necessary to allow the sacred powers to continue the process of creation. Furthermore, the Skiris believed that although the victim died, her spirit became a star in the heavens, where she would shine brightly forever as one of Morning Star's wives.[17]

"THEY INTEND TO WIPE US OUT AND BURN OUR VILLAGE": GENOCIDAL WARFARE WITH THE PAAHIKSUKAT (LAKOTAS) AND SAAHE (CHEYENNES)

Although the Pawnees saw warfare as a contest between spiritual powers that sometimes ended with a human sacrifice, nothing prepared them for genocidal conflict with the Lakotas and Cheyennes, who, supplied with guns and horses, invaded their territories in the seventeenth and eighteenth centuries. Warfare with the Lakotas and Cheyennes was particularly traumatic because it resulted in disturbingly high mortality rates. The Lakotas especially made it no secret that they desired to wipe the Pawnees from the face of the earth.

To apply the term "genocide" to this war is certain to raise eyebrows. Still, it most accurately describes the actions of the Lakotas and the Cheyennes, who at this time posed a greater threat to the Pawnee people than the U.S. Army or Euro-American settlers. To be sure, whites endangered Pawnee culture and existence by exploiting natural resources (such as wood, grass, and game), by introducing diseases, and by advocating the destruction of Pawnee ways of life. But the Lakotas and Cheyennes intended to physically exterminate the Pawnees, and their actions to accomplish this had a devastating and demoralizing effect on the Pawnee people.[18]

Today the Pawnees, Lakotas, and Cheyennes enjoy friendly relations and admire each other's cultural accomplishments, but this was not the case in the nineteenth century, when they fought bitter wars of annihilation against each other. To be sure, the Lakotas and Cheyennes fell victim to genocide at the hands of Euro-American invaders. The massacres of Cheyennes at Sand Creek (1864) and Lakotas at Wounded Knee (1890) are only two examples of acts of genocide. The deliberate destruction of the bison, violation of treaty rights, appropriation of territories, harassment by settlers, systematic dismantling of culture by the U.S. government's "civilization" program, the placement of children in boarding schools or non-Indian foster families, sterilization programs, economic neglect by the federal government, and so on meet present-day criteria of genocide and ethnocide (the intentional destruction of a people's cultural identity). Still, the evidence is compelling that the Lakotas and Cheyennes were capable of perpetrating genocidal acts as well.[19]

This should not come as a surprise. Genocide scholars argue that mass killings and attempts to wipe out social groups can be found in "all stages of human existence, and nearly all parts of the world have known genocide at one time or another, often repeatedly."[20] American Indians were no exception. Among examples of acts of genocide are the aforementioned Crow Creek Massacre in South Dakota in 1325, the Haudenoshaunee (Iroquois) wars against the Hurons, and the destruction of Awat'ovi Pueblo by other Puebloans in 1700.[21]

To be fair, Native-against-Native genocide was often linked to European and Euro-American settler colonialism. For example, the presence of Euro-Americans forced the Haudenoshaunee into ever-more-destructive wars of conquest to secure trapping and hunting territories.[22] The Awat'ovi had endangered the Pueblo moral order by aligning themselves too closely with the Spanish and by mixing Catholic religion with traditional Pueblo religious practices. Likewise, the war between the Pawnees and the Lakotas and Cheyennes was predicated on the expansion of white settlements to the east and the white man's guns and horses, which made the plains an attractive area for the Lakotas and Cheyennes to settle as well.

Considering acts of genocide perpetrated against American Indians *by the United States*, genocide scholar Adam Jones distinguishes between (1) genocidal massacres; (2) biological warfare, using pathogens (especially smallpox) to which the indigenous people had no resistance; (3) spreading of disease via the "reduction" of Indians to densely crowded and unhygienic settlements; (4) slavery and forced/indentured labor, especially though not exclusively in Latin America, in conditions often rivaling those of Nazi concentration camps; (5) mass population removals to barren reservations, sometimes involving death marches en route and generally leading to widespread mortality and population collapse upon arrival; (6) deliberate starvation and famine, exacerbated by destruction and occupation of the Native land base and food resources; and (7) forced education of indigenous children in white-run schools, where mortality rates sometimes reached genocidal levels. Some of these very same acts, however, were also committed against the Pawnees by their Native enemies.

Based on Jones's admittedly presentist standards, there is no doubt that U.S. policies had genocidal outcomes. These policies forced the Pawnees onto ever-shrinking reservations before their final relocation to Oklahoma, where many died from lack of food, poor sanitation, inadequate medical care, exhaustion, and homesickness. Later, the U.S. government forced Pawnee children to attend distant boarding schools, where many died from diseases such as tuberculosis. Still, although on occasion settlers murdered Pawnees and caused the impoverishment of the Pawnee people, state-sponsored genocidal massacres of Pawnees did not occur.

In contrast, the Lakota genocide of the Pawnees was almost entirely military. Lakotas massacred Pawnees on various occasions, and their attacks also forced the Pawnees to reorganize into densely packed and unhygienic towns to protect themselves more efficiently. The result of this reorganization was a greater susceptibility to infectious diseases, which weakened and further demoralized the people. The Lakotas also threatened the Pawnees with starvation and famine by plundering or destroying Pawnee food stores, killing women working in their gardens to disrupt food production, and stealing Pawnee horses or ambushing hunters to disrupt annual summer hunts.

One might argue that this was just part of Plains Indian warfare, but the matter is not so simple. From the perspective of the Pawnees, the main invaders at this time were not the whites but the nomadic tribes who sought to establish their dominance on the plains. Like the Comanches in the South and the Blackfeet in the North, the Lakotas and Cheyennes sought to impose their supremacy on the central plains at the expense of sedentary tribes such as the Pawnees and the Arikaras.[23] The Lakotas waged war against them to obtain monopolies on buffalo, horses, and the gun trade. As buffalo populations dwindled, warfare intensified further, much like the Haudenoshaunee wars against the Hurons had intensified in the American Northeast.[24]

On various occasions, the Lakotas stated their determination to "wipe out" the Pawnee Nation completely. Of course, this could simply have been rhetoric used to intimidate enemies or to raise one's own courage. Indeed, Plains Indian tribes frequently wished each other "dead and gone," but the Lakotas (and to a lesser extent the Cheyennes) backed up their words with actions.

The Lakotas and Cheyennes brought Pawnee society to the brink of collapse with military strategies of annihilation and attrition. The desire to annihilate the Pawnee people prompted the Cheyennes in 1830 to carry sacred arrows, their most revered sacred tribal objects, into battle against the Pawnees, believing the arrows would give them near-invincible powers.[25] In a remarkable feat of bravery, the Pawnees captured the sacred arrows, thus forcing the Cheyennes to abandon the fight and scale back (but not abandon) future attacks against them.[26]

If large-scale attacks were dangerous, the attritional effect of small-scale raids targeting Pawnee women was perhaps even more disruptive. The loss of women meant not only reduced reproductive power but loss of agricultural productivity as well. Furthermore, because the Pawnees suffered from a chronic lack of weapons, they were unable to defend themselves or their families adequately. In 1832 Indian agent John Dougherty noted that the Skiri Pawnees had a total of seven guns to protect themselves. Despite heroic resistance with bows and arrows, the Skiris were "soon convinced that they could not compete against powder & Ball."[27]

Lakota and Cheyenne attacks caused great anxiety among agency and mission personnel as well. In 1837 Pawnee missionary Samuel Allis (1805–83) wrote, "The Agt. is here now thinks it not safe to settle among them until something is done to effect a peace between them and the Sioux."[28] Four years later, Allis reported that the Pawnees numbered about seven thousand souls but that they "are wasteing away fast." Allis believed that warfare was one of the main causes, for he wrote next: "There was a war party of Loups [Skiris] fought with the Shiennes [Cheyennes] last spring, when 50 of them were killed, and also many of the Shiennes."[29] In September 1842, agency farmer George Belcher Gaston wrote, "The Pawnees have returned from their summer hunt & are verry poor & in consequence of government neglecting to send them such Annuitys as they want & the distruction of their village by the Sioux they are allmost discouraged though I think they will rebuild their village."[30]

On June 27, 1843, the Lakotas staged a massive attack against the Pawnees in which they captured all Pawnee horses (about two hundred) and set fire to twenty of the forty-one lodges in the town. The Pawnees defended themselves well in this "Battle of Burned Town," but the Lakotas were superiorly armed and mounted. The outcome was devastating. The Pawnees suffered sixty-seven people dead and twenty-six wounded. Among the casualties were some of the best and bravest men. However, women and children were killed as well when they ran in a panic from their lodges toward the river. The loss of horses and property was great as well. Losing their mounts meant that the Pawnees would not be able to go on their annual summer hunt.[31] "It would take some 8,000 or 10,000 [dollars]," Missionary John Dunbar (1804–1857) estimated, "to make the property of the Pawnees as good as the day before the fight."[32] Dunbar concluded his report by stating, "The Sioux boast that they intend to exterminate the tribes south of them—as the Pawnees, Delawares, Shawnees, Kickapoos, Potawatomies, &c."[33] After the June 27 attack, the Pawnees moved their village. "When I informed the Pawnees of the Sioux' threat to exterminate them," Dunbar wrote on November 14, 1843, "they moved up to the village where the Loups settled about two miles above where they have remained ever since."[34]

That the Lakotas were serious about their threat is evident from Allis's report from July 21, 1843, in which he estimated that the Lakotas had killed "from 200 to 250 Pawnees" and stolen some four hundred horses since the first of March. "We are at the entire mercy of the Sioux," he lamented.[35] If Allis's numbers are correct, and between 200 and 250 of an estimated 7,000

Pawnees were killed in less than five months (a mortality rate of 2.85 to 3.57 percent), at this rate, the entire Pawnee nation would be completely eradicated within a decade and a half. In reality, the extermination was much faster, because the economic and reproductive power of the Pawnees (the ability to hunt, cultivate gardens, bear children, and care for children) was affected by stress and deprivation, resulting in a more exponential rate of population decline.

Occasionally the Lakotas employed scorched earth tactics that affected Pawnee subsistence. Allis reported that the barrage of attacks by enemy tribes resulted in severe economic losses and loss of food supplies. "All of their corn is *veery much* injured," he wrote, and he concluded that the Pawnees were in real danger of starving to death.[36] Less than a year later, Dunbar wrote that over the past year, the Skiris "were so harassed by the Sioux, that they raised little or no corn; and in the winter the [Skiris] and the larger part of the [Pitahawiratas], who hunted together, were repeatedly attacked by the Sioux, who succeeded in preventing them from hunting much, and indeed took from many of them all the provisions they had, and everything else of any value." Meanwhile, the Otoes, who had been targeted by the Lakotas as well, plundered the Pawnee fields in their absence. In their desperation, the Pawnees began to steal corn from the missionaries.[37] Disrupting Pawnee hunts continued year after year. In 1847, for example, Lakota warriors reportedly killed eighty-three Pawnee hunters.[38]

Fear of Lakota and Cheyenne ambushes prevented the Pawnees from participating in the Fort Laramie peace conference in 1851. A reporter for the *Missouri Republic* wrote that the Pawnees "are now almost the only tribe upon which the Sioux, Cheyennes and Arrapahoes make war." He concluded: "It is probable that they will suffer very much this winter."[39]

Despite promises in the 1857 treaty to protect the Pawnees if they moved north of the Platte River, the federal government failed to commit enough troops to defend the Pawnee reservation. Thus Lakota threats of extermination continued into the 1860s.[40] After one attack in June 1860, Pawnee agent J. L. Gillis wrote in desperation, "[T]here will soon be a vacancy in the Agency or no use for an Agent, for, as in the expressive language of the Indian, the Pawnees will soon be wiped out."[41]

Despite desperate calls from concerned Indian agents like Gillis, each year the attackers returned, killing women and seriously disrupting the Pawnee economy. The war culminated in the tragedy near present-day Trenton, Nebraska, where a large Lakota war party wiped out sixty-nine Pawnee men, women, and children on their summer hunt while government agents stood by helplessly. The tragedy at "Massacre Canyon" on August 5, 1873, was an important reason for the Pawnees leaving their Nebraska homelands to settle in Oklahoma.

From the Pawnee perspective, the behavior of the Lakotas and Cheyennes was unmistakably genocidal. This does not provide an after-the-fact justification for U.S. conquest of the Lakotas and Cheyennes. Instead, one might argue that by not providing the Pawnees with protection as promised in its treaties, the United States was in fact criminally negligent and complicit in the destruction of the Pawnee people. Indeed, the United States indirectly benefited when the Pawnees decided to leave their ancestral homelands for Oklahoma.[42]

PAWNEE DIPLOMATIC EFFORTS TO PREVENT ANNIHILATION

Before enemy pressure forced them to leave Nebraska, the Pawnees had considered other strategies. As early as 1816, they hoped to establish closer trading and diplomatic ties with the United States to counterbalance the Lakota and Cheyenne threat. One of the first steps to remove diplomatic obstacles with the United States was to end the sacrifice of a human captive in the Morning Star ceremony. In 1816 and 1819, two Pawnee chiefs, Piitariisaaru' (Man Chief) and his father, Riiciriisaaru' (Knife Chief), tried to prevent the sacrifice of a captive in the ceremony.[43]

The strategy seemed to work at first. In 1821 several chiefs went on a tour to Baltimore, Philadelphia, New York, and Washington, D.C. Among them was Man Chief, who received a medal commemorating his daring rescue of the captive woman in 1816.[44] Treaties of friendship followed in 1825 and 1833. In the 1833 treaty, the Pawnees agreed to cede their territory south of the Platte River to the United States in exchange for annual payments, schools, and "twenty-five guns, with suitable ammunition, [to be placed] in the hands of the [government] farmers of each village, to be used in case of an attack from hostile bands."[45] Agency farmers, however, were reluctant to hand out the weapons for fear they might be used to start wars. Indeed, as pointed out above, the United States reneged on its promises to defend the Pawnee people. Not until the United States itself became embroiled in war with the Lakotas and Cheyennes in the mid-1860s did it reluctantly reach out to the Pawnees for mutual assistance.[46] Until that time, however, the Pawnees had to face the Lakotas and Cheyennes alone.

In 1834 the Pawnees also allowed the aforementioned ministers Samuel Allis and John Dunbar to establish a Christian mission among the Pawnees.

Both came from Massachusetts and went west on behalf of the American Board of Commissioners for Foreign Mission of the Presbyterian Church in Boston. During their first year, Dunbar joined the South Band Pawnees, while Allis joined the Skiris to learn the respective North and South Band languages. In 1839 they constructed permanent buildings on the Loup River, about one hundred miles from the town of Bellevue, Nebraska. Despite their energy and enthusiasm, they were unsuccessful in converting Pawnees to Christianity. Still, the Pawnees learned important lessons, and the rise of Pahukatawa shows some intriguing parallels with the death and resurrection of Jesus Christ. Although the missionaries wrote letter after letter about the devastation wreaked upon the Pawnees by the Lakotas, their pleas for government action fell upon deaf ears. Indeed, Lakota pressure, coupled with internal tensions, caused Dunbar and Allis to abandon the mission in 1846.[47]

A third option was to seek an alliance with the Arikara Indians. In July 1825, a Skiri delegation under Knife Chief visited the Arikaras.[48] Details of the meeting were not recorded, but it appears that Knife Chief invited the Arikaras to join the Skiris in Nebraska to form a common defense against the Lakotas. The Arikaras declined at this time, but after a series of Lakota attacks in 1832, the Arikara leaders agreed to move south to live with their Skiri relatives. Chief Big Axe of the Skiris was pleased to see them, for he hoped they would provide military assistance. Allis estimated the number of Arikaras at twenty-two hundred.[49]

Despite providing additional manpower against the Lakotas, the Arikaras were reluctant to take up arms against the Cheyennes, with whom they were friendly. Worse, Arikara relations with the South Band Pawnees were strained. In the spring of 1835, some Arikara young men stole some Kitkehahki horses and Arikara hunting expeditions trespassing into Pawnee hunting grounds irritated South Band chiefs.[50] In December 1835, the Arikara relationship with the Skiris also came under pressure. That winter the Skiris were unable to find any buffalo on account of the Arikaras, who camped between them and the buffalo herds. The Arikaras refused a Skiri invitation to hunt together. By 1836 relations were so poor that the Arikaras decided to leave the Pawnee country, move north, and settle near Fort Clark, a fur trading post on the Missouri River.[51]

Though the Arikaras had been an annoyance, their departure left the Pawnees to face the Lakotas and Cheyennes alone again. They received help from an unexpected quarter: a scalped man named Pahukatawa returned from the dead to help his people. He became the greatest prophet that the Pawnees ever had.

"I WAS BROUGHT TO LIFE AGAIN THAT I MIGHT SAVE MY PEOPLE FROM STARVATION AND FROM THEIR ENEMIES": PAHUKATAWA, THE PAWNEE PROPHET

One day in the early 1830s, a Lakota war party surprised five Pawnee Indians trapping beaver. Four of the Pawnees escaped to the hills, but the Lakotas killed the remaining man and dismembered his body. When the Pawnees returned later that spring to collect the bones of their slain friend, they found only arrows and bullets. His remains had disappeared.

Several years later, the slain man's spirit returned from the dead. His name was Pahukatawa (Hills along the Banks of a River, or Knee Print by the Water).[52] He had come to help his people, who at this time were extremely desperate as a result of the war with the Lakotas and Cheyennes. Pahukatawa gave the people strength and hope. He promised to protect them from diseases and inspire them to many victories against their enemies, thus preserving the Pawnees from extinction.

Because he had survived death and mutilation, Pahukatawa was in effect the ultimate scalped man. Several versions of his story exist. The main sources include Roaming Scout, a Skiri Pawnee priest; James R. Murie, who conducted much ethnographical work in the early 1900s; Lone Chief, a Skiri chief and owner of the Morning Star bundle; John Brown Dunbar, son of the Presbyterian missionary to the Pawnees in the 1830s and 1840s; George Bird Grinnell, an ethnographer; and Samuel Osborne, son of a Pawnee scout and a graduate of Haskell Institute. Although their accounts differ in details, they agree with each other in outline.[53]

According to these sources, Pahukatawa was the son of Hikus (Breath) and brother of Kawaharu (Wind Ready to Give), both of whom were stars in the northern sky. His mother was an ordinary woman, providing an interesting parallel with Jesus, who was the Son of God and born of the Virgin Mary. Although the tale of his origins may have been apocryphal, Pahukatawa eventually assumed his station in the northern sky alongside Hikus and Kawaharu.[54]

The sources provide conflicting accounts about Pahukatawa's death. According to Roaming Scout, Pahukatawa died while trapping beavers.[55] Lone Chief stated that he was killed while hunting,[56] and in Samuel Osborne's version, Pahukatawa was looking for horses when the Lakotas surprised him. In any case, when his friends returned the next spring to recover his remains, they found only arrows, bullets, and other rubbish, but no corpse. Grinnell added that the Lakotas had thrown Pahukatawa's body parts into a river.

All accounts agree that the animals took pity on Pahukatawa and put him back together, by dancing around him until he was alive again. But the animals could not find Pahukatawa's scalp or brains because crows had eaten them. They replaced the brains with some downy feathers, but Pahukatawa would have trouble speaking thereafter.

It is unclear in what year Pahukatawa returned from the dead, but according to Lone Chief, the spirit first visited an old friend. Samuel Osborne, however, claimed that Pahukatawa first visited his mother, who had cried so much over the loss of her son that she had gone blind. Pahukatawa restored her vision as the first of a series of miracles. Most sources claim that Pahukatawa visited a man, possibly his brother. Only Murie provides a name for this individual: "Coming Sun," a name bestowed by Pahukatawa himself.[57]

According to Murie, Pahukatawa first appeared as a voice, which told the man he would soon name Coming Sun to meet him on a hill and offer tobacco in his honor. Instead of finding Pahukatawa, Coming Sun encountered a mountain lion, then a bear, and finally the leader of an enemy war party. Each time, Coming Sun backed away in fear. Pahukatawa scorned him for his cowardice but gave him one last chance. When he appeared as a charging buffalo bull, Coming Sun closed his eyes and stood his ground. When he opened his eyes, Pahukatawa stood before him dressed in a fine buffalo robe and buckskin leggings.[58] He wore "a whole eagle on his back and in his right hand held a staff six feet long upon which was tied eagle down." Pahukatawa blessed Coming Sun with the power of prophecy. Pahukatawa told him to repeat his words to the people. "I have great power from the gods in the heavens and on the earth," he told Coming Sun. "I was brought to life again that I might save my people from starvation and from their enemies."[59]

Pahukatawa left the robe, leggings, staff, and eagle amulet behind. It was at this point that he bestowed the name Coming Sun on the man he had revealed himself to. The name symbolized rebirth after the dormant but revitalizing stage of night. Indeed, the name symbolizes a new era in Pawnee life: through Coming Sun, Pahukatawa presented himself as a savior.[60]

One night, Pahukatawa warned Coming Sun about an upcoming attack by the Lakotas and other tribes. "They will make war upon us," Pahukatawa said. "I have come to tell you so you can warn the people." He added that the Lakotas and their allies "intend to wipe us out and burn our village." The next day Coming Sun alerted Chief Big-Eagle, and the chiefs and headmen gathered in council. There Pahukatawa's spirit appeared to them in a fire, first as a buffalo sitting down, next as an eagle, and briefly as a person. Pahukatawa instructed Coming Sun to perform the One Horn Buffalo Dance (One Horn).[61]

Pahukatawa returned over subsequent days. One time he instructed the people to build "a high embankment around the village." Another time he said that the enemy was so near that it was time for the people to dance and imitate the animals. On this occasion, he also noticed skeptics among the Skiris: "They are now coming in and I must make myself visible to them for many still doubt me," he said. "They do not believe I am here."[62] While dancing, each dancer asked for a brave deed in battle. Some wanted to kill enemies; others asked for coups or scalps. An old man wished to strike twelve men and take a prisoner, whom he pledged to hand over to the women of the tribe so that they could torture him. Pahukatawa promised to grant all their wishes.

Not everyone believed Pahukatawa's prophecies. In fact, many did not think that Pahukatawa was real. Among them was a young man who asked Pahukatawa to be wounded or killed in the upcoming battle. Of this young man, Pahukatawa said, "That young man has no faith in me, but what he says will come true."[63]

On the day of the battle, Pahukatawa first appeared as a buffalo to alert the people that the enemy had launched the attack. Then he took the shape of a rain cloud to wet the enemy's weapons and render them useless. Finally he appeared in the shape of a wolf to signal to the people that they should get behind the breastworks. In Samuel Osborne's account, Pahukatawa also appeared as the wind.

All happened as Pahukatawa had prophesied. The old man struck twelve enemies and captured the war leader. The young man who had mocked Pahukatawa with his wish to die in battle also received what he had asked for.

In return for his help, Pahukatawa demanded that the people honor him with the One Horn Buffalo Dance. "When I was living among you, I valued the One Horn of you people—the dance named One Horn. You must dance that One Horn," he said. "When one dances it, one must be painted with white clay and one must wear on his head the scalp of a buffalo bull."[64]

The name of the dance probably referred to the single buffalo horn that dancers attached on the right side of their war bonnets. The members of this dance (*raris arika*) were young men eligible to go to war. According to Murie, the dance "was only held when Pahukatawa ordered it and then only before an attack by the enemy." Each dancer imitated a particular animal and was painted in the color of his particular spirit guardian. Murie specifically listed crows (black), jackrabbits (white), buffalo, and bears (yellow or red). A large drum painted according to Pahukatawa's instructions provided the rhythm. It was black, with four buffalo skull designs on the side and four flints tied inside. The purpose of the war dance was "to teach the men how to act during battle and to remind them that there was a being who watched over them and gave them courage."[65]

Murie recorded the lyrics of two One Horn Dance songs from White Horse, a member of the Pitahawirata band, who had learned the songs from the Skiris.[66] The songs relate episodes from the Pahukatawa story.

First Song	**Second Song**
Here I do speak	The same I do say
The dance is coming	The dance is coming
As he tells of the vision	The same it is the place
(chorus)	(chorus)
The dance is coming	The dance is coming
The dance is coming	The dance is coming
The dance is coming	The dance is coming
The dance is coming	The dance is coming
The dance is coming	The dance is coming
The dance is coming	The dance is coming
Now they are happy in spirit	Oh, I am indeed pitiable
The dance is coming	The dance is coming
Now (that) they have smoked	My grandfather is listening (to my song)
(chorus)	(chorus)
Now I tell of it	Now I tell of him
The dance is coming	The dance is coming
The one who has flares	A person wonderful
(chorus)	(chorus)
Now it has stopped	Now it has stopped
The dance is coming	The dance is coming
The old One Horn Dance	(The song of) the person who is different
(chorus)	(chorus)

These were probably the opening songs of a larger set of songs belonging to the One Horn Dance. Other songs may have told of the many wonderful things that Pahukatawa did for his people. In any case, the One Horn Dance strengthened the people.[67]

But the faction of disbelievers remained strong. After a while, feeling unappreciated and ignored, Pahukatawa left. The accounts vary on the exact circumstances of his departure. In Lone Chief's version, Pahukatawa departed because one day nobody wished to smoke with him.[68] Roaming Scout explained that Pahukatawa left to live among other Indians after some Skiris had spoken disrespectfully about him. According to Murie, Coming Sun's successor one night refused to visit with Pahukatawa because he was sleepy. In any case, offended by these slights, Pahukatawa left earth and ascended to the northern sky. He would stay there forever but said that "he would help the people when they called on him."[69] This completed Pahukatawa's transformation from human to spirit to star power.

The Reverend Samuel Allis provided an entirely different (and probably inaccurate) version of events. According to Allis, by 1836 Pahukatawa had sided with the Lakotas against his own people:

> They had a skirmish with the Sioux, but had no success from the fact that there was an Indian with the Sioux who was once a Pawnee. He had been killed in battle by their enemies, and left on the battlefield to be devoured by the wolves and ravens. The wolves finally gathered his bones together, and restored him to life, when he went among other tribes, on account of the barbarous treatment of his own people in leaving him to be so devoured. And whenever he came to war with the enemy it was useless for the Pawnees to fight, for their guns would flash in the pan, and their bow-strings break. His name was Pahocatawa—I do not know the meaning. He will probably exist as long as there is a Pawnee; they report having seen him several times. They also say that if an Indian or squaw is scalped alive in any tribe, he or she is discarded, and goes to live with a scalped tribe under ground—probably meaning dugouts.[70]

Allis's description, with its claim that Pahukatawa had been restored to life by wolves and that he was immediately antagonistic to the Pawnees, is problematic. Allis also described Pahukatawa as a sort of "devil." This negative description is not entirely surprising because Allis believed that Pahukatawa competed with Jesus Christ for the devotion of the Pawnee people. Perhaps

Allis was also inspired by Skiri traditionalists who saw in Pahukatawa a rival to Morning Star and who spoke badly of him.

Grinnell's sources believed that before he ascended to the heavens, Pahukatawa lived among the Arikaras.[71] The Arikara version of the Pahukatawa story is very different from that of the Pawnees. The Arikaras said that the Cheyennes had killed him and that he was brought back to life by a mysterious mist or cloud that carried his body away. In any event, after abandoning the Pawnees, he joined the Arikaras, among whom he lived for a long time. He even had one or more children by an Arikara woman. Pahukatawa's Arikara grandson told Grinnell that he had once seen Pahukatawa. "He was described as a man, having feet like a wolf, and wearing a robe made of wolf skins," Grinnell wrote. "The old man who told this—whose name was also Pahukatawá—went toward the form, intending to speak to it, but when he came close to it, it suddenly disappeared."[72]

Among the Pawnees meanwhile, Pahukatawa became a revered celestial power. According to the Skiri Pawnee smoke sacrifice, he was the seventh of the major powers to receive smoke, after Tiiraawaahat; Morning Star; Evening Star; the big black meteoric star; his father, Hikus; and his brother Kawaharu. Interestingly, he received smoke before Sun and Moon. One head priest explained the significance of the smoke offering:

> Now priests, young men, and you chiefs who rule over the people, this offering will be made to Ready To Give; the son of Ready To Give stands there. When he was upon the earth, he taught us to keep our villages clean so that disease would not enter them. It was he who came to warn our people of the approach of the enemy. He assists his father [Hikus] in sending buffalo. He assists the warriors to capture ponies. When we are near the village of the enemy, ponies come out on account of his power. He is Pahukatawa (Knee Prints Upon The River Bank).[73]

"HE WAS KILLED . . . EVEN AS CHRIST WAS KILLED": PAHUKATAWA, MORNING STAR, AND JESUS

Although present-day Pawnees vow that he was important and wonderful, Pahukatawa remains a mystery to this day. The ethnohistorical record is sparse about his life and death. However, by placing Pahukatawa in the context of his time, it is possible to gain more insight into his mystery. For example, his reappearance more or less coincided with the arrival of the first Christian missionaries among the Pawnees in the mid-1830s. Equally intriguing is that

Pahukatawa's rise as a sacred power coincided with a crisis in the worship of Morning Star, the powerful cosmic warrior whose marriage to Evening Star had resulted in the creation of the Pawnee people.[74]

Many present-day Pawnees compare Pahukatawa to Jesus. Like Jesus, Pahukatawa rose from the dead, performed miracles such as healing sick and heartbroken people, and eventually ascended to heaven. Early scholars also noted similarities between Jesus Christ and Pahukatawa. In the 1880s John Brown Dunbar believed that Pawnee religion had appropriated ideas from Christianity. "Much of their system," Dunbar wrote, "has been manifestly borrowed, perhaps remotely, from the Christian religion."[75] Undoubtedly Dunbar was referring specifically to the worship of Pahukatawa.

Dunbar, who grew up among the Pawnees in the 1830s and early 1840s, observed that the Pawnees listed Pahukatawa after Tiiraawaahat and "spirits" as one of the most important powers at that time.[76] Dunbar's account depicted Pahukatawa as both savior *and* "devil," who sometimes aided the enemy because his friends had abandoned him at the time of his death. In other words, Dunbar's Pahukatawa is ambivalent. But the ambivalence that baffled Dunbar reflects the controversial status that Pahukatawa enjoyed among the Skiri Pawnees in the 1830s and 1840s.[77]

Roaming Scout also saw many similarities between Pahukatawa and Jesus. According to Roaming Scout, Pahukatawa said, "There is another person, a person who lives there in the east [Jesus]. You will learn that he is like I am. He knows of the Heavens. . . . You people are going to learn from him. I am just like that one." There can be no doubt that he was referring to Jesus Christ.[78]

The link between Jesus and Pahukatawa should not be surprising. After all, the Pawnees had invited Allis and Dunbar among them to learn more about the white man's religion. Even though they did not reject Christianity, the Pawnees did not convert either. Instead, it appears as if the lessons of Christianity found a new expression in Pahukatawa. Like Jesus, he was born of a heavenly father and an earthly mother. Also like Jesus, as mentioned by Osborne, Pahukatawa was a healer. According to Murie, Pahukatawa carried a staff, which immediately bring to mind portraits of Jesus holding a shepherd's staff. Like Jesus also, not everyone immediately accepted him as a savior; he was tortured and murdered. Finally, like Jesus, Pahukatawa ascended to the heavens.

Still, major differences between Jesus and Pahukatawa make the comparison problematic. Pahukatawa was not a peacemaker but a patron power of warriors. He promised not eternal life in the hereafter but survival on earth. He promised to help the people to victory against their enemies. In this regard, Pahukatawa resembled Morning Star more closely than Jesus.

Rather than treating Pahukatawa as a form of Christian–Pawnee *syncretism*, it seems more accurate to view him as a form of religious *synthesis*. Syncretism involves the blending of two or more religions, in which one religion absorbs ("colonizes") the other.[79] Examples of syncretism are the Ghost Dance and peyote religions of the late nineteenth century, in which Jesus Christ plays an important role.[80] In contrast, in synthesis, something entirely new is created. It is radically different from both the indigenous and the alien religion. Even though Pahukatawa shared certain commonalities with Jesus Christ and Morning Star, he was nevertheless a completely separate power. He was an entirely new addition to the Pawnee pantheon. This would also explain why Christians like Allis and traditionalist Skiri Pawnees objected to him when he first appeared. Still, although some initially viewed him with suspicion, Pahukatawa eventually found acceptance among all Pawnees and so revitalized the Pawnee people. Unlike the revitalizing Ghost Dance and peyote religions, however, Pahukatawa resulted not from Euro-American acculturation pressures but from genocidal warfare with the Lakotas and Cheyennes. This makes him rather unique in the literature of American Indian revitalization movements.[81]

My theory that Pahukatawa arose in response to genocidal warfare, and that he displayed both traditional elements (borrowed from scalped men and Morning Star) and new elements (Jesus Christ) to become something entirely new, throws new light upon a famous event in Pawnee history: the attempt by Knife Chief and Man Chief to end the sacrifice of a human to Morning Star. As mentioned earlier, the first attempt to prevent the sacrifice of a female captive in 1816 may have served diplomatic purposes. Although contemporary white audiences depicted the rescue as a dramatic last-minute event, in reality, twenty-year-old Man Chief probably announced his intentions to free the captive in advance, thus risking the wrath of Morning Star and the scorn of Skiri supporters of the sacrifice.[82]

Around this time, Knife Chief and Man Chief also rescued another captive, a Spanish boy, and ransomed him back to Oklahoma. By 1827, however, both these chiefs were dead. When the Skiris prepared to sacrifice a captive Cheyenne girl that year, Indian agent John Dougherty directed a rescue operation, but he watched helplessly when angry Skiris killed the captive before the rescuers could make their escape.[83]

The attempts to interfere with the sacrifice caused much resentment and opposition among conservative Skiris. If Knife Chief, Man Chief, and other reformers sought to make a favorable impression with the United States, then they scored a diplomatic success: Man Chief became a celebrity when he visited the eastern states in 1821.[84] However, while eastern audiences celebrated Man Chief, many people at home considered his actions highly controversial. His rescue attempts created serious tensions between traditionalist Skiris and those who supported Man Chief, the reformer.

The Skiri people were in a difficult position: their Morning Star ceremony was under scrutiny internally and externally (including by South Band Pawnees and the U.S. government). In this situation, Pahukatawa appeared with his message of hope and promise to assist them against the Lakotas. However, Skiri traditionalists, who favored Morning Star, rejected Pahukatawa, depicting him as a false power. Eventually they accused him of actively assisting the Lakotas.[85]

The traditionalists suffered a major blow in 1838 when a Skiri war party returned with twenty Lakota women and children who carried the lethal smallpox virus with them. Soon the disease devastated the Pawnees, killing mostly children under thirteen or fourteen years of age. According to missionary Dunbar, the Skiris hoped to reverse their misfortune by sacrificing one of the captives to Morning Star.[86] This decision backfired terribly. "As soon as the report of this sacrifice reached the Sioux," wrote Father Pierre-Jean DeSmet, who traveled the region at this time, "they burned with the desire to avenge their honor, and bound themselves by oaths that they would not rest until they had killed as many Pawnees as their innocent victim had bones or joints in her body."[87] True to their word, the Lakotas forged an alliance with the Cheyenne, Arapaho, Kiowa, Kiowa Apache, and Comanche tribes in 1840, with the objective to punish the Pawnees.[88]

In the aftermath of this dual calamity, a growing number of Skiris turned toward Pahukatawa and the One Horn Dance. Although the Skiris continued to perform the Morning Star ceremony by substituting the human captive with cloth and other objects, Pahukatawa's One Horn Dance became more prominent in the Pawnee ceremonial repertoire.

The tensions between "traditionalists" and "reformers" may explain John Brown Dunbar's and Samuel Allis's observations that some Skiri Pawnees viewed Pahukatawa as an "evil" spirit while others considered him a savior. Traditionalists who favored a strict observation of the Morning Star religion attributed bad luck and misfortune to Pahukatawa in an attempt to undermine his growing popularity. At the same time, One Horn Dancers and others championed the worship of Pahukatawa.

It appears, then, that Pahukatawa was not fully accepted as a true sacred power until 1838 or shortly thereafter. From this time on, he would receive smoke offerings during Skiri bundle ceremonies.[89]

The worship of Pahukatawa declined after the Pawnees moved to Oklahoma and the threat of genocidal warfare disappeared. It was revived, however, during the Ghost Dance years in the early 1890s, after social circumstances had changed once again.

This time, the Pawnees faced a different kind of genocide: the destruction of their language and culture (ethnocide) at the hands of Euro-American agents of "civilization." Pahukatawa returned once more to give the people hope. This "second coming," however, showed a Pahukatawa who was closer to Jesus than to Morning Star. In *The Pawnee Ghost Dance Hand Game* (1933), Alexander Lesser reported that the Pawnees now interpreted Pahukatawa in distinctly Christian terms. While talking about the smoke offering in the One Horn Dance, a priest told Lesser, "Pahukatawa is the Holy Ghost." The priest added:

> The Holy Ghost is placed in the North, the same way as the North Star. Everything is supposed to go around him. The Holy Ghost is also thought to be the Morning Star in the East because God sent Christ in the East.[90]

Lesser believed that Pawnee conceptions of Pahukatawa and the Holy Ghost were inconsistent because they linked Pahukatawa with Jesus's crucifixion while also associating Jesus with the Morning Star. However, this merely suggests that Pawnee philosophers in the 1890s were trying to synthesize the different teachings into a single coherent system. One man told Lesser, "This man [Pahukatawa] was killed in spite of his good ways, even as Christ was killed, in spite of the fact that he knew everything that happened and would happen on earth and in heaven." According to this source, a spirit bird raised Pahukatawa up to heaven, "and he came to life again." Later "he went away [and] became the Morning Star."[91]

It is difficult to reconstruct the history of Pahukatawa beliefs from the early twentieth century to the present, but it is safe to say that he never truly left the Pawnee people. The Pawnee people today continue to hold Pahukatawa in awe. However, as in the past, he is viewed with a mix of reverence and fear. Some Pawnees consider him to be so sacred that they will not speak his name out loud but will only whisper it softly.[92] Other Pawnees refuse to say his name at all because they fear he might return and cause trouble. These Pawnees treat his name with extreme reverence and caution. Still, all present-day Pawnees agree that he was a powerful being who "represented what was mysterious and holy."[93] As Pawnee historian Roger C. Echo-Hawk explains:

The story of Pahukatawa today carries many resonations in Pawneeland. For some it is a curious tale of the ancient mysteries and hidden powers of the world. For others it serves as an enduring reminder of the ceremonial and religious cycles that long ago shaped what it meant to be Pawnee. But for many Pawnees of the early twentieth century, Pawnee mysticism and Christian mysticism found common ground in the story of a man who died and became a divinity. For these Pawnees, Pahukatawa helped to open an ideological door, a narrative passageway that both affirmed Pawnee tradition and validated new forms of religious life.[94]

CONCLUSION

As I try to show in this chapter, the trauma of warfare with the Lakotas and Cheyennes resulted in a dramatic increase in the number of scalped men among the Pawnees. Originally, the Pawnees viewed these unfortunate beings as terrifying "monsters" who could cause harm to the people. However, as the wars with the Lakotas and Cheyennes took on more genocidal characteristics, scalped people were increasingly seen as potential sources of spiritual power.

Genocidal warfare caused a great spiritual crisis among the Pawnees. Traditional powers such as Morning Star no longer seemed to provide sufficient protection. Desperate for new ways to counter the enemy threat, Skiri chiefs Man Chief and Knife Chief sought to abolish the practice of human sacrifice to Morning Star to obtain the support of the United States. In the mid-1830s, the Pawnees also welcomed Presbyterian missionaries John Dunbar and Samuel Allis among them, to add Christian ideas to their arsenal of spiritual powers against the Lakotas and Cheyennes. Although Allis and Dunbar were unable to convert the people to Christianity, the Pawnees learned about intriguing Christian doctrines such as the resurrection of a savior spirit. It appears that the main reason that Allis and Dunbar failed to convert Pawnees was the fact that Jesus did not provide the protection the Pawnees so desperately longed for.

But when the Pawnees were at their most desperate, the animal powers came to the rescue. The animals revived a man slain and dismembered by the Lakotas. His name was Pahukatawa, and he had come to help his people against their enemies. However, his return was not accepted by everyone right away. Traditionalist Skiris saw in him a rival to Morning Star and accused him of conspiring against the Skiri people and their traditions, even of assisting the Lakotas against them. This traditionalist camp lost ground in 1838, however, when the sacrifice of a Lakota captive to Morning Star caused the Lakotas and Cheyennes to further escalate their war against the Pawnee people. The worship of Morning Star would continue, but the Skiris stripped the ceremony devoted to him of human sacrifice. At the same time, the Skiris accepted the power of Pahukatawa, whose worship spread to all the Pawnee bands.

Scholars have had difficulty explaining the seemingly contradicting and ambiguous nature of Pahukatawa. One reason is that he had been so controversial among the Pawnees themselves. Placing him in the geopolitical context of the wars with the Lakotas and Cheyennes makes it possible to explain the ambiguities. Pahukatawa has features of both scalped men, Morning Star, and Jesus. He was a result of synthesis rather than syncretism. Christian ideas of the resurrection may have inspired some part of his story, but Pahukatawa was in every respect a completely new member in Pawnee cosmology.

The worship of Pahukatawa faded after the Indian wars ended in the 1870s. But when white agents of "civilization" sought to eradicate traditional Pawnee culture, Pahukatawa returned a second time. Again he reappeared to give the people hope, but this time he was more compatible with Christianity. Indeed, it appears that some Pawnee theologians tried to incorporate Pahukatawa, Morning Star, and Jesus into a single coherent religion. Still, most Pawnees carried on viewing him as a distinct and separate sacred power. They continue to do so to this day.

In a way, with Pahukatawa this book comes full circle. Whereas the monsters in earlier chapters were enemies of the people that had to be slain by cunning warrior heroes, in the Pahukatawa story we see an interesting evolution from a "monstrous" scalped man to a savior who inspires both reverence and awe.

Conclusion

"We Na Netsu Ut"
(Now the Gut Passes)

"History," Dutch historian Johan Huizinga once wrote, "is the manner in which a culture reflects on its past." Of course, different cultures have different ways of remembering things. What one civilization considers important and worthy to remember might be different from that of another. The form in which things are remembered may also differ from society to society.

Although Western historical methods have become the standard in much of the world today, indigenous forms of history are no less valuable. Indeed, oral traditions and myths provide valuable insights into the way indigenous cultures reflected on their past. They not only present different perspectives, but are useful, if underutilized, sources of information as well.

What deters many mainstream historians from using oral traditions in the manner shown in this book is the degree of interpretation required to analyze them. I am certain that many scholars feel that I stray too deeply into the realm of speculation on too many occasions. I understand their apprehension. Still, I did so on purpose in the hope that this approach might yield results. Although some critics may argue that my findings are fanciful, I nevertheless remain convinced that my conclusions are reasonable and worthy of consideration. They are intended, as Julie Cruikshank wrote, to "make connections that are not always straightforward."[1]

Critics will say that it is difficult to extrapolate historical facts from these oral traditions, especially if one does not know the context in which they were told. While this is true, I nevertheless believe that the attempt to explain these particular stories as works of history is worthwhile. I suspect that the use of oral traditions and indigenous knowledge will remain controversial. They must indeed be used with care, as one should do with all types of evidence. However, to not use them at all is shortsighted and ethnocentric.

Of course, by interpreting and rationalizing these stories as I have done, I may be guilty of trying to explain them according to non-Indian modes of thought. In the act of interpreting these stories, I may have appropriated and reformulated their ideas.[2] I tried hard to avoid this problem by reconstructing Caddoan ideas about oral traditions and myths. Still, my interpretations are very much my own and not necessarily Caddoan. The simple fact is that, like all forms of verbal or written texts, these stories do not speak for themselves; it is the historian who speaks for them. Thus they are always subjected to interpretation. It is the nature of historical inquiry.

In any case, the Caddoan monsters stories featured in this book allow us to draw a few conclusions about them. One of the most important discoveries is that, although these tribes were linguistically and culturally related, they have very different sets of monsters. In simple terms, these monsters represented different historical traumas that were unique to each tribe. The differences in monster iconography show that each tribe had a different history to tell.

As this study has shown, Whirlwind and certain animal monsters in Arikara oral traditions represented epidemic diseases. The cannibal man with the iron-nosed mask was a member of the De Soto expedition, which contacted and devastated the Caddo people in 1541. The Wichita story of the witch-woman who captured the chief's son described events leading up to and including the San Sabá Massacre of 1758. Several historical figures could have been the model for the Flint Monster in Pawnee tradition. Most likely he was a coat-of-mail-wearing enemy, possibly Spanish but more likely an American Indian enemy. The appearance of scalped men took place at a time when the Sioux waged a devastating war of extermination against the Pawnees, and out of these unfortunates emerged Pahukatawa, a new culture hero who exhibited both traditional and Christian traits.

Despite the fantastic content of these stories, there is almost certainly a historical core to them. To be sure, these stories are not history in the Western, Rankean sense of the word. Yet they are not merely products of lively imaginations either. The evidence presented in this book strongly suggests that these stories were inspired by real events.

A surprising discovery is that the time-depth of the stories is relatively shallow. Historians often believe that these stories refer to ancient times. In truth, the monsters in this book all come from post-contact times. The Arikara creation account too, although it started in deep time, has a monster that stands for the smallpox epidemic of the mid- to late 1700s. This shows that the Arikaras continued to incorporate relatively recent events into their cosmic history.

Most mainstream historians—if they are willing to do so—look at oral traditions after they consult most of the traditional sources, to see if the two kinds of sources match. I did the reverse: I looked at the oral traditions first before checking for possible matches in colonial records. Although the stories have an archaic literary flavor, which caused Dorsey and other scholars to mistake them for ancient myths, some of the texts discussed here actually refer to events that took place in the more recent past.

A good example is the Pawnee story of the Flint Monster. As the analysis in this book shows, the monster most likely represented an armor-wearing Spaniard or (more likely) an armor-wearing Indian. This would locate the story between about 1690 and 1852. However, the story ends with people choosing to become certain types of animals. At this point the story takes on a distinctly mythological character, which further explains why Dorsey viewed it as a cosmological tale. But the story of the transformation of the people into animals seems oddly disconnected from everything that preceded it. It is possible that this segment was added later to give the story additional significance. Or perhaps it merely referred to the breaking up of the Skiri Pawnees into different groups. Here there are new avenues of investigation.

There is, however, another explanation concerning why stories such as the Flint Monster account assumed mythological traits. One must remember that to the Caddoan Indians, historical events could not be separated from the supernatural. If the boundary between natural and supernatural could be crossed, it was also possible for the historical to cross into the mythological realm and vice versa: for the mythological to creep into the historical. If through this process the Flint Monster story became part of the corpus of Skiri Pawnee creation stories, it is also possible that the story of the transformation of the people into animals became part of the original Flint Monster account.

A similar process took place with Whirlwind in the Arikara creation account. If the account refers to deep time (indeed, Pawnee scholar Roger Echo-Hawk suggests that the story of the Arikaras' emergence from the ground and journey across a lake, a heavy timber, and a great chasm refers to their entrance into America across the Bering Strait and their crossing of the Rocky Mountains some ten thousand years ago), the story of Whirlwind brings this ancient story into the post-contact era. In short, stories of the traumatic experience of epidemics became part of the sacred stories of creation. Likewise, mythological elements (if they were such) could also find their way into historical accounts.

Interestingly, although the monsters appear in symbolic form, the type of disaster determined the iconographic image that the Caddoan historian-storytellers created. The image of the powerful and unstoppable Whirlwind among the Arikaras symbolized the magnitude of devastation and trauma caused by epidemic infectious diseases. The epidemic of 1780–81, especially, rapidly killed people in enormous numbers, scattering survivors as communities and families broke up to escape the ravages of infection. The image of Whirlwind was not only a mnemonic or literary device allowing Arikara storytellers to remember the account, but it most accurately described the magnitude of devastation wreaked upon the Arikara people. At the same time, it also served as a model of explanation: to the Arikaras it represented a force of nature unleashed by the sinful attitudes of the people; it was the wrath of the sacred powers for the people's failure to worship properly or adequately. In light of this, the Arikaras could not have picked a better symbol. The snakes also symbolized disease. In this case, the painful (and poisonous) snakebites resembled the marks and scars of smallpox pustules. The attack by bears, finally, symbolized the ravenous and indiscriminate violence of an epidemic infection.

The monsters from the other accounts, in contrast, are to be taken both *literally* and *literarily*. They are often surprisingly literal depictions of threats people encountered. Of course, De Soto's men were not cannibals, but the sheer scale and horror of their actions (including cutting off victims' limbs, burning victims over fires, hanging them from trees like jerked meat, and the occasional massive slaughter of Caddo Indians during battle) make the analogy not that implausible. Indeed, Spanish chroniclers and European artists such as Theodore de Bry, who were equally unfamiliar with American Indian military practices, also used the image of cannibalism to explain horrendous, "barbaric" Native behaviors such as dismembering the corpses of opponents killed in battle. Both sides, then, accused the other of monstrous acts, and anthropophagy seemed the most logical explanation for these abominable behaviors.

The witch-woman of the Wichita story represents a Christian Madonna, who to the Wichitas was not a mother figure but the chief of Spanish religious invaders who kidnapped Wichita children in her name. She was present at the San Sabá Mission in the form of a painting only, but to the Wichitas she was as real as she was to the monks who had brought her image with them. The four headless men of the account represent the Spanish missionaries and staff who occupied the mission post. Although only one of them was decapitated (or two if one includes the decapitated statue of Saint Francis), their headless state may also be attributed to their tonsures.

The scalped men in Pawnee and Arikara stories, like the Spanish monks from San Sabá, were no longer human but were spirits who had the potential of causing harm. There is ample evidence of people who survived scalping.

Hence this monster too is realistic and not a creation of the subconscious. Indeed, as warfare intensified, scalped men became potential sources of power. The greatest of all scalped men, Pahukatawa, was considered a savior who eventually assumed a place in the Pawnee pantheon of sacred powers, although as we have seen, his rise there (to some degree at the expense of Morning Star) was not uncontroversial.

In short, these monsters were not imaginary creations but were based on real threats and dangers. These threats were external. In fact, they were all linked to some aspect of European contact. Even Sioux warfare against the Pawnees was linked to European invasion and colonization because dispossessed eastern tribes pushed the Sioux westward. In addition, European innovations such as guns and horses allowed the Sioux to adopt a successful way of life (horse nomadism) that brought them into conflict with the semisedentary Pawnees. Therefore even the Sioux–Pawnee conflict cannot be detached from European contact. Indeed, the Pawnees would side with the United States in a military alliance against the Sioux and other nomadic tribes in the 1860s and 1870s.

Of course, the twentieth century created its own monsters. Ironically, these monsters were peculiarly bureaucratic: health-care specialists who performed sterilizations on Native women, doctors who tested new and experimental therapies on unsuspecting Indian patients, social workers who removed Indian children from their families and placed them in non-Indian foster homes, engineers whose hydro-technological projects dislocated entire communities, a Kafkaesque BIA bureaucracy that treated Indians as statistics rather than people, and so on. Although these bureaucracies supposedly worked for the common good, many Indian people saw in them new monsters. Modern-day monsters wear lab coats, business attire, or overalls, and their weapons are pens, syringes, and calculators. Although less imaginative and fantastical in appearance, they are nevertheless terrifyingly powerful.

It seems appropriate to end this book about oral traditions using the traditional Pawnee words at the end of a Trickster story. I hope this book has stimulated readers to look at these old stories again. Perhaps, like me, readers will discover hidden meanings or new things in them. In any case, I have said enough. It is high time to pass the gut: "We na netsu ut!"

Notes

PREFACE

1. Old-Man-That-Chief quoted in Weltfish, *Lost Universe*, 251.
2. Parks, "Roaming Scout Texts," n.p.

INTRODUCTION

1. In the past there were more Caddoan tribes, such as the Kitsai, but they disappeared or were absorbed into one of the aforementioned groups.
2. Rogers and Sabo, "Caddo," 626–28. See also the entries on the Pawnees, Arikaras, Wichitas, and Kitsais in DeMallie, *Handbook of North American Indians*, vol. 13, *Plains*, 365–90, 515–47, 548–66, 567–71.
3. Wissler and Spinden, "Pawnee Human Sacrifice," 48–55. Ralph Linton challenged the Wissler–Spinden hypothesis. See Linton, "Origin of the Skidi Pawnee Sacrifice," 457–66. However, ethnologist George Bird Grinnell pointed out that the Arikara version of this ceremony had replaced the sacrifice of humans with something else. Grinnell, *Story of the Indian*, 124; Gilmore, "Study in the Ethnobotany," 330–31.
4. Parks, "Caddoan Languages," 80–93; Parks, "Northern Caddoan Languages," 197–213.
5. For the Arikara version of their separation from the Pawnees, see Parks, *Traditional Narratives*, 363–65.
6. Dorsey, *Traditions of the Skidi Pawnee*, xiii.
7. Rogers and Sabo, "Caddo," 616, 619–20.
8. Jackson and Urban, "Mythology and Folklore," 713.
9. Echo-Hawk, "Ancient History," 267–90. It must be noted, however, that the Caddo Indians believe they emerged from the earth at the mouth of the Red River.
10. For a brief but excellent overview of the development of the field, see Krech, "From Ethnohistory," 85–91. Older high points in the historiography of ethnohistory include Sturtevant, "Anthropology, History, and Ethnohistory," 1–51; Hudson, "Folk History and Ethnohistory," 52–70; and James Axtell, "Ethnohistory," 3–15. For a more current position on the problem of ethnohistory, see Miller and Riding In, *Native Historians Write Back*.

11. John Swanton and R. B. Dixon, "Primitive American History," *American Anthropologist*, 16, no. 3 (1914): 376–412.

12. Lowie, "Oral Tradition and History," 597–99.

13. Dixon, "Dr. Dixon's Reply," 599–600.

14. Swanton, "Dr. Swanton's Reply," 600.

15. An example of such an attitude is Luther Standing Bear, who wrote in his autobiography, "[Whites] are not in a position to write accurately about the struggles and disappointments of the Indian. . . . No one is able to understand the Indian race like an Indian." Standing Bear, *My People*, n.p. Apart from the inherent ethnocentrism, I also take issue with Standing Bear's implication that a Lakota can speak with authority to non-Indian audiences about other tribes.

16. Lowie, "Oral Tradition and History," 161–281. Lowie based some of his findings on experiments on how stories change as they are reproduced. This research was conducted by F. C. Bartlett in the early 1920s; Bartlett, "Some Experiments," 243–58. See also Robert H. Lowie, "Some Cases of Repeated Reproduction," in *The Study of Folklore*, ed. Alan Dundes (Englewood Cliffs, N.J.: Prentice-Hall, 1965), 259–64.

17. Hallowell, "Temporal Orientation," 667.

18. Hyde, *Red Cloud's Folk*, ix.

19. Hyde, *Pawnee Indians*, 32.

20. Nabokov, *Forest of Time*, 16.

21. Thompson, "Myths and Folktales," 482–88; Raglan, "Myth and Ritual," 454–61; Bascom, "Myth-Ritual Theory," 103–14; Bidney and Raglan, "Reply to Bascom," 359–61; Bascom, "Rejoinder to Raglan and Bidney," 79–80; Hyman, "Reply to Bascom," 152–55; Bascom, "Rejoinder to Hyman," 155–56.

22. Thomas, *Skull Wars*.

23. Alice Kehoe quoted in Mason, *Inconstant Companions*, 237.

24. Ibid., 10–13.

25. Ibid., 49.

26. Ibid., 107.

27. Ibid., 116.

28. Ibid., 164, 165, 177, 178, 179.

29. Ibid., 169.

30. Ibid., 252.

31. Psychoanalysts have made significant contributions to the study of folklore. For a brief but excellent introduction on the value of psychoanalysis, see Jones, "Psychoanalysis and Folklore," 88–102. Among advocates of the psychological approach to oral traditions are folklorist Alan Dundes as well as anthropologist Clyde Kluckhohn. See Alan Dundes, ed., *The Study of Folklore* (Englewood Cliffs, N.J.: Prentice-Hall, 1965), 158–68, 206–15.

32. Murphy and Wasik, *Rabid*. For the original rabies–vampire hypothesis, see Gómez-Alonso, "Rabies," 856–59.

33. Vansina, *Oral Tradition*, 197–99.

34. Ibid., 160.

35. Ibid., 173.

36. Ibid., 160.
37. Ibid., xii.
38. Nabokov, *Forest of Time*, 26.
39. Ibid., 10–11, 26, 32, 33.
40. Miller, "Ethnography of Speaking," 224.
41. For an example of this approach, see Galloway, *Choctaw Genesis*, 324–37.
42. Nabokov, *Forest of Time*, 47, 76.
43. Barber and Barber, *When They Severed Earth from Sky*.
44. Ibid., 244.
45. Ibid., 2.
46. Roger Echo-Hawk, "Ancient History," 267–90.

47. Echo-Hawk speculates that, depending on the complexity of the culture, these traditions can go back as far as forty thousand years. Using archaeological, historical, and linguistic data, Echo-Hawk sets out to prove that the Arikara creation accounts relate the migration of proto-Caddoans from the Arctic Circle to the Great Basin, the Rocky Mountains, and the Grand Canyon and to their ultimate locations on the Great Plains and (in the case of the Caddo tribe) in the southeastern woodlands. At various points during this ancient, pre-Columbian migration, different groups split off, establishing what would eventually become the tribes known to us today.

48. Nabokov, *Forest of Time*, 50.
49. Cook-Lynn, "History, Myth, and Identity," 330.
50. Walters, *Talking Indian*, 80. See also Nabokov, *Forest of Time*, 56.
51. Cook-Lynn, "History, Myth, and Identity," 337.
52. For a critique of non-Native historians and anthropologists and how they have colonized Native American studies, see Mihesuah, *Natives and Academics*.
53. Echo-Hawk, "Ancient History," 287.
54. Cook-Lynn, "History, Myth, and Identity," 331. Indeed, Lynn calls for a move away from Americanization and a return to true Native American knowledge and literature: "For Indians in America today, real empowerment lies in First Nation ideology, not in individual liberation of Americanization." Ibid., 341. When non-Native scholars use oral traditions, they can open themselves up to criticisms from Native communities, as Peter Nabokov discovered when he reissued "The Origin Myth of Acoma Pueblo." This book, which first appeared in 1946, was based on information furnished by Acoma Pueblo's Edward Proctor Hunt, a Christian convert and assimilated Indian who had been banned from the Acoma community. Nabokov's republication of this work earned him the scorn of Acoma Pueblo, which charged him with colonizing the intellectual property of the Acomas. Despite Nabokov's defense that the book resides in the public domain and is freely available on the Internet, and that he removed the most sacred parts of the work (the images), the Acomas called his work a modern-day version of grave robbing. They charged that Nabokov was building his career on the backs of the Acoma people. The fact that one member of the pueblo transmitted the story to persons calling themselves anthropologists without consent of the whole pueblo did not matter, said one of the pueblo attorneys pursuing the case: "[Hunt's] violation does not sanitize [Nabokov's] action." Consequently, the Acomas demanded that publication of the book should

be halted. Khristiaan D. Villela, "Controversy Erupts over Peter Nabokov's publication of 'The Origin Myth of Acoma Pueblo,'" *Santa Fe New Mexican*, January 15, 2016, www.santafenewmexican.com (accessed October 13, 2016); Lucas Iberico Lozada, "The Professor and the Pueblo: Was the Disclosure of Acoma Traditions Exploitation or Scholarship?" *Santa Fe Reporter*, January 27, 2016, www.sfreporter.com/santafe/article-11510-the-professor-and-the-pueblo.html (accessed October 13, 2016); Alex Jacobs, "Don't Buy This Book! Acoma Pueblo vs. Peter Nabokov: When the Sacred Is Made Profane," *Indian Country Today*, February 11, 2016.

55. Fogelson, "On the Varieties of Indian History," 106–7.

56. Jeffrey Cohen, "Monster Culture," 17. The body of literature on monsters (and the "monstrous races") is large and growing. Mostly, however, it focuses on European perceptions and concepts. See, for example, Kaplan, *Science of Monsters*; Friedman, *Monstrous Races*; Beal, *Religion and Its Monsters*; Jeffrey Cohen, *Of Giants*; and Greenblatt, *Marvelous Possessions*.

57. The exception is the omnipotent and omnipresent God of Judeo–Christian–Islamic tradition, who is particularly terrifying because he lies beyond our comprehension. He is unpredictable and embodies both "good" by being merciful and "mercilessness" by destroying us in the end.

58. Asma, *On Monsters*, 14.

59. Ibid., chapters 9–11.

60. Ibid., 188.

61. Hoffman and Oliver-Smith, *Catastrophe and Culture*, 6.

62. Ibid., 9.

63. Ibid., 113, 19 (respectively). Hoffman further argues that, especially in cases of cyclical disasters (recurring droughts, earthquakes, and so on), disaster symbolism creates not only "monsters" but also "mothers." Usually, people have offended the "mother" (as in Mother Nature), who subsequently sends a monster to punish them. In this view, monsters take a position between nature and culture as something that is neither.

64. Oliver-Smith, "'What Is a Disaster?'" 22, 23, 26, 28.

65. See, for example, McPherson, *Viewing the Ancestors*, and Lankford, *Looking for Lost Lore*.

66. Deloria Jr., *Spirit and Reason*, 344.

67. Mason, *Inconstant Companions*, 164–65.

CHAPTER 1. CADDOAN STORYTELLERS AND STORYTELLING TRADITIONS

1. Tedlock, *Spoken Word*, 9.

2. One scholar suggested that translating Native texts is "the central act of European colonization and imperialism in America." Eric Cheyfitz quoted in Swann, *Born in the Blood*, 1. The various essays in this volume detail the problems associated with translating Native oral texts into non-Native and written forms. See also Asad, "Concept of Cultural Translation."

3. Foley, "Foreword."

4. On the different forms of collaborations and (ethical) issues arising from such work, see the various essays in Evers and Toelken, *Native American Oral Traditions*.

5. Toelken, *Anguish of Snails*, 5–6. Like Toelken, I acknowledge a scholarly and intellectual debt to the communities whose oral traditions I analyze in this book. For that reason, I contacted tribal communities to solicit their comments, criticisms, and suggestions. I was not always successful. Ideally, one ought to visit the communities and make face-to-face contact. Contacting tribes by email or social media is not nearly as effective, but because I am located in the Middle East, I had to rely mostly on indirect contact. An additional problem is that there are many different Native voices, and it is hard to discern who speaks with the most authority. While doing fieldwork on the Fort Berthold Indian Reservation in North Dakota, I was introduced to the rather heated debate over the true nationality of Sakakawea (aka Sacajawea) between Shoshones and Hidatsas. Both sides claimed her as their own. Lewis and Clark described her as a Shoshone who had been captured by the Hidatsas. The Hidatsas claim that she was Hidatsa by birth, captured by the Shoshones before she was recaptured and repatriated by her own people. The issue poses a vexing problem for the scholar. Present-day Hidatsas are very frustrated with Lewis and Clark for bringing the lie that she was not one of theirs into the world. Meanwhile, an Arikara friend asked me what Lewis and Clark had to gain by hiding her true identity. In any case, the most diplomatic thing the scholar can do is to present both arguments.

6. Ibid., 10.

7. Ibid., 14.

8. Tedlock pioneered "ethnopaleography" when he took an old text (the Popol Vuh) back to the Mayan people to compare it to modern spoken arts and to "obtain commentaries from contemporary readers." Tedlock, *Spoken Word*, 16.

9. Dundes, *Sacred Narrative*, 1, 8–9.

10. See Lauri Honko, "The Problem of Defining Myth," in Dundes, *Sacred Narrative*, 41–52.

11. Bronislaw Malinowski, "The Role of Myth in Life," in Dundes, *Sacred Narrative*, 199.

12. G. S. Kirk, "On Defining Myths," in Dundes, *Sacred Narrative*, 53–61. See also J. W. Rogerson, "Slippery Words: Myth," in the same volume, 62–71.

13. See, for example, Lankford, *Native American Legends of the Southeast*.

14. One of Linderman's Crow Indian sources once told a story that Linderman eventually recognized as a Sanskrit story. Intrigued by this fact, Linderman asked his Crow collaborator how it was possible that these distant cultures knew almost identical stories. The Indian simply remarked, "These things are beyond us." Linderman, *Plenty-coups*, 205–6.

15. Th. P. van Baaren, "The Flexibility of Myth," in Dundes, *Sacred Narrative*, 223.

16. Ramsey, *Reading the Fire*, 139.

17. Clements, *Native American Verbal Art*, 1.

18. For an excellent introduction on the variety and complexity of trickster figures, see Hynes and Doty, *Mythical Trickster Figures*, especially chapters 1–3. See also Krupat, *All That Remains*, chapter 1: "Trickster Tales Revisited."

19. My view of theory corresponds with what mythographer and classicist G. S. Kirk wrote in 1973: "One of the chief impediments to progress has been the preoccupation . . . that all myths have the same kind of origin and function, and that what students of mythology should be pursuing is some all-embracing theory of myth." Kirk argued that

myths may have many functions. Therefore one should recognize myth "as a broad category, within which special forms and functions will require different kinds of explanation." In this sense, theories are problematic because of their tendency for "overdetermination": "The analysis to be applied to a myth must be both flexible and multiform, and it must not reject earlier ideas because of their formal limitations or for fear of the bogey of 'eclecticism.'" G. S. Kirk quoted in Dundes, *Sacred Narrative*, 54. James G. Frazer observed in 1935, "A superstructure of theory is always transitory, being constantly superseded by fresh theories which make nearer and nearer approaches to the truth without ever reaching it. On the shore of the great ocean of reality men are perpetually building theoretical castles of sand, which are perpetually being washed away by the rising tide of knowledge. I cannot expect my own speculations to be more lasting than those of my predecessors. The most that a speculative thinker can hope for is to be remembered for a time as one of those long line of runners, growing dimmer and dimmer as they recede in the distance, who have striven to hand on the torch of knowledge with its little circle of light glimmering in the illimitable darkness of the unknown." James G. Frazer, *Creation and Evolution in Primitive Cosmogonies* (London: Macmillan, 1935), viii.

20. Arnold Krupat, *Red Matters: Native American Studies* (Philadelphia: University of Pennsylvania Press, 2002), xi. In the absence of the original native-language versions, the language I seek to translate in this book is the language of metaphor.

21. Ibid., 71.

22. Krupat also notes that "modern western cultures tend to privilege historical difference; for Us, it is the uniqueness of the moment, its qualitative difference from the past out of which it comes and the future to which it leads, that gives it its particular historicity. Traditional Native cultures, however, tend to privilege historical identity or sameness." Ibid., 53, 59.

23. Parks, "Roaming Scout Texts," 162–65.

24. Old-Man-That-Chief quoted in Weltfish, *Lost Universe*, 251.

25. Stands In Timber and Liberty, *Cheyenne Voice*, 461. Strictly speaking, Stands In Timber was not an oral historian because he also committed certain stories to paper.

26. Carla Gerona, "Caddo Sun Accounts," 348; Carter, *Caddo Indians*, 8–9.

27. Stands In Timber and Liberty, *Cheyenne Voice*, 464.

28. Standing Bear, *Land of the Spotted Eagle*, 27. On page 227, Standing Bear elaborates on this point: "Irreparable damage has been done by white writers who discredit the Indian. Books have been written of the native American, so distorting his true nature that he scarcely resembles the real man; his faults have been magnified and his virtues minimized; his wars, and his battles, which, if successful, the white man chooses to call 'massacres,' have been told and retold, but little attention has been given to his philosophy and ideals. Books, paintings, and pictures have all joined in glorifying the pioneer—the hunter, trapper, woodsman, cowboy, and soldiery—in their course of conquest across the country, a conquest that could only have been revitalized by committing untold offenses against the aboriginal people."

29. Linderman, *Plenty-coups*, 33.

30. Nabokov, *Forest of Time*, 36.

31. Dorsey, *Traditions of the Skidi Pawnee*, xxii–xxiii.

32. Weltfish, "Pawnee Field Notes." See also Weltfish, *Lost Universe*, 352–60.
33. See also Miller, "Ethnography of Speaking," 224.
34. Stands In Timber and Liberty, *Cheyenne Memories*, 16.
35. Weltfish, *Lost Universe*, 56.
36. Ibid., 359.
37. Dorsey, "Arikara Story-Telling Contest."
38. Dorsey, *Mythology of the Wichita*, 252–57, 274–75.
39. Chafe, "Introduction to the Paperback Edition."
40. Dorsey, *Mythology of the Wichita*, 23.
41. Dorsey, *Traditions of the Skidi Pawnee*, xxii.
42. Ibid., xxii.
43. Ibid., xxiii.
44. Dorsey, *Pawnee Mythology*, 9–10.
45. Ibid., 10.
46. Dorsey, *Mythology of the Wichita*, 22.
47. Ibid., 23.
48. G. K. Chesterton, "The Red Angel," in *Tremendous Trifles* (London: Methuen, 1909), chapter 17.
49. Carla Gerona, "Caddo Sun Accounts," 349.
50. Wallace Chafe, "Introduction to the Paperback Edition," xiii.
51. Parks and DeMallie, "Plains Indian Native Literatures," 106.
52. DeMallie and Parks, "George A. Dorsey," 59–60.
53. Dorsey quoted in DeMallie and Parks, "George A. Dorsey," 62.
54. Cole, *Captured Heritage*, 174. Cole offers a scathing criticism of Dorsey. According to Cole, Dorsey's frantic pace in collecting artifacts was caused by his competition with Boas. Cole writes that Dorsey's expeditions were more accurately "raids" for "plunder" in which he "handled [Indian] graves most unmercifully." Dorsey's greatest strength was his ability to manipulate his superiors and coax them to provide more money for research: "Dorsey's success in moving a reluctant executive rested upon his political skills, his ability to deal with the business and philanthropic mind [of men like Marshall Field, Edward Ayer, and others], and his persuasive dramatization of the anthropological world." In short, Dorsey was a maverick for publicity and self-promotion rather than an accomplished scholar. His charm ultimately got him in trouble when he "induced a girl 'of good family' to go with him on an overseas excursion," which caused a public scandal that led to his wife filing for divorce. The scandal and supposed financial mismanagement forced Dorsey to resign his position at the Field Museum in 1915. Cole, *Captured Heritage*, 175, 181, 209, 211.
55. Dorsey quoted in Almazan and Coleman, "George Amos Dorsey," 89.
56. DeMallie and Parks, "George A. Dorsey," 61.
57. Dorsey quoted in Almazan and Coleman, "George Amos Dorsey," 90.
58. DeMallie and Parks, "George A. Dorsey," 71.
59. Ibid., 70.
60. Ibid., 72.
61. Parks, "Biography of James R. Murie," 22.

62. Ibid., 22–23.

63. Ibid., 23. See also Parks and DeMallie, "Plains Indian Native Literatures," 107–10.

64. Dorsey quoted in Almazan and Coleman, "George Amos Dorsey," 91.

65. Douglas Parks, Murie's biographer, wrote: "Murie's work, given his time and circumstances, was truly remarkable. He worked long and diligently in the tedious detail of recording the culture of the Pawnee, particularly his own band, the Skiri. Whatever his shortcomings in terms of professional training, the overriding conclusion remains that were it not for James R. Murie, the unusual wealth of ethnography that we now possess for the Pawnee would in all likelihood not exist. . . . He made it his life's goal to record and preserve the religious and ceremonial ritual of the Pawnee, and he spent nearly a quarter of a century involved in that endeavor. We shall forever be in debt for his perseverance and dedication." Parks, "Biography of James R. Murie," 27.

66. Martha Royce Blaine, *Some Things Are Not Forgotten: A Pawnee Family Remembers* (Lincoln: University of Nebraska Press, 1997), 113.

67. Ibid., 63–64. Pawnee scholar Roger Echo-Hawk believes that Murie's "conciliatory" tone in this letter was actually intended to assuage the agent's fears that the Ghost Dancers were planning to rise up against the whites. After all, the tragedy at Wounded Knee had happened only a few years earlier. By asserting that there was a strong and "loyal" faction among the Pawnees, and that the Ghost Dancers were only a small and relatively harmless group, Murie argued against military intervention on the agency. Roger C. Echo-Hawk, personal communication, April 5, 2014.

68. Gary McAdams, personal communication, May 6, 2015.

69. Ibid., May 6, 2015; April 14, 2015.

70. Ibid., May 6, 2015.

71. Ibid.

72. Ibid.

73. Ibid., May 6, 2015; April 14, 2015.

74. Ibid., May 6, 2015.

75. Southwell and Lovett, *Photographs of Annette Ross Hume*, 35.

76. De Lancey W. Gill photo collection at the National Anthropological Archives.

77. Dorsey, *Mythology of the Wichita*, xiii, 298–99.

78. Dorsey, *Traditions of the Skidi Pawnee*, 359.

CHAPTER 2. "THE WHIRLWIND IS COMING TO DESTROY MY PEOPLE"

1. Dorsey, *Traditions of the Arikara*, 21.

2. Melvin R. Gilmore, "Uses of Plants"; "Real Indians in the 'Movies,'" *New York Times*, September 23, 1924. For biographical information on Gilmore, see Welsh, "Introduction," xi–xxii. See also "Oldest Indians Alone Can Tell of Long Sacred Native Dances," *Fargo Forum*, December 9, 1922; Melvin R. Gilmore, "Account of the Piraskani Ceremony of the Arikara at Armstrong, ND, September 1922" (unpublished manuscript, American Indian Studies Research Institute, Indiana University, Bloomington, n.d.); Will, "An Arikara Sacred Ceremony," 266–67.

3. DeMallie and Parks, "George A. Dorsey." See also Almazan and Coleman, "George Amos Dorsey and His Comrades."

4. George A. Dorsey to Commissioner of Indian Affairs William A. Jones, cited in Parks, *Traditional Narratives of the Arikara Indians*, 18.

5. Dorsey, *Traditions of the Arikara*, 15.

6. For information on the Congregational mission, see Case and Case, *100 Years at Ft. Berthold*. For the Catholic mission, see Kardong, *Catholic Life at Fort Berthold*; Foley, *Father Francis M. Craft*; and Pfaller, *St. Joseph Mission*. In 1952 Eagle Rises Up (aka Frank Heart) told a story of Jesus that was handed down to him by his grandfather Two Crows. According to the story, Jesus had first appeared to the Arikaras, who did not give him a proper welcome. Offended, Jesus then granted his teachings and powers to the white man. According to Eagle Rises Up, Jesus was a handsome white man with a yellow beard. He said, "I am the person that you desired to see. You did not see me but I came so that you could see me. Now you see me. I will tell you that I have been offended that the people did not welcome me. I came purposely to visit you people and to leave you with this blessing that you would be blessed with the talent to make things and to develop things so that you would not remain poor but you would be gainful in the use of your talents but since your people have ignored me and not welcomed me I have decided to turn this blessing over to that people that is white and will give to them that blessing that you have rejected. Although this man is white and has been wayward, heinous, yet I will give to him this blessing that you are rejecting because of your failure to welcome me and greet me when you saw me. I have decided to leave this talent to this white person so he can develop and become useful and be gainful in use of his talent." Eagle Rises Up, "The Appearance of a Stranger."

7. The main primary sources are Dorsey, *Traditions of the Arikara*; Curtis, "The Arikara," especially pages 80–86; Gilmore, "The Arikara Book of Genesis"; Grinnell, *Story of the Indian*, 186–94; and Grinnell, "Pawnee Mythology." Another version of Two Crows's account was recorded in Wilson, "Arikara Cosmogony."

8. Dorsey, *Traditions of the Arikara*, 31.

9. For an example of problems of translation and interpretation, see Judith Berman, "Oochalan-Woman's Robe: Fish, Blankets, Masks, and Meaning in Boas's Kwakw'ala Texts," in Brian Swann, *On the Translation of Native American Literatures*, 125–62.

10. DeMallie and Parks, "George A. Dorsey."

11. For an excellent overview of Arikara archaeology, see Rogers, *Objects of Change*; Meleen, *A Report on an Investigation*; Hoffman, *The La Roche Sites*; Lehmer and Jones, *Arikara Archeology*; Krause, "Plains Village Tradition," 206; and Wood, "Plains Trade," 98–109. For the presence of white, mostly French fur traders among the Arikaras at this time, see Jantz and Owsley, "White Traders in the Upper Missouri," 189–201. However, Wesley R. Hurt, who excavated the Swan Creek site, reported that there was no evidence of direct contact with Europeans. Hurt, *Report of the Investigation*.

12. Lehmer, "Plains Village Tradition"; Holder, *The Hoe and the Horse*, 85.

13. Delisle, "Carte du Mexique"; Parks, "Bands and Villages," 215, 217, 220, 228; Norall, *Bourgmont*, 110; Lehmer, *Introduction to Middle Missouri Archaeology*, 168, 169–70;

Tucker, *Indian Villages*, plate xv. In 1719 Jean Baptiste Bénard de La Harpe learned from the Tawakonis (Wichitas) that the Arikaras were numerous, that they inhabited seven villages, and that they formed part of forty-five villages of Pawnees. According to La Harpe, the Arikaras also fought a "cruel war" with neighboring tribes, such as the Canecys, the Padoucas, and some Panis, but the exact identity of these tribes has never been established satisfactorily. Pierre Margry, *Decouvertes et Etablissements* 289–90, 293.

14. Margry, *Decouvertes et Etablissements*, 407–12; Burpee, *Journals and Letters*, 18–23, 413. It is possible that this was a Pawnee rather than an Arikara band.

15. For the etymology of "Snake" Indians, see Kavanagh, "Comanche," 886, 902–3; and the chapters on the Shoshones in D'Azevedo, *Handbook of North American Indians*, 262, 279, 305, 334.

16. Although guns changed Arikara military tactics (ambushes rather than pitched, close-formation battles became more common), the cultural values associated with warfare did not change fundamentally. From all appearances, the gun merely reinforced existing Arikara cultural traits in hunting and warfare. The introduction of the gun did not leave an impression on Arikara oral tradition. In fact, the introduction of the bow and arrow was far more significant. Garavaglia and Worman, *Firearms of the American West*, 343–60; Gluckman, *Identifying Old U.S. Muskets*; Hamilton, *Indian Trade Guns*; Ewers, *Plains Indian History*, 48–50; Secoy, *Changing Military Patterns*; Malone, *Skulking Way of War*; Starkey, *European and Native American Warfare*. The same is true for the arrival of the horse. Although horses turned the Arikaras from foot soldiers into cavalrymen and allowed people to travel greater distances in search of buffalo herds during the annual summer hunt, the semi-sedentary lifestyle of the Arikaras did not lend itself to the maintenance of large herds because horses required fresh grass for forage and thus needed to be moved around often and sometimes over great distances. Instead, the Arikaras preferred to sell surplus horses as soon as possible. When they lacked horses, the Arikaras preferred to trade for them rather than steal them from enemy tribes. In this case, the Arikaras used corn (Neešaanu's greatest gift to the people) to obtain what they needed. Some research shows that the arrival of the horse may actually have intensified Arikara horticulture, as the Arikaras preferred to buy horses and even the buffalo meat and robes that increased agricultural production offered them. Because corn remained supreme, it is not surprising that the introduction of the horse went unrecorded in Arikara oral tradition. Wilson, "The Horse and the Dog"; Ewers, *The Horse in Blackfeet Indian Culture*; Wissler, "Influence of the Horse"; Roe, *The Indian and the Horse*; Hanson, "Adjustment and Adaptation"; Levy, "Is This a System?"; Bridges, "Prehistoric Arthritis," 76, 81–82. The only mythological reference to horses is in a story told by Not Afraid of the Enemy" (Alfred Morsette), but there are some problems with this account. See Parks, *Traditional Narratives of the Arikara Indians*, 101, 134–37. The increase in corn production actually resulted in an increase in joint problems among Arikara women. Wescott and Cunningham, "Temporal Changes."

17. It is possible that European fur traders carried the smallpox virus directly to the Arikaras, although it may also have been transferred along existing Native trade routes.

18. Gilmore, *Prairie Smoke*, 166–72; Gilmore "Study in the Ethnobotany," 330–31; Gilmore, "Account of the Piraskani Ceremony." For Arikara relations with the Cheyennes,

see Grinnell, *Cheyenne Indians,* 1:6, 8–9, 37–38, 47, 240, 251–52, 302; 2:190, 205, 338; Moore, Liberty, and Strauss, "Cheyenne;" John Stands In Timber and Liberty, *Cheyenne Memories,* 16.

19. For excellent discussions of Sioux history and culture, see DeMallie and Sturtevant, *Handbook of North American Indians,* 718–820; Hassrick, *The Sioux*; Gibbon, *The Sioux*; Anderson, "Early Dakota Migration."

20. Warren W. Caldwell, "Fortified Villages."

21. Sioux winter counts provide fragmentary information but suggest that conflicts between the two nations were common after the first recorded battle around 1694. Howard, "Memoir 11"; Mallery, *Picture-Writing,* 297. Some of the better-known winter counts that note conflicts between the Sioux and the Arikaras are in Curtis, "High Hawk's Winter-Count"; Howard, *British Museum Winter Count*; Vestal, *Warpath*; Thornton, "Rosebud Reservation"; and Waggoner, "Oglala Sioux Winter Count."

22. Trimble, "Infectious Disease," 50. Although it is unclear how these diseases reached the Arikara settlements, it seems likely that germs traveled along the old trade routes that connected the Arikaras to the various corners of the continent.

23. Europeans introduced a large number of diseases into the Americas, including chickenpox, bubonic plague, yellow fever, whooping cough, cholera, mumps, malaria, diphtheria, typhus, influenza, measles, and smallpox. Frequently, two or more diseases struck at the same time, multiplying mortality by an unknown factor. Epidemics followed each other so fast that populations did not have enough time to recover. Thornton, *American Indian Holocaust,* chapters 2 and 3. In effect, there was "an epidemic of epidemics" in the eighteenth century. Mark Braun, personal communication, September 13, 2005. (Braun holds an MD and an MA in bioanthropology and teaches at the School of Medicine, Indiana University, Bloomington. He studies the impact of infectious diseases introduced by Europeans and Africans into Native American populations during the early period of colonization of the Americas.) Several historical sources comment on the decline of the Arikaras. In 1785 the governor-general of Spanish Louisiana, Esteban Rodriguez Míro, reported that the Arikaras lived ninety leagues upstream of the mouth of the Niobrara River, where they had seven villages and some nine hundred warriors. Nasatir, *Before Lewis and Clark,* 123, 126–27; Parks, "Arikara," 366. Míro's figures were probably based on outdated information. A more reliable estimate comes from French fur trader Jean Baptiste Truteau, who visited the Arikaras in the mid-1790s. Truteau wrote that before the epidemics, the Arikaras had been able to muster about four thousand warriors but that the disaster had reduced their fighting strength to a mere five hundred. Truteau also noted that since the epidemics, Arikara attitudes toward fur traders had changed. They formerly had called all white men "spirits" because of the powerful objects they carried. But "now they think of us simply in connection with the items of merchandise that we bring them [and] that are so necessary to them." See DeMallie et al., *Fur Trader.*

24. Fenn, *Pox Americana,* 16–18.

25. Mark W. Braun, personal communication, September 13, 2005.

26. Abel, *Tabeau's Narrative,* 124, 126.

27. Moulton, *Journals of the Lewis and Clark Expedition,* 3:156–57. For an Arikara perspective see Yellow Bird, "Now I Will Speak."

28. The plagues that devastated the Arikaras between 1750 and 1781 may have resulted in a population decline of almost 90 percent. One reason is that the diseases disproportionately affected the young, who were the future reproductive group. A succession of diseases, then, had a snowball effect upon the reproductive capacities of the group. Mark Braun, personal communication, September 13, 2005.

29. Lehmer, *Middle Missouri Archaeology,* 170. The Arikaras eventually lost their Cheyenne allies as well. Jablow, *The Cheyenne,* 65, 78–89.

30. Although the identity of the attackers cannot be established with absolute certainty, only the Sioux were strong enough to launch an attack of this magnitude against a heavily fortified Arikara village. This was not an ordinary hit-and-run attack. Searching for a cause of the attack, researchers discovered that the number of young victims was relatively small. Based on this finding, they concluded that the purpose of the attack was to capture children under the age of five. Perhaps the attackers were trying to replenish their own numbers and to replace loved ones lost to smallpox and other diseases. Owsley, Berryman, and Bass, "Demographic and Osteological Evidence," 128.

31. DeMallie et al., *Fur Trader.*

32. Some scholars called these Sioux trading visits "friendly raiding parties." According to Truteau, the Arikaras tolerated the Sioux "owing to fear, wishing to avoid (making) too great a multitude of enemies among the Sioux nation who would certainly overpower them." Truteau added that the Sioux visit the Arikaras "and make great promises to live in good unity and in good accord with them in order to smoke their tobacco, to eat their maize, to freely hunt the bison and beaver on their lands in the autumn and winter; and in the spring they withdraw to the other river bank from which they return usually to kill [the Arikaras] or steal their horses." DeMallie et al., *Fur Trader.* Less than a decade later, Pierre Antoine Tabeau, who was not disposed to be friendly with the Arikaras, wrote that the Sioux saw in the Arikaras "a certain kind of serf, who cultivates for them and who, as they say, takes, for them, the place of women." Abel, *Tabeau's Narrative,* 130–31.

33. Fogelson, "Ethnohistory of Events and Nonevents."

34. Dorsey, *Traditions of the Arikara,* 17.

35. Ibid., 32.

36. Ibid., 21–22.

37. Ibid., 29.

38. Ibid., 21.

39. Ibid., 22.

40. Dorsey, *Traditions of the Skidi Pawnee,* 15.

41. Dorsey, *Pawnee Mythology,* 133–34.

42. Ibid., 410–11.

43. See the story "Coyote and the Origin of Death" in Dorsey, *Traditions of the Caddo,* 15.

44. Dorsey, *Mythology of the Wichita,* 135, 231, 296–97.

45. In the account by Hawk, the animal that threatened the people was Cut Nose. "This was an animal that had been a man, and he had gotten away from the people, but he was now trying to kill these people. His horns were long, and they seemed to touch the heavens." Dorsey, *Traditions of the Arikara,* 33. Based on this description, one might

see the horns as stylized whirlwinds or, because at this time the Arikaras had been under the influence of Christian missionaries for three decades, distinguish a resemblance to Satan. But Cut Nose was apparently an ancestor of the buffalo. In his time, buffalos hunted and ate people. Because he was formerly a man, one could also see him as a sort of cannibal, which is an image very common among the more distantly related Caddo Indians.

46. Ibid., 125–26. For a slightly different and more modern version of the story, see Alfred Morsette, "The Foolish Ones Who Killed the Beloved Snake Child," in Parks, *Traditional Narratives of the Arikara Indians*, 209–12.

47. It is possible that the "snake" might refer to the Missouri River itself and that the disease might have made it to the Arikara settlements by way of the river. The Arikaras believed in a serpent-like monster named Nuutawáčeš, which lived in the Missouri River and had to be appeased by sacrifices of tobacco. See Gilmore, *Prairie Smoke*, 38–39. See also Dorsey, *Traditions of the Arikara*, 79–80.

48. Dorsey, *Traditions of the Arikara*, 126–27.

49. For an excellent and highly engaging history of rabies, see Murphy and Wasik, *Rabid*.

50. It is possible that this event refers to a war with an enemy tribe, or perhaps to a "civil war" among the Arikara people themselves. In both these cases, a murder may have caused a cycle of devastating revenge killings. The people hiding in their cellars may be those who sought to escape or to remain neutral in the conflict.

51. In the story of the bears, there is an interesting twist. By having intercourse with the woman, the bear was actually transferring his power to her husband. But when the husband attacked the bear in a fit of jealousy, this power was denied and the bears retaliated. In other words, human "sin" (greed, jealousy, and so on) caused these misfortunes. Parks, *Traditional Narratives of the Arikara*, 205.

52. Melvin R. Gilmore, "Arikara Book of Genesis," 102–3.

53. Dorsey, *Traditions of the Arikara*, 17.

54. Ibid., 21.

55. Ibid., 37–38.

56. In Star's version, it was not Mother Corn but an unnamed woman who saved the people by turning herself into the cedar tree. Ibid., 21.

57. Ibid., 17.

58. Ibid., 32.

59. Ibid., 134–36.

60. Ibid., 33.

61. Kelton, *Cherokee Medicine*, 12.

62. *Arikara Ceremonies* (New York: Museum of the American Indian, Heye Foundation, 1924).

63. Hartley B. Alexander, "Lucky-in-the-House," *Theatre Arts Monthly* 17, no. 8 (August 1933), 616–26, and by the same author, *The World's Rim: Great Mysteries of the North American Indians* (Lincoln: University of Nebraska Press, 1953), 25–41.

64. George F. Will, "Magical and Sleight of Hand Performances by the Arikara," *North Dakota Historical Quarterly* 3, no. 1 (October 1928), 50–65; "Arikara Ceremonials,"

North Dakota Historical Quarterly 4, no. 4 (July 1930), 247–65; "Notes on the Arikara Indians and Their Ceremonies," *Old West Series* 3 (1934), 5–48; and "An Arikara Sacred Ceremony," *North Dakota History* 16, no. 4 (October 1949), 265–68.

CHAPTER 3. "THE SPIDERS WHO RECOVERED THE CHIEF'S GRANDSON"

1. "The Spiders Who Recovered the Chief's Grandson," in Dorsey, *Mythology of the Wichita*, 183.
2. For an excellent introduction to Wichita history and culture, see Newcomb, "Wichita."
3. From "The Spiders Who Recovered the Chief's Grandson," in Dorsey, *Mythology of the Wichita*, 177–87.
4. Dorsey, *Mythology of the Wichita*, preface and foreword.
5. Ibid., 2.
6. It is not clear if Ahahe's account specifically related a story from the Waco past or if it described an event from one of the other Wichita groups. Almazan and Coleman, "George Amos Dorsey."
7. Dorsey, *Mythology of the Wichita*, 182.
8. Ibid., 181.
9. For a brief but excellent discussion of the transformation of the intertribal slave trade, see Barr, "From Captives to Slaves."
10. For an excellent discussion of the southwestern Indian slave trade see Brooks, *Captives and Cousins*, and Reséndez, *Other Slavery*. See also Carocci and Pratt, *Native American Adoption*, and Gallay, *Indian Slave Trade*.
11. Brooks, *Captives and Cousins*, 50.
12. Historian Carl J. Ekberg estimated that nearly two-thirds of all Indian slaves in Canada in the early 1700s were "Panis." French officials eventually used the term "Panis" to designate any kind of Indian slave from west of the Missouri River. Still, the majority of these slaves belonged to the Caddoan language family, which included the Caddos, Wichitas, Kitsais, South Band Pawnees, Skiri Pawnees, and Arikaras. Ekberg, *Stealing Indian Women*, 10, 11, 13, 48. See also Wedel, *Wichita Indians*, 53–72.
13. Brooks, *Captives and Cousins*, 49.
14. Ibid., 50.
15. See Barr, "From Captives to Slaves." See also Brooks, *Captives and Cousins*, 59–79. For a recent discussion on the rise of the Comanches on the southern plains see Hämäläinen, *Comanche Empire*.
16. The Wichitas forged an alliance with the Comanches in the 1750s, but because Ahahe says that both villages "made their living by raising crops of corn," it seems unlikely that the Comanches were meant. Dorsey, *Mythology of the Wichita*, 177.
17. Newcomb, "Wichita," 550.
18. Dorsey, *Mythology of the Wichita*, 183.
19. Barnes, *True Story of Punishment*, chapter 3; Abbott, *Rack, Rope and Red-Hot Pincers*, 3, 123–47, 195, 219–22, 232. Another intriguing form of pole torture was tying a victim to the mouth of a cannon, which was charged with ball, shrapnel, grapes, or a blank charge. Needless to say, when the gun went off, the victim's body would be torn to

pieces. This form of execution was rare, although it was reportedly used by the Spanish in Chile during the Mapuche Rebellion (1553–1558), and the Portuguese executed a Brazilian Native leader in this manner in 1618. It does not quite fit the description of slowly burning the child to death either.

20. Thomas, *After Coronado*, 12–14, 33–39.
21. Dorsey, *Mythology of the Wichita*, 181–82.
22. The best primary source collection on the Coronado expedition is Flint and Cushing-Flint, *Documents of the Coronado Expedition*. For a modern history of the Coronado expedition see Hoig, *Came Men on Horses*. Hoig also provides useful overviews of the expeditions by Fray Agustín Rodríguez (1581) and Antonio de Espejo (1582), the illegal expedition staged by Captains Francisco Leyva de Bonilla and Antonio Gutiérrez de Humaña in 1593, and, finally, an expedition led by Don Juan de Oñate in 1601. For primary sources on the Gaspar Castaño de Sosa expedition of 1590, see Hammond, *Rediscovery of New Mexico*, especially 245–97. The Leyva–Humaña expedition held the most promise for my purposes. There are several parallels or common themes between the Wichita myth and the Humaña: (1) the presence of harquebuses and possibly a cannon; (2) the apparent hostility between Humaña and the Wichitas; (3) the presence of a large river by which Humaña might have tried to escape; (4) the tactics used by the Wichitas in their battle with the Spaniards; (5) the burned feet of the surviving Spaniard, which correspond with the burns of the captive child. Of course, there are also some major problems: (1) There was no old woman present, and it seems doubtful that Humaña or his men kept clearly visible images of the blessed Virgin Mary; (2) clearly the French were not present at this time, in which case Spider-Man must have been some other figure; (3) the details are too obscure to positively identify Humaña with the myth. For example, it is unknown if the Wichitas decapitated any of the men in Humaña's party. See Hammond, *Rediscovery of New Mexico*, 323–26; Hoig, *Came Men on Horses*, 181–82, 201–3.
23. Although it is now more than half a century old, the best and most complete account of the massacre is still Weddle, *San Sabá Mission*.
24. Weddle, *San Sabá Mission*, part 2.
25. Ibid., 70.
26. Simpson, *San Sabá Papers*, 51, 66, 92, 95–96.
27. Weddle, *San Sabá Mission*, 71.
28. Simpson, *San Sabá Papers*, 74; Weddle, 72–73.
29. Ibid., 85. Others—Father Molina especially—claimed that the Indians entered the stockade by removing the bars that locked the gate. Weddle, *San Sabá Mission*, 73–75.
30. Simpson, *San Sabá Papers*, 87–88.
31. Ibid., 75.
32. Ibid., 75, document 29, testimony by Joseph Vazquez.
33. The soldiers in Colonel Parrilla's command were so spooked that they undertook the unusual step of requesting removal of the fort to safer territory. In effect, this request amounted to mutiny. Parrilla had to apply all his diplomatic skills to keep the situation from getting out of control. Simpson, *San Sabá Papers*, 107–9.
34. Ibid., 86, 87.
35. Hämäläinen, *Comanche Empire*, 43–44.

36. Dunn, "Apache Mission," 413.
37. Ratcliffe, "'Escenas de Martirio,'" 517–23.
38. Simpson, *San Sabá Papers*, 86.
39. See also Barr, *Peace Came in the Form of a Woman*; Kavanagh, *Comanche Political History*; Hämäläinen, *Comanche Empire*; Canonge, *Comanche Texts*.
40. Juan Cortina quoted in Robert S. Weddle, *After the Massacre*, 2.
41. Simpson, *San Sabá Papers*, 44, 52, 66, 74, 90.
42. Ibid., 76.
43. Ibid., 137–38.
44. Dorsey, *Mythology of the Wichita*, 183. Ahahe also explains that there was an "open space" within the village, which corresponds with the little plaza in front of the mission church at San Sabá.
45. Ratcliffe, "'Escenas de Martirio,'" 526–28.
46. V. Kay Hindes et al., *Rediscovery of Santa Cruz*, 73.
47. Dorsey, *Mythology of the Wichita*, 182.
48. According to one art historian, "José de Páez inundated the second half of the eighteenth century with his paintings. Among his infinity of pictures, some have interest . . . but it is difficult to name one that is entirely respectable." Manuel Toussaint quoted in Bernard L. Fontana, "Pictorial Images," 933.
49. Dorsey, *Mythology of the Wichita*, 183.
50. "Fr. Maria Ano de los Dolores to the Reverend Fathers of the Rio Grande Missions, 21 March 1758," in Boyd, McWilliams, and Wade, *Spanish Colonial Documents*, 199.
51. Weddle, *San Sabá Mission*, 88.
52. Simpson, *San Sabá Papers*, 98.
53. Weddle, *After The Massacre*, 5. The number of Spaniards killed is still a matter of debate. Juan M. Romero de Terreros argues that twelve men were killed and nine wounded. Terreros, "Destruction of the San Sabá Apache Mission," 624–25.
54. Simpson, *San Sabá Papers*, 56. It is also possible that the "headless men" were enemies enslaved by the Wichitas. Following their contact with the French, the Wichitas themselves became slave raiders and slave traders. Until this time, they had been the victims of slave raids. According to some sources, they sometimes retaliated by torturing and cannibalizing captives for supposed religious purposes. "By the mid-eighteenth century," anthropologist William Newcomb wrote, "captives had become an important article of commerce [for the Wichitas], and cannibalism disappeared prior to the nineteenth century." Newcomb, "Wichita," 557.
55. Terreros, "Destruction of the San Sabá Apache Mission," 623. It is possible that more corpses were scalped before they were burned.
56. Ibid., 625.
57. Simpson, *San Sabá Papers*, 52.
58. Ibid., 69.
59. Ibid., 44.
60. Dorsey, *Mythology of the Wichita*, 183.
61. Simpson, *San Sabá Papers*, 47.
62. Ibid., 49.

63. Ibid., 48.
64. Ibid., 64.
65. Ibid., 65.
66. Ibid., 82–83.
67. Historians consider the San Sabá Massacre a pivotal event in borderlands history. Scholar Juan M. Romero de Terreros called it a "historical breakthrough." Terreros gives three reasons for this assertion. First, the massacre involved fifteen hundred to two thousand warriors, which was an unprecedented number. Second, this was the first time a broad alliance of Wichitas, Comanches, Tonkawas, and men from other tribes had acted together. Third, these Indians were unusually well armed (more than 50 percent of them carried guns in the attack). Finally, "San Sabá is the only instance, during the 150 years of Spain's effective presence in Texas, where a mission was fully destroyed and a sizable part of its thirty inhabitants killed." Never before had Indians attacked a mission with such devastating consequences. Terreros, "Destruction of the San Sabá Apache Mission," 626–27.

CHAPTER 4. DEATH OF THE FLINT MONSTER

1. Dorsey, *Traditions of the Skidi Pawnee*, 29.

2. See Mishkin, *Rank and Warfare*; Starkey, *European and Native American Warfare*; Malone, *Skulking Way of War*.

3. Archaeological finds support the fact that chain mail armor was indeed common in Plains Indian warfare through the centuries. Wedel, "Chain Mail." See also Bleed et al., "Scale Armor."

4. The census records do list a Kitkehahki man named Curley Chief (age sixty-three in 1889–90), but this man had passed away by 1900. The same records also list a young Kitkehahki man named Curley Hair or Buck-skah-ree-wih (age twenty-one in 1889–90), who was Curley Chief's nephew. He told Murie several traditional stories that were published by Dorsey. NARA, Microcopy 595.

5. Other stories by Curly-Head include a version of "The Girl Who Married a Star" (story 16, endnote 119), as well as "The Boy Who Disobeyed the Stars" (story 17), "The Boy and the Thistles" (story 29), and "The Boy Who Conquered the Buffalo" (story 30). See Dorsey, *Traditions of the Skidi Pawnee*; 60–65, 65–68, 104–9, 109–11.

6. The closely related Wichita Indians have a similar version of this story, but instead of a flint-covered monster, the animal who carries off people is "Mountain-Lion (Woxis), or Spike-Tail." Other important details are missing from this story, which implies that the Wichitas obtained a trimmed-down version of the Pawnee story. See "The Story of Not-Know-Who-You-Are," told by Ahahe in Dorsey, *Mythology of the Wichita*, 224–28.

7. Attaching cloth either over or under the mail made it more comfortable to wear and allowed for the embroidery of heraldic emblems. Heraldic emblems often represented martial qualities (lion = courage, dragon = strength, fox = cunning). Emblems were often combined when families intermarried. To document, register, and regulate heraldry, the College of Heralds was instituted in England in 1484. With the development of the chain-mail-piercing longbow in the fourteenth century, full plate armor became necessary.

At first, large plates of iron were held together by leather straps. Steel plate armor probably developed when designers added plates to protect joints such as elbows and knees. It is unclear exactly when plate armor for the torso appeared; illustrations from the era do not offer any insights because this armor was often worn underneath a surcoat. A coat of plates was called a brigandine. Brigandines were eventually replaced by larger breastplates. By the late 1300s, both cavalry and infantry widely used the cuirass, in which breastplate and back plate were connected by leather straps. To prevent an opponent's sword, saber, or knife from sliding along the slippery plate surface into the throat, armor smiths often riveted a V-shaped bar just below the neck. Greaves, protective plates for the shins, also appeared around this time, as did sabatons, which protected the feet. In the 1390s, the gorget or bevor, made of "overlapping plates of metal and formed to cover the neck from the shoulders to the chin," came into use, although many soldiers continued to use chain mail collars. This time also saw the development of plate armor for arms and hands, including plate gauntlets with "narrow metal plates secured together with internal leathers and rivets and attached to a leather glove." Eventually the plates became fewer and larger. Thus a full suit of armor consisted of (1) a cuirass consisting of a breastplate and back plate; (2) a gorget to protect the neck or throat; (3) vambraces to protect the arms; (4) gauntlets to guard the hands and wrists; (5) cuisses and greaves for leg protection; and (6) sabatons to protect the feet. Scholars often refer to two different types of armor: the German and Italian styles. In reality, both styles were made and worn in both Italy and Germany. New carburizing techniques made the steel harder and also made it possible to generate a "high shine," which found its expression in the "white knight" from European folk traditions. DeVries and Smith, *Medieval Military Technology*, 72–77.

    8. "Eventually, the gauntlet consisted of only a single plate to protect the back and sides of the hand, molded to the shape of the knuckles and the base of the thumb, and separate smaller plates to protect the fingers and the thumb. All the plates continued to be attached by rivets to a leather glove." Gauntlets underwent a significant transformation in the fifteenth century: "The gauntlet changed only after 1430, from a relatively simple cover for the top of the hand to a mitten which encompassed the entire hand. This was achieved by surrounding the entire hand with armor and by extending the metacarpal plates to the tips of the fingers. The number of plates depended on the flexibility desired—the more plates the better the flexibility—although the right gauntlet, which covered the weapon-wielding hand, was always more flexible than the left. At the same time, the 'hour-glass' shape of the cuffs fell out of fashion, and the cuff now extended further up the lower arm, overlapping the lower cannon." DeVries and Smith, *Medieval Military Technology*, 77–83.

    9. Ibid.; Wedel, "Chain Mail," 189.

    10. Bleed et al., "Scale Armor"; Peter Bleed, personal communication, September 11, 2015.

    11. DeVries and Smith, *Medieval Military Technology*, 83.

    12. Wedel, "Chain Mail," 189.

    13. DeVries and Smith, 85.

14. Ibid., 90.

15. Gardner, *Five Centuries*, 217.

16. Hammond and Rey, *Obregón's History*, 232.

17. "Among certain plains Indian tribes the personal name Iron Shirt often occurs. This name refers to coats of mail brought to the southern United States by the Spaniards in very early days and which passed into the hands of the Indians and were worn by them. There are several traditions of this kind. Armor of a certain sort was used by Indians of the Pacific Slope, but no armor of metal was ever known to the aborigines except as it came through the white men. Most of the traditions of these coats of mail are vague, yet of some we have definite knowledge." Grinnell also mentioned coats of mail among the Kiowas and Comanches. In 1858 the Caddo Indians killed a Comanche who wore a coat of mail. According to Grinnell, French explorer Robert Cavalier, sieur de La Salle, had found a shirt of mail in the hands of Indians occupying villages on the Mississippi River in the 1680s. Grinnell, *Fighting Cheyennes*, 71–72. Chain mail made its way up as far as the northern plains. Fur trader Hugh Monroe told how he met a Pikuni Blackfeet chief named Lone Walker (chief of the Small Robes band), who showed him a Spanish sword and coat of mail. Etched in the sword was "Francisco Alvarez. Barcelona. 1693." Lone Walker had acquired these items in the "always-summer land," where he had traveled as a young man to steal horses. In a fight, he had killed the man who wore the iron shirt and carried the sword. Lone Walker explained: "That is a strong shirt. Arrows cannot pierce it. It has saved my life three different times in battle with the enemy." Schultz, *Rising Wolf*, 145–46. I did not find the name Francisco Alvarez in Gardner's compendium on armorers. Hence it is probably the name of the original owner of the sword. See Gardner, *Five Centuries of Gunsmiths*, part 5. Walter McClintock mentioned that among the Blackfeet Indians there was a chief named Iron Shirt. Technically, this man did not truly wear chain mail but rather "a buckskin shirt with pieces of shining metal." His grandson received the same name. Neither of these men were killed in battle with the Pawnees in the manner described in the Skiri myth. McClintock, *Old North Trail*, 422, 431–32. Perhaps this was the same man observed by Prince Maximilian at Fort MacKenzie in 1833: "In front of the Indians we saw three or four chiefs in red and blue uniforms, trimmed with lace, and wearing round hats with plumes of feathers. The most distinguished among them was Mexkehme-Sukahs (the iron shirt), dressed in a scarlet uniform, with blue facings and lace, with a drawn sabre in his hand; riding without stirrups, he managed, with great dexterity, his light bay horse, which was made very restiff by the firing of the musketry." Thwaites, *Early Western Travels*, 88. Artist Carl Bodmer, who accompanied the prince on the expedition, drew or painted a portrait of this chief. The family name Iron Shirt is still carried by Blackfeet Indians today.

18. Loomis and Nasatir, *Pedro Vial*. See also John and Benavides, "Inside the Comancheria."

19. Ibid., 29.

20. Flint and Cushing Flint, *Documents of the Coronado Expedition*; Flint, *Great Cruelties*; Flint, *No Settlement*; Flint and Cushing Flint, *Coronado Expedition*; Flint and Cushing Flint, *Latest Word*. For a short introduction on Coronado as well as subsequent expeditions, see Hoig, *Came Men on Horses*, 139–45.

21. Flint and Cushing Flint, *Documents of the Coronado Expedition*, 135–51.

22. Ibid., 140, 145.

23. Ibid., 517.

24. We can safely eliminate the expeditions by Fray Agustín Rodríguez (1581) and Antonio de Espejo (1582) as possible sources for the Flint Monster's true identity. Fray Agustín Rodríguez was a Franciscan who in 1581, escorted by one officer and nine soldiers, set out from Santa Barbara, Mexico, with two fellow friars, nineteen Indian servants, ninety horses, and six hundred head of stock to establish a mission. Although all three friars were murdered by Indians, this expedition did not contact the Pawnees. We can exclude the Antonio de Espejo expedition for similar reasons. Although Espejo entered Texas, he seems to have gone no further than present-day Fort Davis, and it does not appear that he contacted a Caddoan group. Hoig, *Came Men on Horses*, 139–45. In 1590 Gaspar Castaño de Sosa, then lieutenant governor of Nueva León, set out with about 170 people to establish a colony in Texas and look for slaves. Castaño fought several engagements with Indians, but he operated primarily in West Texas and New Mexico, far away from the Pawnees, although his slave raids may have indeed encountered Caddoan traders or hunters. The accounts of Castaño's expedition do not provide clear links with Curly-Head's account. See Hoig, *Came Men on Horses*, 148–52. For primary sources on this expedition, see Hammond, *Rediscovery of New Mexico*, especially 245–97.

25. Hoig, *Came Men on Horses*, 152.

26. Hammond, *Rediscovery of New Mexico*, 323–26; Hoig, *Came Men on Horses*, 181–82, 201–3, 230.

27. Wedel, "Chain Mail," 194.

28. He ruled with an iron fist. For example, when the Acoma Pueblos rebelled in 1599, Oñate quashed the rebellion and ordered severe punishments for "all those of fighting age . . . as a warning to everyone in this kingdom." Oñate ordered his men to cut off one foot of every Acoma male over the age of twenty-five; these men also had to serve twenty-five years as slaves. Acoma women were sent to monasteries and convents in Mexico, and many of them never saw their home again. Elderly men and women were turned over as slaves to the Querecho Apaches. Hoig, *Came Men on Horses*, 157, 198, 204.

29. Ibid., 148, 207, 221–38.

30. Kavanagh, *Comanche Political History*, 105. For example, in 1858 Texas Rangers killed a Comanche chief named Pohebits Quasho (Iron Jacket) and cut up his coat of mail for souvenirs. At the Battle of Adobe Walls in 1864, the United States Army killed a young Kiowa or Comanche warrior wearing a Spanish coat of mail. One of the signatories on the Treaty of Little Arkansas in 1865 was a Plains Apache chief named Iron Shirt. Hoig, *Came Men on Horses*, 98.

31. In the sources, the name appears in several versions: Camisa de Fierro, Camisa de Hierro, and Camisa de Yierro. Kavanagh, *Comanche Political History*, 500.

32. John and Benavides, "Inside the Comancheria," 37–38.

33. Kavanagh, *Comanche Political History*, 120.

34. Ibid., 140–43, 149, 178.

35. Hämäläinen, *Comanche Empire*, 160–61.

36. Cheyenne expert George Bird Grinnell reported that in 1838 that the Cheyennes "possessed a suit of Spanish armor which appears to have been in the possession of the tribe, or of their allies, the Arapahoes, for thirty or more years before that." One of these Cheyennes wore this shirt in 1844 during a fight with eastern Indian trappers at Shawnee Creek, a tributary of the Arickaree fork of the Republican River. Grinnell, *Fighting Cheyennes*, 71–72. The Smithsonian Institution archives contain an "Anonymous Cheyenne drawing of Iron Shirt killed by Pawnee warriors in battle." The drawing dates to the 1880s, but the event depicted took place long before. However, this Iron Shirt could not be the Flint-Monster from the Skiri myth because the man in the drawing was killed by a gun volley. There is another Cheyenne named Iron Shirt. In the early decades of the twentieth century, Thomas Marquis showed photographs to John Wooden Legs, who helped Marquis identify the men in the pictures. One of the pictures showed "Iron Shirt" and his family. Although this Iron Shirt died a natural death, his uncle and brother were both nicknamed Iron Shirt. Liberty, *Northern Cheyenne Album*, 233.

37. The Pawnees sometimes used the name Iron Shirt for Alights on the Cloud, but Grinnell also lists his name as "Touching Cloud" and "He Who Mounts the Clouds." Reportedly, he was one of the "most important men" among the Cheyennes. In 1851 he attended the negotiations at Fort Laramie. The Pawnees were not represented at the negotiations, but when a Pawnee chief later suggested making peace with the Cheyennes, Alights on the Cloud refused and the peace was never concluded. After Fort Laramie, Alights on the Cloud (aka Iron Shirt) visited Washington, D.C. Grinnell, *Fighting Cheyennes*, 70–71.

38. Ibid., 74, 80. Elsewhere Grinnell states that Mexicans traded objects with the Indians, including the coat of mail that Alights on the Cloud wore. "It was from one of these Mexican traders that the so-called 'iron shirt'—a coat of mail—was obtained by an Arapaho or a Flathead and finally passed into the possession of the Cheyennes, who retained it until the year 1852, when Alights On The Cloud, who was then wearing it, was killed and the shirt was captured by the Pawnees and destroyed." Grinnell, *Cheyenne Indians*, 35–36.

39. Grinnell's main informants were Bald-Faced Bull, Iron Shirt, and Kiowa Woman. Grinnell, *Fighting Cheyennes*, 75–76.

40. These were not the sacred arrows that the Pawnees had captured from the Cheyennes around 1844. George E. Hyde argued that the hero was a fifteen-year-old Kitkehahki by the name of Big Spotted Horse. In an endnote, Hyde also explains the discrepancies between the different accounts: "George Bent of the Cheyennes described this armor to the present writer as a long leather coat with small discs sown all over it, overlapping like shingles on a roof. Dr. George Bird Grinnell states (*The Fighting Cheyennes*, pp.78–9) that a Pitahauerat Pawnee on foot shot Alights-on-the-Clouds [sic] with a magic arrow, and he gives old Eagle Chief of the Skidis as his authority. Many old Cheyennes in 1912 (and some of them were in this fight) agreed that Alight-on-the-Clouds was killed by a left-handed Pawnee who was riding a horse when he shot the arrow. Captain L. H. North heard this story over and over, and the Pawnees (around 1863–73) always said that it was Big Spotted Horse, mounted, who killed the Cheyenne. Captain North knew

Eagle Chief very well and found it difficult to believe that he had given a different version to Grinnell; indeed North suggested that the interpreter (Tom Morgan) had twisted old Eagle Chief's words and given Grinnell a false interpretation. It may be noted that Tom Morgan was the man who produced this story of the magic arrow, and that he said it was his own father who killed the Cheyenne." Hyde, *Pawnee Indians*, 232–34. The above quote is on page 237.

41. Grinnell, *Fighting Cheyennes*, 79.

42. Ibid., 79.

43. Frances Densmore, *Pawnee Music*, 60.

44. Ibid., 59.

45. Mooney's complete entry states: "Summer 1852. *Á'pätáte* (*K'a-t'ógyä* or *Hánt'ógyä-k'ía*) *Ehótal-de Pai*, 'Summer that Touch-the-Clouds (Knife-shirt, or Iron-shirt-man) was killed.' There was no sun dance this year. The Pawnee warriors killed a Cheyenne chief who wore a cuirass, and the tree with leaves shows that it occurred during the summer. At a great Cheyenne camp upon a stream, apparently in Kansas or Nebraska, known to the Kiowa as Há'ntso P'a, 'Cannon-ball (literally, metal rock) river,' the Cheyenne, Arapaho, and some Dakota had made medicine for a combined expedition against the Pawnee, to which they invited the Kiowa and Apache, who were camped at the time on Konyä'daldä P'a, 'Black-hill river,' in Kansas, north of the Arkansas. About half the warriors of the two latter tribes accepted the invitation, and the united force, moving with all their women, children, and tipi outfits, started against the Pawnee. They met the enemy, but were defeated, with the loss of the Cheyenne chief Wóifdóĭsh, 'Touch-the-clouds,' called by the Kiowa *Á'pätáte*, 'Far-up,' otherwise known as *Hánt'ógyä-k'ía*, 'Iron-shirt-man,' from a cuirass which he wore and which had probably been procured originally from Mexico, where the Kiowa once captured another. The official report for the year thus notices the encounter: A war party of Osages, Kioways, and Kaws, consisting of about four hundred warriors, went in pursuit of the Pawnees while out on their last hunt. They overtook the Pawnees and attacked them, but, being greatly outnumbered by the Pawnees, they ingloriously fled, leaving on the ground one war chief killed, and having killed and scalped one Pawnee woman (*Report*, 81)." Mooney, "Calendar History," 294–95.

46. The problem with Hyde's claim that the hero was a Kitkehahki by the name of Big Spotted Horse is that Hyde used only secondhand sources such as Luther North. Hyde, *Pawnee Indians*, 237.

47. Ewers, *The Horse in Blackfoot Indian Culture*; Wissler, "Influence of the Horse"; Roe, *The Indian and the Horse*; Gilbert L. Wilson, "The Horse and the Dog"; Holder, *The Hoe and the Horse*.

48. The division of the people into eastern and western villages is also typical of Skiri Pawnee cosmology. According to the Skiri creation story, Morning Star lived in the east while Evening Star lived in the west. When these two sacred powers came together, they gave birth to the first human being.

49. There is widespread confusion about the identity of the Padoucas. Spanish sources applied the name Padoucas to the Plains Apaches, but French sources identified the Padoucas with the Comanches. The confusion of terms resulted from the fact that

the Comanches pushed away and replaced the Apaches on the plains in the eighteenth century, causing the French, who arrived on the plains later than the Spanish, to misidentify them. For the debate on the Padoucas, see Grinnell, "Who were the Padouca?" and Secoy, "Identity of the 'Paduca.'"

50. Foster and McCollough, "Plains Apache."

51. Hotz believed that the tepee-dwelling defenders were Apaches and that the attackers were Opatas or Pimas. Hotz, *Indian Skin Paintings*, 13–78.

52. Hyde, *Pawnee Indians*, 46.

53. Thomas, *After Coronado*, 13–14.

54. Ibid., 4, 19.

55. Apache warriors continued to use chain mail, or at least carried the name Iron Shirt, until the 1860s. In 1864 a Kiowa Apache (or Plains Apache) chief named Iron Shirt died when his tepee burned down during the Battle of Adobe Walls against American soldiers under command of Kit Carson. According to the sources, when Carson ordered his men to burn the village, Iron Shirt refused to leave the tepee, preferring to die by fire. A year later, in 1865, another Apache chief named Iron Shirt—possibly the son of the slain chief at Adobe Walls—signed a treaty with the Cheyennes and Arapahos. Palmer, *Apache Peoples*, n.p.; Kappler, *Indian Affairs*, 891–92. Two years after that, this same man signed the Medicine Lodge Treaty of 1867. He is listed under the name Ba-zhe-ech (Iron Shirt), and he agreed to peace with the Comanches, including Ten Bears, and the Kiowas under Satank and Satanta. Kappler, *Indian Affairs*, 982–84.

56. Thomas, *After Coronado*, 31–32, 36–39, 129–37, 163–65, 183–87, 228. For a recent interpretation see Christopher Steinke, "Leading the 'Father.'" It is unlikely that Curly-Head's account refers to the Villasur expedition, because Villasur was the aggressor and because the Spanish no longer wore mail armor at this time. Of course, it is possible that one of the Indian allies wore chain mail.

57. Roger C. Echo-Hawk, personal communication, April 5, 2014.

58. Paul Wilhelm, Duke of Württemberg, *Travels in North America, 1822–1824*, trans. W. Robert Nitske, and ed. Savoie Lottinville (Norman: University of Oklahoma Press, 1973), 389. "Die am Wolfs-Fluess aber waren niemals gegen franzoesische Creolen oder Amerikaner boesgesinnt, waehrend ihr Hass gegen Spanier oder Mexikaner keine Grenzen kennt, und sie gegen die oestliche Bevoelkerung der Provincias internas, laengs des Rio bravo und Texas, einen unversoehnlichen Verfolgungskrieg fuehren. Es scheint, als staemmen diese Volker, sowie de Comaches [*sic*], Arapahoras und andere Indianos Llaneros bravos aus dem jetzt von Neu-Spaniern besetzten Gebiete, und als habe sie das Schwert ihrer Eroberer aus ihren frueheren Wohnsitzen verdraengt, wogegen einige andere mit ihnen verwandte indianische Staemme, welche die unzugaenglichsten Gebirge und waldigsten Gegenden der Cordillera wie den Bolson de mapini, die Sierra das grullas u.s.w. bewohnen, ihre Selbstaendigkeit nur der Wildheit des von ihnen bewohnten Landes verdanken, von welchem Schlupfwinkeln aus sie ebenfalls durch ununterbrochene Raubzuge die Geissel der benachtbarten Ranchos [Ranchos werden Niederlassungen genannt, in welchen Vieh und Pferde gezogen werden] werden." Paul Wilhelm, Herzog von Wuerttemberg, *Erste Reise nach dem noerdlichen Amerika in*

den Jahren 1822 bis 1824 (Stuttgart: Verlag der J. O. Cotta'schen Buchhandlung, 1835), 370.

59. Wilhelm, *Travels in North America*, 390. "Die Pahnis sind stoltz auf den grossen Schaden, den sie laengsther den spanischen Abkoemmlingen verursacht, sowie darauf, dass sie schon in den frueheren Zeiten der Eroberung harte Kaempfe mit den Conquistadores gefochten haben; auch besitzen sie eine Menge Trophaeen von den letzteren." Wilhelm, *Erste Reise*, 370.

60. Wilhelm, *Travels in North America*, 392. "Es wurde mir ein junger Indianer zugefuehrt, welcher gebrochen Spanisch sprach. Dieser Indier war in der Naehe der Mission von San Antonio gefangen genommen und von den Spaniern bis in das Innere von Neu-Spanien geschleppt worden. Daselbst wurde er getauft und fand hernach Gelegenheit, zu entfliehen und zu seinen Landsleuten zurueckzukehren,—ein Beweis von den Scharfsinn und der Schlauheit der Indianer." Wilhelm, *Erste Reise*, 373.

61. Wilhelm, *Travels in North America*, 394. "Mein Vater! Die langen Messer [gen] Osten haben uns Gutes gethan und lieben uns; die baertigen Leute [gen] Westen und den Bergen aber hassen die rothen Leute und haben uns seit Vaeter Zeiten vertrieben und getoedtet; darum trinken wir ihr Blut und hassen sie, den unser Land war [gen] Abend." Wilhelm, *Erste Reise*, 374.

62. Wilhelm, *Travels in North America, 1822–1824*, 395. "Ferner zeigte mir der Priester alte spanische Waffen aus dem 16ten Jahrhunderte, welche, seiner Angabe nach, vor langer Zeit in den Kriegen, welche die Pahnis in den Gebirgen [gen = zu?] Westen mit den Spaniern bestanden hatten, erobert worden waren. Er sprach von mehreren Indianern der Nation, welche auf ihren Streifzuegen bis an die Muendungen des Bravo-Stromes gekommen waren. Ich fand nachher Gelegenheit, selbst einige zu sehen, und ueberzeugte mich von der Wahrheit dieser Aussage." Wilhelm, *Erste Reise*, 375.

63. In an endnote, Dorsey stated that the double balls were used in a game: "In this [game] two small buckskin balls, attached to each other by a string about eight inches in length, are tossed by means of slender sticks slightly curved at one end." Dorsey also noted, "The idea of magic flight through space by means of the ball or arrow is not uncommon," and he referred to myths from the Arapahos, Wichitas, and others. See, for example, Dorsey, *Mythology of the Wichita*, 64–65, 220, 237.

64. Gilles Havard, personal communication, September 13, 2015. See also Gilles Havard, *Empire et Métissages: Indiens at Français dans le Pays d'en Haut, 1660–1715* (Paris: Septentrion, Presses de l'Université, 2003), 544, 654.

65. Jantz and Owsley, "White Traders in the Upper Missouri."

66. Thomas, *After Coronado*, 4, 19.

67. See Back, "Dress of the First Voyageurs," 2–19.

68. Meanwhile, the transformation of Coyote-Man's family into "coyotes" may refer to the division between Skiri Pawnees and a group that later joined the Arikaras. The word for "coyote" and "wolf" is the same in both Pawnee dialects: *ckirihki*. The division between the Skiris and the Arikaras was a process that took place between 1450 and 1650, with the formation of new groups that would break away from the Skiri. Some of these joined the Arikara tribe later.

69. Ramsey, *Reading the Fire*, 159–69.

CHAPTER 5. THE OLD MAN WITH THE IRON-NOSED MASK

1. Dorsey, *Traditions of the Caddo*, 58–59.

2. The Caddos are the southernmost branch of the tribes belonging to the Caddoan Indian language family. At the time of contact, the different Caddo groups (Hasinai, Kadohadacho, Natchitoches, and some smaller groups) occupied territory in southwestern Arkansas, southeastern Oklahoma, northern Louisiana, and northeastern Texas. Although the Caddos shared many similarities with their plains relatives, anthropologists usually include them in the southeastern culture area. See Rogers and Sabo, "Caddo." For a general history see Carter, *Caddo Indians*. According to scholars, the Caddos separated from the northern Caddoans about three thousand to thirty-five hundred years ago, the Wichita separated from the northern Caddoan group some nineteen hundred to two thousand years ago, and the Pawnees and Arikaras separated some three hundred to four hundred years ago. Following their separations, these tribes not only occupied different territories but also had different historical experiences, which are reflected in their oral traditions. The masked cannibal with the iron nose does not appear in the oral traditions of the other Caddoan tribes. Parks, "Caddoan Languages."

3. The major primary sources for the De Soto expedition were published in Clayton, Knight, and Moore, *De Soto Chronicles*.

4. According to linguist and Caddo expert Wallace Chafe, the name Tula is not Caddo because the Caddo language does not contain the consonant *l*. Chafe speculates that the name was probably given by one of De Soto's guides, who was most likely a speaker of a Muskogean language. Chafe also translated Naguatex (pronounced "Nawidish") as "place of salt." He positively identified it as a Caddo village. See Chafe, "Caddo Names in the de Soto Documents," 225. Archaeologist Frank Schambach believes that Tula was a Tunica settlement. Most scholars, however, continue to follow John Swanton, who claimed that Tula was Caddo. Frank Schambach, "The End of the Trail: The Route of Hernando de Soto's Army through Southwest Arkansas and East Texas," *Arkansas Archaeologist* 27 (1989): 9–33.

5. Despite certain theories to the contrary, it is unlikely that the concurrent Coronado expedition made contact with the Caddo Indians. Swanton, *Source Material*, 32–35.

6. Clews Parsons, *Notes on the Caddo*, 35. See also Gerona, "Caddo Sun Accounts," 358–62. For Wing's description of the Caddo medicine men, see "The Origin of the Medicine Men," in Dorsey, *Traditions of the Caddo*, 23.

7. See also Gerona, "Caddo Sun Accounts," 360.

8. Dorsey, *Traditions of the Caddo*, 58–59.

9. Ibid., 59–61.

10. Swanton, *Source Material*, 35. As stated in chapter 4, the process of turning a historical event into myth might begin almost instantly. See Ramsey, *Reading the Fire*, chapter 9.

11. Speck, "Ethnology of the Yuchi Indians," 140.

12. Mooney, *Myths of the Cherokee*, 319–21.

13. Curtin, *Seneca Indian Myths*, especially 4–5, 122–23, 154–55.

14. Ibid., 1–7, 47–51, 122–23, 152–55, 216–17, 247–55, 360–65, 457–73, 509–11.

15. Stevenson, *Sia*, 45.

16. Opler, *Myths and Tales*, 79.

17. Ibid., 168.

18. Duncan and Diaz-Granados, "Of Masks and Myths."

19. La Vere, *Caddo Chiefdoms*, 26–27, 28.

20. Hall, *Archaeology of the Soul*, chapter 18 and 145–54. See also Duncan and Diaz-Granados, "Of Masks and Myths."

21. Possibly this is a reference to a sweat lodge.

22. Dorsey, *Traditions of the Caddo*, 31–36.

23. Saunt, "History until 1776," 130. Historian and De Soto expert Paul E. Hoffman does not agree entirely: "Clearly, some Old World diseases did reach epidemic levels among the southeastern Indians during the sixteenth century, but whether that was before or after or because of De Soto remains to be tested, as do their full effects on the political and social structures that De Soto's men recorded." Clayton, Knight, and Moore, *De Soto Chronicles*, 12.

24. Ibid., 58, 125, 129.

25. Chamberlain, "American Indian Legends."

26. Swanton, *Source Material*, 118.

27. Mooney, *Myths of the Cherokee*, 254, 262, 286–87.

28. The *Handbook of North American Indians*, volume 14, *Southeast*, does not mention "Flying Squirrel" in connection with any of the southeastern tribes.

29. Brightman and Wallace, "Chickasaw," 485.

30. Despite having brought along pigs that provided sustenance, De Soto's expedition on several occasions endured "great vicissitudes and extreme need," as one source, the "Gentleman from Elvas," wrote. Still, it is unlikely that they ever had to resort to cannibalism. Clayton, Knight, and Moore, *De Soto Chronicles*, 80.

31. Ibid., 143.

32. Ibid., 135–36.

33. Ibid., 126–27. See also Hudson, *Knights of Spain*, 320–25.

34. Dorsey, *Traditions of the Caddo*, 58–59, 59–61.

35. Hudson, *Knights of Spain*, 368.

36. Clayton, Knight, and Moore, *De Soto Chronicles*, 142–47; Hudson, *Knights of Spain*, chapter 15.

37. Wallace Chafe, personal communication, April 10, 2013.

38. Indeed, the "witch episode" seems oddly out of place with the rest of the narrative. While adding to the drama of the story, it also confuses the plotline. After all, the witch had supposedly killed the brothers. But in the next scene, Coyote informs the boy that his brothers are in fact alive. The witch now disappears from the story altogether. It is possible that this storyteller wove two separate stories together.

39. Clayton, Knight, and Moore, *De Soto Chronicles*, 91.

40. Ibid., 50.

41. Peterson, *Arms and Armor*, 103, 106–7. It is doubtful that many of De Soto's men were still wearing chain mail armor by the time they met the Caddos. According to De

Soto scholar Paul E. Hoffman at Louisiana State University, "Given what we know of the last stages of the expedition, it is possible that many of the men were in buckskins or other Native American 'fabrics' by the time they reached East Texas." Paul E. Hoffman, personal communication, April 8, 2013.

42. Peterson, *Arms and Armor*, 115. See also Calvert, *Spanish Arms and Armour*; Blair, *European Armour*; and Wise, *Conquistadores*.

43. Pyhrr, LaRocca, and Breiding, *Armored Horse in Europe*, 8–18.

44. Ibid., 7.

45. Inventories of the Coronado expedition into the American Southwest, which coincided with De Soto's expedition into the Southeast, list a great number of iron weapons. The sharp nose could refer to the swords, daggers, metal-tipped lances, and halberds. Cabrillo National Monument, "Conquistador Clothing," National Park Service, 2015, www.nps.gov/cabr/historyculture/conquistador-clothing.htm (accessed August 1, 2017).

46. Peterson, *Arms and Armor*, 7–11.

47. Ibid., 93.

48. Ibid., 92.

49. Clayton, Knight, and Moore, *De Soto Chronicles*, 459.

50. See also Chafe, "Caddo."

51. Clayton, Knight, and Moore, *De Soto Chronicles*, 412.

52. Ibid., 412.

53. Ibid., 412–13.

54. Ibid., 413.

55. A vara is a unit of length that is no longer commonly used. In the past, there were differences in the exact length between various regions. It appears that in Spanish Texas, a vara measured about 33.3 inches or 0.84667 meters—slightly under one yard.

56. Clayton, Knight, and Moore, *De Soto Chronicles*, 416.

57. Ibid., 416.

58. Ibid., 417–19. Juan Páez was not very lucky in his duels with Indians. Later he received another painful wound in battle with an Aays warrior, and while marching back to the Mississippi River, lost his horse and was wounded in his foot in a duel with another warrior. Hudson, *Knights of Spain*, 367, 377.

59. According to Garcilaso, the Spaniards remained at Tula for twenty days to recover from their wounds. During this time they sent out patrols that "captured many Indians, both men and women, of all ages." But these Indians "showed themselves to be so obstinate and ungovernable, as we have said, that it was necessary to kill the men who were capable of fighting. The women, boys, and children they let go, since they could not carry them off." Despite this last claim by Garcilaso, several Spaniards nevertheless carried off Tulans into slavery. Clayton, Knight, and Moore, *De Soto Chronicles*, 419, 420.

60. Milanich and Hudson, *Hernando de Soto*, 6–7.

61. For an excellent discussion of this problem, see Lankford, "Legends of the Adelantado."

62. Lankford, *Native American Legends*, 136.

CHAPTER 6. FROM "MONSTER" TO SAVIOR

1. Murie, *Ceremonies of the Pawnee*, 40.

2. Dorsey recorded a story among the Caddos in which a man named Red-Mountain-Lion was scalped. Unlike Pawnee custom, the Caddos allowed this man to live among them, even though "he was always foolish." Eventually, however, it became necessary for the people to kill this man in old age because "he became more foolish and did many evil things." Dorsey, *Traditions of the Caddo*, 72.

3. Melvin R. Gilmore, "The Plight of Living Scalped Indians," *Papers of the Michigan Academy of Science, Arts, and Letters* 19 (1933): 39–45.

4. Axtell and Sturtevant, "Unkindest Cut"; van de Logt, "'The Powers of the Heavens.'"

5. Willey, *Prehistoric Warfare on the Great Plains*; Willey and Emerson, "Osteology and Archaeology"; Zimmerman and Bradley, "Crow Creek Massacre."

6. Dorsey, *Traditions of the Skidi Pawnee*, 78. Stories of scalped men snatching women were also popular among the Arikaras. One story, a never-before-published school assignment, was told by Stella Bear, an Arikara who attended Hampton Institute in Virginia, from 1897 to 1903. In this story, a scalped man appeared as a boogeyman who frightened young girls:

> One beautiful evening, a party of Indian maids were playing near the edge of the woods, when suddenly a peculiar looking man sprang out of the woods, and giving one loud war whoop ran up to the girls and said in angry tones, "Many years ago, your people and my people had a fight. Many lives were lost on both sides. I was there."
>
> As he said this, he removed the fox fur that was around his head and touching his head, he asked them if they noticed anything. The youngest of the girls spoke up and said, "I see your scalp lock is gone." By this time the girls were trembling with fear, "Yes" he said, "It was taken by one of your people and now I am going to have my revenge."
>
> When he said this, the frightened girls scattered in different directions, he following after them. He soon overtook a pretty girl, the chief's only child. Instead of killing her, he stuck his fist into her mouth to keep her cries from being heard and then carried her into a cave which was on a side of a high cliff.
>
> The girls ran back to the camp and told what had happened. Soon everything was in confusion. The young braves mounted their horses and were soon speeding towards the place where the girls had been. The women and even children were waiting and all that night not a soul slept except the little children.
>
> Early in the morning the men returned from their hunt but had failed to find any trace of the girl.
>
> Day after day the chief looked for his daughter but without success. He gave then gave up all hopes of ever finding her.

It was ten years then since the disappearance of the girl and the people moved away from that place to a new hunting place. In the fall when the people were on their way back, they stopped at a beautiful ravine and camped there for the night.

That night when the camp fires had gone out and the people had gone to bed, a strange singing was heard nearby. The men got up and watched but saw nothing and all believed that it was some dead person's spirit that haunted the ravine.

The next day the people were not able to go on with their journey for the horses needed a rest so all agreed to remain there another night.

That evening, when the sun had gone down, two figures were seen creeping through the tall prairie-grass and the people noticed that one was of a young woman. Two men, armed with bows & arrows went through the ravine and came up on the other side. They cautiously crept up to the two figures that were hiding in the grass.

All at once, one of the men shouted, "Chief, Son of the Star, your daughter is found!" The people ran and when they saw the girl they cried with joy and brought her to the camp. The person that was with her disappeared as soon as the two men approached them. It was the man who had taken her away many years ago. He had brought the girl back only to see her tribe once more for that night she passed into the happy hunting ground above. (Stella Bear file, Hampton University Archives)

For a history of Arikara students at Hampton Institute, see Hultgren and Molin, "'Long Rides across the Plains.'"

7. Weltfish, *Lost Universe*, 294.

8. Dunbar, "Pawnee Indians," 339–40.

9. William Riding In, "One-Hair and the Scalped Men," in Weltfish, *Caddoan Texts*, 240.

10. Parks, "Historical Character Mythologized."

11. Weltfish, chapter 39.

12. For the most thorough treatment of Skiri Pawnee religion, see Dorsey and Murie, "The Pawnee." For the significance of visions, see Hultkrantz, *Religions of the American Indians*, introduction and chapter 5.

13. Dorsey, *Pawnee Mythology*, especially 13–44; Murie, *Ceremonies of the Pawnee*, 183.

14. For Pawnee cosmology, see Murie, *Ceremonies of the Pawnee*.

15. Murie, "The New Fire Ceremony," in *Ceremonies of the Pawnee*, 136–54.

16. Dorsey and Murie, "Notes on Skidi Pawnee Society," 101–7.

17. Murie, "Human Sacrifice to the Morning Star," in *Ceremonies of the Pawnee*, 114–36; Ross, *Das Menschenopfer der Skidi-Pawnee*.

18. See Wishart, *Unspeakable Sadness*; Martha Royce Blaine, *Pawnee Passage, 1870–1875* (Norman: University of Oklahoma Press, 1990).

19. The discussion of genocide and the American Indian is contentious. Because the 1948 United Nations definition of genocide emphasizes the physical destruction of a people, some scholars argue that the U.S. government did not commit genocide, since

Indian policy was not aimed at the physical destruction of American Indian nations. See Chalk and Jonassohn, *History and Sociology of Genocide*, 23. See also Lewy, "Were American Indians the Victims of Genocide?"; Anderson, "Native Peoples of the American West." Anderson argues that U.S. policy was more accurately "ethnic cleansing" rather than "genocide." Recently, however, historian Roxanne Dunbar-Ortiz disputed this position, arguing that the United States did in fact pursue a *policy* of genocide because its support of "Settler-colonialism is a genocidal policy." Roxanne Dunbar-Ortiz, *Indigenous Peoples' History of the United States*, 1–14; Echo-Hawk, *In the Courts of the Conqueror*, especially chapter 6.

20. Jones, *Genocide*, xxiv, xxvii, 6.
21. For an excellent discussion of the Awat'ovi massacre, see Brooks, *Mesa of Sorrows*.
22. Blick, "Iroquois Practice of Genocidal Warfare."
23. White, "Winning of the West." See also Pekka Hämäläinen, *Comanche Empire*.
24. Calloway, "Inter-tribal Balance."
25. Roger C. Echo-Hawk, personal communication, April 5, 2014.
26. Dorsey, "How the Pawnee Captured."
27. Jensen, *Pawnee Mission Letters*, 107.
28. Ibid., 204.
29. Ibid., 284.
30. Ibid., 310, 315–17.
31. Other factors, such as the weather and the poor condition of their horses, aggravated the situation for the Pawnees. In the summer of 1843, John Dunbar, Allis's colleague, wrote that there were plenty of buffalo around but that the Pawnees' horses were so poor after an exceptionally long winter that buffalo could not be hunted. Ibid., 325.
32. Ibid., 332.
33. Ibid., 333.
34. Ibid., 343.
35. Ibid., 335–36, 339, 340.
36. Ibid., 359.
37. Ibid., 491, 543.
38. Hyde, *Pawnee Indians*, 223–29.
39. *New York Daily Tribune*, February 25, 1852; Chittenden and Richardson, *Life, Letters and Travels*, 687–88.
40. J. L. Gillis to commissioner of Indian Affairs, June 22, 1860, Pawnee Agency ledger book, 7–8. Material in the possession of Bill Coons, member of the Pawnee Nation, Houston, Texas.
41. J. L. Gillis to commissioner of Indian Affairs, June 24, 1860, Pawnee Agency ledger book, 9.
42. Riding In, "Betrayal of 'Civilization.'"
43. Hyde, *Pawnee Indians*, 160–61.
44. Kappler, *Indian Affairs*, 156–59.
45. Ibid., 417.

46. Reeder, "Wolf Men of the Plains," 352.

47. Jensen, *Pawnee Mission Letters,* xi–xxxii; Wedel, *Dunbar-Allis Letters,* vii–xvi; Hyde, *Pawnee Indians,* 191.

48. Jensen and Hutchins, *Wheel Boats on the Missouri,* 130.

49. Wedel, *Dunbar-Allis Letters,* 697, 701.

50. This information is based on Colonel Henry Dodge's journal and report of his 1835 expedition to the Rocky Mountains, *American State Papers: Military Affairs,* vol. 6 (1861; repr., Buffalo, N.Y.: William S. Hein, 1998), 130–46.

51. Wedel, *Dunbar-Allis Letters,* 707; Annie Heloise Abel, *Chardon's Journal at Fort Clark, 1834–1839* (Lincoln: University of Nebraska Press, 1997), 80, 100.

52. Murie, "Pawnee Indian Societies," 616; Dunbar, "Pawnee Indians," 736.

53. Murie, "Roaming Scout Texts," text 9; Dorsey, *Traditions of the Skidi Pawnee,* 49–51. Samuel Osborne's account of Pahukatawa, here called Powhohatawa, appeared in Haskell's campus newspaper, *Indian Leader* 18, no. 33 (May 1915): 12–13; also available at www.roger-echo-hawk.com/resources/Powhohatawa.html. Additional stories featuring Pahukatawa include "The Son of Wind, Ready-To-Give," "The Boy Who Preferred Woman to Power," and "The Skeleton-Man and the Sun Dance," in Dorsey, *Pawnee Mythology,* 90–95, 102–4, 408–9. In the last story, Pahukatawa is credited with instituting the Sun Dance.

54. Dorsey and Murie, "Pawnee," chapter 17.

55. Murie, "Roaming Scout Texts," text 9.

56. Dorsey, *Traditions of the Skidi Pawnee,* 49–51, 337.

57. Murie, "Roaming Scout Texts," text 9.

58. The sacred leggings were symbols of war. They were kept in the "Wonderful Leggings bundle," which had clear associations with warfare. Along with the sacred leggings (one of which was white, the other black), the bundle included seven reeds containing sacred power. The reeds were painted with white clay and staked into the ground during approaching storms. After smoke offerings and smudging of the objects, the bundle was closed again. The bundle was "now ready when war parties set out." Dunbar, "Pawnee Indians," 755–56; Murie, *Ceremonies of the Pawnee,* part 1, 65.

59. Murie, "Pawnee Indian Societies," 618.

60. Dorsey, *Traditions of the Skidi Pawnee,* 50.

61. Murie, "Pawnee Indian Societies," 619.

62. Ibid., 620, 621.

63. Ibid., 621; Murie, "Roaming Scout Texts," text 9.

64. Murie, "Roaming Scout Texts," text 9.

65. Murie, "Pawnee Indian Societies," 616, 617.

66. Martha Royce Blaine implied that the "Buffalo Horn Dance" (*A ri ka*) originally belonged to the repertoire of the Pitahawiratas. The Skiris would invite Pitahawirata singers to contribute to their One Horn Dance. Blaine, *Some Things Are Not Forgotten,* 195–96.

67. Murie, *Ceremonies of the Pawnee,* part 2, 433–34. Pahukatawa also provided the people with medicine to restore their health. Apparently they performed the dance until

at least 1948. Samuel Osborne, "Powhohatawa," *Pawnee Writings*, 2009, www.roger-echo-hawk.com/resources/Powhohatawa.html (accessed 1 August 2017).

68. Dorsey, *Traditions of the Skidi Pawnee*, 51.

69. Murie, "Pawnee Indian Societies," 623.

70. Allis, "Forty Years among the Indians," 145.

71. Grinnell, *Pawnee Hero Stories*, 142–60; Hyde, *Pawnee Indians*, 195–96. James Murie stated "that the Arikara claim that Pahukatiwa was of their tribe." See Dorsey, *Traditions of the Skidi Pawnee*, 337–38.

72. Grinnell, "Pawnee Mythology," 128; Grinnell, "Notes and Queries," 90–92, especially 90.

73. Dorsey and Murie, "Notes on Skidi Pawnee Society," chapter 12.

74. See, for example, Duke, "Morning Star Ceremony."

75. Dunbar, "Pawnee Indians," 735.

76. Ibid., 736.

77. George Bird Grinnell also saw similarities between Pahukatawa and Jesus. But Grinnell also believed that, unlike Jesus, Pahukatawa did not willfully sacrifice himself but "gained his immortality . . . by the exhibition of a selfish cowardice." Grinnell, "Pawnee Mythology," 128.

78. Murie, "Roaming Scout Texts," text 9.

79. Leopold and Jensen, *Syncretism in Religion*, 41, 61, 67.

80. For an excellent discussion, see Lesser, *Pawnee Ghost Dance Hand Game*. See also Blaine, *Some Things Are Not Forgotten*, 63–64.

81. Wallace, "Revitalization Movements."

82. Murie, *Ceremonies of the Pawnee*, 114–36.

83. Melburn D. Thurman, "The Timing of the Skidi-Pawnee Morning Star Sacrifice," *Ethnohistory* 30, no. 3 (1983): 155–63; Thurman, "Skidi Pawnee Morning Star Sacrifice," 268–80.

84. Overland, *Making and Meaning of an American Classic*, 17, 56–60, 79, 83–84.

85. Parks and DeMallie, "Plains Indian Native Literatures," 116.

86. Jensen, *Pawnee Mission letters*, 220.

87. Chittenden and Richardson, *Life, Letters and Travels*, 988; Wedel, *Dunbar-Allis Letters*, 631.

88. Cheney, *Sioux Winter Count*, According to the Swift Bear and High Hawk winter counts, the Sioux and their allies killed one hundred Skiris that year. Lucy Cohen, "Even in Those Days"; Curtis, "High Hawk's Winter Count," 175.

89. Weltfish, *Lost Universe*, 152–53.

90. Lesser, *Pawnee Ghost Dance Hand Game*, 282.

91. Ibid., 282–83. Archaeoastronomist Von Del Chamberlain believes that Pahukatawa was either Beta Persei or Gamma Cephei. But it is not possible to identify Pahukatawa on the famous Pawnee "star chart" (a map of the heavens painted on a buffalo skin), now held in the Field Museum in Chicago. Chamberlain, *When Stars Came Down to Earth*, 111–12, 204, 237.

92. Walter R. Echo-Hawk, personal communication, September 21, 2016.

93. Adrian Spottedhorsechief, personal communication, September 21, 2016.
94. Roger C. Echo-Hawk, personal communication, September 21, 2016.

CONCLUSION

1. Cruikshank, *Do Glaciers Listen?*, 50.
2. Ibid., 259.

Bibliography

PERSONAL COMMUNICATION

Braun, Mark, September 13, 2005.
Chafe, Wallace, April 10, 2013.
Echo-Hawk, Roger C., April 25, 2008; September 21, 2016.
Echo-Hawk, Walter R., September 21, 2016.
Flint, Richard, March 9, 2014.
Havard, Gilles, September 13, 2015.
Hoffman, Paul E., April 8, 2013.
Spottedhorsechief, Adrian, September 21, 2016.
Weddle, Robert, March 4, 2014.

ARCHIVAL MATERIALS, FILMS, ELECTRONIC RESOURCES,
AND UNPUBLISHED WORKS

American Indian Studies Research Institute. "AISRI Dictionary Portal." Indiana University, Bloomington, n.d. http://zia.aisri.indiana.edu/~dictsearch/.
Caddo Nation. "Welcome to the Official Website of the Caddo Nation." Caddo Nation, 2017. http://caddonation-nsn.gov/icw/.
Dorsey, George A., and James R. Murie. "The Pawnee: Society and Religion of the Skidi Pawnee." Unpublished manuscript, circa 1906. Original at the Field Museum Library Archives, Chicago; copy at the American Indian Studies Research Institute, Indiana University, Bloomington.
Eagle Rises Up. "The Appearance of a Stranger Among the Arikaras." Unpublished story, March 31, 1952. Transcription at American Indian Studies Research Institute, Indiana University, Bloomington.
Gilmore, Melvin R. "Account of the Piraskani Ceremony of the Arikara at Armstrong, ND, September 1922." Unpublished manuscript, circa 1922. Transcription at American Indian Studies Research Institute, Indiana University, Bloomington.
———. *Arikara Ceremonies*. Film. Heye Foundation, Museum of the American Indian, 1924.
Hampton University Archives. Stella Bear file.

Lewy, Guenter. "Were American Indians the Victims of Genocide?" History News Network, 2017. http://historynewsnetwork.org/article/7302.

Murie, James R. "Roaming Scout Texts." Edited by Douglas R. Parks. Unpublished manuscript, circa 1906. American Indian Studies Research Institute, Indiana University, Bloomington.

National Archives and Records Administration (NARA). Microcopy 595, "Indian Census Rolls, 1885–1940." Roll 386, "Ponca (Ponca, Oto and Missouri, Pawnee, and Tonkawa Indians), 1886–90."

National Anthropological Archives, Smithsonian Institution. De Lancey W. Gill Photo Collection. Accession number NAA INV 06255400, OPPS NEG 01331.

Osborne, Samuel. "Powhohatawa," *Indian Leader* 18, no. 33 (May 1915): 12–13. www.roger-echo-hawk.com/resources/Powhohatawa.html.

Parks, Douglas R., ed. "Roaming Scout Texts, Free Translations." Unpublished manuscript. American Indian Studies Research Institute, Indiana University, Bloomington.

Pawnee Nation of Oklahoma. "Indian Child Welfare." Pawnee Nation of Oklahoma, 2015–17. www.pawneenation.org/page/home/divisions/division-of-health-community-services/indian-child-welfare.

Reeder, William S., Jr. "Wolf Men of the Plains: Pawnee Indian Warriors, Past and Present." PhD diss., Kansas State University, 2001.

Weltfish, Gene. "Pawnee Field Notes, Summer 1935." Unpublished field notes, 1935. American Indian Studies Research Institute, Indian University, Bloomington.

Wilson, Gilbert L. "The Arikara Cosmogony." Unpublished notes. Gilbert L. Wilson files. American Indian Studies Research Institute, Indiana University, Bloomington.

BOOKS AND ARTICLES

Abbott, Geoffrey. *Rack, Rope and Red-Hot Pincers: A History of Torture and Its Instruments.* London: Headline Book Publishing, 1993.

Abel, Annie Heloise. *Tabeau's Narrative of Loisel's Expedition to the Upper Missouri.* Norman: University of Oklahoma Press, 1968.

Alexander, Hartley B. "Lucky-in-the-House." *Theatre Arts Monthly* 17, no. 8 (August 1933): 616–26.

———. *The World's Rim: Great Mysteries of the North American Indians.* Lincoln: University of Nebraska Press, 1953.

Allis, Samuel. "Forty Years among the Indians and on the Eastern Borders of Nebraska." *Transactions and Reports of the Nebraska State Historical Society* 2 (1887): 133–66.

Almazan, Tristan, and Sarah Coleman. "George Amos Dorsey and His Comrades." *Fieldiana Anthropology*, n.s., 36 (September 30, 2003): 87–97.

Anderson, Gary Clayton. "Early Dakota Migration and Intertribal War: A Revision." *Western Historical Quarterly* 11, no. 1 (January 1980): 17–36.

———. "The Native Peoples of the American West: Genocide or Ethnic Cleansing?" *Western Historical Quarterly* 47, no. 4 (Winter 2016): 407–33.

Asad, Talal. "The Concept of Cultural Translation in British Social Anthropology." In *Writing Culture: The Poetics and Politics of Ethnography,* edited by James Clifford and George E. Marcus, 141–64. Berkeley: University of California Press, 1986.

Asma, Stephen T. *On Monsters: An Unnatural History of Our Worst Fears.* New York: Oxford University Press, 2009.

Axtell, James. "Ethnohistory, an Historian's Viewpoint." In *The European and the Indian: Essays in the Ethnohistory of Colonial North America*, edited by James Axtell, 3–15. New York: Oxford University Press, 1982.

Axtell, James, and William C. Sturtevant. "The Unkindest Cut, or, Who Invented Scalping." *William and Mary Quarterly*, 3rd ser., 37, no. 3 (July 1980): 451–72.

Back, Francis. "The Dress of the First Voyageurs, 1650–1715." *Museum of the Fur Trade Quarterly* 36, no. 2 (Summer 2000): 2–19.

Barber, Elizabeth Wayland, and Paul T. Barber. *When They Severed the Earth from Sky: How the Human Mind Shapes Myth.* Princeton, N.J.: Princeton University Press, 2004.

Barnes, Henry Elmer. *The True Story of Punishment: A Record of Man's Inhumanity to Man.* Montclair, N.J.: Patterson Smith, 1972.

Barr, Juliana. "From Captives to Slaves: Commodifying Indian Women in the Borderlands." *Journal of American History* 92, no. 1 (June 2005): 19–46.

———. *Peace Came in the Form of a Woman: Indians and Spaniards in the Texas Borderlands.* Chapel Hill: University of North Carolina Press, 2007.

Bartlett, F. C. "Some Experiments on the Reproduction of Folk Stories. In *The Study of Folklore*, edited by Alan Dundes, 243–58. Englewood Cliffs, N.J.: Prentice-Hall, 1965.

Bascom, William. "Rejoinder to Hyman." *Journal of American Folklore* 71, no. 280 (1958): 155–56.

———. "Rejoinder to Raglan and Bidney." *Journal of American Folklore* 71, no. 279 (1958): 79–80.

———. "The Myth-Ritual Theory." *Journal of American Folklore* 70, no. 276 (1957): 103–14.

Beal, Timothy K., *Religion and Its Monsters.* New York: Routledge, 2002.

Bidney, David, and Lord Raglan. "Reply to Bascom." *Journal of American Folklore* 70, no. 278 (1957): 359–361.

Blaine, Martha Royce. *Some Things Are Not Forgotten: A Pawnee Family Remembers.* Lincoln: University of Nebraska Press, 1997.

Blair, C. *European Armour.* London: B. T. Batsford, 1958.

Bleed, Peter, Lindsay Long, Jessica Long, Madeleine Roberg, and David Killick. "Scale Armor on the North American Frontier: Lessons from the John G. Bourke Armor." *Plains Anthropologist* 60, no. 235 (August 2015): 199–222.

Blick, Jeffrey P. "The Iroquois Practice of Genocidal Warfare (1534–1787)." *Journal of Genocide Research* 3, no. 3 (2001): 405–29.

Boyd, Douglas K., Jennifer K. McWilliams, and Mariah F. Wade, eds. *Spanish Colonial Documents Pertaining to Mission Santa Cruz de San Sabá (41MN23), Menard County, Texas.* Austin: Texas Department of Transportation, 2007.

Bridges, Patricia S. "Prehistoric Arthritis in the Americas." *Annual Review of Anthropology* 21 (1992): 67–91.

Brightman, Robert A., and Pamela S. Wallace. "Chickasaw." In *Handbook of North American Indians.* Vol. 14, *Southeast*, edited by Raymond Fogelson and William Sturtevant, 478–98. Washington, D.C.: Smithsonian Institution, 2004.

Brooks, James F. *Captives and Cousins: Slavery, Kinship, and Community in the Southwest Borderlands.* Chapel Hill: University of North Carolina Press, 2001.

———. *Mesa of Sorrows: A History of the Awat'ovi Massacre.* New York: W. W. Norton, 2016.

Burpee, Lawrence J., ed. *Journals and Letters of Pierre Gaultier de Varennes de la Vérendrye and His Sons.* Toronto: Champlain Society, 1927.

Caldwell, Warren W. "Fortified Villages in the Northern Plains." *Plains Anthropologist* 9, no. 23 (February 1964): 1–7.

Calloway, Colin G. "The Inter-tribal Balance of Power on the Great Plains, 1760–1850." *American Studies* 16, no. 1 (1982): 25–47.

Calvert, Albert F. *Spanish Arms and Armour.* London: John Lane, 1907.

Canonge, Elliott. *Comanche Texts.* Norman: Summer Institute of the University of Oklahoma, 1958.

Carocci, Max, and Stephanie Pratt, eds. *Native American Adoption, Captivity, and Slavery in Changing Contexts.* New York: Palgrave Macmillan, 2012.

Carter, Cecile Elkins. *Caddo Indians: Where We Come From.* Norman: University of Oklahoma Press, 1995.

Case, Harold, and Eva Case, comp. *100 Years at Ft. Berthold: The History of the Fort Berthold Indian Mission, 1876–1976.* Bismarck, N.Dak.: H. W. Case, 1977.

Chafe, Wallace. "Caddo." In *The Native Languages of the Southeastern United States,* edited by Heather K. Hardy and Janine Scancarelli, 323–50. Lincoln: University of Nebraska Press, 2005.

———. "Caddo Names in the de Soto Documents." In *The Expedition of Hernando de Soto West of the Mississippi, 1541–1543: Proceedings of the de Soto Symposia, 1988 and 1990,* edited by Gloria A. Young and Michael P. Hoffman, 222–26. Fayetteville: University of Arkansas Press, 1993.

———. "Introduction to the Paperback Edition." In *Traditions of the Caddo,* by George A. Dorsey, xix–xx. Lincoln: University of Nebraska Press, 1997.

Chalk, Frank, and Kurt Jonassohn. *The History and Sociology of Genocide: Analyses and Case Studies.* New Haven, Conn: Yale University Press, 1990.

Chamberlain, A. F. "American Indian Legends and Beliefs about the Squirrel and the Chipmunk." *Journal of American Folklore* 9, no. 32 (1896): 48–50.

Chamberlain, Von Del. *When Stars Came Down to Earth: Cosmology of the Skidi Pawnee Indians of North America.* Los Altos, Calif.: Ballena Press, 1982.

Cheney, Roberta C. *Sioux Winter Count: A 131-Year Calendar of Events.* Happy Camp, Calif.: Naturegraph, 1998.

Chittenden, Hiram Martin, and Alfred Talbot Richardson, eds. *Life, Letters and Travels of Father Pierre-Jean DeSmet, S. J., 1801–1873.* New York: Francis P. Harper, 1905. Reprint, New York: Klaus Reprint, 1969.

Clayton, Lawrence A., Vernon J. Knight, and Edward C. Moore, eds. *The De Soto Chronicles: The Expedition of Hernando de Soto to North America in 1539–43.* 2 vols. Tuscaloosa: University of Alabama Press, 1995.

Clements, William M. *Native American Verbal Art: Texts and Contexts.* Tucson: University of Arizona Press, 1996.

Clews Parsons, Elsie. *Notes on the Caddo: Memoirs of the American Anthropological Association,* no. 57, supplement, *American Anthropologist* 43, no. 3, part 2 (1941).

Cohen, Jeffrey Jerome. "Monster Culture (Seven Theses)." In *Monster Theory: Reading Culture,* edited by Jeffrey Jerome Cohen, 3–25. Minneapolis: University of Minnesota Press, 1996.

———. *Of Giants: Sex, Monsters, and the Middle Ages.* Minneapolis: University of Minnesota Press, 1999.

Cohen, Lucy Kramer. "Even in Those Days Pictures Were Important." *Indians at Work* 9, no. 6 (February 1942): 31.

Cole, Douglas. *Captured Heritage: The Scramble for Northwest Coast Artifacts.* Seattle: University of Washington Press, 1985.

Cook-Lynn, Elizabeth. "History, Myth, and Identity in the New Indian Story." In *Handbook of Critical Indigenous Methodologies,* edited by Norman K. Denzin, Yvonna S. Lincoln, and Linda Tuhiwai Smith, 329–46. Los Angeles: Sage, 2008.

Cruikshank, Julie. *Do Glaciers Listen? Local Knowledge, Colonial Encounters, and Social Imagination.* Seattle: University of Washington Press, 2005.

Curtin, Jeremiah. *Seneca Indian Myths.* New York: E. P. Dutton, 1923.

Curtis, Edward S. *The North American Indian.* Vol. 5, *The Mandan. The Arikara. The Atsina.* New York: Johnson Reprint Corporation, 1970.

———. "High Hawk's Winter-Count." In *The North American Indian.* Vol. 3, *The Teton Sioux. The Yanktonai. The Assiniboin,* 159–82. New York: Johnson Reprint Company, 1970.

D'Azevedo, Warren L., ed. *Handbook of North American Indians.* Vol. 11, *Great Basin.* Washington, D.C.: Smithsonian Institution, 1986.

Delisle, Guillaume. "Carte du Mexique et de la Florida des Terres Angloises et des Isles Antilles du Cours et des Environs de la Riviere de Mississipi." Paris: Chez l'Auteur sur le Quai de l'Horloge, 1703.

Deloria, Vine, Jr. *Spirit and Reason: The Vine Deloria Jr. Reader.* Golden, Colo.: Fulcrum, 1999.

DeMallie, Raymond J., and Douglas R. Parks. "George A. Dorsey and the Development of Plains Indian Anthropology." In *Anthropology, History, and American Indians: Essays in Honor of William Curtis Sturtevant,* edited by William L. Merrill and Ives Goddard, 59–74. Washington, D.C.: Smithsonian Institution Press, 2002.

DeMallie, Raymond J., Douglas R. Parks, and Robert Vézina, eds. *A Fur Trader on the Upper Missouri: The Journal and Description of Jean-Baptiste Truteau, 1794–1796.* Lincoln: University of Nebraska Press, 2017.

DeMallie, Raymond, and William Sturtevant, eds. *Handbook of North American Indians.* Vol. 13, *Plains,* parts 1 and 2. Washington, D.C.: Smithsonian Institution, 2001.

Densmore, Frances. *Pawnee Music.* Smithsonian Institution Bureau of American Ethnology Bulletin 93. Washington, D.C.: Government Printing Press, 1929.

DeVries, Kelly, and Robert Douglas Smith. *Medieval Military Technology.* 2nd ed. Toronto: University of Toronto Press, 2012.

Dixon, R. B. "Dr. Dixon's Reply." *American Anthropologist* 17, no. 3 (1915): 599–600.

Dodge, Henry. "Report on the Expedition of Dragoons, under Colonel Henry Dodge, to the Rocky Mountains in 1835." *American State Papers: Military Affairs* 6 (1861):130–46.

Dorsey, George A. "An Arikara Story-Telling Contest." *American Anthropologist*, n.s., 6, no. 2 (1904): 210–43.

———. "How the Pawnee Captured the Cheyenne Medicine Arrows." *American Anthropologist* 5 (1903): 644–58.

———. "The Skidi Rite of Human Sacrifice." *Congress Internationale des Americanistes*, session 15, part 2 (1906): 65–70.

———. *The Mythology of the Wichita*. Washington, D.C.: Carnegie Institution, 1904. Reprint, Norman: University of Oklahoma Press, 1995.

———. *The Pawnee Mythology*. Washington, D.C.: Carnegie Institution, 1906.

———. *Traditions of the Arikara*. Washington, D.C.: Carnegie Institution, 1904.

———. *Traditions of the Caddo*. Lincoln: University of Nebraska Press, 1997.

———. *Traditions of the Skidi Pawnee*. Boston: American Folk-Lore Society, 1904. Reprint, New York: Krause Reprint, 1969.

Dorsey, George A., and James R. Murie. "Notes on Skidi Pawnee Society." Edited by Alexander Spoehr. *Field Museum of Natural History, Anthropological Series* 27, no. 2 (September 1940): 67–119.

Douglas, Walter Bond. *Manuel Lisa: With Hitherto Unpublished Material*. Edited by Abraham P. Nasatir. New York: Argosy-Antiquarian, 1964.

Duke, Philip, ed. "The Morning Star Ceremony of the Skiri Pawnee as Described by Alfred C. Haddon." *Plains Anthropologist* 34, no. 125 (August 1989): 193–203.

Dunbar, John B. "Pitalesharu—Chief of the Pawnees." *Magazine of American History* 5, no. 5 (November 1880): 343–45.

———. "The Pawnee Indians: Their Habits and Customs." *Magazine of American History* 8 (1882): 734–53.

Dunbar-Ortiz, Roxanne. *An Indigenous Peoples' History of the United States*. Boston: Beacon Press, 2014.

Duncan, James R., and Carol Diaz-Granados. "Of Masks and Myths." *Midcontinental Journal of Archaeology* 25, no. 1 (Spring 2000): 1–26.

Dundes, Alan, ed. *Sacred Narrative: Readings in the Theory of Myth*. Berkeley: University of California Press, 1984.

Dunn, William E. "The Apache Mission on the San Sabá River: Its Founding and Failure." *Southwestern Historical Quarterly* 17, no. 4 (April 1914): 379–414.

Echo-Hawk, Roger. "Ancient History in the New World: Integrating Oral Traditions and the Archaeological Record in Deep Time." *American Antiquity* 65, no. 2 (April 2000): 267–90.

Echo-Hawk, Walter R., Jr. *In the Courts of the Conqueror: The 10 Worst Indian Law Cases Ever Decided*. Golden, Colo.: Fulcrum Publishing, 2010.

Ekberg, Carl J. *Stealing Indian Women: Native Slaves in the Illinois Country*. Urbana: University of Illinois Press, 2007.

Evers, Larry, and Barre Toelken, eds. *Native American Oral Traditions: Collaboration and Interpretation*. Logan: Utah State University, 2001.

Ewers, John C. *The Horse in Blackfeet Indian Culture: With Comparative Material from Other Western Tribes*. Washington, D.C: Smithsonian Institution Press, 1955.

———. *Plains Indian History and Culture: Essays on Continuity and Change*. Norman: University of Oklahoma Press, 1997.

Fenn, Elizabeth. *Pox Americana: The Great Smallpox Epidemic of 1775–82*. New York: Hill & Wang, 2002.

Fletcher, Alice C. *The Hako: Song, Pipe, and Unity in a Pawnee Calumet Ceremony*. Lincoln: University of Nebraska Press, 1996.

Flint, Richard. *Great Cruelties Have Been Reported: The 1544 Investigation of the Coronado Expedition*. Dallas: Southern Methodist University Press, 2002.

———. *No Settlement, No Conquest: A History of the Coronado Entrada*. Albuquerque: University of New Mexico Press, 2008.

Flint, Richard, and Shirley Cushing-Flint, eds. *The Coronado Expedition to Tierra Nueva: The 1540–1542 Route across the Southwest*. Niwot: University Press of Colorado, 1997.

———. *Documents of the Coronado Expedition, 1539–1542*. Dallas: Southern Methodist University Press, 2005.

———. *The Latest Word from 1540: Peoples, Places, and Portrayals of the Coronado Expedition*. Albuquerque: University of New Mexico Press, 2011.

Fogelson, Raymond D. "The Ethnohistory of Events and Nonevents." *Ethnohistory* 36, no. 2 (Spring 1989): 133–47.

———. "On the Varieties of Indian History: Sequoyah and Traveller Bird." *Journal of Ethnic Studies* 2, no. 1 (1974): 105–12.

Foley, John Miles. "Foreword." In *Native American Oral Traditions: Collaboration and Interpretation*, edited by Larry Evers and Barre Toelken, vii–viii. Logan: Utah State University Press, 1986.

Foley, Thomas W. *Father Francis M. Craft: Missionary to the Sioux*. Lincoln: University of Nebraska Press, 2002.

Fontana, Bernard L. "Pictorial Images of Spanish North America." *Journal of the Southwest* 42, no. 4 (Winter 2000), 927–61.

Foster, Morris W., and Martha McCollough. "Plains Apache." In *Handbook of North American Indians*. Vol. 13, *Plains,* part 2, edited by Raymond J. DeMallie, 926–40. Washington, D.C.: Smithsonian Institution, 2001.

Friedman, John B. *The Monstrous Races in Medieval Art and Thought*. Syracuse, N.Y.: Syracuse University Press, 2000.

Gallay, Alan. *The Indian Slave Trade: The Rise of the English Empire in the American South, 1670–1717*. New Haven, Conn.: Yale University Press, 2002.

Galloway, Patricia, *Choctaw Genesis*, 1500–1700. Lincoln: University of Nebraska Press, 1995.

Garavaglia, Louis A., and Charles G. Worman. *Firearms of the American West, 1803–1865*. Niwot: University Press of Colorado, 1998.

Gardner, Robert E. *Five Centuries of Gunsmiths, Swordsmiths and Armourers, 1400–1900*. Columbus, Ohio: Walter F. Heer, 1948.

Gerona, Carla. "Caddo Sun Accounts across Time and Place." *American Indian Quarterly* 36, no. 3 (Summer 2012): 348–76.

Gibbon, Guy. *The Sioux: The Dakota and Lakota Nations.* Oxford, UK: Blackwell Publishing, 2003.
Gilmore, David D. *Monsters: Evil Beings, Mythical Beasts, and All Manner of Imaginary Terrors.* Philadelphia: University of Pennsylvania Press, 2009.
Gilmore, Melvin R. "Uses of Plants by the Indian of the Missouri River Region." In *Thirty-Third Annual Report of the Bureau of American Ethnology.* Washington, D.C.: Government Printing Office, 1919. Reprint, Lincoln: University of Nebraska Press, 1991.
———. "The Arikara Book of Genesis." *Papers of the Michigan Academy of Science, Arts, and Letters* 12 (1929): 95–120.
———. *Prairie Smoke.* Saint Paul: Minnesota Historical Society Press, 1987.
———. "A Study in the Ethnobotany of the Omaha Indians." *Collections of the Nebraska State Historical Society* 17 (1913): 314–57.
Gluckman, Arcadi. *Identifying Old U.S. Muskets, Rifles and Carbines.* Harrisburg, Pa.: Stackpole Books, 1965.
Gómez-Alonso, Juan. "Rabies: A Possible Explanation for the Vampire Legend." *Neurology* 51 (September 1998): 856–59.
Greenblatt, Stephen. *Marvelous Possessions: The Wonder of the New World.* Chicago: University of Chicago Press, 1991.
Grinnell, George Bird. *The Cheyenne Indians: Their History and Ways of Life.* Lincoln: University of Nebraska Press, 1972.
———. "Development of a Pawnee Myth." *Journal of American Folklore* 5, no. 17 (1892): 127–34.
———. *The Fighting Cheyennes.* New York: Charles Scribner's Sons, 1915.
———. "Notes and Queries: Arikara Creation Myth." *Journal of American Folk-Lore* 22, no. 83 (1909): 90–92.
———. *Pawnee Hero Stories and Folk-Tales: With Notes on the Origin, Customs and Character of the Pawnee People.* Lincoln: University of Nebraska Press, 1961.
———. "Pawnee Mythology." *Journal of American Folklore* 6 (1893): 113–30.
———. *The Story of the Indian.* New York: D. Appleton and Company, 1908.
———. "Who Were the Padouca?" *American Anthropologist* 22, no. 3 (1920): 248–60.
Hall, Robert L. *An Archaeology of the Soul: North American Indian Belief and Ritual.* Urbana: University of Illinois Press, 1997.
Hallowell, A. Irving. "Temporal Orientation in Western Civilization and in a Pre-Literate Society." *American Anthropologist* 39, no. 4 (1937): 647–70.
Hämäläinen, Pekka. *Comanche Empire.* New Haven, Conn.: Yale University Press, 2008.
Hamilton, T. M., comp. *Indian Trade Guns: The Missouri Archeologist,* vol. 22. Columbia: University of Missouri Press, 1960.
Hammond, George P., ed. *The Rediscovery of New Mexico: The Exploration of Chamuscado, Espejo, Castaño de Sosa, Morlete, and Leyva de Bonilla and Humaña.* Coronado Cuarto Centennial Publications, 1540–1940, vol. 3. Albuquerque: University of New Mexico Press, 1966.
Hammond, George P., and Agapito Rey, eds. *Obregón's History of 16th Century Explorations in Western America.* Los Angeles: Wetzel Publishing, 1928.

Hanson, Jeffrey R. "Adjustment and Adaptation on the Northern Plains: The Case of Equestrianism among the Hidatsa." *Plains Anthropologist* 31, no. 112 (May 1986): 93–107.

Hassrick, Royall B. *The Sioux: Life and Customs of a Warrior Society.* Norman: University of Oklahoma Press, 1964.

Hindes, V. Kay, Mark R. Wolf, Grant D. Hall, and Kathleen Kirk. *The Rediscovery of Santa Cruz de San Sabá, A Mission for the Apache in Spanish Texas.* Lubbock: Texas Historical Foundation and Texas Tech University, 1995.

Hoffman, J. J. *The La Roche Sites.* Publications in Salvage Archaeology 11. Lincoln, Neb.: River Basin Surveys/Museum of Natural History, Smithsonian Institution, 1968.

Hoffman Susanna M., and Anthony Oliver-Smith, eds. *Catastrophe and Culture: The Anthropology of Disaster.* Santa Fe, N.Mex.: School of American Research Press, 2001.

Hoig, Stan. *Came Men on Horses: The Conquistador Expeditions of Francisco Vázquez de Coronado and Don Juan de Oñate.* Boulder: University Press of Colorado, 2013.

Holder, Preston. *The Hoe and the Horse on the Plains: A Study of Cultural Development among North American Indians.* Lincoln: University of Nebraska Press, 1991.

Hotz, Gottfried. *Indian Skin Paintings from the American Southwest: Two Representations of Border Conflicts between Mexico and the Missouri in the Early Eighteenth Century.* Norman: University of Oklahoma Press, 1970.

Howard, James Henri. *The British Museum Winter Count.* London: British Museum, 1979.

———. "Memoir 11: Yanktonai Ethnohistory and the John K. Bear Winter Count." *Plains Anthropologist* 21, no. 73, part 2 (August 1976): 1–78.

Hudson, Charles. "Folk History and Ethnohistory." *Ethnohistory* 13, no. 1/2 (1966): 52–70.

———. *Knights of Spain, Warriors of the Sun: Hernando de Soto and the South's Ancient Chiefdoms.* Athens: University of Georgia Press, 1997.

Hultgren, Mary Lou, and Paulette Fairbanks Molin. "'Long Rides across the Plains': Fort Berthold Students at Hampton Institute." *North Dakota History* 61, no. 2 (Spring 1994): 10–36.

Hultkrantz, Åke. *The Religions of the American Indians.* Berkeley: University of California Press, 1980.

Hurt, Wesley R. *Report of the Investigation of the Swan Creek Site, 39WW7, Walworth County, South Dakota, 1954–1956.* Pierre: South Dakota Archaeological Commission, 1957.

Hyde, George E. *Red Cloud's Folk.* Norman: University of Oklahoma Press, 1937.

———. *The Pawnee Indians.* Norman: University of Oklahoma Press, 1988.

Hyman, Stanley Edgar. "Reply to Bascom." *Journal of American Folklore* 71, no. 280 (1958): 152–55.

Hymes, Dell. *"In Vain I Tried to Tell You": Essays in Native American Ethnopoetics.* Philadelphia: University of Pennsylvania Press, 1981.

Hynes, William J., and William G. Doty, eds. *Mythical Trickster Figures: Contours, Contexts, and Criticisms.* Tuscaloosa: University of Alabama Press, 1993.

Irving, Washington. *A Tour on the Prairies.* Edited by John Francis McDermott. Norman: University of Oklahoma Press, 1956.

Jablow, Joseph. *The Cheyenne in Plains Indian Trade Relations, 1795–1840.* Lincoln: University of Nebraska Press, 1994.

Jackson, Jason Baird, and Greg Urban. "Mythology and Folklore." In *Handbook of North American Indians.* Vol. 14, *Southeast*, edited by Raymond Fogelson and William Sturtevant. Washington, D.C.: Smithsonian Institution, 2004.

Jantz, Richard L., and Douglas W. Owsley. "White Traders in the Upper Missouri: Evidence from the Swan Creek Site." In *Skeletal Biology in the Great Plains: Migration, Warfare, Health, and Subsistence*, edited by Douglas W. Owsley and Richard L. Jantz, 189–201. Washington, D.C.: Smithsonian Institution Press, 1994.

Jensen, Richard E., ed. *The Pawnee Mission Letters, 1834–1851.* Lincoln: University of Nebraska Press, 2010.

Jensen, Richard E., and James S. Hutchins. *Wheel Boats on the Missouri: The Journals and Documents of the Atkinson-O'Fallon Expedition, 1824–26.* Helena: Montana Historical Society Press, 2001.

John, Elizabeth A. H. *Storms Brewed in Other Men's Worlds: The Confrontation of Indians, Spanish, and French in the Southwest, 1540–1795.* Lincoln: University of Nebraska Press, 1981.

John, Elizabeth A. H., and Adan Benavides Jr., eds. "Inside the Comancheria, 1785: The Diary of Pedro Vial and Francisco Xavier Chaves." *Southwestern Historical Quarterly* 98, no. 1 (July 1994): 26–56.

Jones, Adam. *Genocide: A Comprehensive Introduction.* 2nd ed. London: Routledge, 2011.

Jones, Dorothy V. "John Dougherty and the Pawnee Rite of Human Sacrifice: April 1827." *Missouri Historical Review* 63, no. 3 (April 1969): 293–316.

Jones, Ernest. "Psychoanalysis and Folklore." In *The Study of Folklore*, edited by Alan Dundes, 88–102. Englewood Cliffs, N.J.: Prentice-Hall, 1965.

Kaplan, Matt. *The Science of Monsters: The Origins of the Creatures We Love to Fear.* New York: Simon and Schuster, 2013.

Kappler, Charles J., comp. and ed. *Indian Affairs: Laws and Treaties.* Vol. 2, *Treaties.* Washington, D.C.: Government Printing Office, 1904.

Kardong, Terrence. *Catholic Life at Fort Berthold, 1889–1989.* Richardton, N.Dak.: Assumption Abbey Press, 1989.

Kavanagh, Thomas W. "Comanche." In *Handbook of North American Indians.* Vol. 13, *Plains*, part 2, edited by Raymond J. DeMallie, 886–906. Washington, D.C.: Smithsonian Institution, 2001.

———. *Comanche Political History: An Ethnohistorical Perspective, 1706–1875.* Lincoln: University of Nebraska Press, 1996.

Kearney, Richard. *Strangers, Gods, and Monsters: Interpreting Otherness.* London: Routledge, 2003.

Kelton, Paul. *Cherokee Medicine, Colonial Germs: An Indigenous Nation's Fight against Smallpox, 1518–1824.* Norman: University of Oklahoma Press, 2015.

Krause, Richard A. "Plains Village Tradition: Coalescent." In *Handbook of North American Indians.* Vol. 13, *Plains*, part 1, edited by Raymond J. DeMallie, 196–206. Washington, D.C.: Smithsonian Institution, 2001.

Krech, Shepard. "From Ethnohistory to Anthropological History." In *Anthropology, History, and American Indians: Essays in Honor of William Curtis Sturtevant*, edited by William L. Merrill and Ives Goddard, 85–91. Washington, D.C.: Smithsonian Institution Press, 2002.

Krupat, Arnold. *All That Remains: Varieties of Indigenous Expression.* Lincoln: University of Nebraska Press, 2009.

———. *Red Matters: Native American Studies.* Philadelphia: University of Pennsylvania Press, 2002.

Lankford, George E. "Legends of the Adelantado." In *The Expedition of Hernando de Soto West of the Mississippi, 1541–1543: Proceedings of the De Soto Symposia, 1988 and 1990*, edited by Gloria A. Young and Michael P. Hoffman, 173–91. Fayetteville: University of Arkansas Press, 1993.

———. *Looking for Lost Lore: Studies in Folklore, Ethnology, and Iconography.* Tuscaloosa: University of Alabama Press, 2008.

Lankford, George E., comp. and ed. *Native American Legends of the Southeast: Tales from the Natchez, Caddo, Biloxi, Chickasaw, and Other Nations.* Tuscaloosa: University of Alabama Press, 2011.

La Vere, David. *The Caddo Chiefdoms: Caddo Economics and Politics, 700–1835.* Lincoln: University of Nebraska Press, 1998.

Lehmer, Donald J. *Introduction to Middle Missouri Archaeology.* Washington, D.C.: National Park Service, 1971.

———. "Plains Village Tradition: Postcontact." In *Handbook of North American Indians.* Vol. 13, *Plains,* part 1, edited by Raymond J. DeMallie, 245–55. Washington, D.C.: Smithsonian Institution, 2001.

Lehmer, Donald J., and David T. Jones. *Arikara Archeology: The Bad River Phase.* Publications in Salvage Archeology 7. Lincoln, Neb.: Museum of Natural History, Smithsonian Institution, 1968.

Leopold, Anita Maria, and Jeppe Sinding Jensen, eds. *Syncretism in Religion: A Reader.* New York: Routledge, 2004.

Lesser, Alexander. *The Pawnee Ghost Dance Hand Game: A Study of Cultural Change.* New York: AMS Press, 1969.

Levy, Jerrold E. "Is This a System? Comment on Osborn's 'Ecological Aspects of Equestrian Adaptations in Aboriginal North America.'" *American Anthropologist* 86, no. 4 (December 1984): 985–91.

Liberty, Margot, ed. *A Northern Cheyenne Album: Photographs by Thomas B. Marquis, Commentary by John Wooden Legs.* Norman: University of Oklahoma Press, 2006.

Linderman, Frank B., *Plenty-coups: Chief of the Crows.* Lincoln: University of Nebraska Press, 1962.

Linton, Ralph. "The Origin of the Skidi Pawnee Sacrifice to the Morning Star." *American Anthropologist* 28, no. 3 (1926): 457–66.

———. *The Sacrifice to the Morning Star by the Skidi Pawnee.* Leaflet 6. Chicago: Field Museum of Natural History, 1922.

Loomis, Noel M., and Abraham P. Nasatir. *Pedro Vial and the Roads to Santa Fe.* Norman: University of Oklahoma Press, 1967.

Lowie, Robert. "Oral Tradition and History." *American Anthropologist* 17, no. 3 (1915): 597–99.

———. "Oral Tradition and History." *Journal of American Folk-Lore* 30, no. 116 (1917): 161–67.

Mallery, Garrick. *Picture-Writing of the American Indians,* vol. 1. Washington, D.C.: Smithsonian Institution, 1893.

Malone, Patrick M. *The Skulking Way of War: Technology and Tactics among the New England Indians.* Baltimore: Johns Hopkins University Press, 1993.

Margry, Pierre. *Decouvertes et Etablissements des Français Dans l'Ouest et Dans le Sud de l'Amerique Septentionale, 1614–1754, Mémoires et Documents Originaux.* Vol. 6, *Exploration des Affluents du Mississippi et Découverte des Montagnes Rocheuses, 1679–1754.* New York: AMS Press, 1974.

Mason, Ronald J. *Inconstant Companions: Archaeology and North American Indian Oral Traditions.* Tuscaloosa: University of Alabama Press, 2007.

McClintock, Walter. *The Old North Trail: Or, Life, Legends and Religion of the Blackfeet Indians.* London: MacMillan, 1910.

McPherson, Robert S. *Viewing the Ancestors: Perceptions of the Anaasází, Mokwič, and Hisatsinom.* Norman: University of Oklahoma Press, 2014.

Meleen, Elmer E. *A Report on an Investigation of the La Roche Site, Stanley County, South Dakota.* Vermillion: University of South Dakota Museum, 1948.

Mihesuah, Devon A., ed. *Natives and Academics: Researching and Writing about American Indians.* Lincoln: University of Nebraska Press, 1998.

Milanich, Jerald T., and Charles M. Hudson. *Hernando de Soto and the Indians of Florida.* Gainesville: University Press of Florida, 1993.

Miller, Susan A., and James Riding In, eds. *Native Historians Write Back: Decolonizing American Indian History.* Lubbock: Texas Tech University Press, 2011.

Miller, Wick R. "The Ethnography of Speaking." In *Handbook of North American Indians.* Vol. 17, *Languages,* edited by Ives Goddard, 222–43. Washington, D.C.: Smithsonian Institution, 1996.

Mishkin, Bernard. *Rank and Warfare among the Plains Indians.* Lincoln: University of Nebraska Press, 1992.

Mooney, James. "Calendar History of the Kiowa Indians." In *Seventeenth Annual Report of the Bureau of American Ethnology to the Secretary of the Smithsonian Institution.* Part 1, *1895–96,* 129–445. Washington, D.C.: Government Printing Office, 1898.

———. "Myths of the Cherokee." In *Nineteenth Annual Report of the Bureau of American Ethnology 1897–98.* Part 1, *1900.* Washington, D.C.: Government Printing Office, 1900.

Moore, John H., Margot P. Liberty, and A. Terry Strauss. "Cheyenne." In *Handbook of North American Indians.* Vol. 13, *Plains,* part 2, edited by Raymond J. DeMallie, 863–85. Washington, D.C.: Smithsonian Institution, 2001.

Moulton, Gary. *Journals of the Lewis and Clark Expedition.* 13 vols. Lincoln: University of Nebraska Press, 1983–2001.

Murie James R. "Pawnee Indian Societies." *Anthropological Papers of the American Museum of Natural History* 11, no. 7 (1914): 543–644.

———. *Ceremonies of the Pawnee*, parts 1 and 2. Edited by Douglas R. Parks. Washington, D.C.: Smithsonian Institution Press, 1981.

Murphy, Monica, and Bill Wasik. *Rabid: A Cultural History of the World's Most Diabolical Virus.* New York: Penguin Books, 2012.

Nabokov, Peter. *A Forest of Time: American Indian Ways of History.* Cambridge: Cambridge University Press, 2002.

———. *Where the Lightning Strikes: The Lives of American Indian Sacred Places.* New York: Viking Penguin, 2006.

Nasatir, Abraham P., ed. *Before Lewis and Clark: Documents Illustrating the History of the Missouri, 1785–1804.* Lincoln: University of Nebraska Press, 1990.

Newcomb, William W., Jr. "Wichita." In *Handbook of North American Indians.* Vol. 13, *Plains,* part 1, edited by Raymond J. DeMallie, 548–66. Washington, D.C.: Smithsonian Institution, 2001.

Norall, Frank. *Bourgmont: Explorer of the Missouri, 1698–1725.* Lincoln: University of Nebraska Press, 1988.

Oliver-Smith, Anthony. "'What Is a Disaster?': Anthropological Perspectives on a Persistent Question." In *The Angry Earth: Disaster in Anthropological Perspective,* edited by Anthony Oliver-Smith and Susanna M. Hoffman, 18–34. New York: Routledge, 1999.

Opler, Morris Edward. *Myths and Tales of the Jicarilla Apache Indians.* Lincoln: University of Nebraska Press, 1994.

Overland, Orm. *The Making and Meaning of an American Classic: James Fenimore Cooper's* The Prairie. New York: Humanities Press, 1973.

Owsley, Douglas W., Hugh Berryman, and William M. Bass. "Demographic and Osteological Evidence for Warfare at the Larson Site, South Dakota." *Plains Anthropologist Memoir* 13 (1977): 119–31.

Palmer, Jessica Dawn. *The Apache Peoples: A History of All Bands and Tribes through the 1880s.* Jefferson, N.C.: McFarland, 2013.

Parks, Douglas R. "Arikara." In *Handbook of North American Indians.* Vol. 13, *Plains,* part 1, edited by Raymond J. DeMallie. Washington, D.C.: Smithsonian Institution, 2001: 365–90.

———. "Bands and Villages of the Arikara and Pawnee." *Nebraska History* 60, no. 2 (Summer 1979), 214–39.

———. "Caddoan Languages." In *Handbook of North American Indians.* Vol. 13, *Plains,* part 1, edited by Raymond J. DeMallie, 80–93. Washington, D.C.: Smithsonian Institution, 2001.

———. "An Historical Character Mythologized: The Scalped Man in Arikara and Pawnee Folklore." In *Plains Indian Studies: A Collection of Essays in Honor of John C. Ewers and Waldo R. Wedel,* edited by Douglas H. Ubelaker and Herman J. Viola, 47–58. Washington, D.C.: Smithsonian Institution Press, 1982.

———. "The Northern Caddoan Languages: Their Subgrouping and Time Depths." *Nebraska History* 60, no. 2 (Summer 1979): 197–213.

Parks, Douglas R., ed. "Biography of James R. Murie." In *Ceremonies of the Pawnee.* Part 1, *The Skiri*, by James R. Murie, 21–28. Washington, D.C.: Smithsonian Institution Press, 1981.

Parks, Douglas R., and Raymond J. DeMallie. "Plains Indian Native Literatures." *Boundary 2* 19, no. 3 (1992): 105–47.

Parks, Douglas R., and Waldo R. Wedel. "Pawnee Geography: Historical and Sacred." *Great Plains Quarterly* 5, no. 3 (1985): 143–76.

Paul Wilhelm, Duke of Württemberg. *Travels in North America, 1822–1824.* Translated by W. Robert Nitske and edited by Savoie Lottinville. Norman: University of Oklahoma Press, 1973.

Paul Wilhelm, Herzog von Wuerttemberg. *Erste Reise nach dem noerdlichen Amerika in den Jahren 1822 bis 1824.* Stuttgart: Verlag der J. O. Cotta'schen Buchhandlung, 1835.

Peterson, Harold L. *Arms and Armor in Colonial America, 1526–1783.* Mineola, N.Y.: Dover Publications, 2000.

Pfaller, Louis. *St. Joseph Mission, Twin Buttes, North Dakota: A Brief History and Picture Review Published after the Dedication of the New Church in June 1972.* Richardton, N.Dak.: Assumption Abbey Press, 1973.

Pyhrr, Stuart W., Donald J. LaRocca, and Dirk H. Breiding. *The Armored Horse in Europe, 1480–1620.* New York: Metropolitan Museum of Art/Yale University Press, 2004.

Raglan, Lord. "Myth and Ritual." *Journal of American Folklore* 68, no. 270 (1955): 454–61.

Ramsey, Jarold. *Reading the Fire: The Traditional Indian Literatures of America.* Seattle: University of Washington Press, 1999.

Ratcliffe, Sam D. "'Escenas de Martirio': Notes on 'The Destruction of Mission San Sabá.'" *Southwestern Historical Quarterly* 94, no. 4 (April 1991): 507–34.

Reséndez, Andrés. *The Other Slavery: The Uncovered Story of Indian Enslavement in America.* Boston: Houghton Mifflin Harcourt, 2016.

Riding In, James. "The Betrayal of 'Civilization' in United States–Native Nations Diplomacy." In *Nation to Nation: Treaties between the United States and American Indian Nations*, edited by Suzan Shown Harjo, 153–71. Washington, D.C.: Smithsonian Institution, 2014.

Roe, Frank Gilbert. *The Indian and the Horse.* Norman: University of Oklahoma Press, 1979.

Rogers, J. Daniel. *Objects of Change: The Archaeology and History of Arikara Contact with Europeans.* Washington, D.C.: Smithsonian Institution Press, 1990.

Rogers, J. Daniel, and George Sabo III. "Caddo." In *Handbook of North American Indians.* Vol. 14, *Southeast,* edited by Raymond D. Fogelson and William C. Sturtevant, 616–31. Washington, D.C.: Smithsonian Institution, 2004.

Ross, Sonja Brigitte. *Das Menschenopfer der Skidi-Pawnee.* Bonn, Germany: Holos Verlag, 1989.

Saunt, Claudio. "History until 1776." In *Handbook of North American Indians.* Vol. 14, *Southeast,* edited by Raymond D. Fogelson and William C. Sturtevant, 128–38. Washington, D.C.: Smithsonian Institution, 2004.

Schultz, James Willard. *Rising Wolf, the White Blackfoot: Hugh Monroe's Story of His First Year on the Plains.* Boston: Houghton Mifflin Company, 1919.

Secoy, Frank Raymond. *Changing Military Patterns of the Great Plains Indians: 17th Century through Early 19th Century.* Lincoln: University of Nebraska Press, 1992.

———. "The Identity of the 'Paduca'; an Ethnohistorical Analysis." *American Anthropologist* 53, no. 4 (1951): 525–42.

Simpson, Lesley B., ed. *The San Sabá Papers: A Documentary Account of the Founding and Destruction of San Sabá Mission.* San Francisco: John Howell Books, 1959.

Southwell, Kristina L., and John R. Lovett. *The Photographs of Annette Ross Hume: Life at the Kiowa, Comanche, and Wichita Agency.* Norman: University of Oklahoma Press, 2010.

Speck, Frank G. "Ethnology of the Yuchi Indians." *Anthropological Publications of the University Museum* 1, no. 1. Philadelphia: University of Pennsylvania, 1919.

Standing Bear, Luther. *Land of the Spotted Eagle.* Lincoln: University of Nebraska Press, 1978.

———. *My People the Sioux.* Lincoln: University of Nebraska Press, 1975.

Stands In Timber, John, and Margot Liberty. *Cheyenne Memories.* New Haven, Conn.: Yale University Press, 1967.

———. *A Cheyenne Voice: The Complete John Stands In Timber Interviews.* Norman: University of Oklahoma Press, 2013.

Starkey, Armstrong. *European and Native American Warfare, 1675–1815.* Norman: University of Oklahoma Press, 1998.

Steinke, Christopher. "Leading the 'Father': The Pawnee Homeland, Coureurs de Bois, and the Villasur Expedition of 1720." *Great Plains Quarterly* 32, no. 1 (Winter 2012): 43–62.

Stevenson, Matilda Coxe. *The Sia.* Eleventh Annual Report of the Bureau of American Ethnology. Washington, D.C.: Smithsonian Institution, 1894.

Sturtevant, William C. "Anthropology, History, and Ethnohistory." *Ethnohistory* 13, no. 1/2 (1966): 1–51.

Swann, Brian, ed. *Born in the Blood: On Native American Translation.* Lincoln: University of Nebraska Press, 2011.

———. *On the Translation of Native American Literatures.* Washington, D.C.: Smithsonian Institution Press, 1992.

Swann, Brian, and Arnold Krupat, eds. *Recovering the Word: Essays on Native American Literature.* Berkeley: University of California Press, 1987.

Swanton, John R. "Dr. Swanton's Reply." *American Anthropologist* 17, no. 3 (1915): 600.

———. *Source Material on the History and Ethnology of the Caddo Indians.* Norman: University of Oklahoma Press, 1996.

Tedlock, Dennis. *The Spoken Word and the Work of Interpretation.* Philadelphia: University of Pennsylvania Press, 1983.

Terreros, Juan M. Romero de. "The Destruction of the San Sabá Apache Mission: A Discussion of the Casualties." *Americas* 60, no. 4 (April 2004): 617–27.

Thomas, Alfred Barnaby. *After Coronado: Spanish Exploration Northeast of New Mexico, 1696–1727, Documents from the Archives of Spain, Mexico and New Mexico.* Norman: University of Oklahoma Press, 1966.

Thomas, David Hurst. *Skull Wars: Kennewick Man, Archaeology, and the Battle for Native American Identity.* New York: Basic Books, 2000.

Thompson, Stith. "Myths and Folktales." *Journal of American Folklore* 68, no. 270 (1955): 482–88.

Thornton, Russell. *American Indian Holocaust and Survival: A Population History since 1492.* Norman: University of Oklahoma Press, 1987.

———. "A Rosebud Reservation Winter Count, circa 1751–52 to 1886–1887." *Ethnohistory* 49, no. 4 (2002): 723–41.

Thurman, Melburn D. "A Case of Historical Mythology: The Skidi Pawnee Morning Star Sacrifice of 1833." *Plains Anthropologist* 15, no. 50, part 1 (1970): 309–11.

———. "The Skidi Pawnee Morning Star Sacrifice of 1827." *Nebraska History* 51, no. 3 (Fall 1970): 268–80.

Thwaites, Reuben Gold, ed. *Early Western Travels, 1748–1846.* Vol. 23, *Part II of Maximilian, Prince of Wied's Travels in the Interior of North America, 1832–1834.* Cleveland, Ohio: Arthur H. Clark, 1906.

Toelken, Barre. *The Anguish of Snails: Native American Folklore in the West.* Logan: Utah State University Press, 2003.

Trimble, Michael K. "Infectious Disease and the Northern Plains Horticulturalists: A Human Behavior Model." *Plains Anthropologist* 34, no. 124 (1989): 41–59.

Tucker, Sara Jones, comp. *Indian Villages of the Illinois Country.* Part 1, *Atlas.* Scientific Papers, Illinois State Museum, vol. 2. Springfield: State of Illinois, 1942.

Van de Logt, Mark. "'The Powers of the Heavens Shall Eat of My Smoke': The Significance of Scalping in Pawnee Warfare." *Journal of Military History* 72, no. 1 (January 2008): 71–104.

Vansina, Jan. *Oral Tradition as History.* Madison: University of Wisconsin Press, 1985.

Vestal, Stanley. *Warpath: The True Story of the Fighting Sioux Told in a Biography of Chief White Bull.* Boston: Houghton Mifflin Company, 1934.

Waggoner, Josephine F. "An Oglala Sioux Winter Count," *Museum of the Fur Trade* 24, no. 4 (1988): 11–14.

Wallace, Anthony F. C. "Revitalization Movements." *American Anthropologist* 58, no. 2 (1956): 264–81.

Walters, Anna Lee. *Talking Indian: Reflections on Survival and Writing.* Ithaca, N.Y.: Firebrand Books, 1992.

Weddle, Robert S. *After the Massacre: The Violent Legacy of the San Sabá Mission.* Lubbock: Texas Tech University Press, 2007.

———. *The San Sabá Mission: Spanish Pivot in Texas.* Austin: University of Texas Press, 1964.

Wedel, Mildred M. *The Wichita Indians 1541–1750: Ethnohistorical Essays.* Reprints in Anthropology 38. Lincoln, Neb.: J & L Reprint Company, 1988.

Wedel, Waldo R. "Chain Mail in Plains Archeology." *Plains Anthropologist* 20, no. 69 (August 1975): 187–96.

———. *The Dunbar-Allis Letters on the Pawnee.* New York: Garland, 1985.

Welsh, Roger L. "Introduction to the Reprint Edition." In *Prairie Smoke,* by Melvin R. Gilmore, xi–xxii. Saint Paul: Minnesota Historical Society Press, 1987.

Weltfish, Gene. *Caddoan Texts, Pawnee, South Band Dialect.* Publications of the American Ethnological Society 17. New York: American Ethnological Society, 1937.

———. *The Lost Universe: Pawnee Life and Culture.* Lincoln: University of Nebraska Press, 1977.

Wescott, Daniel J., and Deborah L. Cunningham. "Temporal Changes in Arikara Humeral and Femoral Cross-sectional Geometry Associated with Horticultural Intensification." *Journal of Archaeological Science* 33 (2005): 1022–36.

White, Richard. "The Winning of the West: The Expansion of the Western Sioux in the Eighteenth and Nineteenth Centuries." *Journal of American History* 65 (September 1978): 319–43.

Wied, Maximilian. *Maximilian, Prince of Wied's Travels in the Interior of North America, 1832–1834,* part 2. In *Early Western Travels, 1748–1846,* vol. 23, edited by Reuben Gold Thwaites. New York: AMS Press, 1966.

———. *Reise in das Innere Nord-America in de Jahren 1832 bis 1834.* Coblenz, Germany: J. Hoelscher, 1841.

Will, George F. "Arikara Ceremonials." *North Dakota Historical Quarterly* 4, no. 4 (July 1930): 247–65.

———. "An Arikara Sacred Ceremony." *North Dakota History* 16, no. 4 (October 1949): 265–68.

———. "Magical and Sleight of Hand Performances by the Arikara." *North Dakota Historical Quarterly* 3, no. 1 (October 1928): 50–65.

———. "Notes on the Arikara Indians and Their Ceremonies." *Old West Series* 3 (1934): 5–48.

Willey, Patrick S. *Prehistoric Warfare on the Great Plains: Skeletal Analysis of the Crow Creek Massacre Victims.* New York: Garland Publishing, 1990.

Willey, Patrick S., and Thomas E. Emerson. "The Osteology and Archaeology of the Crow Creek Massacre." *Plains Anthropologist* 38, no. 145 (1993): 227–69.

Wilson, Gilbert L. "The Horse and the Dog in Hidatsa Culture." *Anthropological Papers of the American Museum of Natural History* 15 (1924): 125–311.

Wise, Terence. *The Conquistadores.* London: Osprey Man-at-Arms, 1980.

Wishart, David. *An Unspeakable Sadness: The Dispossession of the Nebraska Indians.* Lincoln: University of Nebraska Press, 1994.

Wissler, Clark. "The Influence of the Horse in the Development of Plains Culture." *American Anthropologist,* n.s., 16, no. 1 (January–March 1914): 1–25.

Wissler, Clark, and Herbert J. Spinden. "The Pawnee Human Sacrifice to the Morning Star." *American Museum Journal* 16 (January 1916): 49–55.

Wood, W. Raymond. "Plains Trade in Prehistoric and Protohistoric Intertribal Relations." In *Anthropology on the Great Plains,* edited by W. Raymond Wood and Margot Liberty, 98–109. Lincoln: University of Nebraska Press, 1980.

Yellow Bird, Loren. "Now I Will Speak (Nawah Ti Waako'): A Sahnish Perspective on What the Lewis and Clark Expedition and Others Missed." *Wicazo Sa Review* 19, no. 1 (Spring 2004), 73–84.

Young, Gloria A., and Michael P. Hoffman, eds. *The Expedition of Hernando de Soto West of the Mississippi, 1541–1543: Proceedings of the de Soto Symposia, 1988 and 1990.* Fayetteville: University of Arkansas Press, 1993.

Zimmerman, Larry J., and Lawrence E. Bradley. "The Crow Creek Massacre: Initial Coalescent Warfare and Speculations about the Genesis of Extended Coalescent." *Plains Anthropologist* 38, no. 145 (1993): 215–26.

Index

Page numbers in *italic* type indicate illustrations.

Aays, 144, 215n58
abducted women and child(ren): accounts of abduction and torture of, 79, 82, 83, 84, 141; Coyote's rescue of, 75, 77–80, 79–80, 82, 85, 86, 96; as Madonna and infant Jesus, 97, 99, 101; mission protection and escape of, 88, 92, 100; official Spanish support of, 81, 83, 113; in Pawnee-Spanish warfare, 114. *See also* Coyote story (Wichita); slavery and slave trade
abduction story. *See* Coyote story (Wichita)
Acoma Pueblo(s), 191n54, 208n28
Adais, 5. *See also* Caddoan oral traditions
adaptations, cultural and physical, 24–25
agriculture, 2–3, 76, 130, 198n16
Ahahe, 75, 78. *See also* Coyote story (Wichita)
Alights on the Cloud, 107, 114–17, *115*, 118, 119, 209nn37–38, 209n40
Allis, Samuel, 167, 169–70, 175
American Indian oral traditions. *See* oral traditions
American Indian Quarterly, 26
American Indian tribes. See *specific tribal names*
American Museum of Natural History, New York, 46
amputation, medical, 161
Anderson, Gary Clayton, 218n19
animal stories, 68–70, 71, 184, 201nn50–51, 212n68
Antelope, F. W., 46
anthropophagy. *See* cannibalism

Anza, Juan Bautista de, 114
Apaches: armor of, 211n55; and Christianity, 89; Cuartelejo band, 126; Jicarilla band, 120, 138; Kiowa band, 179, 211n55; Lipan band, 83, 89;Pawnee warfare, 119–21; slave trade of, 80–81, 83, 92. *See also* abducted women and child(ren); San Sabá Massacre (1758)
appropriation and Native traditions, 11, 18, 177, 184
Arapaho traditions, 46
archaeological sites and collections, 45–46, 109, 139, 159, 205n3, 220n91
Arikara oral traditions: animal stories of, 68–70, 71, 184, 186, 201nn50–51, 212n68; classification system for, 42; Dorsey's collection of, 42, 47, 49, 60; Pahukatawa in, 176, 220n71; religion, 70–74; scalped men in, 157, 159, 162, *163*, 216n6; storytelling sources of, 60–62; Whirlwind story in, 5, 26–28, 67–74, 184, 185–86
Arikaras: 1780s massacre of, 66; cultural overview of, 2–6, 61–62, 189n3; epidemic diseases and effects on, 27, 63, 65–74, 198n17, 199nn22–23, 200n28; on fur traders, 199n23; intertribal relations of, 63–66, 170, 198n13, 199n21, 200nn29–30, 200n32; medicine among, 70–71, *71, 73*; population of, 60–61, 65, 199n23, 200n28; territory of, 2, *4*; weapons and horses of, 198n16
armor technologies. *See* metal armor

241

arrowheads, 109, 110. *See also* bows and arrows
Asma, Stephen T., 23
Awat'ovi Pueblo(s), 165
Aztecs, 139

Baaren, Th. P. van, 34–35
Barber, Elizabeth Wayland and Paul T., 16–17
Battle of Adobe Walls, 208n30, 211n55
Battle of Tula, 143, 146–51, 215n59
Bear Hactcin, 138
Bear's Tail, 62, 67
bear stories, 68–69, 70, 138, 186, 201nn50–51
Beowulf, 19, 34, 103–4
bevor, 108–9, 206n7
Big Crow, 68
Big Spotted Horse, 209n40, 210n46
Blackfeet, 166, 207n17
"Black Pawnees." *See* Wichitas
Blaine, Garland James, 50
Blaine, Martha Royce, 50, 219n66
Blaine, Wichita, 118
Boas, Franz, 35, 45
Bodmer, Carl, 207n17
body modification, 76, 148
Botone, Marjorie Louise Brown, 51, 52–53
Bourgmont, Étienne de Veniard Sieur de, 63
Bourke, John Gregory, 108–9
bows and arrows, 146, 167, 198n16. *See also* arrowheads
brigandine, 206n7
Brightman, Robert, 142
Brooks, James, 81
Bry, Theodore de, 153
bull boats, 123–24
Bureau of Indian Affairs, 187. *See also* census rolls (Bureau of Indian Affairs)
burgonets, 145. *See also* helmets
byrnie, 108

Cabello y Robles, Domingo, 110–11, 113
Cabrera, Miguel, 93
Caddoan monster stories: about, 24, 136, 184–87; stone coat tradition in, 107–8, 111, 137–38, 205n6. *See also* monster theories

—Arikara: animal stories, 68–70, 71, 184, 186, 201nn50–51, 212n68; Pahukatawa, 176, 220n71; scalped men stories, 157, 159, 162, 163, 216n6; Whirlwind story, 5, 26–28, 67–74, 184, 185–86. *See also* Arikara oral traditions
—Caddo: scalped men stories, 157, 216n2. *See also* Caddoan oral traditions; masked cannibal stories (Caddo)
—Pawnee: scalped men stories, 157, 159–64, 186–87; Whirlwind story, 67–68. *See also* Pahukatawa story (Pawnee); Pawnee oral traditions
—Skiri Pawnee: scalped men stories, 157, 159–64, 186–87. *See also* Flint Monster story (Skiri Pawnee); Skiri (Skidi) Pawnee oral tradition
—Wichita: stone coat monsters, 205n6; Whirlwind and Wind stories, 68. *See also* Coyote story (Wichita); Wichita oral traditions
Caddoan oral traditions: classification systems for stories of, 42–44; coats of mail in, 207n17; Dorsey's collection of, 45, 47, 132, 216n2; as historical sources, 6–11, 183–87; scalped men in, 157, 216n2. See also *specific tribes*
Caddos: battles of, 143, 145–50; body modifications by, 148; cultural overview of, 2–6, 189n1 (intro.); introduction of horses to, 144; migration and territory of, 2, *4*, 130, 191n47, 213n2. *See also* masked cannibal stories (Caddo)
Cadohadachos, 5
Cahinnios, 5
Calahorra of Nacogdoches, Joseph de, 83
Camisa de Hierro, 113–14, 208n31. *See also* Iron Shirt
Cannibal chief. *See* Páez, Juan
cannibalism, 142–43, 186, 201n45, 204n54, 214n30
cannibal stories. *See* masked cannibal stories (Caddo)
Carbine and Lance (Nye), 54
Carranza, Juan de, 149
Carrying the Shield in Front, 117, 118
Carson, Kit, 211n55
Carter, Cecile Elkins, 38

Cassirer, Ernst, 34
Castaño de Sosa, Gaspar, 88, 208n24
Castillo, García del, 111
Catholicism, 165
Cavalier, Robert, 207n17
Cedar Tree ceremony, 72–74, *73*
celibacy, 85
census rolls (Bureau of Indian Affairs), 51, 60–61, 78, 104, 205n4. *See also* population statistics
Ceremonies of the Pawnee (Murie), 49
Chafe, Wallace, 45, 144, 213n4
chain mail armor. *See* metal armor
Chamberlain, Von Del, 220n91
Chawi Pawnees, 3. *See also* Pawnees
Cherokees, 66–67, 72, 107, 137, 142
Chesterton, G. K., 44
Cheyennes, 107, 158, 209n36, 210n45; Pawnee warfare, 158, 164–70. *See also* Alights on the Cloud
Chickasaws, 142
Chief Big Axe, 170
Chief Big Eagle, 172
children. *See* abducted women and child(ren)
"child(ren) of the sun," 122–23. *See also* Wonderful Boy
Christianity: and Apaches, 89; God of, 23, 192n57; influence on ceremonies and stories, 27, 44, 61, 132, 184, 186, 201n45; of Murie, 47–48, 50; and Pahukatawa as sacred power, 24, 27, 170, 176–78, 180, 184; and Pawnees, 158, 169–70, 180–82; and slave trade, 81. *See also* Franciscan missionaries; Jesus Christ
classification systems, 42–44
Clements, William M., 35
clubs (weapon), 68, 95, 147, 148–49, 150–51
coats of armor. *See* metal armor
Cohen, Jeffrey Jerome, 22
Cole, Douglas, 46, 195n54
collaboration in recording and interpreting stories, 31–32, 193n5
colonialism and Native traditions, 18–22, 165, 191n54, 192n2
Comanches: armor of, 207n17; as Flint Monsters, 113–14; Indian Agency of, 52, 53; migration of, 64; relations with Wichitas, 52, 81, 87, 92, 101, 202n16; and slave trade, 83. *See also* San Sabá Massacre (1758)
Coming Sun, 172, 175
Contatanacapara, 114
Cook-Lynn, Elizabeth, 19, 21, 191n54
corn cultivation, 2–3, 76, 130, 198n16, 202n16
corn mill, *131*, 135–36, 145, 147, 149
corn pestles. *See* clubs (weapon)
Coronado, Francisco Vázquez de: contact with Caddos, 213n5; contact with Wichitas, 76; introduction of chain mail armor and horses by, 109, 119; muster and inventories of, 111, 145, 146, 215n45; research on, 77, 88, 111
Cortinas, Juan, 95
cosmology of Pawnees, 39, 43, 74, 152, 158–59, 162–63, 182, 210n48. *See also* Morning Star; Pahukatawa story (Pawnee)
Cota de Malla, 114
coureurs de bois, 86, 104, 121, 123–27
Coyote (Caddo hero), 145, 147–50, 152
Coyote (Wichita hero): encounter with headless men, 79, 82, 86, 97; help from Spider-Man, 26, 76, 84; identity of, 94; portrayals of, 92, 93, *93*; rescue of abducted child(ren) by, 75, 77–80, 82, 85, 86, 96. *See also* Coyote story (Wichita)
Coyote, as character in oral traditions, 35, 39, 40, 41, 42–43, 212n68
"Coyote and the Six Brothers" story, 129, 134–36, 214n38. *See also* masked cannibal stories (Caddo)
Coyote-Man (Skiri Pawnee hero), 105, 123, 212n68
Coyote story (Wichita): analyzed components of story, 81–87; connection to San Sabá Massacre, 27, 88, 92–102, 184; summary, 77, 78–80. *See also* Coyote (Wichita hero)
creation story. *See* Whirlwind story (Arikara)
Creeks, 141
crinet, 109

crossbows, 111, 146, 150
Crow Creek Massacre (1325), 159, 165
cruelty and torture by Spanish, 84–85, 143, 203n19, 208n28
Cruikshank, Julie, 183
crupper, 109
Cuartelejo Apaches, 126. *See also* Apaches
cuirass, 109, 206n7, 210n45
cultural adaptations, 24–25
cultural history, overview, 2–6
Curley Hair, 205n4
Curly Chief, 205n4
Curly-Head, 103, 104–5, 205nn4–5. *See also* Flint Monster story (Skiri Pawnee)
Cut Nose, 200n45

Davis, Richard, 47, 49
decapitation, 86, 91, 97–98, 120, 186, 203n22. *See also* headless men; scalping
deceased persons and historical recording, 39
Delawares, 78, 115, 167
Deloria, Vine, Jr., 10, 13, 21, 27
DeMallie, Raymond J., 45, 46
Densmore, Frances, 117–18
DeSmet, Pierre-Jean, 179
De Soto–Moscoso expedition: armor and weaponry of, 144–46, 214n41; battles of, 143–44, 146–51; cannibalism by, 142–43, 214n30; connection to masked cannibal stories, 136, 141–53, 184; cruelty and torture by, 143–44; introduction of horses by, 144; introduction of iron by, 141; summary of, 27, 129–32. *See also* masked cannibal stories (Caddo)
The Destruction of Mission San Sabá (painting by Páez), 93, *93*, 97
DeVoto, Bernard, 8
disaster theories, 24–25, 192n63
diseases. *See* epidemic diseases
Dixon, R. B., 6–7
doctors' societies and medicine men, 70–71, *71*, *73*, 132, 161 187
dog stories, 69–70, 71, 144
Dolores, Maria Ano de los, 98
Dorsey, George: career and criticisms of, 44–47, 54–55, 195n54; editorializing by, 40, 45; ethnographic interpreters of, 32,

45, 46, 47–49, 53; on Flint Monster story, 103; *The Mythology of the Wichita*, 43, 47, *52*, 53, 54, 76–77; *Pawnee Mythology*, 43, 49; *Traditions of the Arikara*, 42, 47, 49, 60; *Traditions of the Caddo*, 45, 47, 132, 216n2; *Traditions of the Skidi Pawnee*, 41–42, 49, 105, 205n5
double balls, 105–6, 123–24, 212n63
Dougherty, John, 166, 178
Doustioni tribe, 5. *See also* Caddoan oral traditions
dragons, 17
Dunbar, John, 167, 169–70, 179, 218n31
Dunbar, John Brown, 171, 177
Dunbar-Ortiz, Roxanne, 218n19
Dundes, Alan, 33
Dunn, William, 92
Dusty Chief, 116, 118

Eagle Chief, 116, 117, 209n40
Eagle Rises Up, 197n6
Ear Ring, 116
Echo-Hawk, Roger C.: on Arikara creation story, 5; on historicity of oral traditions, 17–18, 21; on migration of Caddoan ancestors, 191n47; on Murie and Ghost Dance, 50, 196n67; on Pahukatawa, 180–81
Ecueracapa, 114
Ekberg, Carl J., 202n12
Eliade, Mircea, 34
El Turco (Pawnee guide), 111–12
emblems, 205n7
Encanguané, 114
epidemic diseases, 65–74; dates of, 60, 63, 65; from fur traders, 198n17, 199n23; intertribal transmission of, 179; population decline from, 199nn22–23, 200n28; from Spanish contact, 141, 152, 214n23; warfare due to, 113–14. *See also* Whirlwind story (Arikara)
Escanjaques, 113
Espejo, Antonio de, 88, 208n24
ethnocide, 164, 180
ethnohistory: challenges in, 33; criticism of, 15–16, 21–22, 38–39, 194n28; methods used in, 6, 14, 18, 26–27, 193n8. *See also* myth; oral traditions

ethnopaleography, 193n8
ethnopoetics, 35–36
Evening Star, 163, 176, 177, 210n48
Eyeish, 5, 144, 215n58

fantastic elements as historical metaphors in oral traditions, 2, 8, 11–12, 60, 194n20. *See also* monsters
Field (Columbian) Museum, Chicago, 45, 49
The Fighting Cheyennes (Grinnell), 115
flanchard, 109
Fletcher, Alice Cunningham, 49
Flint Monster story (Skiri Pawnee): background of, 27, 103–4; identity of Flint Monster in, 104, 107, 111–19, 184; identity of Wonderful Boy in, 104, 122–27; summary of, 105–7, 119, 185. *See also* metal armor
Flores, Joseph Antonio, 98, 99
Flying Squirrel, 134, 135, 141–42, 214n28
flying squirrel stories, 142
Fogelson, Raymond, 21–22, 66
Foley, John Miles, 31
A Forest of Time (Nabokov), 15
Fort Berthold Reservation, 59. *See also* Arikaras
Four Horns, 62, 67, 71
Four Rings, 62, 69
Franciscan missionaries, 75–76, 81, 85, 88–92, 111, 208n24. *See also* Christianity
Frazer, James G., 194n19
French explorers and traders: Arikara attitude on, 199n23; *coureurs de bois*, 86, 104, 121, 123–27; influence of and introduction of guns by, 80–81, 94–96, 101; and slave trade, 81
Freud, Sigmund, 23, 33–34

gambeson, 109, 110
García, Joseph, 98
Garcilaso de la Vega, 147–50, 215n59
garroting, 85
Gaston, George Belcher, 167
gauntlets, 104, 108, 111, 121, 206nn7–8
genocide, 158, 159, 164–70, 181, 217n19
Géno^{N}skwa, 137–38

Gerona, Carla, 44
Ghost Dance (religious movement), 50, 178, 180, 196n67
Ghost-Man, 68
Gill, Lancey W., 53
Gillis, J. L., 168
Gilmore, David D., 22
Gilmore, Melvin, 73
Gilmore, Melvin Randolph, 3, 59
Giraud, Rene, 23
Godoy, Diego de, 149
gorgets, 108–9, 206n7
greaves, 206n7
Grinnell, George Bird: ethnographic sources of, 49, 116; *The Fighting Cheyennes*, 115; on human sacrifice, 189n3; on metal armor and identity of Iron Shirt, 110, 207n17, 209nn36–40; on Pahukatawa, 171, 176, 220n77
Guachoyas, 143
guns, introduction of, 80–81, 94–96, 128, 198n16. *See also* weaponry
Gutiérrez, Joseph, 95
Gutíerrez, Juan Antonio, 90, 91, 98, 100
Guttiérrez, Jusepe, 112

Hachaxas, 114
Hais, 144, 215n58
The Hako (Fletcher), 49
halberds, 146, 150, 215n45
Hallowell, A. Irving, 7
Hampton Normal and Agricultural Institute, 47–48
Hand (Arikara storyteller), 61, 62, 67, 70
harquebuses, 111, 113, 146, 203n22
Hasinais, 5, 213n2
hauberk, 108
Haudenoshaunee, 165, 166
Háweniyo, 137
Hawk (Arikara storyteller), 62, 70, 72, 200n45
headless men: encounter with Coyote, 79, 82, 86, 97; identity of, 77–78, 85, 98, 186, 204n54; portrayals of, *93*, 98. *See also* Coyote story (Wichita); decapitation
Heart, Frank, 197n6
helmets, 95, 108, 136, 137, 145. *See also* masks and maskettes; metal armor

heraldry, 205n7
heroes and tradition, role of, 24
Hikus, 171, 176
Hills along the Banks of a River. *See* Pahukatawa story (Pawnee)
history. *See* ethnohistory; myth; oral traditions
Hoffman, Paul E., 214n23, 214n41
Hoffman, Susanna M., 24, 192n63
Holder, Preston, 63
Horn, Strieby, 74
Hornbostel, Erich von, 45
horses: armor protection for, 109, 145–46; introduction of, 80, 119, 144, 198n16; Pawnee's use of, 119
Huiziga, Johan, 183
Humaña, Antonio Gutiérrez de, 112, 203n22
human sacrifice, 3, 158, 163, 169, 178, 179, 189n3
Hume, Annette Ross, 53
Hunt, Burgess, 45, 47, 51–54, *52*, 76, 78
Hunt, Edward Proctor, 191n54
Hyde, George E., 7–8, 209n40, 210n46
Hyman, Stanley Edgar, 8
Hymes, Dell, 35

identity: difference *vs.* sameness in historical, 194n22; and scholarly research, 193n5
Iksa' Fáni', 142
influenza. *See* epidemic diseases
Iowa Indians, 64, 126, 139
iron, introduction of, 141
Iron Jacket, 110
iron-nosed masks. *See* masks and maskettes
Iron Shirt: as Apache warrior, 211n55; as Blackfeet chief, 207n17; as Cheyenne warrior, 209n36; as Comanche warrior, 107, 113, 207n17; as Pawnee warrior, 209n37; versions of name, 110, 113–14, 208n31

Jesus Christ: "abduction" of infant, 97, 99, 101; Arikara story about, 61, 197n6; Caddo story of, 132–33; parallels with Pahukatawa, 24, 170, 175, 177, 220n77; sacred rise of, 23. *See also* Christianity
Jicarilla Apaches, 120, 138

Jones, Adam, 165
Judeo-Christian-Islamic God, 23, 192n57. *See also* Christianity
Jung, Carl, 23, 34

Kadas, 40
Kadohadachos, 213n2
Kawaharu, 171, 176
Kaws, 64, 116
Kehoe, Alice Beck, 9
Kelton, Paul, 72
Kennewick Man, 8–9
Kiowa Apache, 179, 211n55
Kiowas: Agency of, 51, 52, 53; armor and warfare of, 115, 116, 179, 207n17, 210n45; census on, 51; migration of, 64, 120; winter counts of, *115*, 118, 199n21, 210n45
Ki-Ri-Ki-Ri-See-Ra-Ki-Wa-Ri. *See* Roaming Scout
Kirk, G. S., 193n19
Kitkehahki Pawnees, 3, 205n4
Kitsais oral traditions, 2, *4*, 189n1 (intro.). *See also* Wichita oral traditions
Kluckhohn, Clyde, 34
Knee Print by the Water. *See* Pahukatawa story (Pawnee)
Knife Chief, 158, 170, 178
Kō'kā'kā, 118
Krupat, Arnold, 35, 36–37

LaFlesche, Francis, 15
La Harpe, Jean Baptiste Benard de, 84, 94, 198n13
Lakotas, 64, 158, 164–70, 184. *See also* Sioux
lances, 83, 136, 146, 147
Lankford, George, 151–52
Leal, Juan, 89–90, 93, 95
leather armor, 146
leggings, sacred, 172, 219n58
Lehmer, Donald, 63
LeMoyne, Jacques, 153
Le Page du Pratz, Antoine, 15
Lesser, Alexander, 180
Le Sueur, Pierre-Charles, 126
Lévi-Strauss, Claude, 34
Lewis and Clark expedition, 66, 193n5

Leyva de Bonilla, Francisco, 88, 112, 203n22
Linderman, Frank B., 39, 193n14
Linton, Ralph, 32, 50
Lipan Apaches, 83, 89. *See also* Apaches; San Sabá Massacre (1758)
lodging, 3, 130, 144
Lone Chief, 171–72
Lone Walker, 207n17
longbow, 108, 145, 146, 205n7
long-nosed maskettes. *See* masks and maskettes
Louis XIV (king), 123, 126
Lowie, Robert, 6–7, 129, 190n16

Madonna, 96–97, 99, 101, 186
magic balls, 105–6, 123–24, 212n63
mail armor. *See* metal armor
maiming practices, 161
Malinowski, Bronislav, 34
Man Chief, 158, 169, 178–79
Many Fox, 71–72
masked cannibal stories (Caddo): connection to De Soto expedition, 136, 141–53, 184; "Coyote and the Six Brothers," 129, 134–36, 214n38; description of masks in, 136, 144; Red Horn myth, 139, 141; summary of, 27, 129–30; tools used in, *131*; twin hero myth, 139–41; "The Young Men and the Cannibals," 129, 132–34, 146–48. *See also* De Soto–Moscoso expedition
masks and maskettes: iron-nosed, 136, 144, 145, 152; long-nosed, 139–41; metal helmets, 95, 108, 136, 137, 145. *See also* metal armor
Mason, Ronald J., 9–11, 13, 28
massacres, 66, 159, 164–65, 168–69. *See also* San Sabá Massacre (1758)
McAdams, Gary, 51, 54
McPherson, Robert S., 27
measles. *See* epidemic diseases
Medicine Lodge ceremony, 72, 162
Medicine Man (Caddo hero), 139–40
medicine men and doctors' societies, 70–71, *71*, *73*, 132, 161 187
memoration, 150
memorization, 38
Menchaca, Don José, 114

metal armor, 107–11, *108*, 205n7, 206n8; archaeological finds of, 108, 109, 205n3; brigadine, 206n7; curiass, 109, 206n7, 210n45; gauntlets, 104, 108, 111, 121, 206nn7–8; gorgets, 108–9, 206n7; helmets, 95, 108, 136, 137, 145; historical records on use of, 120, 207n17, 208n30, 209n36; for horses, 109, 145–46; shields, 144, 146, 149; tribal advantage of, 128; worn by De Soto–Moscoso expedition, 144–46, 214n41. *See also* Flint Monster story (Skiri Pawnee); masked cannibal stories (Caddo); masks and maskettes; weaponry
metal weaponry, introduction of, 103, 104, 128, 141. *See also* guns, introduction of
Mexkehme-Sukahs, 207n17
Miller, Wick R., 15
Míro, Esteban Rodriguez, 199n23
Mission Santa Cruz de San Saba. *See* San Sabá Massacre (1758)
Molina, Miguel, 88, 90–91, 92, 94, 95, 203n29
Monroe, Hugh, 207n17
Monsters: Evil Beings, Mythical Beasts, and All Manner of Imaginary Terrors (Gilmore), 22
monster stories. *See* Caddoan monster stories
monster theories, 1–2, 187, 192n56; of Asma, 23; of Cohen, 22; of Gilmore, 22–23; of Giraud, 23; as historical metaphors in oral traditions, 2, 8, 11–12, 194n20; Judeo-Christian-Islamic God in, 192n57; of psychoanalysts and psychologists, 22, 23–24, 190n31. *See also* Caddoan monster stories
Monster Theory: Reading Culture (Cohen), 22
Mooney, James, 137, 142, 210n45
Mora y Ceballos, Francisco de la, 81
Morgan, Tom, 117, 118, 210n40
Morning Star, 210n48; and Jesus, 180; offerings to, 3, 41, 122, 163–64, 169, 176, 179; and Pahukatawa, 24, 158–59, 177; rise and fall of worship of, 181–82
mortar and pestle, *131*, 149. *See also* corn mill
Moscoso y Alvarado, Luis de, 131, 143–44. *See also* De Soto–Moscoso expedition

Mother Corn: ceremony and offerings to, 59, 62, 70, 72–74, *73*; as supreme power, 63, 67
mounds, 5, 19, 130, 139
Moving Fire. *See* Spider-Man
Murie, James Rolfe, *48*; career of, 47–51, 196n65; ethnographic work of, 32, 38, 45, 46, 49–50, 60; on Pahukatawa, 157, 171, 172, 174; publications by, 49; reputation and attitudes of, 50–51, 196n67
muskets, 95, 99, 146
"Muster Roll of the Expedition" (Coronado), 111
mutilation. *See* cruelty and torture by Spanish; decapitation; scalped men stories
myth: disciplinary study of, 26–28, 33–35; *vs.* history, 2, 6–11, 77; mythologizing process, *12*, 16–17, 33, 136, 213n10; *vs.* oral traditions, 12–13; origins of, 8, 193n19. *See also* Caddoan monster stories; oral traditions
The Mythology of the Wichita (Dorsey), 43, 47, *52*, 53, 54, 76–77

Nabokov, Peter, 15–16, 19, 191n54
Natchez, 15
Natchitoches, 5, 213n2
National Museum of Natural History (Smithsonian), Washington, D.C., 45
Native American Church (peyote religion), 53, 178
Native American Graves Protection and Repatriation Act (NAGPRA), 9, 17
Native beliefs. *See* religion
Navajos, 107, 119, 120, 121
Neešaanu NačitákUx (the Great Chief Above), 59, 63, 70–71
Newcomb, William, 204n54
New Fire Ceremony, 163
"Norteño" Indians, 89
North, L. H., 209n40
Notes on the Caddo (Parsons), 132
Nuestra Señora de Refugio, 96–97, 99, 101
Nuño de Tobar, Captain, 143
"Nûñ'yunu'wï, The Stone Man" story (Cherokee), 137

Nuutawáčeš, 201n47
Nye, Wilbur S., 54

Obregón, Baltasar, 109
Old-Man-That-Chief, 38
Oliver-Smith, Anthony, 25
Oñate, Don Juan de, 88, 112–13, 208n28
One Horn Buffalo Dance and songs, 172, 173–75, 179, 219n66
On Monsters: An Unnatural History of Our Worst Fears (Asma), 23
Opler, Morris, 138
Oral Tradition as History (Vansina), 13
Oral Tradition: A Study in Historical Methodology (Vansina), 13
oral traditions: challenges to interpreting Arikara stories, 61–62; classifications systems for, 42–44; collaboration in recording and interpreting, 31–32, 193n5; and colonialism, 20–22, 191n54, 192n2; concerns about writing of, 11, 18–20, 31, 35, 177, 184; diagram of history and, *12*; Echo-Hawk on, 17–18, 21; ethnopoetics on, 35–36; fantastic elements as historical metaphors in, 2, 8, 11–12, 60, 194n20; mythologizing process in, 16–17, 33; Nabokov on, 15–16, 19; performance of, 31–35; on sexuality, xii, 24, 25, 55, 87; significance of, 18–19; as sources of history, 6–11, 26–27, 36–37, 183–87; storytelling conventions, 37–42; study of folklore in, 33–34; Vansina on, 13–15; and vitality, xiii, 37–38; word of caution on reading stories of, 54–55. *See also* Caddoan oral traditions; ethnohistory; myth
"The Origin Myth of Acoma Pueblo", 191n54
"The Origin of the Arikara." *See* Whirlwind story (Arikara)
Osages, 64, 81, 83, 85, 116
Osborne, Samuel, 171–72, 219n53
Otoes, 64, 121, 168
Ouachitas, 5. *See also* Caddoan oral traditions
Our Lady of Refuge, 96–97, 99, 101
outbreaks. *See* epidemic diseases
Owl, 72

Padoucas, 127, 198n13, 210n49
Páez, José de, 93, *93*, 97, 204n48, 215n58
Páez, Juan, 147–51
Pahukatawa story (Pawnee): Allis on, 175–76; among Arikara, 176, 220n71; archaeoastronomer on, 220n91; Echo-Hawk on, 180–81; Grinnell on, 171, 176, 220n77; influence of Christianity on, 24, 27, 170, 176–78, 180–81, 184; medical cures by, 177, 219n67; One Horn Buffalo Dance and songs in, 172, 173–75, 179, 219n66; Osborne on, 171–72, 219n53; sacred rise of, 171–73, 177, 179; shape-shifting in, 173; summary of, 157–59, 162, 181–82, 184. *See also* scalped men stories
Panis Indians, 126, 198n13
Panis slave trade, 81, 202n12
Parker, Quanah, 53
Parks, Douglas, 43, 45, 46, 49, 162
Parrilla, Don Diego Ortiz de, 88–89, 90, 95, 98, 100, 203n33
Parsons, Elsie Clews, 132
The Pawnee Ghost Dance Hand Game (Lesser), 180
The Pawnee Indians (Hyde), 8
Pawnee Indian Societies (Murie), 49
Pawnee Music (Densmore), 117
Pawnee Mythology (Dorsey), 43, 49
Pawnee oral traditions: classification system for, 43; cultural overview of, 2–6; importance of Pahukatawa in, 157–58; publications of, 8, 41–42, 43, 49, 105, 117, 180; scalped men stories in, 157, 159–64, 186–87; storytelling conventions of, 39–40, 41; Whirlwind in, 67–68. *See also* Skiri (Skidi) Pawnee oral tradition
Pawnees: acquisition of horses by, 119; and Christianity, 158, 169–70, 176–78, 180–82; cosmology of, 39, 43, 74, 152, 158–59, 162–63, 182, 210n48; genocide and annihilation of, 158, 159, 164–70, 181, 184, 218n31; human sacrifice tradition of, 3, 163, 169, 178, 179, 189n3; introduction of metal weapons to, 103, 104, 128; metal armor used by, 107–11, *108*, 120, 128; territory of, 2, *4*;

US goverment relations, 158, 169–70, 178–79, 181, 187; warfare of, 113, 115–17, 119–22, 210n45. *See also* Skiri (Skidi) Pawnees
Peña, Juan de Dios, 114
performance of oral traditions, 31–37
pestle, *131*
peyote religion, 53, 178
peytral, 109
physical adaptations, 24–25
Piitariisaaru, 169
Pima Indians, 15
Pitahawirata Pawnees, 3, 174
plagues. *See* epidemic diseases
Pohebits Quasho, 208n30
pole torture, 77, 84–85, 202n19
population statistics, 60–61, 65, 78, 167–68, 199n23. *See also* census rolls (Bureau of Indian Affairs)
postmortem intestinal gases, 16–17
pounder. *See* corn mill
"Primitive American History" (Swanton and Dixon), 6–7
psychoanalysts and psychologists, monster theories of, 22, 23–24, 33–34, 190n31

Qsa-Hi-Wa-Ski- A-Gu-Na-Ur-I-Sa. *See* Hunt, Burgess
Quivira, 113

rabies, 69
Radcliffe-Brown, Alfred, 34
Raglan, Lord, 8
Ramirez, Juan, 109
Ramsey, Jarold, 127–28
Rayados, 113
Reading the Fire (Ramsey), 127
redemption story. *See* Coyote story (Wichita)
Red Fox, 114
Red Horn myth, 139, 141
Rees. *See* Arikaras
religion: of Arikara, 70–74; of Caddo, 152; cosmology of Pawnees, 39, 43, 74, 152, 158–59, 162–63, 182, 210n48; Ghost Dance, 50, 178, 180, 196n67; peyote, 53, 178; syncretism *vs.* synthesis in, 178, 180, 182. *See also* Christianity; cosmology of Pawnees; oral traditions

Riding In, William, 161–62
Riiciriisaaru, 169
Roaming Scout, *37*; as ethnographic source, 49; on Pahukatawa, 171, 175, 177; on vitality and oral traditions, xiii, 37–38
Rodríguez, Agustín, 88, 208n24

sabatons, 206n7
sacred leggings, 172, 219n58
sacred stories. *See* oral traditions
sacred texts, scholarship on, 18–22, 60
Sahnish. *See* Arikara oral traditions
Saint Francis of Assisi, 98
Sakakawea (Sacajawea), 193n5
Sa-Ku-Ru-Ta. *See* Murie, James Rolfe
Salazar, Francisco de, 149
Sanánat. *See* Sioux
Sand Creek Massacre (1864), 164
San Luis de las Amarillas Presidio, 91, 95
San Sabá Massacre (1758): connection to Coyote story, 27, 88, 92–102, 184; description of incident, 75–76, 77, 88–92, 203n29, 203n33, 204n44, 204n53; painting of, 93, *93*, 97; significance of, 205n67
Santa Cruz de San Sabá. *See* San Sabá Massacre (1758)
Santee Sioux, 64
Santiesteban, José, 75–76, 89, 91, *93*, 98. *See also* San Sabá Massacre (1758)
scale mail armor. *See* metal armor
"Scalped-Man Loses His Wife" story (Pawnee), 159–60
scalped men stories: of Arikara, 157, 159, 162, 163, 216n6; of Caddo, 216n2; of Pawnee, 157, 159–164, 186–87; summary of, 157–59. *See also* Pahukatawa story (Pawnee)
scalping, 98, 100, 105, 117, 118–19, 159, 216n2. *See also* decapitation
scholarship on Native traditions, 18–22
seasons and storytelling, 39–40
Semalitsa, 127
Senecas, 107, 137
sexuality: abstinence of, 85; portrayals in oral traditions of, xii, 24, 25, 55, 87
shaffrons, 109, 145, 146
shields, 144, 146, 149. *See also* metal armor

Sia Pueblos, 138
Silvestre, Gonzalo, 149–50
Sioux: –Arikara relations, 64–66, 199n21, 200n30, 200n32; effects of epidemic diseases among, 66; –Pawnee warfare, 158, 159, 164–70, 181, 184, 220n88; winter counts of, 199n21, 220n88. *See also* Lakotas
Skidi Pawnee Society (Murie), 49
Skiri (Skidi) Pawnee oral tradition: Dorsey's collection on, 41–42, 49, 105, 205n5; on Pahukatawa, 176; scalped men stories in, 157, 159–64, 186–87; storytelling seasons of, 39. *See also* cosmology of Pawnees; Flint Monster story (Skiri Pawnee)
Skiri (Skidi) Pawnees: cultural overview of, 3, 118; warfare of, 113, 115–17, 158, 159, 164–70, 181, 184, 220n88. *See also* Pawnees
slavery and slave trade: of Acoma Puebloans, 208n28; Caddos in, 141, 142, 145, 215n59; New Mexico markets, 119; of "Panis," 81, 202n12; Spanish Colonization Law on, 113; Wichitas in, 78, 80–81, 83, 89, 92, 101, 204n54. *See also* abducted women and child(ren)
smallpox. *See* epidemic diseases
"Snake" Indians, 63, 68
snake stories, 68, 70, 186, 201n47
"Some Things Are Not Forgotten" (Blaine), 50
songs, 117
South Band Pawnees, 170, 179
Southern Workman, 48
Spanish explorers and colonials: armor worn by, 108, 109, 110, 144–45; cruelty and torture used by, 84–85, 143, 203n19, 208n28; infectious diseases from, 141, 152; introduction of horses by, 80–81; introduction of iron by, 141; and slavery, 81, 83, 113, 141, 142, 145. *See also specific conquistadors and expeditions*
Speck, Frank G., 137
Spider-Man, 75, 79, 84, 94. *See also* Coyote story (Wichita)
"The Spiders Who Recovered the Chief's Grandson" story (Wichita). *See* Coyote story (Wichita)

Spider-Woman, 77, 79, 82, 83. *See also* Coyote story (Wichita)
Spinden, Herbert, 3
Spoehr, Alexander, 49
Squirrel, 142. *See also* Flying Squirrel
Squirrel Clan, 142
Standing Bear, Luther, 38–39, 190n15, 194n28
Stands All Night (or Standing All Night), 40
Stands in Timber, John, 38, 194n25
Star (Arikara storyteller), 62, 67, 70
starvation, 65
Stella Bear, 216n6
sterilization programs, 187
Stevenson, Matilda Coxe, 138
sticks. *See* clubs (weapon)
"stone coat" monsters, 107–8, 111, 137–38, 205n6. *See also* Flint Monster story (Skiri Pawnee)
Stone Coat people, 137–38
storytelling. *See* oral traditions
Strangers, Gods, and Monsters (Giraud), 23
street divisions, tribal, 83
suffering, 65. *See also* epidemic diseases
Sun Dance, 219n53
Sun King, 123, 126
Swann, Brian, 35
Swanton, John, 6–7
syncretism *vs.* synthesis, religious, 178, 180, 182

Talking Hactcin, 138
Taovaya Wichitas, 89, 110, 111
"Tattooed Pawnees." *See* Wichitas
tattooing, 76, 148
Tatum, John, 53
Tedlock, Dennis, 31, 35, 193n8
tents, 144
Terreros, Alonso Giraldo de, 75, 88, 90, *93*, 98. *See also* San Sabá Massacre (1758)
Terreros, Juan M. Romero de, 205n67
Terreros, Pedro Romero de, 93
textile armor, 108, 205n7, 215n41. *See also* metal armor
Thompson River Indians, 127–28
Tiiraawaahat, 163, 176
Tisné, Charles Du, 119
Tlascaltecans, 88

tobacco cultivation, 3
Toelken, Barre, 32–33, 35
Tonkawas, 88, 143, 205n67
torture, 77, 84–85, 141, 202n19, 208n28
Touching Cloud, 118. *See also* Alights on the Cloud
tradition, role of heroes and, 24
Traditions of the Arikara (Dorsey), 42, 47, 49, 60
Traditions of the Caddo (Dorsey), 45, 47, 132, 216n2
Traditions of the Skidi Pawnee (Dorsey), 41–42, 49, 105, 205n5
Truteau, Jean Baptiste, 199n23, 200n32
Tsa'Bisu. *See* Wing (Caddo storyteller)
Tulans, 143, 146–51, 213n4, 215n59
twin hero myth, 139–41
Two Crows, 62, 197n6
Two Hawks, 62, 68

Ulibarri, Juan de, 126–27
United States government: BIA census rolls, 51, 60–61, 78, 104, 205n4; ethnocide policies by, 164, 180; genocide policies by, 165, 187, 217n19; Pawnee relations, 158, 169–70, 178–79, 181, 187; on religious freedom, 46

vambraces, 206n7
vampires, 16–17
Vansina, Jan, 13–15
vara (measurement), 148, 215n55
Vazquez, Joseph, 91, 100
Veniard, Étienne de, 63
Vérendrye, François and Louis-Joseph de la, 63, 68
Vergara, Juan Pérez de, 111
Vial, Pedro, 110–11, 113–14

Wallace, Pamela, 142
Walters, Anna Lee, 19
Warden, Cleaver, 46
Water Monster, 139–40
weaponry: arrowheads, 109, 110; bows and arrows, 146, 167, 198n16; clubs, 68, 95, 147, 148–49, 150–51; crossbows, 111, 146, 150; halberds, 146, 150, 215n45; harquebuses, 111, 113, 146, 203n22;

weaponry (*continued*)
  introduction of guns, 80–81, 94–96, 128, 198n16; introduction of metal weapons, 103, 104, 128, 141; inventories of Spanish expeditions, 146, 215n45; lances, 83, 136, 146, 147; longbow, 108, 145, 146, 205n7; muskets, 95, 99, 146; in U.S.–Pawnee treaties, 169. *See also* metal armor
Wearing Horns, 118
Weddle, Robert S., 89, 98
Wedel, Mildred M., 26
Wedel, Waldo, 112
Weltfish, Gene, 38, 39–40, 161–62
When They Severed Earth from Sky (Barber and Barber), 16–17
Whirlwind in Pawnee stories, 67–68
Whirlwind story (Arikara), 5, 26–28, 67–74, 184, 185–86. *See also* Arikara oral tradition
White Horse, 67, 174
Wichita oral traditions: classification system for, 43, 76–77; Dorsey's publication of, 43, 47, *52*, 53, 54, 76–77; stone coat monsters in, 205n6; storytelling conventions of, 40–41; whirlwinds and Wind in, 68. *See also* Coyote story (Wichita)
Wichitas: cannibalism among, 204n54; census on, 51; cultural overview of, 2–6, 76, 78; relations with Comanches, 52, 81, 87, 92, 101, 202n16; and slave trade, 78, 80–81, 83, 89, 92, 101, 204n54; territory of, 2, *4*. *See also* San Sabá Massacre (1758)

Wilson, John, 53
Wing (Caddo storyteller), 129, 132. *See also* "The Young Men and the Cannibals" story (Caddo)
Winnebagos, 139
winter counts, 8, *115*, 118, 199n21, 210n45, 220n88
Wissler, Clark, 3
witch-woman story. *See* Coyote story (Wichita)
wolf story, 138
"The Woman Who Married a Star" (Hunt), 53
Woman-Who-Wears-Shell-Rattles, 80, 87
women. *See* abducted women and child(ren)
Wonderful Boy, 104, 105–7, 119, 122–27. *See also* Flint Monster story (Skiri Pawnee)
Wonderful Man, 44
Wood, D. J. M., 50
Wounded Knee Massacre (1890), 164

Yacatecuhtli, 139
Yankton Sioux, 64
Yatasis, 5. *See also* Caddoan oral traditions
Yellow Bird, Loren, 74
"The Young Men and the Cannibals" story (Caddo), 129, 132–34, 146–48. *See also* masked cannibal stories (Caddo); Wing (Caddo storyteller)

Zaldívar, Vicente de, 113

Printed in the USA
CPSIA information can be obtained
at www.ICGtesting.com
LVHW090415170824
788482LV00004B/331